Atlantic Lives

Atlantic Lives offers insight into the lived experiences of a range of actors in the early modern Atlantic World. Organized thematically, each chapter features primary source selections from a variety of non-traditional sources, including travel narratives from West Africa, the Caribbean, and Latin America. The fully revised and expanded second edition goes into even greater depth in exploring the diverse roles and experiences of women, Native Americans, and Africans, as well as the critical theme of emerging capitalism and New World slavery. New chapters also address captivity experiences, intercultural religious encounters, and interracial sexuality and marriage. With classroom-focused discussion questions and suggested additional readings accompanying each chapter, *Atlantic Lives* provides students with a wide-ranging introduction to the many voices and identities that comprised the Atlantic World.

Timothy J. Shannon is Professor of History at Gettysburg College in Gettysburg, Pennsylvania.

Atlantic Lives

A Comparative Approach to Early America

Second Edition

Timothy J. Shannon

Routledge
Taylor & Francis Group

NEW YORK AND LONDON

Second edition published 2019
by Routledge
52 Vanderbilt Avenue, New York, NY 10017

and by Routledge
2 Park Square, Milton Park, Abingdon, Oxon, OX14 4RN

Routledge is an imprint of the Taylor & Francis Group, an informa business

First edition published by Pearson 2003

Library of Congress Cataloging-in-Publication Data
A catalog record for this book has been requested

ISBN: 978-1-138-57772-5 (hbk)
ISBN: 978-1-138-57773-2 (pbk)
ISBN: 978-1-351-26624-6 (ebk)

Typeset in Goudy
by Wearset Ltd, Boldon, Tyne and Wear

For my students

Contents

Preface

This book has grown out of a course I started teaching in 1997 at Gettysburg College. At that time, the History Department had decided to revamp its introductory courses. In particular, the World History survey was at once too familiar and too daunting to students and instructors. It required covering an enormous amount of material at a breakneck speed, without providing the depth necessary to introduce students to the study of history at the college level. Those of us who had taught the World History course decided we would slice up the pie, each of us developing a new course that would deal with history on an intercontinental scale, but in a time-frame small enough to allow in-depth concentration on specific themes and ideas. As a historian of Early America, I decided to focus on the interaction between Europe, Africa, and the Americas, from the Age of Columbus through the Age of Revolutions. It was an idea that would have appealed to Goldilocks: if World History was too big for what I hoped to accomplish and the standard US History survey too small, then the Atlantic World seemed just right.

As soon as I began teaching the course, I became aware that the subject lacked a good, comprehensive textbook. There were many books on particular aspects of the course—the Atlantic Slave Trade, the Columbian Exchange, Atlantic Migrations—that my students and I found useful and thought-provoking, but I could find no single, overarching narrative that could guide the students through the semester. As I thought about how I would design such a text, it also occurred to me that I would like to have my students reading more of the primary sources of Atlantic history, so that they might meet and listen to many of the individuals who lived this history first hand. As I taught the course in ensuing years, I collected references for such primary sources: slave and captivity narratives, travel journals and diaries, political tracts and promotional pamphlets, letters, and autobiographies. Ultimately, I decided to combine my ideas for a narrative text and primary source collection into one project, the result of which you are reading now.

This book presents a history of the Atlantic World from about 1450 to 1830. After the Introduction, the chapters follow a rough chronological order, but are conceived and organized thematically. The objective of this design is to provide both the skeleton of a narrative overview of the Atlantic World and an introduction to the major topics in the field. Each chapter presents reading selections from two or three primary sources related to its topic. I have chosen to devote the bulk of the book's content to these sources because they provide comparative, first-person perspectives on the issues at hand. Whenever possible, I have incorporated the narratives of people who traveled between the Americas, Africa, and Europe. Their voices give immediacy to the subject matter in a way that a textbook narrative cannot. Too often, the teaching of history loses its human content as students and instructors focus on -isms (feudalism, mercantilism, capitalism, industrialism, and so on) instead of individuals. This book has its share of -isms, but I hope that readers will find in these selections the voices and personalities of those individuals whose lives shaped and were shaped by the history of the Atlantic World.

Preface to the Second Edition

It has been fifteen years since the first edition of *Atlantic Lives*, and the scholarship on Atlantic World history has expanded in depth and breadth. Several textbooks covering the field have appeared during that time, but this book remains one of the very few primary sources readers available on the topic. New source selections make up approximately one-third of this edition, and nearly every chapter features at least one. The number of chapters has also increased in order to provide more comprehensive coverage of such topics as captivity, religion, and sexuality. These new source selections expand the ethnic, racial, and gender diversity of voices represented in this volume, reflecting more fully the human mosaic that knits the Atlantic World together. It is my sincere hope that instructors and students will find in these pages an interesting and useful introduction to Atlantic World history by reading the words of the people who made it.

I would like to thank Eve Setch and Eve Mayer at Routledge for their support of this project, and Ted Meyer for his help in completing the revision process. I would also like to thank Rebekah Grimes for her work in transcribing sources and the Reference and Interlibrary Loan departments at Musselman Library at Gettysburg College for their help in accessing materials. I remain indebted to my students, whose reading, questioning, and interpreting of this material challenge me to see it anew.

Acknowledgments

A faculty Development and Research Grant from Gettysburg College helped support the research for this project. I would like to thank Lauren Rocco, Amber Moulton, and Jen Chesney for their work as research assistants. Also, my thanks to Susan Roach and Linda Isenberger for their help in locating materials, and to Barbara Sommer for sharing her expertise in Latin American history and to Charlie Zabrowski for his help in the Latin translations. My students have helped me identify many of the reading selections included here and to refine my own ideas about the content and meaning of Atlantic history. The kind folks at the Ragged Edge Coffee House (the real reason to visit Gettysburg) supplied my caffeine and a nice place to work, when I could get away from the office. This book has been much improved by the thoughtful commentary of the following reviewers: John Thornton, Millersville University; Edward H. Tebbenhoff, Luther College; Robert A. Becker, Louisiana State University; Melissa Walker, Converse College; Brenda Thompson Schoolfield, Bob Jones University; David Armitage, Columbia University; Anna Bates, Aquinas College; Armand S. La Potin, State University of New York College at Oneonta; Jessica Kross, University of South Carolina; B. R. Burg, Arizona State University; Hal M. Friedman, Henry Ford Community College; H. Warren Gardner, University of Texas of the Permian Basin; Peter Moore, University of Georgia; Constance M. McGovern, Frostburg State University; James H. Williams, Middle Tennessee State University; Michael P. Gabriel, Kutztown University; and Wade Shaffer, West Texas A&M University who reviewed it for Longman; and I also appreciate the advice and assistance of Ashley Dodge and Jacob Drill during the editing and production stages.

Colleen thought this project was a good idea from the start, and it would not have been completed without her encouragement. Caroline and Daniel supplied welcome diversion from beginning to end, and Elizabeth joined them just in time to make the Acknowledgments (good work, kid!). I thank them all for their patience whenever I pleaded for five more minutes.

TIMOTHY J. SHANNON

Introduction
What Is Atlantic History?

By anyone's accounting, David George led a remarkable life. He was born of African parents in Essex County, Virginia in the mid-eighteenth century and spent his early years working as a plantation slave. As a young man, he ran away and found work in South Carolina and then in Georgia. When his freedom seemed in jeopardy, he escaped into the Georgia backcountry, only to be captured by Creek Indians, who re-enslaved him. He worked for several months for a Creek chief, who spoke some English and arranged to sell George back to his original master, 800 miles away in Virginia. George fled again before that transaction could be completed but ended up working as a slave for a master on the Savannah River. There, he was introduced to Christianity by another slave, and after his conversion, became a Baptist minister.

When the British invaded Georgia during the American Revolution, George again sought his freedom. Now married and the father of two children, he abandoned his patriot master and sought refuge for himself and his family among the British. George survived the siege of Savannah and a case of smallpox, and at the end of the war, he accepted a British offer for free passage to Nova Scotia, along with other white and black loyalist refugees. In Nova Scotia, he became a leader of the black community, despite the persecution he faced from whites for preaching before interracial audiences.

His travels were not over yet. After enduring several years of hard times in Nova Scotia, George decided to move again, this time to Africa. In 1792, he joined about 1,000 other black loyalists in founding the colony of Sierra Leone. As conceived by British anti-slavery advocates, Sierra Leone would be populated by former slaves from British colonies, who would bring Christianity and European civilization to Africa and help to end the slave trade there. George continued to work as a minister in Sierra Leone, often mediating when resentments flared between his fellow settlers and British agents. He died there in 1810.

What are we to make of David George? During his life, he moved between freedom and slavery not once, but several times. He participated in two colonizing ventures on opposite sides of the Atlantic: Nova Scotia and Sierra Leone. At various times, he lived among Indians, American slaves and slaveholders, British soldiers, and West Africans. He pursued liberty during the American Revolution, but not in a fashion typically associated with that conflict; he became a loyalist rather than a patriot and preserved his freedom by leaving the United States instead of remaining there. His travels took him hundreds, and then thousands, of miles from his place of birth. Over all that time and distance, how did he come to identify himself? Was he an African who lived in America, or an American who lived in Africa? In a brief autobiographical narrative he composed in the 1790s, George expressed consciousness of his race, noting his parents' African origins and his introduction to Christianity by a "man of my own color," but his most insistent self-identification was as a Christian. After his conversion, he sought the company of other Baptists, black and white, and he worked closely with whites to organize the black loyalist emigration to Sierra Leone.

David George's life defied the conventions by which historians typically tell the story of early America. He was not an immigrant who became American by adopting the New World as his homeland. Neither was he a slave who gained freedom by taking up arms in the patriot cause during the War of Independence. He was a slave who converted to Christianity and learned to read and write the English language, but who also abandoned America to live in the country of his ancestors. George's story is too expansive and too contradictory to be told only in the context of the thirteen colonies that became the United States. It demands a much larger geographic arena for its action and a framework for its themes and events that can connect and explain his experiences in the American South, Nova Scotia, and Sierra Leone.

Atlantic history provides that framework. Focusing on the period between 1450 and 1830—from the earliest European encounters with sub-Saharan Africa to the demise of the Atlantic Slave Trade—Atlantic history examines the ramifications of long-distance contact, exchange, and conflict between human populations in Europe, Africa, and the Americas. While the term Atlantic history has only recently gained widespread currency in academic conferences, graduate programs, and college catalogues, historians have been pursuing it in various ways for quite some time. The first scholars to define it as a field of inquiry were interested in the trans-Atlantic revolutionary movement of the late eighteenth century. They explored ideological links between the French Revolution and the North and South American colonial wars of independence. Some of the most prolific practitioners of Atlantic history have been scholars who recognized the need to move beyond traditional geographic boundaries when writing about the Atlantic Slave Trade, which forcibly dispersed Africans throughout the Americas and the Caribbean. Attempting to survey the demographic, economic, and cultural impact of this migration on both sides of the Atlantic requires evaluating data from the Old World as well as the New and from a variety of regions within the Western Hemisphere. Uncovering the economics that governed the Atlantic Slave Trade often meant dealing with commodities rather than nations, that is, studying the rise of an international plantation complex that produced sugar, tobacco, coffee, and other cash crops for world markets.

Likewise, those historians who have investigated the biological and ecological consequences of contact between the Old World and the New have often found national borders irrelevant to their purposes. Microbes, plants, and animals moved into new environments oblivious to man-made boundaries, and their introduction to an ecosystem could wreak havoc regardless of the political or religious differences that have divided human societies. When historians have tried to measure the impact of such biological exchange on human populations, they have often done so on an international or intercontinental scale. Human migrations are another topic fit for analysis on a trans-Atlantic scale. What historical forces created the displaced peoples who moved between the Old World and the New? How did the experience of forced migration differ from that of voluntary migration? What were the varieties of bound or indentured labor that could bring a person across the Atlantic? What effect did such migrations have on the indigenous populations who encountered them?

Some of these questions have already been addressed in the familiar narratives of the European colonization of the Americas. Each European colonial power produced its own national heroes for this story, from Spain's conquistadors to England's Pilgrims to France's missionaries. These nationalist narratives, however, fall short in several respects. All emphasize the exceptional quality of their subjects' experiences, be it their superior bravery, piety, or humanity. In doing so, they also downplay the consistencies and similarities between these stories that would allow for comparative analysis across national or ethnic borders. Nationalist narratives tend to leave many groups involved in colonization out of the story; they hide or obscure the roles played by stateless people in building the connections between the Old World and the New. For example, many of the sailors whose labor made trans-Atlantic shipping possible were people of mixed ethnicity or no fixed nationality, who lived their lives in flux between two or more places that they might have called home. Pirates, slaves, and fur traders lived and worked among hybrid populations that combined African, European, and Native American identities. Such communities did not fit easily into national categories, and they often ignored whatever claims distant powers made to dominion over them, yet their importance in shaping the Atlantic World is undeniable.

What distinguishes Atlantic history from previous narratives is its transnational quality. Rather than splitting the story of the colonization of the Americas into discreet national units that would have made sense to only a fraction of the people involved, it asks questions that are best answered by taking a comparative perspective on the evidence. How did the Native American response to European missionaries differ in various regions of the Americas, and what circumstances explain those differences? Why did some New World slave societies create large bi-racial populations that occupied a middling social status between freedom and slavery while others did not? Did the colonial wars of independence originate from common grievances against European empires? If so, why were the results of those wars so different? Contemplating these questions reduces the emphasis on exceptionalism that has shaped nationalist narratives of early America and helps us recapture the connections and overlaps that contemporaries would have recognized between these topics.

Let us return to the story of David George. His life illustrates several of the topics that make up the backbone of Atlantic history: slavery, the plantation economy, migrations, and revolutions. More significantly, he illustrates this notion of transnationality, of the movement of peoples and their identities across geographic, cultural, and political borders. George's life was marked by his ability to reinvent himself. He ran away from slavery no fewer than three times to assume the life of a free man. He became a part of the loyalist exodus to Nova Scotia by choosing to align himself with the British cause in the War of Independence. He thought of himself as a Christian and as an African, and that identity led him to emigrate to Sierra Leone. His life reflected a willing, even restless, movement between social and political categories that at first seemed hard and fast. The history of the Atlantic World is the story of David George writ large, of intercontinental exchanges and conflicts between human societies set in motion by the collision of Europe, Africa, and the Americas.

In a way, it is not surprising that historians have latched onto the concept of Atlantic history in recent years. There is much about the Atlantic World that seemed to anticipate the issues and problems of our own. Just as the Atlantic World was made possible by technologies and migrations that broke down previous barriers to human contact and exchange, so too our modern world has been reshaped by an explosion of global relationships. The earth's population is more integrated than ever before. Intercontinental travel occurs with an ease and regularity that few would have expected even fifty years ago. International corporations make products, from cars to clothes to films, which are aimed as much at international audiences as local ones. The Internet and World Wide Web have a global reach and impact, but so do AIDS, greenhouse emissions, and overpopulation. Just as the generations that followed Columbus had to deal with a world that was suddenly much larger than they had previously thought, so too must we deal with a world that is shrinking before our eyes, bringing formerly isolated peoples into contact and conflict with each other, turning local and regional problems into international ones. We should not expect the study of Atlantic history to provide solutions to our current crises, but it can help us understand how human societies in the past have created and dealt with problems of similar global dimensions.

Suggested Readings

David George's autobiography can be found in John Rippon, *The Baptist Annual Register, Including Sketches of the State of Religion Among Different Denominations of Good Men at Home and Abroad* (London, 1793–1802), 473–484. For more on the black loyalists and the Sierra Leone colony, see Ellen G. Wilson, *The Loyal Blacks* (New York: G. P. Putnam's Sons, 1976).

For essays about the challenges and promises of Atlantic history, see Alison Games, "Atlantic History: Definitions, Challenges, and Opportunities," *American Historical Review* 111

(June 2006): 741–757; David Armitage, "Three Concepts of Atlantic History," in David Armitage and Michael J. Braddick (eds.), *The British Atlantic World, 1500–1800* (New York: Palgrave, 2002), 11–29; and Nicholas Canny, "Writing Atlantic History; or, Reconfiguring the History of Colonial British America," *Journal of American History* 86 (1999): 1093–1114. Other works that are useful for conceptualizing Atlantic history include Jack P. Greene and Philip D. Morgan (eds.), *Atlantic History: A Critical Reappraisal* (New York: Oxford University Press, 2009); Bernard Bailyn, *Atlantic History: Concept and Contours* (Cambridge, MA: Harvard University Press, 2005); and John K. Thornton, *A Cultural History of the Atlantic World* (Cambridge: Cambridge University Press, 2012).

1 Into the Atlantic Crucible

Figure 1.1 Columbus Arrives in America.

This allegorical image depicts Christopher Columbus arriving in America, where he encounters a Native American woman on a hammock. A number of exotic animals are also present in the scene, and in the background, three individuals roast a human leg over a fire. How does this image reflect the impressions of America Columbus conveyed in the Santángel letter (Selection 2)?

Source: Theodor Galle, engraver, "America," Plate 2 from *Nova Reperta* (*c*.1600).

Introduction

The year of Christopher Columbus's first voyage to the Americas, 1492, might seem like a logical point at which to date the origin of the Atlantic World. Columbus's voyage was certainly a momentous event in world history, but the foundations of the Atlantic World are to be found in trends and circumstances that were altering Europe's relations with the outside world long before the famed navigator set sail.

Columbus had learned his trade plying the ports of the Mediterranean Sea, the highway of exchange between North Africa, the Near East, and southern Europe in the fifteenth century. He was a native of Genoa, which along with the other Italian city-states of Venice and Florence, dominated Europe's access to the consumer goods of this Mediterranean marketplace: silks, porcelain, and spices from Asia; cloth and sugar from India; and gold, ivory, and slaves from Africa. Italian merchants secured these items through Muslim middlemen, who controlled the caravan routes to sub-Saharan Africa and China.

The impetus for Columbus and other explorers to navigate the Atlantic Ocean (see Map 1.1) came from the gradual unraveling of this Mediterranean system after 1350. The spread of the bubonic plague devastated populations along its major trade routes, and the decline of Mongol power in China closed the access to the Far East that Europeans had enjoyed since the early thirteenth century. In 1453, the conquest of Constantinople by the Turkish Ottoman Empire dealt a severe blow to European interests in the eastern Mediterranean. When Columbus sailed west across the Atlantic almost forty years later, he was expecting to arrive in China, thus opening a new route to Asia that would bypass entirely the Muslim peoples in North Africa and the Near East. He was not alone in this quest. Since the fourteenth century, Portuguese and Spanish ships had been nudging their way into the uncharted waters of the Atlantic, hoping to open direct trade with the kingdoms of sub-Saharan Africa and ultimately to find a sea route to India, the Spice Islands, and China. When Columbus made his fateful voyage, the idea of sailing to the Far East was very old; what was new was his willingness to abandon a southern route along the African coast for a bold foray west across the Atlantic.

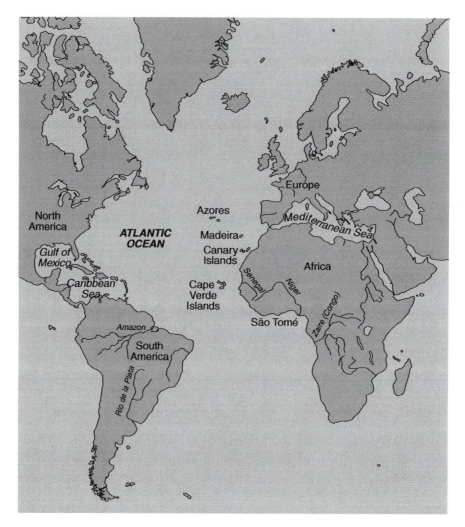

Map 1.1 The Atlantic World.

The Atlantic Ocean, bordered by Europe, Africa, North America, and South America.

So, in a sense, the origins of the Atlantic World lay in a century-long effort by Europeans to go east, not west, in pursuit of exotic goods. That pursuit brought them into contact with strangers of varying languages, ethnicities, and religions, which in turn influenced their encounters with the native peoples of Africa and the Americas. In Africa, for example, European traders and explorers expected to discover kingdoms of great wealth, for they knew that the trans-Saharan trade supplied Muslim merchants in North Africa with their gold. The legend of Prester John, a Christian ruler surrounded by Muslim enemies, led European rulers to sponsor expeditions to West Africa in the hope of discovering a profitable new ally and trading partner. Columbus himself was a reader of Marco Polo, whose famous thirteenth-century account of China and India shaped Columbus's mental picture of the people he expected to meet across the Atlantic. Numerous other medieval travel narratives describing faraway lands and the monstrous peoples who inhabited them influenced European attitudes about the world beyond the Mediterranean.

If such accounts encouraged flights of fantasy, brutal encounters with foreign peoples closer to home taught lessons about conquest and expansion. During the fifteenth and sixteenth centuries, the Spanish, Portuguese, and English gained such first-hand experience in the Canary Islands, São Tomé, and Ireland, respectively. These eastern Atlantic islands became the laboratories of European overseas colonization, and the fate of indigenous peoples there—forced labor, displacement, and religious conversion—foreshadowed what waited for Native Americans on the other side of the Atlantic.

The readings in this chapter offer differing perspectives on these early encounters between the peoples of Europe, Africa, and the Americas. In the first selection, a Portuguese ship captain describes meeting Africans along the coast of West Africa. His purpose is trade, but he is also willing to employ force when he encounters resistance. In the second selection, Christopher Columbus reports on the native peoples he encountered in the Caribbean during his first voyage to America and assesses their potential as subjects and Christian converts. In the last selection, a North American Indian recounts his people's version of the Europeans' arrival. As you read these selections, look for similarities and differences in the ways that Africans, Native Americans, and Europeans reacted to each other. What motives brought them together? How did they attempt to overcome language and cultural barriers between them?

Selection 1: An Early Portuguese Encounter with West Africans

The Portuguese and Spanish pioneered Western Europe's navigation of the Atlantic. Merchants and monarchs in these countries were anxious to secure new trade routes to Asia and Africa that would bypass the Arab merchants who controlled overland access to those regions in North Africa and the Near East. In particular, Dom Henrique (Prince Henry the Navigator) of Portugal sponsored voyages of exploration to sub-Saharan Africa in hope of finding a sea route to Asia and establishing direct contact with the African kingdoms that supplied gold, ebony, ivory, slaves, and other goods to the Mediterranean trade.

One of the adventurers he sponsored was a Venetian named Alvise da Cà da Mosto, who explored coastal West Africa in two voyages in 1455 and 1456. Cà da Mosto met a variety of peoples in his travels, some of whom expressed an interest in trading with him and others who were openly hostile. In the passages below, he describes two such encounters from his first voyage: a successful negotiation with a kingdom south of the Senegal River; and an aborted attempt to sail up the Gambia River.

Credit: *The Voyages of Cadamosto and Other Documents in Western Africa in the Second Half of the Fifteenth Century*, ed. G. R. Grone (London: Hakluyt Society, 1937), 35–36, 48–49, 50–51, 58–61.

I passed beyond this river of Senega in my caravel and sailed to the country of Budomel, fifty miles by the coast from the said river: all this coast is low, without mountains. This name Budomel is the title of the ruler [not the name of the country]. It is called "Terra de Budomel," that is to say the land of that lord, or count.

At this place I made my caravel fast, in order to have converse with this ruler, for certain Portuguese who had had dealings with him had informed me that he was a notable and an upright ruler, in whom one could trust, and who paid royally for what was brought to him. Since I had with me some Spanish horses, which were in great demand in the country of Blacks, not to mention many articles such as woollen cloth, Moorish silk and other goods, I made up my mind to try my fortune with this lord.

Accordingly, I cast anchor at a place on the coast of this country, called "le Palme de Budomel," which is a roadstead, not a port. This done, I caused my negro interpreter to announce my arrival, with horses and goods for his service if he had need of them. To be brief, this lord, being informed of this, took horse and rode down to the sea-shore, accompanied by fifteen horsemen and one hundred and fifty footmen. He sent to me to say that it would please him if I would go ashore to see him, and that he would treat me with honour and esteem. Having heard of his high reputation I went thither. He entertained me to a great feast, and after much talk I gave him my horses, and all that he wished from me, trusting to his good faith. He besought me to go inland to his house, about two hundred and fifty [twenty-five] miles from the shore. There he would reward me richly, and I might remain for some days, for he had promised me 100 slaves in return for what he had received. I gave him the horses with their harness and other goods, which together had cost me originally about three hundred ducats [gold coins]. I therefore decided to go with him, but before I left he gave me a handsome young negress, twelve years of age, saying that he gave her to me for the service of my chamber. I accepted her and sent her to the ship. My journey inland was indeed more to see interesting sights and obtain information, than to receive my dues.

Since it fell to me to spend many days on shore, I decided to go to see a market, or fair, at no great distance [from the spot where I was lodged]. This was held in a field, on Mondays and Fridays, and I went two or three times to it. Men and Women came to it from the neighbourhood country within a distance of four or five miles, for those who dwelt farther off attended other markets. In this market I perceived quite clearly that these people are exceedingly poor, judging from the wares they brought for sale—that is, cotton, but not in large quantities, cotton thread and cloth, vegetables, oil and millet, wooden bowls, palm leaf mats, and all the other articles they use in their daily life. Men as well as women came to sell, some of the men offering their weapons, and others a little gold, but not in any quantity. They sold everything, item by item, by barter, and not for money, for they have none. They do not use money of any kind, but barter only, one thing for another, two for one, three for two.

These negroes, men and women, crowded to see me as though I were a marvel. It seemed to be a new experience to them to see Christians, whom they had not previously seen. They marvelled no less at my clothing than at my white skin. My clothes were after the Spanish fashion, a doublet of black damask, with a short cloak of grey wool over it. They examined the woollen cloth, which was new to them, and the doublet with much amazement: some touched my hands and limbs, and rubbed me with their spittle to discover whether my whiteness was dye or flesh. Finding that it was flesh, they were astounded.

To this market I went to see further strange sights, and also to find out whether any came thither with gold for sale, but altogether, as I have said, there was little to be found.

***

The women of this country are very pleasant and light-hearted, ready to sing and to dance, especially the young girls. They dance, however, only at night by the light of the moon. Their dances are very different from ours.

These negroes marvelled greatly at many of our possessions, particularly at our cross-bows, and, above all, our mortars. Some came to the ship, and I had them shown the firing of a mortar, the noise of which frightened them exceedingly. I then told them that a mortar would slay more than a hundred men at one shot, at which they were astonished, saying that it was an invention of the devil's. The sound of one of our country pipes, which I had played by one of my sailors, also caused wonderment. Seeing that it was decked out with trappings and ribbons at the head, they concluded that it was a living animal that sang thus in different voices, and were much pleased with it. Perceiving that they were misled, I told them that it was an instrument, and placed it, deflated, in their hands. Whereupon, recognising that it was made by hand, they said that it was a divine instrument, made by God with his own hands, for it sounded so sweetly with so many different voices. They said they had never heard anything sweeter.

They were also struck with admiration by the construction of our ship, and by her equipment—mast, sails, rigging, and anchors. They were of opinion that the portholes in the bows of ships were really eyes by which the ships saw whither they were going over the sea. They said we must be great wizards, almost the equal of the devil, for men that journey by land have difficulty in knowing the way from place to place, while we journeyed by sea, and, as they were given to understand, remained out of sight of land for many days, yet knew which direction to take, a thing only possible through the power of the devil. This appeared so to them because they do not understand the art of navigation [the compass, or the chart].

They also marvelled much on seeing a candle burning in a candlestick, for here they do not know how to make any other light than that of a fire. To them the sight of the candle, never seen before, was beautiful and miraculous. As, in this country, honey is found, they suck the honey from the comb, and throw away the wax. Having bought a little honeycomb, I showed them how to extract the honey from wax, and then asked whether they knew what it was that remained. They replied that it was good for nothing. In their presence, therefore, I had some candles made, and lighted. On seeing this, they showed much wonderment, exclaiming that we Christians had knowledge of everything.

In this country they have no musical instruments of any kind, save two: the one is a large Moorish "tanbuchi," which we style a big drum; the other is after the fashion of a viol; but it has, however, two strings only, and is played with the fingers, so that it is a simple rough affair and of no account.

***

The following morning, at about the third hour, we on the other two ships, made sail with a favourable wind and tide to seek our consort and in God's name to enter the river, hoping that in the country farther upstream we might find more civilized people than those we had seen in the canoes. Having joined our consort, she made sail in company and we began to enter the river: the small caravel led the way over the shallows, we following one behind the other.

Having sailed about four miles upstream, we suddenly perceived several canoes coming up behind us (I do not know from whence they came) as fast as they were able. Seeing this, we turned upon them, and being dubious of their poisoned arrows of which we had been informed we protected our ships as best we could, and stood to arms at our stations, although we were poorly equipped. In a short time they reached us. I, being in the leading ship, split the canoes into two sections, and thrust into the midst of them: on counting the canoes, we found they numbered seventeen, of the size of considerable boats. Checking their course and lifting up their oars, their crews lay gazing as upon a marvel. We estimated on examination that there might be about one hundred and fifty at most; they appeared very well built, exceedingly black, and all clothed in white cotton shirts: some of them wore small white caps on their heads, very like the German style, except that on each side they had a white wing with a feather in the middle of the cap, as though to distinguish the fighting men. A negro stood in the prow of each canoe, with a round shield, apparently of leather, on his arm. They made no movement towards us, nor we to them; then they perceived the other two vessels coming up behind me, and advanced towards them. On reaching them, without any other salute, they all threw down their oars, and began to shoot off their arrows.

Our ships, seeing the attack, at once discharged four bombards: hearing these, amazed and confounded by the roar, they threw down their bows, and gazing some here, some there, stood in astonishment at the sight of the shots falling into the river about them. After watching thus for a considerable while, and seeing no more they overcame their fear [of the thunder claps after many shots had been fired], and taking up their bows, began afresh to shoot with much ardour, approaching to within a stone's throw of the ships. The sailors began to discharge their cross-bows at them: the first to do so was a bastard son of the Genoese, who hit a negro in the breast so that he immediately fell dead in the canoe. His companions perceiving this pulled out the arrow and examined it closely, in astonishment at such a weapon: but this did not restrain them from shooting vigorously at the ships, the crews of which replied in like fashion so that in a short space a great number of negroes were wounded. By the grace of God, however, not one of the Christians was hit.

When they saw the wounded and dead, all the canoes with one accord made for the stern of the small caravel, where a stiff fight was waged, for her crew were few and ill-armed. Seeing this I made sail for the small vessel and towed her between our two larger ships amidst a discharge of bombards and cross-bows. At this, the negroes drew off: we, lashing our three ships together by chains, dropped anchor, which, [as the water was calm] held all three.

We then attempted to parley with the Negroes.

***

After much gesticulating and shouting by our interpreters, one of the canoes returned within bowshot. We asked of those in it the reason for their attack upon us, notwithstanding that we were men of peace, and traders in merchandize, saying that we had peaceful and friendly relations with the negroes of the Kingdom of Senega, and that we wished to be on similar terms with them, if they were willing: further, that we had come from a distant land to offer fitting gifts to their king and lord on behalf of our king of Portugal, who desired peace and friendship with them. We besought them to tell us in what country we were, what lord ruled over it, and the name of the river, and told them they might come in peace and confidence to take our wares, for we were content that they should have as much or as little as they pleased.

They replied that they had had news of our coming and of our trade with the negroes of Senega, who, if they sought our friendship, could not but be bad men, for they firmly believed that we Christians ate human flesh, and that we only bought negroes to eat them: that for their part they did not want our friendship on any terms, but sought to slaughter us all, and to make a gift of our possessions to their lord, who they said was three days distant. Theirs was the country of Gambra, and to the river, which was very large, they gave a name which I do not recall.

At this moment the wind freshened; realizing the ill will they bore us, we made sail towards them. They, anticipating this move, scattered in all directions for the land, and thus ended our engagement with them.

Thereupon, we debated [took the advice of our chief men, who formed the ship's council] whether we should proceed farther up the river, if possible for at least one hundred miles, in the hope of finding better disposed peoples. But our sailors, who wished to return home and not to essay further dangers, began with one accord to murmur, declaring that they would not consent to such a course, and that what had been done was sufficient for the voyage.

When we saw that this was their general desire we agreed to give way in order to avoid dissension, for they were pig-headed and obstinate men. Accordingly on the following day, we departed thence, shaping our course for Cape Verde to return, in God's name, to Spain.

Selection 2: First News of Native Americans in Europe

In early 1493, as he was sailing back from his first voyage to America, Christopher Columbus wrote an account of the indigenous peoples he had encountered in the Caribbean. He sent this report to his patrons, King Ferdinand and Queen Isabella of Spain, by way of the king's finance minister Luis de Santángel. The Santángel letter, as it became known, soon found its way into print and became the first widely circulated news about America in Europe. Columbus's contradictory descriptions of Indians as guileless innocents and fearsome cannibals profoundly influenced European approaches to the New World for generations to come.

Credit: *The Spanish Letter of Columbus to Luis de Sant' Angel* (London: G. Norman and Son, 1893), 10–14, 16–17.

Sir,

As I know that you will have pleasure of the great victory which our Lord hath given me in my voyage, I write you this, by which you shall know that in twenty days I passed over to the Indies with the fleet which the most illustrious King and Queen, our Lords, gave me: where I found very many islands peopled with inhabitants beyond number. And, of them all, I have taken possession for their Highnesses, with proclamation and the royal standard displayed; and I was not gainsaid. On the first which I found, I put the name Sant Salvador, in commemoration of his high Majesty, who marvelously hath given all of this: the Indians call it Guanaham. The second I named the Island of Santa Maria de Concepcion, the third Ferrandina, the fourth, Fair Island, the fifth La Isla Juana; and so for each one a new name. When I reached Juana, I followed its coast westwardly, and found it so large that I thought it might be the mainland province of Cathay [China]. And as I did not thus find any towns and villages on the sea-coast, save small hamlets with the people whereof I could not get speech, because they all fled away forthwith, I went on further in the same direction, thinking I should not miss of great cities or towns. And at the end of many leagues, seeing that there was no change, and that the coast was bearing me northwards, whereunto my desire was contrary since the winter was already confronting us, I formed the purpose of making from thence to the South, and as the wind also blew against me, I determined to wait for other weather and turned back as far as a port agreed upon; from which I sent two men into the country to learn if there were a king, or any great cities. They travelled for three days, and found innumerable small villages and a numberless population, but naught of ruling authority; wherefore they returned. I understood sufficiently from other Indians whom I had already taken, that this land in its continuousness, was an island; and so I followed its coast eastwardly for a hundred and seven leagues as far as where it terminated; from which headland I saw another island to the east, ten or eight leagues distant from this, to which I at once gave the name La Spañola ... In this, there are many spiceries, and great mines of gold and other metals.

The people of this island, and of all the others that I have found and seen, or not seen, all go naked, men and women, just as their mothers bring them forth; although some women cover a single place with the leaf of a plant, or a cotton something which they make for that purpose. They have no iron or steel, nor any weapons; nor are they fit thereunto; not because they be not a well-formed people and of fair stature, but that they are most wondrously timorous. They have no other weapons than the stems of reeds in their seeding state, on the end of which they fix little sharpened stakes. Even these, they dare not use; for many times has it happened that I sent two or three men ashore to some village to parley, and countless numbers of them sallied forth, but as soon as they saw those approach, they fled away in such wise [ways] that even a father would not wait for his son. And this was not because any hurt had ever done to any of them: on the contrary, at every headland where I have gone and been able to hold speech with them, I gave them of everything which I had, as well cloth as many other things, without accepting aught therefor; but such they are, incurably timid. It is true that since they have become more assured, and are losing that terror, they are artless and generous with that they have, to such a degree as no one would believe but him who had seen it. Of anything they have, if it be asked for, they never say no, but do rather invite the person to accept it, and show as much lovingness as though they would give their hearts.

And whether it be a thing of value or one of little worth they are straightaways content with whatsoever trifle of whatsoever may be given them in return for it. I forbade that anything so worthless as fragments of broken platters, and pieces of broken glass, and strap-buckles, should be given to them; although when they were able to get such things, they seemed to think they had the best jewel in the world, for it was the hap [good fortune] of a sailor to get, in exchange for a strap, gold to the weight of two and a half castellanos [gold coins], and others much more for other things of far less value; while for new blancas [copper coins] they gave everything they had, even though it were [the worth of] two or three gold castellanos, or one or two arrobas [25 or 50 pounds] of spun cotton. They took even pieces of broken barrel hoops, and gave whatever they had, like senseless brutes; insomuch that it seemed to me ill. I forbade it, and I gave gratuitously a thousand useful things that I carried, in order that they may conceive affection, and furthermore may be made Christians; for they are inclined to the love and service of their Highnesses and of all the Castilian nation, and they strive to combine in giving us things which they have in abundance, and of which we are in need. And they know no sect or idolatry; save that they all believe that power and goodness are in the sky, and they believed very firmly that I, with these ships and crews, came from the sky; and in such opinion, they received me at every place where I landed, after they had lost their terror. And this comes not because they are ignorant: on the contrary, they are men of very subtle wit, who navigate all those seas, and who give a marvelously good account of everything, but because they never saw men wearing clothes nor the like of our ships.

And as soon as I arrived in the Indies, in the first island that I found, I took some of them by force, to the intent that they should learn [our speech] and give me information of what there was in those parts. And so it was, that very soon they understood [us] and we them, what by speech or what by signs; and those [Indians] have been of much service. To this day I carry them [with me] who are still of the opinion that I come from heaven [as appears] from much conversation which they have had with me. And they were the first to proclaim it wherever I arrived; and the others went running from house to house and the neighboring villages, with loud cries of "Come! come to see the people from heaven!" Then, as soon as their minds were reassured about us, every one came, men as well as women, so that there remained none behind, big or little; and they all brought something to eat and drink, which they gave with wondrous lovingness …

It seems to me that in all those islands, the men are all content with a single wife; and to their chief or king they give as many as twenty. The women, it appears to me, do more work than the men. Nor have I been able to learn whether they held personal property, for it seemed to me that whatever one had, they all took share of, especially of eatable things. Down to the present, I have not found in those islands any monstrous men, as many expected, but on the contrary all the people are very comely; nor are they black like those in Guinea, but have flowing hair; and they are not begotten where there is an excessive violence of the rays of the sun. It is true that the sun is there very strong, notwithstanding that it is twenty-six degrees distant from the equinoctial line. In those islands, where there are lofty mountains, the cold was very keen there, this winter; but they endure it by being accustomed thereto, and by the help of the meats which they eat with many and inordinately hot spices. Thus I have not found, not had any information of monsters, except of an island which is here the second in the approach to the Indies, which is inhabited by a people whom, in all the islands, they regard as very ferocious, who eat human flesh. These have many canoes with which they run through all the islands of India, and plunder and take as much as they can. They are no more ill-shapen than the others, but have the custom of wearing their hair long, like women; and they use bows and arrows of the same reed-stems, with a point of wood at the top, for lack of iron which they have not. Amongst those other tribes who are excessively cowardly, these are ferocious; but I hold them as nothing more than the others.

This is enough; and [thanks to] eternal God our Lord who gives to all those who walk His way, victory over things which seem impossible; and this was signally one such, for although men have talked or written of those lands, it was all by conjecture, without confirmation from eyesight, importing just so much the hearers for the most part listened and judged that there was more fable in it than anything actual, however trifling. Since thus our Redeemer has given to our most illustrious King and Queen, and to their famous kingdoms, this victory in so high a matter, Christendom should take gladness therein and make great festivals and give solemn thanks to the Holy Trinity for the great exaltation they shall have by the conversion of so many peoples to our holy faith; and next for the temporal benefit which will bring hither refreshment and profit, not only to Spain, but to all Christians. This briefly, in accordance with the fact. Dated, on the caravel, off the Canary Islands, the 15 February of the year 1493.

At your command,
The Admiral.

Selection 3: An Indian Perspective on the Europeans' Arrival in North America

The Iroquois (also known as the Six Nations) were a powerful confederacy of Indian peoples who inhabited the region south of Lake Ontario in modern-day New York. During the seventeenth and eighteenth centuries, they encountered Dutch, French, and English colonizers and became adept at using the commercial and imperial rivalries between these newcomers to extend their own power in northeastern America. At first with the Dutch and then with the English, the Iroquois established an alliance known as the Covenant Chain, which preserved peace and trade between Indians connected to their confederacy and their colonial neighbors. According to Iroquois custom, this "chain" was "brightened" by colonial officials and Indians who met at periodic conferences to exchange presents, settle differences, and renew their friendship.

One such conference convened in the frontier town of Lancaster, Pennsylvania in 1744. Delegations from Pennsylvania, Maryland, and Virginia met with the Iroquois to discuss trade and to acquire land. One of the Iroquois speakers at this conference was Canasatego, who in a speech addressed to the Maryland governor, recounted the arrival of the Europeans to his people's homelands. Canasatego's version of this story is an excellent example of how Indians incorporated their version of the European–Indian encounter into their own oral traditions.

The spelling has been modernized.

Credit: *A Treaty, Held at the Town of Lancaster, in Pennsylvania, by the Honourable the Lieutenant-Governor of the Province, and the Honourable the Commissioners for the Provinces of Virginia and Maryland, with the Indians of the Six Nations, in June, 1744* (Philadelphia, PA: B. Franklin, 1744), 11–13.

"Brother, the Governor of Maryland,
"When you mentioned the Affair of the Land Yesterday, you went back to old Times, and told us, you had been in Possession of the Province of Maryland, above One Hundred Years; but what is a Hundred Years, in Comparison of the Length of Time since our Claim began?

Since we came out of this Ground? For we must tell you, that long before a Hundred Years, our Ancestors came out of this very Ground, and their Children have remained here ever since.

"You came out of the Ground in a Country that lies beyond the Seas; there you may have a just Claim, but here you must allow us to be your elder Brethren, and the Lands to belong to us long before you knew any Thing of them.

"It is true, that above One Hundred Years ago the Dutch came here in a Ship, and brought with them several Goods, such as Awls, Knives, Hatchets, Guns, and many other Particulars, which they gave us: And when they had taught us how to use their Things, and we saw what Sort of People they were, we were so pleased with them, that we tied their Ship to the Bushes on the Shore; and afterwards, liking them still better the longer they stayed with us, and thinking the Bushes too slender, we removed the Rope and tied it to the Trees; and as the Trees were liable to be blown down by high Winds, or to decay of themselves, from the Affection we bore them, again removed the Rope, and tied it to a strong and big Rock: [Here, the Interpreter said, they mean the Oncido (Oneida) Country] And not content with this, for its further Security, we removed the Rope to the big Mountain, [Here, the Interpreter says, they mean the Onondago Country] and there we tied it very fast, and rolled Wampum [shell beads] about it; and to make it still more secure, we stood upon the Wampum, and sat down upon it, to defend it, and to prevent any Hurt coming to it, and did our best Endeavors, that it might remain uninjured for ever.

"During all this Time, the New-comers the Dutch, acknowledged our Right to the Lands and solicited us from time to time, to grant them part of our Country, to enter into League and Covenant with us, and to become one People with us.

"After this, the English came into the Country, and as we were told, became one People with the Dutch: About two Years after the Arrival of the English, an English Governor came to Albany; and finding what great Friendship subsisted between us and the Dutch, he approved it mightily, and desired to make as strong a League, and to be upon as good Terms with us, as the Dutch were, with whom he was united, and to become one People with us; and by his further Care in looking into what had passed between us, he found, That the Rope which tied the Ship to the great Mountain, was only fastened with Wampum, which was liable to break and rot, and to perish in a Course of Years: He therefore told us, that he would give us a Silver Chain, which would be much stronger, and would last for ever: This we accepted, and fastened the Ship with it, and it has lasted ever since.

"Indeed, we have had some small Differences with the English, and during these Misunderstandings, some of their young Men would, by way of Reproach, be every now and then telling us, that we should have perished, if they had not come into the Country, and furnished us with Strouds [a type of woolen cloth], Hatchets, Guns, and other Things necessary for the Support of Life: But we always gave them to understand, that they were mistaken; that we lived before they came amongst us, and as well or better, if we may believe what our Forefathers have told us: We had then Room enough, and Plenty of Deer, which was easily caught; and though we had not Knives and Hatchets, and Guns, such as we have now, yet we had Knives of Stone, and Hatchets of Stone, and Bows and Arrows, and these served our Uses as well then, as the English ones do now: We are now straightened, and sometimes in want of Deer, and liable to many more Inconveniences, since the English came among us…."

Discussion Questions

1. Compare Cà da Mosto's description of Africans with Columbus's description of Indians: can you find similarities between them that suggest a common approach Europeans took toward strangers they encountered in the Atlantic World? What differences between these accounts suggest potentially different paths for the European-African and European-Indian encounters that would follow?

2. Compare the Africans' reactions to Cà da Mosto with the Indians' reactions to Columbus. According to these two narratives, what did native peoples find impressive about Europeans? What did they find suspect?

3. According to Canasatego, what first attracted the Iroquois to the Dutch ship that arrived in their homelands? How has that relationship changed since the arrival of the English? On what grounds does Canasatego challenge the colonists' claim to the land?

4. In all three of these selections, trade provides a common context for encounter between natives and newcomers. What commercial objectives are evident in Cà da Mosto's and Columbus's accounts? What prejudices are revealed in their descriptions of trade with these strangers? How does Canasatego's description of the European-Indian encounter reflect a different perspective on this exchange?

Suggested Readings

For overviews of European society on the eve of Columbus's voyage, see William D. Phillips, Jr. and Carla Rahn Phillips, *The Worlds of Christopher Columbus* (Cambridge: Cambridge University Press, 1992); and Janet L. Abu-Lughod, *Before European Hegemony: The World System A.D. 1250–1350* (New York: Oxford University Press, 1989). For European reactions to the New World, see J. H. Elliott, *The Old World and the New, 1492–1650* (Cambridge: Cambridge University Press, 1970); and Stephen Greenblatt, *Marvelous Possessions: The Wonder of the New World* (Chicago, IL: University of Chicago Press, 1991). For early encounters between Europeans and sub-Saharan Africans, see John Thornton, *Africa and Africans in the Making of the Atlantic World, 1400–1680* (Cambridge: Cambridge University Press, 1992); and Donald R. Wright, *The World and a Very Small Place in Africa* (Armonk, NY: M. E. Sharpe, 1997). For Native Americans on the eve of European contact, see Charles C. Mann, *1491: New Revelations of the Americas before Columbus* (New York: Knopf, 2005). For the Iroquois-European encounter described by Canasatego in his speech, see Daniel K. Richter, *Ordeal of the Longhouse: The Peoples of the Iroquois League in the Era of European Colonization* (Chapel Hill, NC: University of North Carolina Press, 1992).

2 The Columbian Exchange

Figure 2.1 Smallpox among the Nahuatl in Sixteenth-Century Mexico.

Of the many diseases transmitted across the Atlantic in the Columbian Exchange, smallpox was the most deadly for Native Americans (see Selection 2). Considered a childhood disease in Europe, in America it led to fatality rates that ranged from 30 to 90 percent of infected populations. This image of Native Americans suffering from smallpox comes from a sixteenth-century Spanish collection about the Aztecs.

Source: Florentine Codex, Book XII folio 54. Bernardino de Sahagún, *Historia general de las cosas de la Nueva España* (1540–1585).

Introduction

The passage of human beings between the Old World and the New led to a much wider transfer of plant and animal life commonly known as the Columbian Exchange. Some of this exchange occurred by design, such as when Old World farmers planted American crops in their fields; other times, the exchange was inadvertent, such as when colonists unwittingly introduced new diseases to Native American populations. Whether purposeful or accidental, such exchanges forever altered the nature of plant, animal, and human life on both sides of the Atlantic. Formerly isolated ecosystems became intertwined and transformed in the process. Some species experienced extinction or near extinction, while others flourished in new surroundings unchecked by natural enemies. While scholars have typically studied the human actors involved in this drama, we cannot appreciate the full impact of the Columbian Exchange without considering the other forms of life it affected.

The most profound changes wrought by the Columbian Exchange resulted from the transmission of microbes from the Old World to the New. European sailors, explorers, traders, and colonists brought to the Americas a number of diseases to which Native Americans had had no previous exposure, and therefore, no natural immunities. Smallpox, measles, influenza, bubonic plague, and others broke out in "virgin-soil epidemics" among these new host populations. Estimating the impact that these diseases had on Native Americans has become a contentious business among scholars, involving debates over the pre-Columbian population of the Americas and the fatality rates associated with virgin-soil epidemics. On the high end, some scholars estimate that as many as 18 million Indians lived in North America prior to 1492, and that Old World microbes reduced that number by as much as 95 percent. More conservative estimates place the pre-Columbian population of North America at 4–7 million, with a 60–70 percent reduction in that number by 1700.

Arriving at a consensus figure is difficult because the record is so fragmentary and the methodologies used to interpret it differ significantly. Any estimates recorded by European observers of native populations were local in nature and did not account for earlier epidemics that may have gone unrecorded. Furthermore, the fatality rates associated with such epidemics varied considerably, depending upon the diseases and the regions and cultures involved. Factors of climate and population density influenced how quickly a disease spread among a new population. Generally speaking, sedentary Indian populations were more vulnerable because they came into sustained contact with the newcomers and had difficulty quarantining the infected. Those Indians who lived in hunter-gatherer societies were more isolated and mobile—factors that impeded the spread of epidemics.

The Columbian Exchange also affected plant and animal life in the Atlantic World. Early European explorers were awestruck by the flora and fauna they encountered in the Americas, the sheer variety of which called into question the biblical stories that informed their understanding of the natural world. The existence of different species in the Americas suggested that life in the Western Hemisphere might be the product of a separate creation, not related to the human and animal descendants of Noah's ark. The tropical climate, lush landscape, and naked peoples encountered by Columbus and other explorers in the American tropics called to mind the Garden of Eden, only in this version, humankind still lived in innocence and bounty.

Such impressions of America as an unspoiled Eden were countered by an impulse to profit from its abundant resources. Forests became lumber and naval supplies. The codfish that teemed in the Grand Banks off New England and Canada became a staple of Old World diets. Furbearing animals, most famously the beaver, were transformed into hats, coats, and gloves for the wealthy. The addictive properties of tobacco made this plant a wildly popular consumer good in Atlantic markets. Everywhere Europeans looked in the Americas, they found plants and animals that they could turn into commodities at home. Colonists also introduced new plants and animals to the American landscape for the same purpose. Sugar, rice, and coffee were Old World crops that became staples of colonial plantation economies. European livestock flourished on American farms and ranches, and these animals carried in their bellies and dung the seeds of plants such as bluegrass and dandelions that spread quickly in American ecosystems.

This invasion of new species transformed Native American subsistence patterns. Pigs damaged unfenced Indian cornfields, and grazing by cattle caused soil erosion. Some Native American peoples became sheep and cattle ranchers, and the horse revolutionized the transportation and hunting of Indians on the Great Plains. Indians who had long used beaver, deer, and buffalo for a variety of purposes—food, clothing, tools, shelter—now hunted them to trade in a trans-Atlantic marketplace. The demands of this market challenged taboos that governed Indian–animal relations and led to overhunting of some species, while the Indians themselves became increasingly dependent on European-manufactured firearms, clothing, and metal wares.

Much of what has been said thus far about the Columbian Exchange would suggest that it was one-sided: Old World microbes, plants, and animals invaded and reshaped the ecological balance of the New World. While it is true that the most obvious environmental changes in the Atlantic World occurred in the Americas, the exchange of organisms did have a significant impact on life in the Old World as well. Most important was the introduction of New World crops to Old World agriculture. American maize, potatoes, peanuts, and manioc diversified and enriched diets in Europe and Africa, making possible a population boom in the Old World that continued well into the twentieth century.

The transmission of microbes across the Atlantic had a much less devastating impact on Old World populations than New. In the wake of Columbus, only one disease ravaged Europe's population with the ferocity of a virgin-soil epidemic. Epidemiologists debate the exact origins of syphilis, but there is no doubt that this sexually transmitted disease, first reported in Europe in the 1490s, spread quickly and with devastating consequences in its new host population. For this reason, some scholars contend that it originated in the Americas and was carried back to the Old World by sailors who had sexual contact with Native American women. It is harder to find evidence of other Native American illnesses that crossed the Atlantic. In part, this is because no significant number of Indians resettled in the Old World, either voluntarily or as a result of enslavement. Thus, Europeans and Africans who stayed at home never faced prolonged exposure to illnesses that may have been endemic to the Americas. Also, infectious diseases in human history have typically evolved in farming societies that rely on domesticated animals for food and milk. Over thousands of years, microbes carried by cows, pigs, sheep, and horses have mutated and adapted to human hosts. At the time of Columbus, the only large animals Native Americans had domesticated were dogs, chiefly for hunting and companionship, and llamas, chiefly as beasts of burden and for their wool. This limited experience with livestock meant that Indians simply had fewer germs to offer to Columbus than he had to offer them.

While the Columbian Exchange continues even today (consider for example the spread of the AIDS virus), its historical legacy for the Atlantic World is quite clear. Old World species derived considerable benefit from contact with the New, by way of access to new land and resources, but the species of the New World suffered considerably. Europeans and Africans displaced Native Americans, while the Old World's demand for American fish, pelts, timber, and other goods tested the sustainability of many American species. Overall, the mixing of species from both sides of the Atlantic has diversified and expanded the world's food supplies and trade, but at the cost of disrupting local ecosystems and human populations.

The readings in this chapter focus on the role microbes, plants, and animals played in encounters between the Old World and the New. The first selection presents an early description of Indian farming, including the "three sisters" (corn, beans, and squash) that were staples of the Indian diet, and tobacco. The second selection focuses on the clash between European and Native American conceptions of human–animal relations and disease transmission. The third selection provides an example of the European fascination with the animal life encountered in the Americas. The fourth selection calls our attention to how the Columbian Exchange continued to affect race relations and notions of racial difference in the Atlantic World long after the period of initial contact and colonization was over. As you read these sources, think about how the Columbian Exchange challenged the mental and physical worlds of the people it involved. How did the collision of microbes, plants, and animals in the Atlantic World shape human experience there?

Selection 1: An Elizabethan Scientist Admires Indian Agriculture

During the 1580s, the English tried twice to establish a colony on Roanoke Island off the coast of modern-day North Carolina. Both ventures failed, but they did give the English their first prolonged interaction with Indians and the American environment. Thomas Hariot was a scientist and mathematician who participated in the first Roanoke expedition of 1585. After returning to England, he published a description of his experiences there to promote the further colonization of Virginia.

While he shared many of the prejudices of his Elizabethan contemporaries about America's native inhabitants, Hariot was nevertheless a careful observer of their culture and society. He expressed great admiration for their agriculture and described in detail their crops and methods of planting. His glowing descriptions of the Indian diet and the fertility of the land must have appealed mightily to English farmers accustomed to eking meager livings out of spent soil and back-breaking labor.

The spelling has been modernized.

Credit: Thomas Hariot, *A Briefe and True Report of the New Found Land of Virginia*, in Richard Hakluyt, *The Principall Navigations, Voiages, and Discoveries of the English Nation* (London: George Bishop, 1589), 753–757.

Such commodities as Virginia is known to yield for victual and sustenance of man's life, usually fed upon by the natural inhabitants, as also by us, during the time of our abode, and first of such as are sowed and husbanded [cultivated]:

Pagatowr, a kind of grain so called by the inhabitants; the same in the West Indies is called Maize. English men call it Guinea Wheat or Turkey wheat, according to the names of the countries from whence the like has been brought. The grain is about the bigness of our ordinary English peas and not much different in form and shape, but of diverse colors, some white, some red, some yellow, and some blue. All of them yield a very white and sweet flower, being used according to this kind, it makes a very good bread. We made of the same in the country some malt, whereof was brewed as good Ale as was to be desired. So likewise by the help of hops thereof may be made as good Beer. It is a grain of marvelous great increase; of a thousand, fifteen hundred, and some two thousand fold …

Okindgier, called by us Beans, because in greatness and partly in shape they are like the Beans in England; saving that they are flatter, of more diverse colors, and some pied. The leaf also of the stem is much different. In taste they are altogether as good as our English peas.

Wickonzówr, called by us Peas, in respect of the beans, for distinction sake, because they are much less [in size], although in form they little differ, but in goodness of taste much, and are far better than our English peas. Both the beans and peas are ripe in ten weeks after they are set. They make them victual either by boiling them all to pieces into a broth, or boiling them whole until they be soft and begin to break as is used in England, either by themselves or mixed together. Sometimes they mingle of the wheat with them. Sometimes also being whole sodden, they bruise or pound them in a mortar, and therefore make loaves or lumps of doughish bread, which they use to eat for variety.

Macócqwer [pumpkins and squash], according to their several forms, called by us Pompions, Melons, and Gourds, because they are of the like forms as those kinds in England. In Virginia such of several forms are of one taste and very good, and do also spring from one seed. There are two sorts: one is ripe in the space of a month, and the other in two months.

There is also an herb which in Dutch is called *Melden*. Some of those that I describe it onto take it to be a kind of Orach [spinach or beets]. It grows about four or five foot high; of seeds thereof they make a thick broth and pottage of a very good taste; of the stalk by burning into ash they make a kind of salt earth, where withal many use sometimes to season their broths. Other salt they know not. We ourselves used the leaves for pot-herbs.

There is also another great herb, in form of a Marigold, about six foot in height, the head with the flower is a span in breadth. Some take it to be *Planta Solis* [sunflowers]; of the seeds hereof they make both a kind of bread and broth.

All the aforesaid commodities for victual are set or sowed, sometimes in grounds apart and severally by themselves, but for the most part together in one ground mixedly, the manner thereof, with the dressing and preparing of the ground, because I will note unto you the fertility of the soil, I think good briefly to describe.

The ground they never fatten with muck, dung, or any other thing, neither plow nor dig it as we in England, but only prepare it in sort as follows. A few days before they sow or set, the men with wooden instruments, made also in form of mattocks or hoes with long handles, with women with short peckers or parers, because they use them sitting, of a foot long and about five inches in breadth, do only break the upper part of the ground to raise up the weeds, grass, and old stubs of corn stalks with their roots, which after a day or two drying in the sun, being scraped up into many small heaps, to save them labor for carrying them away, they burn into ashes … And this is all the husbanding of their ground that they use.

Then their setting or sowing is after this manner. First for their corn, beginning in one corner of the plot, with a pecker they make a hole, wherein they put four grains, with that care they touch not one to another (about an inch asunder) and cover them with the mold again, and so throughout the whole plot, making such holes and using them after such manner, but with this regard, that they be made in ranks, every rank differing from the other half a fathom or a yard, and the holes also in every rank, as much. By this means there is a yard spare ground between every hole, where according to discretion here and there, they set as many Beans and Peas, and in diverse places also among the seeds of *Macócqwer*, *Melden*, and *Planta Solis*.

The ground being thus set … doth there yield in crop of … corn, beans, and peas, at the least two hundred London bushels, besides the *Macócqwer*, *Melden*, and *Planta Solis*; when as in England, forty bushels of our wheat yielded out of such an acre is thought to be much.

I thought also good to note this unto you, that you which shall inhabit and plant there, may know how specially that country corn is there to be preferred before ours. Besides the manifold ways of applying it to victual, the increase is so much that small labor and pains is needful in respect that must be used for ours. For this I can assure you, that according to the rate we have made proof of, one man may prepare and husband so much ground (having once borne corn before) with less than four and twenty hours labor, as shall yield him victual in a large proportion for twelve months …

There is an herb which is sowed apart by itself and is called by the inhabitants *uppówoc*. In the West Indies it has diverse names, according to the several places and countries where it grows and is used. The Spaniards generally call it Tobacco. The leaves thereof being dried and brought into powder, they use to take the fume or smoke thereof by sucking it through pipes made of clay, into their stomach and head, from whence it purges superfluous phlegm and other gross humors, opens all the pores and passages of the body, by which means the use thereof, not only preserves the body from obstructions, but also, if any be, so that they have not been of too long continuance, in short time breaks them, whereby their bodies are notably preserved in health and know not many grievous diseases wherewithal we in England are oftentimes afflicted.

This *uppówoc* is of so precious estimation among them, that they think their gods are marvelously delighted therewith. Whereupon sometime they make hallowed fires and cast some of the powder therein for a sacrifice. Being in a storm upon the waters, to pacify their gods, they cast some up into the air and into the water. So a weir for fish being newly set up, they cast some therein into the air likewise, but all done with strange gestures, stamping, sometime dancing, clapping of hands, holding up of hands, and staring up into the heavens, uttering therewithal and chattering strange words and noises.

We ourselves during the time we were there used to suck it after their manner, as also since our return, and have found many rare and wonderful experiments of the virtues thereof, of which the relation would require a volume by itself; the use of it by so many of late men and women of great calling as else and some learned physicians also, is sufficient witness.

Selection 2: The Exchange of Furs and Microbes in New France

The Society of Jesus was a Catholic religious order founded in the sixteenth century for the purpose of winning converts throughout the world. Jesuits, as its members were known, spearheaded the missionary effort in French Canada. Their annual reports, which were published in Paris to gain financial and political support for their cause, detailed their efforts to learn Indian languages, ingratiate themselves to Indian communities, and gain converts by persuasion and example. Collected and published in a series known as the *Jesuit Relations*, these reports are one of the most important sources on early contact and exchange between Europeans and Indians.

The Jesuits were most concerned with the Indians' spiritual beliefs, but in documenting those, they invariably described other aspects of native life, such as human–animal relations and medicine. In the first passage below, from 1634, Father Paul Le Jeune reports on taboos that governed Indian hunting practices and one Indian's reaction to the fur trade. In the second, from 1653, Father Francesco Bressani describes how the outbreak of new diseases affected the Hurons' reception of the Jesuits.

Credit: Reuben G. Thwaites, ed., *The Jesuit Relations and Allied Documents: Travels and Explorations of the Jesuit Missionaries in New France, 1610–1791*, 73 vols (Cleveland, OH: Burrows Brothers, 1896–1901), Vol. 6: 211–213, 297–299; Vol. 39: 125–135.

The Savages do not throw to the dogs the bones of female Beavers and Porcupines,—at least, certain specified bones; in short, they are very careful that the dogs do not eat any bones of birds and of other animals which are taken in the net, otherwise they will take no more except with incomparable difficulties. Yet they make a thousand exceptions to this rule, for it does not matter if the vertebrae or rump of these animals be given to the dogs, but the rest must be thrown into the fire. Yet, as to the Beaver which has been taken in a trap, it is best to throw its bones into a river. It is remarkable how they gather and collect these bones, and preserve them with so much care, that you would say their game would be lost if they violated their superstitions. As I was laughing at them, and telling them that Beavers do not know what is done with their bones, they answered me, "Thou does not know how to take Beavers, and thou wishest to talk about it." Before the Beaver was entirely dead, they told me, its soul comes to make the round of the Cabin of him who has killed it, and looks very carefully to see what is done with its bones; if they are given to the dogs, the other Beavers would be apprised of it and therefore they would make themselves hard to capture. But they are very glad to have their bones thrown into the fire, or into a river; especially the trap which has caught them is very glad of this. I told them that the Hiroquois [Iroquois], according to the reports of the one who was with us, threw the bones of the Beaver to the dogs, and yet they took them very often; and our Frenchmen captured more game than they did (without comparison), and yet our dogs ate these bones. "Thou hast no sense," they replied, "dost thou not see that you and the Hiroquois cultivate the soil and gather its fruits, and not we, and that therefore it is not the same thing?" I began to laugh when I heard this irrelevant answer. The trouble is, I only stutter, I take one word for another, I pronounce badly; and so everything usually passes off in laughter. What great difficulty there is in talking with people without being able to understand them.

***

The Castor or Beaver is taken in several ways. The Savages say that it is the animal well-beloved by the French, English and Basques,—in a word, by the Europeans. I heard my host say one day, jokingly, *Missi picoutau amissou*, "The Beaver does everything perfectly well, it makes kettles, hatchets, swords, knives, bread; and, in short, it makes everything." He was making sport of us Europeans, who have such a fondness for the skin of this animal and who fight to see who will give the most to these Barbarians, to get it; they carry this to such an extent that my host said to me one day, showing me a very beautiful knife, "The English have no sense; they give us twenty knives like this for one Beaver skin."

***

[I]t was a common opinion that we were the authors of a kind of pestilence which was not usual in the country, and almost utterly ruined it. They founded their suspicion, or rather, certain belief, first, on the ground that the supposed magicians and the principal men of the country assured them of it, and the people easily believe without other examination; secondly, on the ground that although, at the beginning, almost all of ours had been attacked by the disease at the same time,—without a physician, or medicine, or convenience of provisions; without other refreshment than a little wild purslane [herb], boiled in clear water without salt; in extreme necessity and dearth of everything,—they had in a few days convalesced, and recovered perfect health; whereas the Barbarians, with all their remedies, both natural and superstitious, nearly all died. And, in truth, our cures in those countries were a singular grace of God. The Father who wrote the letter copied herein, a little above, being asked what remedy he had employed for the many and dangerous wounds he had received from the Hiroquois,—of which expert Physicians in Europe have said that they would not, without great fear, have undertaken the cure,—answered that he had used no other than a most austere but necessary diet, and his teeth,—with which, having no other instrument, he tore away even to the quick the putrid flesh, in order to eradicate the gangrene which was already forming in three several places of his lacerated hands. [B]ecause, although ours remained almost all the time with the diseased, and those the most filthy and dangerous ones, who were dying on our hands, no one caught the contagion; so that they accounted us Demons, and believed that we had made *fœdus cum morte, et pactum cum Inferno* [an agreement with death, and a pact with Hell]. There had been started at Kebek [Quebec] a Seminary for Huron Youths, which, we believed, would be of great use for propagating our Holy Faith in the country; but there the young men have not great influence, and more easily allow themselves to be perverted than to convert the others, so that, afterward, the mature men were preferred to the youths. To begin this, it was necessary to make great gifts to the parents of the Young men; and, besides that, to persuade them themselves to dwell with us. The Father who had charge of them told someone, in persuading him to remain at Kebek, that he warned him, indeed, that perhaps on returning to his own country he would die in the universal disease, which was ruining it. It is not certain whether the Father went so far; but it is not true that he might believe so, because many traders that year had been infected, as it was believed, with the contagion; and the malady had already assailed many of those Barbarians. Whether true or not, the young man having returned to that country, and seeing the spread of the disease, of course told the Captains that the Father who had wished to keep him at Kebek had predicted the same,—so that he concluded that he was an accomplice therein, and with his companions, the author. Some added that we had for this purpose brought from France a corpse, which we were carefully keeping in our house as something precious,—making allusion to the Most Holy Sacrament, which we kept in our Chapel; we had spoken of this to our Christians, on which account they wished to visit and seek everywhere this corpse, the origin of the pestilence. They said the same thing about some images, etc.; the prayers that we made, and the masses which we said at an early hour, with closed doors; the litanies; even walking abroad,—a new thing in those countries,—were superstitions which we practiced in order to destroy them. It was necessary to stop a small striking clock, which served to regulate our time,—for they regarded it as a Demon which, by striking, gave a sign to death for killing them. They found a superstition even in a little streamer hung at the crest of a pine, and believed that the disease was cast from that flag, wherever the wind drove it; and, because it turned about, now in one direction, now in another, they said therefore that there was no place untainted in the country; they supposed that we had enveloped the malady therein, so as to carry it into the country. "This disease," said many, "has not been engendered here; it comes from without; never have we seen Demons so cruel. The other maladies lasted two or three moons" (they reckon time by moons, like the Hebrews); "this has been persecuting us for more than a year. Ours are content with one or two in a family; this, in many, has left no more than that number,—and, in many, none at all. The loss from the old ones was repaired in a few years, of which we lost not the memory; this would require whole ages to repeople us." I omit the fables which they spread abroad about persons come to life again, who accused and condemned us, together with all the mysteries of the holy Faith, etc.

And this was not simply a popular opinion with people of small account, but it was that of the Captains themselves, and of the most intelligent men, who several times called a council to resolve upon the death of all of ours, and came to announce it to us. Father Brebeuf, the Superior, was repeatedly examined in the public councils, and harshly treated; and thinking the matter already decided, he made,—after the necessary preparations, and the vows made to God, appropriate to the time; and a letter written to Kebek, and consigned to one of our friends, who was already showing us compassion,—on the day when their execution was expected, and according to the usage of the country, a feast which they call "the Farewell." Every dying man makes this, whether he die naturally, or by a violent death, like the captives,—who, having received the news of their death, must say Farewell to their friends: and for this purpose the master of the captive prepares a feast, to which he invites the principal persons of the country, of whom the captive, already destined to the fire, takes leave; a dying man does the same. Ours did so in order to show themselves ready for death, which they did not fear; and they were expecting nothing else than the execution of the sentence which condemned them as sorcerers, and as the assassins of the entire country. Then an unlooked-for Ambassador came to invite Father Brebeuf to the council again, where the principal men of all those nations were assembled. After a very long examination, and a still longer discourse, though interrupted, by the Father,—who spoke more of the Faith than of the pestilence, warning them, with wonderful fearlessness, that not we, but the justice of the God whom we preach, provoked by their sins, was the sole cause of their troubles which would last until they appeased him with the requisite submission and penance,—they so changed their opinion that they sent him away, as it were absolved. Many—notwithstanding the replies of some Captains who called him "a troublesome fellow, who was always repeating the same thing," "one unworthy to live," etc.—requested of the Father, as he went out, to be instructed in the Faith; and, on leaving the same cabin, he saw killed at his feet, with a hatchet-blow, a Barbarian who was most hostile to the Faith. Now, as it was getting late, the Father thought that the murderer had deceived himself, and had taken the dead man for him: and, having stopped, he said to him, "Was it not perhaps for me that this blow was intended?" "No," answered the other, "go on; this man was a sorcerer, and not thou." Let the reader imagine the thanks which were rendered to God at the sight of the Father, who regarded himself as a man risen from the dead; and at the hope of being able to continue the conversion of those wretched people in their extreme necessity.

Selection 3: A Military Officer Contemplates Life in a Beaver Lodge

Thomas Anburey was an Anglo-Irish officer in the British Army who came to America in 1776. As a soldier and prisoner of war, he traveled extensively in Canada and the United States before returning home in 1781. His memoir, published in 1789, provides an engaging tour of the American landscape and its plant, animal, and human life.

Like many of his contemporaries, Anburey often described the new animal species he encountered by ascribing human attributes to them. Nowhere is this more evident than in his description of the beaver, an animal that many Europeans believed exhibited anthropomorphic social habits and engineering skills. Anburey described life in a beaver lodge as cozy, cooperative, and contented, its bliss interrupted only by human marauders, who hunted these animals to satisfy their tastes for luxury and fashion. Anburey is a good example of the curiosity that the New World environment inspired in Europeans and the misgivings some of them expressed about its despoliation by profit-seekers.

Credit: Thomas Anburey, *Travels Through the Interior Parts of America*, 2 vols (London: William Lane, 1789), Vol. 1: 241–248, 251–253.

But it was no sooner understood that Canada was stored with Beavers, than the savages, urged on by a more lucrative interest, directed their war against an animal the most harmless, who molests no living creature, and is neither carnivorous nor sanguinary. This is [has], I am sorry to observe, become an object of man's most earnest pursuit, and the one that the savages hunt after with the greatest eagerness and cruelty; a circumstance entirely owing to the unmerciful rapaciousness which luxury has made necessary in skins, for all the polished nations of Europe.

This animal is by nature adapted for social life, being endowed with an instinct in the preservation and propagation of its species; it is generally about three or four feet long, mostly weighing from forty to sixty pounds; the hinder feet are webbed, which enables it to swim, and in the fore feet the toes are divided; its tail is oval, very flat, and covered with scales; the head resembles that of a rat, in which are four very sharp teeth, with these it will gnaw through trees of a great circumference.

This animal is divested of turbulent passions, without a desire of doing injury to any one, free from craft, scarcely defending itself, unless it lives in society; it never bites, except when caught, and as nature has not supplied it with any weapons of defence, by a natural instinct as it were, it forms societies, and has various contrivances to secure its ease, without fighting, and to live without committing, or suffering an injury; although this peaceable, and you may say almost tame animal, enters into society, it is nevertheless independent, every want being supplied by itself, and therefore it is a slave to none. It will not serve, nor does it pretend to command, every care seems directed by an instinct, that at the same time, as it labors for the general good, it lives for itself alone. To learn the nature of the societies of these animals, as it was related to me by my landlord, may afford you the same entertainment it did me.

In the month of June or July, they assemble from all quarters, to the number of two or three hundred, near some lake or pool of water, to build their habitations against winter, the construction of which, from the complication and manner of disposing the materials, one would be led to imagine to be beyond the capacity of any one but an intelligent being, and especially in their constructing of dams, when they cannot meet with a lake or pool; in this case they fix upon some river, when the first of their labour is to make a dam, which they generally do in the shallowest part of the stream, for that purpose felling trees with the four sharp teeth that I have already described; five or six of them will gnaw a large one through, and to mark to you the wonderful sagacity of these industrious brutes, they contrive it so that it always falls in the water: having laid this foundation, they fell smaller trees, which they roll to this great one, but what appears the most wonderful is, the manner they sink the piles in the water, to prevent the stream's carrying away the trees, they lay across. Their contrivance is this, with their nails they dig a hole in the ground, or at the bottom of the water, with their teeth they rest the stake against the bank of the river, or against the tree that lies across, and with their feet they raise the stake and sink it with the sharp end (which these sensible animals make to it) in the hole that they have made, where it stands up; and to render these stakes or piles more secure, they interweave branches of small trees, and with their tails wisk up a kind of mortar with clay, and fill the vacant space of the interwoven branches.

After this work is finished by the body at large, each one considers of some lodging for himself; an hut being built upon piles on the sides of the Lake, capable of containing from two or three to ten or fifteen, (for they divide themselves into companies, and build these huts accordingly;) which are formed with walls and partitions of about two feet thick and as many in height, arched over, and the whole so plaistered with clay, that the smallest breath of air cannot penetrate through them; each apartment is made large enough to contain two, a male and female; each hut has two entrances, one towards the land, and the other on the side towards the stream, the former for them to go into the woods to fetch provisions, and the latter to escape from their enemy, that is to say MAN, the destroyer of cities and commonwealths. The inside of their apartments has no other furniture than the flooring of grass covered with the boughs of the fir, and these animals are so cleanly, that no filth of any kind is ever seen in these apartments.

In each hut there are store houses proportionate to the number of its inhabitants; every one knows its own, and never steals from his neighbour. Each party, that is to say, the male and female, live in their own habitations; they have no jealousies or quarrels; the provisions of the community are collected and expended without any contest, and rest satisfied with the simple food that their labors procure them. The only passion they have is that of conjugal affection, wherein a most excellent example is held forth to that all-wise and all sufficient man, who is led away by every gust of passion and vanity.

Two of these animals, in the course of their labours in the summer months, match together, unite by inclination and reciprocal choice, and agree to pass the winter, and like too many couples who hastily enter into matrimony with equally as good motives, but forgetting what should make the happiness lasting, that of laying up a stock to guard against an inclement season.

The happy couple retire to their hut about the end of autumn, which has been observed to be no less favorable to love than spring; for if the season of flowers invites the feathered tribe to propagate in the woods, the season of fruits as powerfully excites the inhabitants of the earth in the reproduction of their species; besides, as winter gives leisure for amorous pursuits, it compensates for the advantages of other seasons.

***

If by chance a sun-shiny day should happen to enliven the gloomy melancholy of the season, the happy couple leave their huts to walk on the borders of the Lake, regaling themselves with some fresh bark, and breathing the salutary exhalations of the earth. At the conclusion of the winter, the mother brings forth the endearing pledges of their affection, while the father ranges the woods, allured by the sweets of the spring, leaving to his little family that portion of room which he took up in his narrow cell. The Beaver generally produces two or three, which the mother suckles, nurses and trains up, for when the father is absent, she takes out the young ones, in her excursions for cray and other fish, and green bark to recruit her own strength and to feed her young, till the season of labor returns; for although these animals are so industrious as to build themselves habitations that would last them a century, they are obliged to rebuild them every year, as the first thing the traders do when they meet with any of their works, is to break down their cabins and the dam, together with their dyke.

There are various methods of taking and destroying these animals, by draining the water from their dykes, and sometimes by snares; they are very seldom shot at, for unless killed on the spot, they are lost to the huntsman, by plunging into the water wounded, when they sink to the bottom and never rise. The most certain and general mode of catching them is by setting traps in the woods, where they perceive them to have been eating the bark of the young trees; they bait these traps with fresh slips of wood, which the Beaver no sooner touches, than a great weight falls and crushes its loins, when the huntsman, who lies concealed near the spot, hastens to kill it.

No doubt but by this time you are heartily tired with so long a detail of this animal; but if I have deviated from the common path of description, I can only say it has proceeded from these two causes, that I cannot sufficiently admire the many virtues it possesses, divested of all manner of vice, and have been lost in the contemplation of that Divine Being, who formed it with all these natural endowments.

Selection 4: Black Philadelphians Face a Yellow Fever Epidemic

When historians study the role of diseases in the Columbian Exchange, they often focus their efforts on the impact that smallpox had on Native American populations, but it is important to remember that the Atlantic Ocean never stopped serving as a highway for microbes, and indeed, continues to do so today. As colonial seaports expanded their trade with the outside world, their populations became vulnerable to diseases transmitted by sailors, immigrants, and other human and animal travelers.

In one such instance, an epidemic of yellow fever broke out in Philadelphia in 1793. Yellow fever is a disease transmitted by mosquitoes and most commonly found in West Africa. It likely arrived in Philadelphia on a ship that had previously stopped in West Africa and the Caribbean, and it spread rapidly among the residents of Philadelphia, which at that time was the largest city in the United States. Dr. Benjamin Rush led efforts to relieve the sick and dying, relying heavily on the eighteenth-century medical practice of bleeding in hopes of removing the contagion from the body. Wealthier citizens fled the city, leaving the poor behind to deal with the crisis. Officials specifically called on the city's black residents to provide care for the sick because they erroneously believed that people of African ancestry carried immunities to the disease. Many responded to this call and worked under Rush's direction, only to face criticism from whites, who accused them of overcharging for their services. In the passage below, two leading members of Philadelphia's black community defend their conduct during the crisis.

Credit: [Absalom Jones and Richard Allen], *A Narrative of the Proceedings of the Black People, during the Late Awful Calamity in Philadelphia* (Philadelphia, PA: William W. Woodward, 1794), 3–6, 15–18.

In consequence of a partial representation of the conduct of the people who were employed to nurse the sick, in the late calamitous state of the city of Philadelphia, we are solicited by a number of those who feel themselves injured thereby, and by the advice of several respectable citizens, to step forward and declare facts as they really were; seeing that from our situation, on account of the charge we took upon us, we had it more fully and generally in our power, to know and observe the conduct and behavior of those that were so employed.

Early in September, a solicitation appeared in the public papers, to the people of colour to come forward and assist the distressed, perishing, and neglected sick; with a kind of assurance, that people of our colour were not liable to take the infection. Upon which we and a few others met and consulted how to act on so truly alarming and melancholy an occasion. After some conversation, we found a freedom to go forth, confiding in him who can preserve in the midst of a burning fiery furnace [i.e., God], sensible that it was our duty to do all the good we could to our suffering fellow mortals. We set out to see where we could be useful. The first we visited was a man in Emsley's alley, who was dying, and his wife lay dead at the time in the house, there were none to assist but two poor helpless children. We administered what relief we could, and applied to the overseers of the poor to have the woman buried. We visited upwards of twenty families that day—they were scenes of woe indeed! The Lord was pleased to strengthen us, and remove all fear from us, and disposed out hearts to be as useful as possible.

In order the better to regulate our conduct, we called on the mayor next day, to consult with him how to proceed, so as to be most useful. The first object he recommended was a strict attention to the sick, and the procuring of nurses. This was attended to by Absalom Jones and William Gray; and, in order that the distressed might know where to apply, the mayor advertised the public that upon application to them they would be supplied. Soon after, the mortality increasing, the difficulty of getting a corpse taken away, was such, that few were willing to do it, when offered great rewards. The black people were looked to. We then offered our services in the public papers, by advertising that we would remove the dead and procure nurses. Our services were the production of real sensibility; we sought not fee nor reward, until the increase of the disorder rendered our labour so arduous that we were not adequate to the service we had assumed. The mortality increasing rapidly, obliged us to call in the assistance of five hired men, in the awful discharge of interring the dead. They, with great reluctance, were prevailed upon to join us. It was very uncommon, at this time, to find any one that would go near, much more, handle, a sick or dead person ...

When the sickness became general, and several of the physicians died, and most of the survivors were exhausted by sickness or fatigue; that good man, Doctor Rush, called us more immediately to attend upon the sick, knowing we could both bleed; he told us we could increase our utility, by attending to his instructions, and accordingly directed us where to procure medicine duly prepared, with proper directions how to administer them, and at what stages of the disorder to bleed; and when we found ourselves incapable of judging what was proper to be done, to apply to him, and he would, if able, attend them himself, or send Edward Fisher, his pupil, which he often did; and Mr. Fisher manifested his humanity, by an affectionate attention for their relief.—This has been no small satisfaction to us; for, we think, that when a physician was not attainable, we have been the instruments, in the hand of God, for saving the lives of some hundreds of our suffering fellow mortals.

We feel ourselves sensibly aggrieved by the censorious epithets of many, who did not render the least assistance in the time of necessity, yet are liberal of their censure of us, for the prices paid for our services, when no one knew how to make a proposal to any one they wanted to assist them. At first we made no charge, but left it to those we served in removing their dead, to give what they thought fit—we set no price, until the reward was fixed by those we had served. After paying the people we had to assist us, our compensation is much less than many will believe.

***

It is even to this day a generally received opinion in this city, that our colour was not so liable to the sickness as the whites. We hope our friends will pardon us for setting this matter in its true state ...

When the people of colour has the sickness and died, we were imposed upon and told it was not with the prevailing sickness, until it became too notorious to be denied, then we were told some few died but not many. Thus were our services extorted *at the peril of our lives*, yet you accuse us of extorting *a little money from you.*

The bill of mortality for the year 1793, published by Matthew Whitehead, and John Ormrod, clerks, and Joseph Dolby, sexton, will convince any reasonable man that will examine it, that as many coloured people died in proportion as others. In 1792, there were 67 of our colour buried, and in 1793 it amounted to 305; thus the burials among us have increased more than fourfold, was not this in a great degree the effects of the service of the unjustly vilified black people? ...

When the mortality came to its greatest stage, it was impossible to procure sufficient assistance, therefore many whose friends, and relations had left them, died unseen and unassisted. We have found them in various situations, some laying on the floor, as bloody as if they had been dipt in it, without any appearance of their having had, even a drink of water for their relief; others laying on a bed with their clothes on, as if they had come in fatigued, and lain down to rest; some appeared, as if they had fallen dead on the floor, from the position we found them in.

Truly our task was hard, yet through mercy, we were enabled to go on.

One thing we observed in several instances—when we were called, on the first appearance of the disorder to bleed, the person frequently, on the opening a vein before the operation was near over, felt a change for the better, and expressed a relief in their chief complaints; and we made it a practice to take more blood from them, than is usual in other cases; these in a general way recovered; those who did omit bleeding any considerable time, after being taken by the sickness, rarely expressed any change they felt in the operation.

We feel a great satisfaction in believing, that we have been useful to the sick, and thus publicly thank Doctor Rush, for enabling us to be so. We have bled upwards of eight hundred people, and do declare, we have not received to the value of a dollar and a half, therefore: we were willing to *imitate* the Doctor's benevolence, who sick or well, kept his house open day and night, to give what assistance he could in this time of trouble.

Discussion Questions

1. According to Hariot, what accounts for the bounty of Indian agriculture? Why do you think his description of the Indians' diet and farming would appeal to potential colonists? What are some of the remarkable properties he attributes to tobacco and smoking?

2. According to the *Jesuit Relations*, how did Indians relate the arrival of epidemic diseases to the European newcomers? How does Bressani's description of Father Brebeuf's escape from execution reflect the Jesuits' interpretation of the meaning of these epidemics?

3. What human qualities does Anburey attribute to the beaver? How does he compare this animal's behavior to human nature? In what ways do you think Anburey may be using this account of the beaver to criticize human society?

4. How did responses to the 1793 yellow fever epidemic in Philadelphia reflect the racial attitudes of the day? How did the city's physicians treat the sick, and do you think their efforts helped or worsened the situation?

Suggested Readings

The work of Alfred W. Crosby, Jr. has profoundly influenced the questions historians ask about the ecological consequences of the Atlantic World. See especially *The Columbian Exchange: Biological and Cultural Consequences of 1492* (Westport, CT: Greenwood Press, 1972); and *Germs, Seeds, and Animals: Studies in Ecological History* (Armonk, NY: M. E. Sharpe, 1994). Peter C. Mancall examines European and Native American views of the natural world in *Nature and Culture in the Early Modern Atlantic* (Philadelphia, PA: University of Pennsylvania Press, 2017). Two environmental histories of North American colonization are William Cronon, *Changes in the Land: Indians, Colonists, and the Ecology of New England* (New York: Hill and Wang, 1983); and Timothy Silver, *A New Face on the Countryside: Indians, Colonists, and Slaves in South Atlantic Forests, 1500–1800* (Cambridge: Cambridge University Press, 1990). The effect of European diseases on Native American populations is described in Noble David Cook, *Born to Die: Disease and New World Conquest, 1492–1650* (Cambridge: Cambridge University Press, 1998). For a critical view of recent estimates of the pre-Columbian population of the Americas, see David P. Henige, *Numbers from Nowhere: The American Indian Contact Population Debate* (Norman, OK: University of Oklahoma Press, 1998). Jared Diamond offers a lucid and convincing explanation for the unequal nature of disease transmission between the Old World and the New in *Guns, Germs, and Steel: The Fates of Human Societies* (New York: W. W. Norton and Company, 1999).

Works that address how New World animal species became commodities in Atlantic World markets include Mark Kurlansky, *Cod: A Biography of the Fish that Changed the World* (New York: Penguin Books, 1997); and Calvin Martin, *Keepers of the Game: Indian–Animal*

Relationships and the Fur Trade (Berkeley, CA: University of California Press, 1978). For a comprehensive review of North American Indians' environmental attitudes and practices, see Sherpard Krech III, *The Ecological Indian: Myth and History* (New York: W. W. Norton and Company, 1999). Readers interested in Hariot's Roanoke colony should refer to Karen Ordahl Kupperman, *Roanoke: The Abandoned Colony* (Savage, MD: Rowman and Littlefield Publishers, 1984); and those interested in learning more about the Jesuits' interaction with the Indians of Canada should see Bruce G. Trigger, *The Children of Aataentsic: A History of the Huron People to 1660*, 2 vols (Montreal: McGill-Queen's University Press, 1976). The Atlantic dimensions of Philadelphia's 1793 yellow fever epidemic are addressed in Billy G. Smith, *Ship of Death: A Voyage that Changed the Atlantic World* (New Haven, CT: Yale University Press, 2013).

3 Captivities

Figure 3.1 An Early American Captivity Narrative.

Mary Rowlandson's account of her captivity among New England Indians during King Philip's War (1675–1676) was first published in 1681 and became a foundational example of the captivity narrative in American literature. During the Revolutionary era, new editions appeared that featured an image of Rowlandson confronting her captors with a musket, although no such incident occurs in the narrative. Why do you think this image of an armed woman became popular in the late eighteenth century?

Source: *A Narrative of the Captivity, Sufferings, and Removes of Mrs. Mary Rowlandson* (Boston, MA: Printed and Sold at John Boyle's Printing-Office, 1773).

Introduction

One important avenue of intercultural contact and exchange in the Atlantic World was the experience of captivity. Often the by-product of war, captivity subjected a person to a startling and violent set of circumstances: being torn away from friends and family, forced to live in unfamiliar surroundings, and immersed into the lives and habits of strangers. Captives who survived their ordeals often described them as not only physically dangerous but also psychologically traumatic, as they witnessed the torture and death of others, feared becoming victims of cannibalism, and struggled with the capricious will of their masters. The experience of captivity, however, could also give people new skills and insights into another culture, enabling them to form intimate relationships across cultural divides and to become valued brokers who could help negotiate trade and diplomacy between different peoples.

Long before contact with Europeans, Native Americans used captivity to incorporate strangers into their societies and to render them more predictable and useful. Indian war parties usually enslaved captives or adopted them to replace deceased loved ones. Adult male captives were always a security risk, and so they were likely candidates to suffer torture and execution to assuage the grief and anger of community members who had lost loved ones. Some Native American cultures practiced ritual cannibalism as a means of assimilating the bravery and fortitude exhibited by enemy warriors when they were tortured to death. Captive women and children, on the other hand, were prime candidates for being "raised up" in the place of deceased family members and adopted into the community. Female captives who married into their captors' families were valued for the reproductive role they played in sustaining the next generation. Child captives learned new languages, manners, and customs more quickly than their adult counterparts, and so were prime candidates for adoption. Some Native American societies also enslaved war captives, putting them to work as laborers or trading them much like any other kind of moveable property. The exchange of war captives played an important role in Native American diplomacy. Repatriated war captives helped cement peace with a former enemy, and captives given to a new ally offered tangible proof of a nation's military power.

The arrival of European colonizers in America placed new pressures on the role of captives in Native American societies. Indigenous peoples coping with epidemic diseases such as smallpox went to war to acquire captives to replenish their collapsing populations. Europeans created a new market for Indian slaves, and Native Americans used firearms acquired in the fur trade to fight deadlier and more expansive wars to supply that demand. For example, between 1675 and 1715, approximately 25,000 Native American slaves were exported from South Carolina to the sugar colonies of the West Indies. Africans also became caught up in this cycle of warfare, captivity, and enslavement in the Southeast, pulling Native Americans closer into Atlantic markets for slaves, furs, and firearms.

From their earliest encounters, Europeans and Native Americans took each other captive for a variety of purposes. Beginning with Columbus, European explorers kidnapped Indians and forced them to work as guides and interpreters for coastal and inland expeditions. Some unlucky Indians were carried against their will back to Europe for public exhibition or forced language training. Squanto, the Indian who famously helped the Pilgrims survive after landing at Plymouth, greeted them in English because he had acquired the language during a long European captivity. Other Indians and colonists acquired similar language skills when they served as hostages exchanged by colonial and Indian neighbors to guarantee each side's good behavior. When European colonists took Indians as prisoners of war, they usually sold them into slavery in the Caribbean sugar islands, but in some regions farther removed from Atlantic slave markets, such as New Mexico and Canada, Indian captives became servants or slaves in colonial households.

Indians who took European captives treated them in much the same manner as they treated Indian captives. They tortured and executed some, enslaved others, and sometimes adopted them into their families and communities. Unlike Europeans, Native Americans did not erect an insurmountable racial barrier between their colonial captives and themselves. If a European learned to talk, dress, and act like a Native American, he or she might acquire the kinship and social connections necessary to ensure full incorporation into the community. As colonial and Native peoples grew more adept at dealing with each other, another option emerged for European captives: they might be ransomed or "redeemed" out of their captivity by government officials or family and friends willing to pay for their return. Such ransoms were usually paid in trade goods, and by the mid-eighteenth century, they had become an important part of the intercultural negotiations over captivity in North America.

Over the long course of the colonial era, many other types of captivity came to define the experience of European, African, and Native American peoples. The Atlantic Slave Trade was of course an inter-hemispheric exercise in captivity, forcing Africans into bondage among strangers on the other side of the ocean. Native Americans who were forced into living and laboring on Christian missions or attending Christian schools faced another kind of captivity. Soldiers and sailors taken prisoner in distant lands or on the high seas also endured captivities and forced labor among strangers. Many autobiographical accounts of such captivities were published in the Atlantic World, sharing a common narrative structure revolving around episodes of misfortune, physical and spiritual trial, and ultimately escape and homecoming. Indian captivity narratives dominated this genre, but other examples included the earliest slave autobiographies (which sometimes included accounts of captivity among Native Americans), and accounts of Christian sailors and soldiers enslaved in the Muslim states of North Africa.

The readings in this chapter present captivity stories from different regions and eras in the Atlantic World. The first selection comes from a German soldier, whose account of life among Indians in sixteenth-century Brazil is one of the earliest examples of the captivity narrative genre. The second selection tells the story of the famous dual captivities of Captain John Smith and Pocahontas in the Jamestown colony. In the third selection, a Pennsylvania woman recounts her capture and adoption by Indians during the Seven Years' War. The fourth selection comes from the earliest African-American autobiography published in North America, and it tells the tale of a New England slave who endured multiple captivities during an ill-fated trip to the Caribbean. As you read these sources, look for commonalities and differences among them. How did the captivity experience differ based on the race and gender of the captives and captors? Why did captivity stories have such an enduring appeal, and how did they shape personal and national identities among the peoples of the Atlantic World?

Selection 1: A German Soldier Fears Being Cannibalized by His Native American Captors

During the mid-sixteenth century, Portugal and France competed over the colonization of Brazil, where they encountered the Tupinamba Indians. Hans Staden was a German adventurer who traveled to South America as part of a Portuguese expedition in 1549. He endured several trials there, including a shipwreck and captivity among the Tupinamba, who were at the time allied with the French. The Tupinamba practiced ritual cannibalism of their war captives, and Staden expected that to be his fate. He tried to convince his captors that he was not Portuguese and therefore not their enemy. After nine months of captivity, he escaped and returned home. Published in 1557, his captivity narrative helped cement the link between American Indians and cannibalism in the European imagination.

Credit: Hans Staden, *The True History of His Captivity, 1557*, ed. and trans. Malcolm Letters (London: George Routledge & Sons, 1928), 62–64, 66–69, 85–89.

As I was going through the forest I heard loud yells on either side of me, such as savages are accustomed to utter, and immediately a company of savages came running towards me, surrounding me on every side and shooting at me with their bows and arrows. Then I cried out: "Now may God preserve my soul." Scarcely had I uttered the words when they threw me to the ground and shot and stabbed at me. God be praised they only wounded me in the leg, but they tore my clothes from my body, one the jerkin [jacket], another the hat, a third the shirt, and so forth. Then they commenced to quarrel over me. One said he was the first to overtake me, another protested that it was he that caught me, while the rest smote me with their bows. At last two of them seized me and lifted me up, naked as I was, and taking me by the arms, some running in front and some behind, they carried me along with them through the forest at a great pace towards the sea where they had their canoes. As we approached the sea I saw the canoes about a stone's-throw away, which they had dragged out of the water and hidden behind the shrubs, and with the canoes were great multitudes of savages, all decked out with feathers according to their custom. When they saw me they rushed towards me, biting their arms and threatening me, and making gestures as if they would eat me. Then a king approached me carrying the club with which they kill their captives, who spoke saying that having captured me from the Perot, that is to say the Portuguese, they would now take vengeance on me for the death of their friends, and so carrying me to the canoes they beat me with their fists. Then they made haste to launch their canoes, for they feared that an alarm might be raised at Brikioka [a Portuguese fort], as indeed was the case.

Before launching the canoes they bound my hands together, but since they were not all from the same place and no one wanted to go home empty-handed, they began to dispute with my two captors, saying that they had all been just as near to me when I was taken, and each one demanding a piece of me and clamouring to have me killed on the spot.

Then I stood and prayed, expecting every moment to be struck down. But at last the king, who desired to keep me, gave orders to carry me back alive so that their women might see and make merry with me. For they intended to kill me "Kawewi Pepicke": that is, to prepare a drink and gather together for a feast at which they would eat me. At these words they desisted, but they bound four ropes round my neck, and I was forced to climb into a canoe, while they made fast the ends of the ropes to the boats and then pushed off and commenced the homeward journey.

***

My captors passed by an island and ran the canoes ashore, intending to spend the night there, and they carried me from the canoe to the land. I could scarcely see, for I had been wounded in the face, nor could I walk on account of the wounds in my leg, but could only lie down on the sand. Then they stood round me and boasted that they would eat me.

So in mighty fear and terror I bethought me of matters which I had never dwelt upon before, and considered with myself how dark is the vale of sorrows in which we have our being. Then, weeping, I began in the bitterness of my heart to sing the Psalm: "Out of the depths have I cried unto thee." Whereupon the savages rejoiced and said: "See how he cries: now is he sorrowful indeed."

Then they considered and decided that the island was not a suitable place in which to spend the night, and they returned to the mainland where there were huts which they had erected previously, and it was night when we came there. The savages beached the canoes and lit a fire and afterwards took me to it. There I had to sleep in a net which they call in their tongue Inni [hammock]. These nets are their beds and they make them fast to two posts above the ground, or if they are in the forest they tie them to two trees. So I lay there with the cord which I had about my neck tied high up in a tree, and they lay round about me all night and mocked me saying in their speech: *Schere inbau ende*, which is to say: "You are my bound beast."

Before daybreak we were once more on our way and rowed all day, so that by Vespers [evening time] we were some two miles from the place where they intended to spend the night.

Then great black clouds arose behind me which were terrible to see, and the savages labored at the oars, striving to reach land and to escape the wind and darkness. But when they saw their efforts were in vain they said to me: *Ne mungitta dee Tuppan do Quabe, amanasu y an dee Imme Ranni me sisse*, which is to say: "Speak with your God that we may escape the wind and rain." I kept silence, but prayed in my heart as the savages required of me: "O almighty God, Lord of heaven and earth, who from the beginning hast succoured those that call upon thee, now among the heathen show thy mercy to me that I may know that thou art with me, and establish thee among these savages who know thee not, that they may see that thou hast heard my prayer."

I lay bound in the canoe and could not turn myself to regard the sky, but the savages looked steadfastly behind them and commenced to say: *Oqua moa amanasu*, which means: "The great storm is departing." Then I raised myself as best I could and looked back and saw that the clouds were passing, and I praised God.

When we came to land they did with me as before and bound me to a tree, and lay about me all night telling me that we were approaching their country where we should arrive on the morrow about evening, at which I rejoiced not at all.

***

When I was daily expecting the return of the others who, as I have reported, were preparing for my death, I heard one day the sound of howling in the huts of the king who was absent. I was much afraid, for I thought that they had now returned, since it is the custom of the savages, when one of them has been absent for not longer than four days, to cry over him with joy when he returns. Presently one of the savages came to me and reported that the brother of him who owned a share in me had returned with the news that the others were all sick, whereat I greatly rejoiced, for I told myself that now God would show his might. Not long afterwards this brother himself came to the hut where I was, and sitting down by me he commenced to cry aloud, saying that his brother, his mother, and his brother's children had all fallen sick, and that his brother had sent him to me with the message that I was to make my God restore them to health; and he added that his brother was persuaded that my God was wrath with them. To which I replied: "My God is indeed angry with you for threatening to eat me, and for going to Mambukabe [a nearby village] to prepare the feast, and for falsely accusing me of being a Portuguese." I told him, further, to return to his brother and bid him come back to the huts and I would intercede with my God to make him well again. He replied that his brother was too ill to come, but that he knew and had observed that if I desired it he would recover. Whereupon I made answer that he must wait until he was strong enough to come home to his huts, and that then he would be restored to health. With this answer he returned to Mambukabe, which is situated four miles from Uwattibi, where I was.

After some days the sick persons all came back. Then I was taken to the king's huts, and he told me how the sickness had come upon them, and that I must have known of it, for he well remembered my saying that the moon was wrath with them. When I heard this I told myself that it was indeed God's doing that I had spoken to the moon on that evening, and I rejoiced greatly and said: "This day is God with me."

I told the king that this misfortune had befallen him because he had threatened to eat me, although I was no enemy of his, and he promised that if he recovered his health no evil should happen to me. But I was at a loss what to ask of God, for it seemed to me that if the savages recovered they would kill me at once, and if they died the others would say: "Let us kill him lest greater misfortunes befall us," as indeed they had already begun to say, and I could only submit the whole matter to God, the king beseeching me anew to make them well again. I went to and fro laying my hands on their heads as they desired me to do, but God did not suffer it and they began to die. A child died first, then the king's mother, an old woman, whose business it was to prepare the pots for the drink with which I was to be eaten. Some days later a brother died, and then again a child, and then another brother, that one who had first brought me news of their illness.

When the king saw that his children and his mother and brother were dead he began to fear that he and his wives would die also, and he begged me to tell my God to make an end of his wrath so that he might live. I comforted him mightily, telling him not to despair, and that when he recovered his health he must give up all thought of killing me, which he promised, giving orders to those in his huts to cease from mocking me and threatening to eat me. He remained sick for a time, but finally he recovered, as did one of his wives who had been stricken, but there died of his family some eight persons, besides others, all of whom had treated me with great cruelty.

There were two kings in two other huts, one called Vratinge Wasu, the other Kenrimakui. Vratinge Wasu dreamed a dream, and in his dream I appeared before him and told him that he would die, and the next morning early he came to me and made complaint to me, but I comforted him, saying that he would live, but that he also must not think of killing me, nor give counsel to others to kill me. He replied that he would not do so, and that so long as those who had captured me did not kill me, so long he would do me no harm, and that even if they killed me he would not eat of me.

The second king, Kenrimakui, also dreamed a dream about me which greatly terrified him, and he called me into his huts and gave me to eat, and then he spoke to me of it and told me how, in one of his expeditions, he had captured a Portuguese whom he had killed with his own hands, after which he had eaten so much of him that his stomach has been afflicted ever afterwards, and that he would never eat another Portuguese. But now he had dreamed about me, and his dream was so terrible that he thought he was about to die. I comforted him also, and told him he would recover, but that he must eat no more human flesh.

The old women about the huts who had done me much injury, beating me and threatening to eat me, now called me *Scheraeire*, which signifies: "Son, do not let me die," saying that when they ill-treated me they thought I was one of the Portuguese whom they hated. Further that they had eaten many Portuguese whose God had never been as angry as mine, and that it was clear that I was not a Portuguese at all.

After this they left me alone for a time, for they did not know what to do with me, nor whether I was in truth a Portuguese or a Frenchman. They remarked that I had a red beard like the Frenchmen, whereas the Portuguese, although they had seen some with red beards, had in general black beards.

When the terror was abated, and one of my masters had recovered, there was no more talk of eating me, but they guarded me closely and would not suffer me to go about unattended.

Selection 2: The Captivities of Captain John Smith and Pocahontas

The story of Captain John Smith and Pocahontas has been romanticized in ways that depart significantly from the historical record, but it is still an important illustration of the role that captivity played in early encounters between European colonizers and Native American peoples. Reconstructing the history of these two captivities is also complicated by our reliance on Smith's often self-aggrandizing account of these events and the comparative silence of Pocahontas in textual sources.

Captain John Smith arrived in the Chesapeake Bay with the first wave of English colonists at Jamestown. A veteran of European wars with the Ottoman Empire, he had already experienced captivity among the Turks, and he liked to tell stories about his adventures in foreign lands. In Jamestown, he led parties that seized food from neighboring Indians, who were part of a confederacy that the English named after its paramount chief, Powhatan. Smith was taken captive by Opechancanough, a Powhatan chief, in December 1607. During his brief stay in the

Indian town of Werowocomoco, Smith met Pocahontas, the ten-year-old daughter of Powhatan. After Smith gained his freedom, Pocahontas visited Jamestown regularly. Smith returned to England in 1609 and began publishing accounts of his travels to promote American colonization. In the meantime, the leaders of Jamestown held Pocahontas hostage for several years to discourage her father from warring against them. During her captivity, she learned English, converted to Christianity, and married the colonist John Rolfe. Her visit to London in 1616 with a large retinue of Powhatan Indians prompted Smith to publish increasingly elaborate accounts of his own captivity. In the *Generall Histoire* (1624), Smith offered the fullest account of his time spent with Pocahontas, both in America and England. Readers should note that in the first passage below, Smith refers to himself in the third person, as if he is an objective observer of the events he is describing, while in the second passage he switches his voice to the first person. The spelling has been modernized.

Credit: Captain John Smith, *The Generall Histoire of Virginia, New-England, and the Summer Isles* (London: Michael Sparkes, 1624), 47–50, 121–123.

He [Smith] demanding for their Captain, they [Smith's captors] showed him Opechancanough, King of Pamaunkee [an Indian nation in the Powhatan confederacy], to whom he gave a round Ivory double compass Dial. Much they marveled at the playing of the Fly and Needle, which they could see so plainly, and yet not touch it, because of the glass that covered them. But when he demonstrated by that Globe-like Jewel, the roundness of the earth, and skies, the sphere of the Sun, Moon, and Stars, and how the Sun did chase the night round about the world continually; the greatness of the Land and Sea, the diversity of Nations, variety of complexions, and how we were to them Antipodes [opposites], and many other such like matters, they all stood as amazed with admiration. Notwithstanding, within an hour after they tied him to a tree, and as many as could stand about him prepared to shoot him, but the King holding up the Compass in his hand, they all laid down their Bows and Arrows, and in a triumphant manner led him to Orapaks [a nearby town], where he was after their manner kindly feasted, and well used.

Their order in conducting him was thus; Drawing themselves all in file, the King in the middle had all their Pieces [guns captured from the English] and Swords borne before him. Captain Smith was led after him by three great Savages, holding him fast by each arm: and on each side six went in file with their Arrows nocked [loaded in their bow strings]. But arriving at the Town … Smith they conducted to a long house, where thirty or forty tall fellows did guard him, and ere long more bread and venison was brought him then would have served twenty men, I think his stomach at that time was not very good; what he left they put in baskets and tied over his head. About midnight they set the meat again before him, all this time not one of them would eat a bit with him, till the next morning they brought him as much more, and then did they eat all the old, and reserved the new as they had done the other, which made him think they would fatten him to eat him…

Two days after a man would have slain him (but that the guard prevented it) for the death of his son, to whom they conducted him [Smith] to recover [cure] the poor man then breathing his last. Smith told them that at Jamestown he had a water would do it, if they would let him fetch it, but they would not permit that; but made all the preparations they could to assault Jamestown, craving his advice, and for recompense he should have life, liberty, land, and women. In part of a Table book [notebook] he wrote his mind to them at the Fort [Jamestown], what was intended, how they should follow that direction to affright the messengers, and without fail send him such things as he wrote for. And an Inventory with them. The difficulty and danger, he told the Savages, of the Mines, great guns, and other Engines [weapons] exceedingly affrighted them, yet according to his request they went to Jamestown, in as bitter weather as could be of frost and snow, and within three days returned with an answer.

But when they came to Jamestown, seeing men sally out as he had told them they would, they fled; yet in the night they came again to the same place where he had told them they should receive an answer, and such things as he had promised them, which they found accordingly, and with which they returned with no small expedition, to the wonder of them all that heard it, that he could either divine, or the paper could speak: then they led him to the Youghtanunds, the Mattapanients, the Payankatanks, the Nantaughtacunds, and Onawmanients [other Indian nations in Powhatan's confederacy] upon the rivers of Rappahannock, and Potomac, over all those rivers, and back again by divers [many] other several Nations, to the Kings habitation at Pamaunkee, where they entertained him with more strange and fearful Conjurations… .

At last they brought him to Meronocomoco [Werowocomoco], where was Powhatan their Emperor. Here more than two hundred of those grim Courtiers stood wondering at him, as he had been a monster; till Powhatan and his train had put themselves in their greatest braveries [dress]. Before a fire upon a seat like a bedstead, he sat covered with a great robe, made of Raccoon skins, and all the tails hanging by. On either hand did sit a young wench of 16 or 18 years, and along on each side the house, two rows of men, and behind them as many women, with all their heads and shoulders painted red; many of their heads bedecked with the white down of Birds; but everyone with something: and a great chain of white beads about their necks. At his entrance before the King, all the people gave a great shout. The Queen of Appamatuck [another Indian town] was appointed to bring him water to wash his hands, and another brought him a bunch of feathers, instead of a towel to dry them: having feasted him after their best barbarous manner they could, a long consultation was held, but the conclusion was, two great stones were brought before Powhatan: then as many as could laid hands on him [Smith], dragged him to them, and thereon laid his head, and being ready with their clubs, to beat out his brain, Pocahontas the King's dearest daughter, when no entreaty would prevail, got his head in her arms, and laid her own upon his to save him from death: where at the Emperor was contented he should live to make him hatchets, and her bells, beads, and copper; for they thought him as well of [good at] all occupations as themselves. For the King himself will make his own robes, shoes, bows, arrows, pots; plant, hunt, or do anything so well as the rest …

Two days after, Powhatan having disguised himself in the most fearful manner he could, caused Captain Smith to be brought forth to a great house in the woods, and there upon a mat by the fire to be left alone. Not long after, from behind a mat that divided the house, was made the most doleful noise he ever heard; then Powhatan more like devil than a man with some two hundred more as black as himself, came unto him and told him now they were friends, and presently he should go to Jamestown, to send him two great guns, and a grindstone, for which he would give him the Country of Capahowosick [a region within Powhatan's confederacy], and forever esteem him as his son Nantaquoud. So to Jamestown with twelve guides Powhatan sent him. That night they quartered in the woods, he still expecting (as he had done all this long time of his imprisonment) every hour to be put to one death or other, for all their feasting. But almighty God (by his divine providence) had mollified the hearts of those stern Barbarians with compassion. The next morning betimes they came to the Fort, where Smith having used the Savages with what kindness he could, he showed Rawhunt, Powhatan's trusty servant two demi-Culverings [small cannon] and a millstone to carry Powhatan: they found them somewhat too heavy but when they did see him discharge them, being loaded with stones, among the boughs of a great tree loaded with Icicles, the ice and branches came so tumbling down, that the poor Savages ran away half dead with fear. But at last we regained some conference with them, and gave them such toys, and sent to Powhatan, his women, and children such presents, as gave them in general full content …

***

That some ten years ago being in Virginia, and taken prisoner by the power of Powhatan their chief King, I received from this great Savage exceeding great courtesy, especially from his son Nanataquaus, the most manliest, comeliest, boldest spirit, I ever saw in a Savage, and his sister Pocahontas, the King's most dear and well-beloved daughter, being but a child of twelve or thirteen years of age, whose compassionate pitiful heart, of my desperate estate, gave me much cause to respect her: I being the first Christian this proud King and his grim attendants ever saw: and thus enthralled in their barbarous power, I cannot say I felt the least occasion of want that was in the power of those my mortal foes to prevent, notwithstanding all their threats. After some six weeks fattening amongst those Savage Courtiers, at the minute of my execution, she hazarded the beating out of her own brains to save mine, and not only that, but so prevailed with her father, that I was safely conducted to Jamestown, where I found about eight and thirty miserable poor and sick creatures, to keep possession of all those large territories of Virginia, such was the weakness of this poor Common-wealth, as had the Savages not fed us, we directly had starved.

And this relief ... was commonly brought us by this Lady Pocahontas, notwithstanding all these passages when inconstant Fortune turned our peace to war, this tender Virgin would still not spare to dare to visit us, and by her our jars [conflicts] have been oft appeased, and our wants still supplied ... it is most certain, after a long troublesome war after my departure, betwixt her father and our Colony, all which time she was not heard of, about two years after she herself was taken prisoner, being so detained near two years longer, the Colony by that means was relieved, peace concluded, and at last rejecting her barbarous condition, [she] was married to an English Gentleman, with whom at this present she is in England; the first Christian ever of that Nation, the first Virginian ever spoke English, or had a child in marriage by an Englishman, a matter surely, if my meaning be truly considered and well understood, [is] worthy a Prince's understanding ...

Being about this time preparing to set sail for New-England, I could not stay to do her service I desired, and she well deserved; but hearing she was at Branford with divers of my friends, I went to see her: After a modest salutation, without any word, she turned about, obscured her face, as not seeming well contented; and in that humor her husband with divers others, we all left her two or three hours, repenting myself to have written she could speak English. But not long after, she began to talk, and remembered me well what courtesies she had done: saying, "You did promise Powhatan what was yours should be his, and he the like to you; you called him father being in his land a stranger, and by the same reason so must I do you," which I though I would have excused, I durst not allow of that title, because she was a King's daughter; with a well set countenance she said, "Were you not afraid to come into my father's Country, and caused fear in him and all his people (but me) and fear you here I should call you father; I tell you then I will, and you shall call me child, and so I will be for ever and ever your Countryman. They did tell us always you were dead, and I knew no other till I came to Plymouth [a seaport on England's southern coast]; yet Powhatan did command Uttamato-makkin [a Powhatan leader who accompanied Pocahontas to England] to seek you, and know the truth, because your Countrymen will lie much."

Selection 3: A Pennsylvania Woman's Adoption into an Indian Family

Mary Jemison was born on the ship that carried her family from Ireland to North America in 1742. Like many Scots-Irish emigrants of that period, the Jemisons settled in the backcountry of Pennsylvania, on land that the Delaware and Shawnee Indians still claimed as their own. During the Seven Years' War (also known as the French and Indian War in North America), Mary, her parents, and three of her siblings were taken captive by a war party of Shawnee and Frenchmen. Her captors took her to an Indian village on the Ohio River, where she was adopted into a Seneca family, learned their language, and married an Indian husband.

She eventually moved with her adopted family to the Genesee River Valley of New York, where she remarried after her first husband's death and bore six more children. In 1823, she told her life story to a newspaper writer, James E. Seaver, who published it in the following year as *A Narrative of the Life of Mrs. Mary Jemison*. The passages from her narrative below describe her experience from the point of her capture until her marriage to her first husband.

Credit: James E. Seaver, ed., *A Narrative of the Life of Mrs. Mary Jemison* (1824; New York: The American Scenic and Historic Preservation Society, 1918), 25–29, 32–40, 44–45.

The party that took us consisted of six Indians and four Frenchmen, who immediately commenced plundering, as I just observed, and took what they considered most valuable; consisting principally of bread, meal, and meat. Having taken as much provision as they could carry, they set out with their prisoners in great haste, for fear of detection, and soon entered the woods....

Mother, from the time we were taken, had manifested a great degree of fortitude, and encouraged us to support our troubles without complaining; and by her conversation seemed to make the distance and time shorter, and the way more smooth. But father lost all his ambition in the beginning of our trouble, and continued apparently lost to every care—absorbed in melancholy. Here, as before, she insisted on the necessity of our eating; and we obeyed her, but it was done with heavy hearts.

As soon as I had finished my supper, an Indian took off my shoes and stockings and put a pair of moccasins on my feet, which my mother observed; and believing that they would spare my life, even if they should destroy the other captives, addressed me as near as I can remember in the following words:

> My dear little Mary, I fear that the time has arrived when we must be parted forever. Your life, my child, I think will be spared; but we shall probably be tomahawked here in this lonesome place by the Indians. O! how can I part with you my darling? What will become of my sweet little Mary? Oh! How can I think of your being continued in captivity without a hope of your being rescued? O that death had snatched you from my embraces in your infancy; the pain of parting then would have been pleasing to what it now is; and I should have seen the end of your troubles! Alas, my dear! My heart bleeds at the thoughts of what awaits you; but, if you leave us, remember my child your own name, and the name of your father and mother. Be careful and not forget your English tongue. If you shall have an opportunity to get away from the Indians, don't try to escape; for if you do, they will find and destroy you. Don't forget, my little daughter, the prayers that I have learned you—say them often; be a good child, and God will bless you. May God bless you my child, and make you comfortable and happy....

My suspicions as to the fate of my parents proved too true; for soon after I left them they were killed and scalped, together with Robert, Matthew, Betsey [Jemison's siblings], and the woman and her two children [neighbors also taken captive], and mangled in the most shocking manner....

In the afternoon we came in sight of Fort Pitt (as it is now called), where we were halted while the Indians performed some customs upon their prisoners which they deemed necessary. That fort was then occupied by the French and Indians, and was called Fort Du Quesne. It stood at the junction of the Monongahela, which is said to signify, in some of the Indian languages, the Falling-in-Banks, and the Alleghany rivers, where the Ohio river begins to take its name. The word O-hi-o, signifies bloody.

At the place where we halted, the Indians combed the hair of the young man [another captive in the war party], the boy, and myself, and then painted our faces and hair red, in the finest Indian style. We were then conducted into the fort, where we received a little bread, and were then shut up and left to tarry alone through the night....

The morning at length arrived, and our masters came early and let us out of the house, and gave the young man and boy to the French, who immediately took them away. Their fate I never learned; as I have not seen or heard of them since.

I was now left alone in the fort, deprived of my former companions, and of everything that was near or dear to me but life. But it was not long before I was in some measure relieved by the appearance of two pleasant looking Squaws of the Seneca tribe, who came and examined me attentively for a short time, and then went out. After a few minutes absence, they returned with my former masters, who gave me to them to dispose of as they pleased.

The Indians by whom I was taken were a party of Shawanees, if I remember right, that lived, when at home, a long distance down the Ohio.

My former Indian masters, and the two Squaws, were soon ready to leave the fort, and accordingly embarked; the Indians in a large canoe, and the two Squaws and myself in a small one, and went down the Ohio....

At night we arrived at a small Seneca Indian town, at the mouth of a small river, that was called by the Indians, in the Seneca language, She-nan-jee, where the two Squaws to whom I belonged resided. There we landed, and the Indians [Jemison's captors] went on; which was the last I ever saw of them.

Having made fast to the shore, the Squaws left me in the canoe while they went to their wigwam or house in the town, and returned with a suit of Indian clothing, all new, and very clean and nice. My clothes, though whole and good when I was taken, were now torn in pieces, so that I was almost naked. They first undressed me and threw my rags into the river; then washed me clean and dressed me in the new suit they had just brought, in complete Indian style; and then led me home and seated me in the center of their wigwam.

I had been in that situation but a few minutes, before all the Squaws in the town came in to see me. I was soon surrounded by them, and they immediately set up a most dismal howling, crying bitterly, and wringing their hands in all the agonies of grief for a deceased relative.

Their tears flowed freely, and they exhibited all the signs of real mourning. At the commencement of this scene, one of their number began, in a voice somewhat between speaking and singing, to recite some words to the following purport, and continued the recitation till the ceremony was ended; the company at the same time varying the appearance of their countenances, gestures and tone of voice, so as to correspond with the sentiments expressed by their leader:

> Oh our brother! Alas! He is dead—he has gone; he will never return! Friendless he died on the field of the slain, where his bones are yet lying unburied! Oh, who will not mourn his sad fate? No tears dropped around him; oh, no! No tears of his sisters were there! He fell in his prime, when his arm was most needed to keep us from danger! Alas! he has gone! and left us in sorrow, his loss to bewail: Oh where is his spirit? His spirit went naked, and hungry it wanders, and thirsty and wounded it groans to return! Oh helpless and wretched, our brother has gone! No blanket nor food to nourish and warm him; nor candles to light him, nor weapons of war:—Oh, none of those comforts had he! But well we remember his deeds!—The deer he could take on the chase! The panther shrunk back at the sight of his strength! His enemies fell at his feet! He was brave and courageous in war! As the fawn he was harmless: his friendship was ardent: his temper was gentle: his pity was great! Oh! our friend, our companion is dead! Our brother, our brother, alas! he is gone! But why do we grieve for his loss? In the strength of a warrior, undaunted he left us, to fight by the side of the Chiefs! His war-whoop was shrill! His rifle well aimed laid his enemies low: his tomahawk drank of their blood: and his knife flayed their scalps while yet covered with gore! And why do we mourn? Though he fell on the field of the slain, with

glory he fell, and his spirit went up to the land of his fathers in war! Then why do we mourn? With transports of joy they received him, and fed him, and clothed him, and welcomed him there! Oh friends, he is happy; then dry up your tears! His spirit has seen our distress, and sent us a helper whom with pleasure we greet. Dickewamis [Jemison's Indian name] has come: then let us receive her with joy! She is handsome and pleasant! Oh! she is our sister, and gladly we welcome her here. In the place of our brother she stands in our tribe. With care we will guard her from trouble; and may she be happy till her spirit shall leave us.

In the course of that ceremony, from mourning they became serene—joy sparkled in their countenances, and they seemed to rejoice over me as over a long lost child. I was made welcome amongst them as a sister to the two Squaws before mentioned, and was called Dickewamis; which being interpreted, signifies a pretty girl, a handsome girl, or a pleasant, good thing. That is the name by which I have ever since been called by the Indians.

I afterwards learned that the ceremony I at that time passed through, was that of adoption. The two Squaws had lost a brother in Washington's war [Anglo-French-Indian hostilities in the Ohio Country], sometime in the year before, and in consequence of his death went up to Fort Pitt, on the day on which I arrived there, in order to receive a prisoner or an enemy's scalp, to supply their loss.

It is a custom of the Indians, when one of their number is slain or taken prisoner in battle, to give to the nearest relative to the dead or absent, a prisoner, if they have chanced to take one, and if not, to give him the scalp of an enemy. On the return of the Indians from conquest, which is always announced by peculiar shoutings, demonstrations of joy, and the exhibition of some trophy of victory, the mourners come forward and make their claims. If they receive a prisoner, it is at their option either to satiate their vengeance by taking his life in the most cruel manner they can conceive of; or, to receive and adopt him into the family, in the place of him whom they have lost. All the prisoners that are taken in battle and carried to the encampment or town by the Indians, are given to the bereaved families, till their number is made good. And unless the mourners have but just received the news of their bereavement, and are under the operation of a paroxysm of grief, anger, and revenge; or unless the prisoner is very old, sickly, or homely, they generally save him, and treat him kindly. But if their mental wound is fresh, their loss so great that they deem it irreparable, or if their prisoner or prisoners do not meet their approbation, no torture, let it be ever so cruel, seems sufficient to make them satisfaction. It is family, and not national, sacrifices amongst the Indians, that has given them an indelible stamp as barbarians, and identified their character with the idea which is generally formed of unfeeling ferocity, and the most abandoned cruelty.

It was my happy lot to be accepted for adoption; and at the time of the ceremony I was received by the two Squaws, to supply the place of their brother in the family; and I was ever considered and treated by them as a real sister, the same as though I had been born of their mother....

Being now settled and provided with a home, I was employed in nursing the children, and doing light work about the house. Occasionally I was sent out with the Indian hunters, when they went but a short distance, to help them carry their game. My situation was easy; I had no particular hardships to endure. But still, the recollection of my parents, my brothers and sisters, my home, and my own captivity, destroyed my happiness, and made me constantly solitary, lonesome, and gloomy....

Not long after the Delawares came to live with us at Wiishto [an Indian village in the Ohio Country], my sisters told me that I must go and live with one of them, whose name was Sheninjee. Not daring to cross them, or disobey their commands, with a great degree of reluctance I went; and Sheninjee and I were married according to Indian custom.

Sheninjee was a noble man; large in stature; elegant in his appearance; generous in his conduct; courageous in war; a friend to peace, and a great lover of justice. He supported a degree of dignity far above his rank, and merited and received the confidence and friendship of all the tribes with whom he was acquainted. Yet, Sheninjee was an Indian. The idea of spending my days with him, at first seemed perfectly irreconcilable to my feelings: but his good nature, generosity, tenderness, and friendship towards me, soon gained my affection; and, strange as it may seem, I loved him! To me he was ever kind in sickness, and always treated me with gentleness; in fact, he was an agreeable husband, and a comfortable companion. We lived happily together till the time of our final separation, which happened two or three years after our marriage, as I shall presently relate.

In the second summer of my living at Wiishto, I had a child at the time that the kernels of corn first appeared on the cob. When I was taken sick, Sheninjee was absent, and I was sent to a small shed, on the bank of the river, which was made of boughs, where I was obliged to stay till my husband returned. My two sisters, who were my only companions, attended me, and on the second day of my confinement my child was born; but it lived only two days. It was a girl: and notwithstanding the shortness of the time that I possessed it, it was a great grief to me to lose it.

After the birth of my child, I was very sick, but was not allowed to go into the house for two weeks; when to my great joy, Sheninjee returned, and I was taken in and as comfortably provided for as our situation would admit of. My disease continued to increase for a number of days; and I became so far reduced that my recovery was despaired of by my friends, and I was concluded that my troubles would soon be finished. At length, however, my complaint took a favorable turn, and by the time the corn was ripe I was able to get about. I continued to gain my health, and in the fall was able to go to our winter quarters, on the Sciota [a tributary of the Ohio], with the Indians.

From that time nothing remarkable occurred to me till the fourth winter of my captivity, when I had a son born, while I was at Sciota: I had a quick recovery, and my child was healthy. To commemorate the name of my much lamented father, I called my son Thomas Jemison.

Selection 4: An African-American Sailor's Serial Captivities

New England slaves sometimes went to sea as wage-earning sailors, their masters allowing them to do so in return for a cut of their pay. Briton Hammon shipped out of Massachusetts in December 1747 for Jamaica, but his winter sojourn to the Caribbean turned into a twelve-year odyssey of shipwreck, captivity, and redemption. Hammon's story is an excellent example of the parallels between early slave narratives and Indian captivity narratives. As you read it, note also how his identities as a Christian and as an American shaped his reactions to and treatment by his captors.

Credit: Briton Hammon, *A Narrative of the Uncommon Sufferings and Surprizing Deliverance of Briton Hammon, A Negro Man, Servant to General Winslow, of Marshfield, New England, Who Returned to Boston, after having been Absent almost Thirteen Years* (Boston, MA: Green and Russell, 1760), 3–13.

On Monday, 25th Day of *December*, 1747, with the leave of my Master, I went from *Marshfield*, with an Intention to go a Voyage to Sea, and the next Day, the 26th, got to *Plymouth*, where I immediately ship'd myself on board of a Sloop, Capt. *John Howland*, Master, bound to *Jamaica* and the *Bay*.—We sailed from *Plymouth* in a short Time, and after a pleasant Passage of about 30 Days, arrived at *Jamaica*; we was detain'd at *Jamaica* only 5 Days, from whence we sailed for the *Bay*, where we arrived safe in 10 Days. We loaded our Vessel with Logwood, and sailed from the *Bay* the 25th Day of *May* following, and the 15th Day of *June*, we were cast away on *Cape-Florida*, about 5 Leagues from the Shore; being now destitute of every Help, we knew not what to do or what Course to take in this our sad Condition:—The Captain was advised, intreated, and beg'd on, by every Person on board, to heave over but only 20 Ton of the *Wood*, and we should get clear, which if he had done, might have sav'd his Vessel and Cargo, and not only so, but his own Life, as well as the Lives of the Mate and Nine Hands, as I shall presently relate.

After being upon this Reef two Days, the Captain order'd the Boat to be hoisted out, and then ask'd who were willing to tarry on board? The whole Crew was for going on Shore at this Time, but as the Boat would not carry Twelve Persons at once, and to prevent any Uneasiness, the Captain, a Passenger, and one Hand tarry'd on board, while the Mate, with Seven Hands besides myself, were order'd to go on Shore in the Boat, which as soon as we had reached, one half were to be Landed, and the other four to return to the Sloop, to fetch the Captain and the others on Shore. The Captain order'd us to take with us our Arms, Ammunition, Provisions and Necessaries for Cooking, as also a Sail to make a Tent of, to shelter us from the Weather; after having left the Sloop we stood towards the Shore, and being within Two Leagues of the same, we espy'd a Number of Canoes, which we at first took to be Rocks, but soon found our Mistake, for we perceiv'd they moved towards us; we presently saw an English Colour hoisted in one of the Canoes, at the Sight of which we were not a little rejoiced, but on our advancing yet nearer, we found them, to our very great Surprize, to be *Indians* of which there were Sixty; being now so near them we could not possibly make our Escape; they soon came up with and boarded us, took away all our Arms, Ammunition, and Provision. The whole Number of Canoes (being about Twenty,) then made for the Sloop, except Two which they left to guard us, who order'd us to follow on with them; the Eighteen which made for the Sloop, went so much faster than we that they got on board above Three Hours before we came along side, and had kill'd Captain *Howland*, the Passenger and the other hand; we came to the Larboard side of the Sloop, and they order'd us round to the Starboard, and as we were passing round the Bow, we saw the whole Number of *Indians*, advancing forward and loading their Guns, upon which the Mate said, "*my Lads we are all dead Men*," and before we had got round, they discharged their Small Arms upon us, and kill'd Three of our hands, viz. *Reuben Young* of *Cape-Cod*, Mate; *Joseph Little* and *Lemuel Doty* of *Plymouth*, upon which I immediately jump'd overboard, chusing rather to be drowned, than to be kill'd by those barbarous and inhuman Savages. In three or four Minutes after, I heard another Volley which dispatched the other five, viz. *John Nowland*, and *Nathaniel Rich*, both belonging to *Plymouth*, and *Elkanah Collymore*, and *James Webb*, Strangers, and *Moses Newmock*, Molatto. As soon as they had kill'd the whole of the People, one of the Canoes padled after me, and soon came up with me, hawled me into the Canoe, and beat me most terribly with a Cutlass, after that they ty'd me down, then this Canoe stood for the Sloop again and as soon as she came along side, the *Indians* on board the Sloop betook themselves to their Canoes, then set the Vessel on Fire, making a prodigious shouting and hallowing like so many Devils. As soon as the Vessel was burnt down to the Water's edge, the *Indians* stood for the Shore, together with our Boat, on board of which they put 5 hands. After we came to the Shore, they led me to their Hutts, where I expected nothing but immediate Death, and as they spoke broken English, were often telling me, while coming from the Sloop to the Shore, that they intended to roast me alive. But the Providence of God order'd it otherways, for He appeared for my Help, *in this Mount of Difficulty*, and they were better to me than my Fears, and soon unbound me, but set a Guard over me every Night. They kept me with them about five Weeks, during which Time they us'd me pretty well, and gave me boil'd Corn, which was what they often eat themselves. The Way I made my Escape from these Villains was this; A Spanish Schooner arriving there from *St. Augustine* [in Florida], the Master of which, whose Name was *Romond*, asked the *Indians* to let me go on board his Vessel, which they granted, and the Captain knowing me very well, weigh'd Anchor and carry'd me off to the *Havanna*, and after being there four Days the *Indians* came after me, and insisted on having me again, as I was their Prisoner;—They made Application to the Governor, and demanded me again from him; in answer to which the Governor told them, that as they had put the whole

Crew to Death, they should not have me again, and so paid them Ten Dollars for me, adding, that he would not have them kill any Person hereafter, but take as many of them as they could, of those that should be cast away, and bring them to him, for which he would pay them Ten Dollars a-head. At the *Havanna* I lived with the Governor in the Castle about a Twelve-month, where I was walking thro' the Street, I met with a Press-Gang who immediately prest me, and put me into Gaol [jail], and with a Number of others I was confin'd till next Morning, when we were all brought out, and ask'd who would go on board the King's Ships, four of which having been lately built, were bound to *Old-Spain*, and on my refusing to serve on board, they put me in a close Dungeon, where I was confin'd *Four Years and seven months*; during which Time I often made application to the Governor, by Persons who came to see the Prisoners, but they never acquainted him with it, nor did he know all this Time what became of me, which was the means of my being confin'd there so long. But kind Providence so order'd it, that after I had been in this Place so long as the Time mention'd above the Captain of a Mer-chantman, belonging to *Boston*, having sprung a Leak was obliged to put into the *Havanna* to refit, and while he was at Dinner at *Mrs. Betty Howard's*, she told the Captain of my deplorable Condition, and said she would be glad, if he could by some means or other relieve me; The Captain told *Mrs. Howard* he would use his best Endeavours for my Relief and Enlargement.

Accordingly, after Dinner, came to the Prison, and ask'd the Keeper if he might see me; upon his Request I was brought out of the Dungeon, and after the Captain had Interrogated me, told me, he would intercede with the Governor for my Relief out of that miserable Place, which he did, and the next Day the Governor sent an Order to release me; I lived with the Governor about a Year after I was delivered from the Dungeon, in which Time I endeavour'd three Times to make my Escape, the last of which proved effectual; the first Time I got on board of Captain *Marsh*, an *English* Twenty Gun Ship, with a Number of others, and lay on board conceal'd that Night; and the next Day the Ship being under sail, I thought myself safe, and so made my Appearance upon Deck, but as soon as we were discovered the Captain ordered the Boat out, and sent us all on Shore—I intreated the Captain to let me, in particular, carry on board, begging, and crying to him, to commiserate my unhappy Condition, and added, that I had been confin'd almost five Years in a close Dungeon, but the Captain would not hearken to any Intreaties, for fear of having the Governor's Displeasure, and so I was obliged to go on Shore.

After being on Shore another Twelvemonth, I endeavour'd to make my Escape the second Time, by trying to get on board of a Sloop bound to *Jamaica*, and as I was going from the City to the Sloop, was unhappily taken by the Guard, and ordered back to the Castle, and there confined.—However, in a short Time I was set at Liberty, and order'd with a Number of others to carry the *Bishop* from the Castle, thro' the Country, to confirm the old People, baptize Chil-dren, etc. for which he receives large Sums of Money.—I was employ'd in this Service about Seven Months, during which Time I lived very well, and then returned to the Castle again, where I had my Liberty to walk about the City, and do Work for my self;—The *Beaver*, an *English* Man of War then lay in the Harbour, and having been informed by some of the Ship's Crew that she was to sail in a few Days, I had nothing now to do, but to seek an Opportunity how I should make my Escape.

Accordingly one Sunday Night the Lieutenant of the Ship with a Number of the Barge Crew were in a Tavern, and *Mrs. Howard* who had before been a Friend to me, interceded with the Lieutenant to carry me on board: the Lieutenant said he would with all his Heart, and immediately I went on board in the Barge. The next Day the *Spaniards* came along side the *Beaver*, and demanded me again, with a Number of others who had made their Escape from them, and got on board the Ship, but just before I did; but the Captain, who was a true *English-man*, refus'd them, and said he could not answer it, to deliver up any *Englishmen* under *English* Colours.—In a few Days we set Sail for *Jamaica*, where we arrived safe, after a short and pleas-ant Passage.

After being at *Jamaica* a short Time we sail'd for *London*, as convoy to a Fleet of Merchant-men, who all arrived safe in the *Downs*, I was turned over to another Ship, the *Arcenceil*, and there remained about a Month. From this Ship I went on board the *Sandwich* of 90 Guns; on board the *Sandwich*, I tarry'd 6 Weeks, and then was order'd on board the *Hercules*, Capt. *John Porter*, a 74 Gun Ship, we sail'd on a Cruize, and met with a *French* 84 Gun Ship, and had a very smart Engagement, in which about 70 of our Hands were Kill'd and Wounded, the Captain lost his Leg in the Engagement, and I was Wounded in the Head by a small Shot. We should have taken this Ship, if they had not cut away the most of our Rigging; however, in about three Hours after, a 64 Gun Ship, came up with and took her.—I was discharged from the *Hercules* the 12th Day of *May* 1759 (having been on board of that Ship 3 Months) on account of my being disabled in the Arm, and render'd incapable of Service, after being honourably paid the Wages due to me. I was put into the *Greenwich* Hospital where I stay'd and soon recovered.—I then ship'd myself a Cook on board Captain *Martyn*, an arm'd Ship in the King's Service. I was on board this Ship almost Two Months, and after being paid my Wages, was discharg'd in the Month of *October*. —After my discharge from Captain *Martyn*, I was taken sick in *London* of a Fever, and was confin'd about 6 Weeks, where I expended all my Money, and left in very poor Circumstances; and unhappy for me I knew nothing of my *good Master's* being in *London* at this my very difficult Time. After I got well of my sickness, I ship'd myself on board of a large Ship bound to *Guinea*, [West Africa] and being in a publick House one Evening, I overheard a Number of Persons talking about Rigging a Vessel bound to *New-England*, I ask'd them to what Part of *New-England* this Vessel was bound? they told me, to *Boston*; and having ask'd them who was Commander? they told me, Capt. *Watt*; in a few Minutes after this the Mate of the Ship came in, and I ask'd him if Captain *Watt* did not want a Cook, who told me he did, and that the Captain would be in, in a few Minutes; and in about half an Hour the Captain came in, and then I ship'd myself at once, after begging off from the Ship bound to *Guinea*; I work'd on board Captain *Watts* Ship almost Three Months, before she sail'd, and one Day being at Work in the Hold, I overheard some Persons on board mention the Name of *Winslow*, at the Name of which I was very inquisitive, and having ask'd what *Winslow* they were talking about? They told me it was *General Winslow*; and that he was one of the Passengers, I ask'd them what *General Winslow*? For I never knew *my good Master*, by that Title before; but after enquiring more particularly I found it must be *Master*, and in a few Days Time the Truth was joyfully verify'd by a happy Sight of his Person, which so overcome me, that I could not speak to him for some Time—My *good Master* was exceeding glad to see me, telling me that I was like one arose from the Dead, for he thought I had been Dead a great many Years, having heard nothing of me for almost Thirteen Years.

Discussion Questions

1. What sort of use did the Tupinamba Indians make of Staden during his stay with them? How did Staden's and his captors' spiritual beliefs shape how they saw each other and interpreted the meaning of his captivity?

2. What did Powhatan expect to happen in exchange for preserving Smith's life? How did Pocahontas's captivity among the Jamestown colonists parallel that of Smith among the Powhatans? Examine closely Pocahontas's conversation with Smith when the two met in London: why do you think she insisted on calling him "father"?

3. Briefly describe the adoption process Jemison experienced in the Ohio country. Why do you think she chose to remain with her captors for the rest of her life?

4. Briefly trace the course of Hammon's captivities from Florida to Cuba. Who helped him acquire his freedom at different points in his odyssey, and why did they intervene on his behalf? How did Hammon's race and religion affect his captivities and redemptions?

Suggested Readings

For more on Hans Staden's captivity in Brazil, see Neil Whitehead and Michael Harbsmeier, eds. and trans., *Hans Staden's True History: An Account of Cannibal Captivity in Brazil* (Durham, NC: Duke University Press, 2008). Collections of captivity narratives from colonial North America include Alden T. Vaughan and Edward W. Clark, eds., *Puritans Among the Indians: Accounts of Captivity and Redemption, 1676–1724* (Cambridge, MA: Harvard University Press, 1981); and Kathryn Zabelle Derounian-Stodola, ed., *Women's Indian Captivity Narratives* (New York: Penguin Books, 1998). Two books that examine the impact of Native American captivity among colonial New Englanders are John Demos, *The Unredeemed Captive: A Family Story from Early America* (New York: Random House, 1994); and Anne M. Little, *The Many Captivities of Esther Wheelwright* (New Haven, CT: Yale University Press, 2016).

For Native American captivity and slavery in the Southeast, see Camilla Townshend, *Pocahontas and the Powhatan Dilemma* (New York: Hill and Wang, 2004); Christina Snyder, *Slavery in Indian Country: The Changing Face of Captivity in Early America* (Cambridge, MA: Harvard University Press, 2010); and Alan Gallay, *The Indian Slave Trade: The Rise of the English Empire in the American South, 1670–1717* (New Haven, CT: Yale University Press, 2002). For the Southwest, see James F. Brooks, *Captives and Cousins: Slavery, Kinship, and Community in the Southwest Borderlands* (Chapel Hill, NC: University of North Carolina Press, 2002). For captivities related to the era of the Seven Years' War, see Ian K. Steele, *Setting All the Captives Free: Capture, Adjustment, and Recollection in Allegheny Country* (Montreal: McGill-Queen's University Press, 2013); Len Travers, *Hodges' Scout: A Lost Patrol of the French and Indian War* (Baltimore, MD: Johns Hopkins University Press, 2015); and Timothy J. Shannon, *Indian Captive, Indian King: Peter Williamson in America and Britain* (Cambridge, MA: Harvard University Press, 2018). For the perils and opportunities faced by seafarers like Briton Hammon, see W. Jeffrey Bolster, *Black Jacks: African American Seamen in the Age of Sail* (Cambridge, MA: Harvard University Press, 1997).

4   Religion and Conversion

Figure 4.1 Kateri Tekakwitha.

Kateri Tekakwitha was one of the young Mohawk converts to Christianity that missionary Father Claude Chauchetière met when he came to Canada in the 1670s (see Selection 2). This image is based on his portrait of her. What information about her conversion do you think he was trying to convey in this image?

Source: From M. de Bacqueville de La Potherie, *Histoire de l'Amerique Septentrionale* (Claude-Charles Le Roy)/Courtesy of Wikimedia Commons.

Introduction

The collision of cultures in the Atlantic World had a spiritual as well as physical dimension. European colonizers, though they were split into Protestant and Catholic camps, shared a perspective on the New World shaped by their Christian heritage and beliefs. They tried to fit the Americas into a cosmology that was rooted in biblical stories of creation and prophecy, even if the existence of Indians challenged such scriptural authority. Consider, for example, the conundrum posed by the nakedness of the Indians that Columbus met in the Caribbean. The Book of Genesis taught that after Adam and Eve had sinned, they clothed themselves; thereafter, they and their descendants equated nakedness with shame. Yet, the Indians Columbus met exhibited no shame in their lack of clothing. Did that mean they inhabited a prelapsarian Garden of Eden into which sin had not entered? Colonizers quickly put such speculation aside for the more practical task of converting Indians into Christian proselytes, initiating a centuries-long spiritual struggle between native and newcomer. In a similar manner, Europeans used the Bible to legitimize the Atlantic Slave Trade, citing the Old Testament story of Ham's Curse, in which Noah condemned the descendants of his son Ham to servitude, as evidence that God sanctioned enslaving Africans. They also defended the institution of slavery on the grounds that it provided a means of converting Africans and making possible their salvation.

Every European nation that colonized the New World paid at least lip service to the notion of converting Native Americans to Christianity. The Catholic powers (Spain, Portugal, and France) devoted far more resources to this task than did the Protestant ones (England, the Netherlands), sponsoring missionaries and claiming spiritual and political authority over large populations of Indian converts. In those regions colonized by Protestant powers, missionary work was not nearly so well funded or organized, but the conversion of indigenous peoples nevertheless remained a fundamental legal and political justification for seizing Indian land and labor.

Whether Catholic or Protestant, missionaries pursued a full-scale cultural conversion of Indians that involved much more than catechizing them in a new faith. Oftentimes, missionaries described their work as "reducing the Indians to civility": breaking down their old cultural habits and values so that they could be remade in a European image. Missionaries expected converts not only to pray like Christians, but also to eat, dress, and work like them. This process entailed separating converts from their unconverted kin and resettling them into communities (*reserves* in New France, praying towns in New England, *reducciones* in New Spain) under the missionaries' supervision, where their gender roles and sexual mores could be remade according to European models. These communities served as buffers for colonial populations against their enemies and as pools from which to draw labor or military assistance when necessary.

Indian conversions were never as numerous or thorough as European missionaries wished they would be. Some elements of Christianity appealed to Indians. Many converts accepted the sacrament of baptism because they believed it would convey spiritual protection against disease and other types of misfortune that followed in the wake of European contact. The religious artifacts used by Catholic missionaries to teach their faith—saints' medals, rings, rosary beads—resembled in color and shape native objects Indians already associated with spiritual well-being, such as wampum beads. Conversion also offered a variety of practical advantages when it came to dealing with the newcomers. Missionaries provided material support in times of need and worked as diplomatic go-betweens on behalf of their converts with colonial authorities. Indians who resettled in French, English, or Spanish mission communities could also expect greater security of tenure in their lands than those Indians who spurned the missionaries' efforts.

There were also elements of Christianity that Indians generally ignored or resisted. The biblical injunction against nakedness, which missionaries usually invoked to convince Indian men and women to dress like Europeans, held little sway among converts, who adopted European clothing in a selective manner that left plenty of flesh exposed. Likewise, converts were not particularly interested in altering their family and sexual practices so that they were in accordance with Christian prohibitions against polygamy and divorce. In general, those Native Americans who accepted Christianity never bowed entirely to new religious orthodoxies, regardless of how forcefully Europeans tried to impose them. Rather, they selectively chose which elements of Christianity appealed to them, creating syncretic faiths that blended old and new spiritual beliefs and practices.

A similar process of religious acculturation and adaptation occurred among the African populations of the Atlantic World. Generally speaking, Catholic powers expended greater effort in converting slaves than Protestant ones, at least to the point of baptizing them and subjecting their spiritual practices to the policing of church authorities. Among free blacks and mixed race peoples in Portuguese and Spanish America, the church became an important institution for cultivating social networks and mutual obligations that could secure a person's place in society, such as through the practice of god-parentage. In those slave societies with significant black majorities in the population, such as the sugar islands of the Caribbean, the continual influx of new slaves by way of the Atlantic Slave Trade allowed for a more sustained and varied transplantation of African religious beliefs and customs in the New World. Vodou and Santeria in Haiti and Cuba respectively are examples of syneretic faiths that emerged out of the meeting of Catholic and African religions in the Caribbean.

In North America, colonial powers paid much less attention to missionary work among African slaves. English slave owners were reluctant to convert slaves for fear that it would encourage them to sue for their freedom. Therefore, slave codes in English colonies explicitly denied any link between baptism and freedom. Nevertheless, slaves and free blacks in North America adopted Christianity as part of their wider acculturation to colonial society. By the mid-eighteenth century, some Protestant denominations were seeking converts among African and Native American populations. Baptists, Methodists, and Moravians (a German sect) preached a message of Christian brotherhood and spiritual equality that transcended racial boundaries. Starting in the 1740s, a Protestant revivalist movement known as the Great Awakening swept through British North America, led by itinerant preachers who moved from town to town and throughout the countryside, trying to reach people outside of traditional churches. The Great Awakening's message of the New Birth—salvation achieved through acceptance of Jesus Christ—appealed to Native Americans and Africans because it encouraged spiritual autonomy and did not require submission to any particular church authority or doctrine. In this manner, syncretic Protestantism took root among North American Indians and slaves in a way that did not require conversion and confinement in mission communities.

The readings in this chapter illuminate the spiritual dimensions of Atlantic World encounters by focusing on the idea of conversion. The first two selections concern the efforts of seventeenth-century Spanish and French missionaries to enforce a new religious orthodoxy on Native Americans. The third and fourth selections are from the era of the Great Awakening. In one, a Native American convert experiences difficulties when he is sent by his European mentor to preach among other Indians. In the other, an African American has a life-changing experience when he happens to attend the sermon of a revivalist preacher. As you read these sources, look for the tensions and negotiations between missionaries and converts: how did the former try to impose their will on the latter, and how did the latter assert control of their own spiritual lives?

Selection 1: A Revolt among Mission Indians in New Mexico

The Spanish established their first settlements north of the Rio Grande in 1598. Throughout the seventeenth century, this province of New Mexico remained an outpost of Spanish power, with a small colonial population centered in Santa Fe, claiming lordship over the Pueblo Indians surrounding them. Franciscan priests established missions among the Pueblos to eradicate native spiritual beliefs and replace them with Christianity. In 1680, after years of enduring forced labor and religious persecution under the Spanish, the Pueblos rebelled, killing several hundred colonists and approximately two-thirds of the missionaries. The surviving colonists fled the province, crossing the Rio Grande back into Mexico. The Spanish did not return until the 1690s, when they faced more armed resistance before finally reasserting control over the region. In the passages below, two eyewitnesses describe the Pueblo Revolt. First, an aged Indian named Don Pedro Nanboa testifies before the Spanish about the causes of the Pueblos' discontent. Second, the governor of New Mexico, Don Antonio de Otermín, describes the Indians' siege of Santa Fe and the bloody battle that followed.

Credit: Charles Wilson Hackett, *Revolt of the Pueblo Indians of New Mexico and Otermín's Attempted Reconquest, 1680–82*, trans. Charmion Clair Shelby, 2 vols (Albuquerque, NM: University of New Mexico Press, 1942), Vol. 1: 60–61, 94, 98–105.

Declaration of one of the rebellious Christian Indians who was captured on the road. [Place of El Alamillo, September 6, 1680.]

In the place of El Alamillo, jurisdiction of El Socorro, on the 6th day of the month of September, 1680, for the prosecution of this case, and so that an Indian who was captured on the road as the camp was marching may be examined, in order to ascertain the plans, designs, and motives of the rebellious enemy, his lordship, the señor governor and captain-general, caused the said Indian to appear before him. He received the oath from him in due legal form, in the name of God, our Lord, and on a sign of the cross, under charge of which he promised to tell the truth concerning what he might know and as he might be questioned. Having been asked his name and of what place he is a native, his condition, and age, he said that his name is Don Pedro Nanboa, that he is a native of the pueblo of Alameda, a widower, and somewhat more than eighty years of age. Asked for what reason the Indians of this kingdom have rebelled, forsaking their obedience to his Majesty and failing in their obligation as Christians, he said that for a long time, because the Spaniards punished sorcerers and idolaters, the nations of the Teguas, Taos, Pecuríes, Pecos, and Jemez had been plotting to rebel and kill the Spaniards and the religious [missionaries], and that they had been planning constantly to carry it out, down to the present occasion. Asked what he learned, saw and heard in the juntas and parleys that the Indians have held, what they have plotted among themselves, and why the Indians have burned the church and profaned the images of the pueblo of Sandia, he said that he has not taken part in any junta, nor has he harmed any one; that what he has heard is that the Indians do not want religious or Spaniards. Because he is so old, he was in the cornfield when he learned from the Indian rebels who came from the sierra that they had killed the Spaniards of the jurisdiction and robbed all their haciendas, sacking their houses. Asked whether he knows about the Spaniards and religious who were gathered in the pueblo of La Isleta, he said that it is true that some days ago there assembled in the said pueblo of La Isleta the religious of Sandia, Jemez, and Zia, and that they set out to leave the kingdom with those of the said pueblo of La Isleta and the Spaniards—not one of whom remained—taking along their property. The Indians did not fight with them because all the men had gone with the other nations to fight at the villa and destroy the governor and captain-general and all the people who were with him. He declared that the resentment which all the Indians have in their hearts has been so strong, from the time this kingdom was discovered, because the religious and the Spaniards took away their idols and forbade their sorceries and idolatries; that they have inherited successively from their old men the things pertaining to their ancient customs; and that he has heard this resentment spoken of since he was of an age to understand. What he has said is the truth and what he knows, under the oath taken, and he signs and ratifies it, it being read and explained to him in his language through the interpretation of Captain Sebastián Montaño, who signed it with his lordship, as the said Indian does not know how, before me, the present secretary.

***

Letter of the governor and captain-general, Don Antonio de Otermin, from New Mexico [to Fray Francisco de Ayeta], in which he gives him a full account of what has happened to him since the day the Indians surrounded him. [September 8, 1680.]

My very reverend father, Sir, and friend, most beloved Fray Francisco de Ayeta: The time has come when, with tears in my eyes and deep sorrow in my heart, I commence to give an account of the lamentable tragedy, such as has never before happened in the world, which has occurred in this miserable kingdom and holy custodia, His divine Majesty having thus permitted it because of my grievous sins. Before beginning my narration, I desire, as one obligated and grateful, to give your reverence the thanks due for the demonstrations of affection and kindness which you have given in your solicitude in ascertaining and inquiring for definite notices about both my life and those of the rest in this miserable kingdom, in the midst of persistent reports which had been circulated of the deaths of myself and the others, and for sparing neither any kind of effort nor large expenditures. For this, only Heaven can reward your reverence, though I do not doubt that his Majesty (may God keep him) will do so.

***

On Tuesday, the 13th of the said month [August], at about nine o'clock in the morning, there came in sight of us in the suburb of Analco, in the cultivated field of the hermitage of San Miguel, and on the other side of the river from the villa, all the Indians of the Tanos and Pecos nations and the Queres of San Marcos, armed and giving war whoops. As I learned that one of the Indians who was leading them was from the villa and had gone to join them shortly before, I sent some soldiers to summon him and tell him on my behalf that he could come to see me in entire safety, so that I might ascertain from him the purpose for which they were coming. Upon receiving this message he came to where I was, and, since he was known, as I say, I asked him how it was that he had gone crazy too—being an Indian who spoke our language, was so intelligent, and had lived all his life in the villa among the Spaniards, where I had placed such confidence in him—and was now coming as a leader of the Indian rebels. He replied to me that they had elected him as their captain, and that they were carrying two banners, one white and the other red, and that the white one signified peace and the red one war. Thus if we wished to choose the white it must be upon our agreeing to leave the country, and if we chose the red, we must perish, because the rebels were numerous and we were very few; there was no alternative, inasmuch as they had killed so many religious and Spaniards.

On hearing this reply, I spoke to him very persuasively, to the effect that he and the rest of his followers were Catholic Christians, asking how they expected to live without the religious; and said that even though they had committed so many atrocities, still there was a remedy, for if they would return to obedience to his Majesty they would be pardoned; and that thus he should go back to his people and tell them in my name all that had been said to him, and persuade them to agree to it and to withdraw from where they were; and that he was to advise me of what they might reply. He came back from there after a short time, saying that his people asked that all classes of Indians who were in our power be given up to them, both those in the service of the Spaniards and those of the Mexican nation of that suburb of Analco. He demanded also that his wife and children be given up to him, and likewise that all the Apache men and women whom the Spaniards had captured in war be turned over to them, inasmuch as some Apaches who were among them were asking for them. If these things were not done they would declare war immediately, and they were unwilling to leave the place where they were because they were awaiting the Taos, Pecuríes, and Teguas nations, with whose aid they would destroy us.

Seeing his determination, and what they demanded of us, and especially the fact that it was untrue that there were any Apaches among them, because they were at war with all of them, and that these parleys were intended solely to obtain his wife and children and to gain time for the arrival of the other rebellious nations to join them and besiege us, and that during this time they were robbing and sacking what was in the said hermitage and the houses of the Mexicans, I told him (having given him all the preceding admonitions as a Christian and a Catholic) to return to his people and say to them that unless they immediately desisted from sacking the houses and dispersed, I would send to drive them away from there. Whereupon he went back, and his people received him with peals of bells and trumpets, giving loud shouts in sign of war.

With this, seeing after a short time that they not only did not cease the pillage but were advancing toward the villa with shamelessness and mockery, I ordered all the soldiers to go out and attack them until they succeeded in dislodging them from that place. Advancing for this purpose, they joined battle, killing some at the first encounter. Finding themselves repulsed, they took shelter and fortified themselves in the said hermitage and the houses of the Mexicans, from which they defended themselves a part of the day with the firearms that they had and with arrows. We having set fire to some of the houses in which they were, thus having them surrounded and at the point of perishing, there appeared on the road from Tesuque a band of the people whom they were awaiting, who were all the Teguas. Thus it was necessary to go to prevent these latter from passing on to the villa, because the casas reales [royal houses] were poorly defended; whereupon the said Tanos and Pecos fled to the mountains and the two parties joined together, sleeping that night in the sierra of the villa. Many of the rebels remained dead and wounded, and our men retired to the casas reales with one soldier killed and the maese de campo [commanding officer], Francisco Gomez, and some fourteen or fifteen soldiers wounded, to attend them and intrench and fortify ourselves as best we could.

On the morning of the following day, Wednesday, I saw the enemy come down all together from the sierra where they had slept, toward the villa. Mounting my horse, I went out with the few forces that I had to meet them, above the convent. The enemy saw me and halted, making ready to resist the attack. They took up a better position, gaining the eminence of some ravines and thick timber, and began to give war whoops, as if daring me to attack them.

I paused thus for a short time, in battle formation, and the enemy turned aside from the eminence and went nearer the sierras, to gain the one which comes down behind the house of the maese de campo, Francisco Gomez. There they took up their position, and this day passed without our having any further engagements or skirmishes than had already occurred, we taking care that they should not throw themselves upon us and burn the church and the houses of the villa.

The next day, Thursday, the enemy obliged us to take the same step as on the day before of mounting on horseback in fighting formation. There were only some light skirmishes to prevent their burning and sacking some of the houses which were at a distance from the main part of the villa. I knew well enough that these dilatory tactics were to give time for the people of the other nations who were missing to join them in order to besiege and attempt to destroy us, but the height of the places in which they were, so favorable to them and on the contrary so unfavorable to us, made it impossible for us to go and drive them out before they should all be joined together.

On the next day, Friday, the nations of the Taos, Pecuríes, Jemez, and Queres having assembled during the past night, when dawn came more than 2,500 Indians fell upon us in the villa, fortifying and intrenching themselves in all its houses and at the entrances of all the streets, and cutting off our water, which comes through the arroyo [stream] and the irrigation canal in front of the casas reales. They burned the holy temple and many houses in the villa. We had several skirmishes over possession of the water, but, seeing that it was impossible to hold even this against them, and almost all the soldiers of the post being already wounded, I endeavored to fortify myself in the casas reales and to make a defense without leaving their walls. The Indians were so dexterous and so bold that they came to set fire to the doors of the fortified tower of Nuestra Señora de las Casas Reales, and, seeing such audacity and the manifest risk that we ran of having the casas reales set on fire, I resolved to make a sally into the plaza of the said casas reales with all my available force of soldiers, without any protection, to attempt to prevent the fire which the enemy was trying to set. With this endeavor we fought the whole afternoon, and, since the enemy, as I said above, had fortified themselves and made embrasures in all houses, and had plenty of harquebuses [muskets], powder, and balls, they did us much damage. Night overtook us and God was pleased that they should desist somewhat from shooting us with harquebuses and arrows. We passed this night, like the rest, with much care and watchfulness, and suffered greatly from thirst because of the scarcity of water.

On the next day, Saturday, they began at dawn to press us harder and more closely with gunshots, arrows, and stones, saying to us that now we should not escape them, and that, besides their own numbers, they were expecting help from the Apaches whom they had already summoned. They fatigued us greatly on this day, because all was fighting, and above all we suffered from thirst, as we were already oppressed by it. At nightfall, because of the evident peril in which we found ourselves by their gaining the two stations where the cannons were mounted, which we had at the doors of the casas reales, aimed at the entrances of the streets, in order to bring them inside it was necessary to assemble all the forces that I had with me, because we realized that this was their [the Indians'] intention. Instantly all the said Indian rebels began a chant of victory and raised war whoops, burning all the houses of the villa, and they kept us in this position the entire night, which I assure your reverence was the most horrible that could be thought of or imagined, because the whole villa was a torch and everywhere were war chants and shouts. What grieved us most were the dreadful flames from the church and the scoffing and ridicule which the wretched and miserable Indian rebels made of the sacred things, intoning the alabado and the other prayers of the church with jeers.

Finding myself in this state, with the church and the villa burned, and with the few horses, sheep, goats, and cattle which we had without feed or water for so long that many had already died, and the rest were about to do so, and with such a multitude of people, most of them children and women, so that our numbers in all came to about a thousand persons, perishing with thirst—for we had nothing to drink during these two days except what had been kept in some jars and pitchers that were in the casas reales—surrounded by such a wailing of women and children, with confusion everywhere, I determined to take the resolution of going out in the morning to fight with the enemy until dying or conquering. Considering that the best strength and armor were prayers to appease the divine wrath, though on the preceding days the poor women had made them with such fervor, that night I charged them to do so increasingly, and told the father guardián and the other two religious to say mass for us at dawn, and exhort all alike to repentance for their sins and to conformance with the divine will, and to absolve us from guilt and punishment. These things being done, all of us who could mounted our horses, and the rest went on foot with their harquebuses, and some Indians who were in our service with their bows and arrows, and in the best order possible we directed our course toward the house of the maese de campo, Francisco Xavier, which was the place where (apparently) there were the most people and where they had been most active and boldest. On coming out of the entrance to the street, it was seen that there was a great number of Indians. They were attacked in force, and though they resisted the first charge bravely, finally they were put to flight, many of them being overtaken and killed. Then turning at once upon those who were in the streets leading to the convent, they also were put to flight with little resistance. The houses in the direction of the house of the said maese de campo, Francisco Xavier, being still full of Indians who had taken refuge in them, and seeing that the enemy with the punishment and deaths that we had inflicted upon them in the first and second assaults were withdrawing toward the hills, giving us a little room, we laid siege to those who remained fortified in the said houses. Though they endeavored to defend themselves, and did so, seeing that they were being set afire and that they would be burned to death, those who remained alive surrendered and much was made of them. The deaths of both parties in this and the other encounters exceeded three hundred Indians.

Finding myself a little relieved by this miraculous event, although I had lost much blood from two arrow wounds which I had received in the face and from a remarkable gunshot wound in the chest on the day before, I immediately had water given to the cattle, the horses, and the people. Because we now found ourselves with very few provisions for so many people, and without hope of human aid, considering that our not having heard in so many days from the people on the lower river would be because of their all having been killed, like the others in the kingdom, or at least of their being or having been in dire straits, with the view of aiding them and joining with them into one body, so as to make the decisions most conducive to his Majesty's service, on the morning of the next day, Monday, I set out for La Isleta, where I judged the said comrades on the lower river would be. I trusted in divine providence, for I left without a crust of bread or a grain of wheat or maize, and with no other provision for the convoy of so many people except four hundred animals and two carts belonging to private persons, and, for food, a few sheep, goats, and cows.

In this manner, and with this fine provision, besides a few small ears of maize that we found in the fields, we went as far as the pueblo of La Alameda, where we learned from an old Indian whom we found in a maizefield that the lieutenant general with all the residents of his jurisdictions had left some fourteen or fifteen days before to return to El Paso to meet the wagons. This news made me very uneasy, alike because I could not be persuaded that he would have left without having news of me as well as of all the others in the kingdom, and because I feared that from his absence there would necessarily follow the abandonment of this kingdom. On hearing this news I acted at once, sending four soldiers to overtake the said lieutenant general and the others who were following him, with orders that they were to halt wherever they should come up with them. Going in pursuit of them, they overtook them at the place of Fray Cristóbal. The lieutenant general, Alonso García, overtook me at the place of Las Nutrias, and a few days' march thereafter I encountered the maese de campo, Pedro de Leiva, with all the people under his command, who were escorting these wagons and who came to ascertain whether or not we were dead, as your reverence had charged him to do, and to find me, ahead of the supply train. I was so short of provisions and of everything else that at best I should have had a little maize for six days or so.

Thus, after God, the only succor and relief that we have rests with your reverence and in your diligence. Wherefore, and in order that your reverence may come immediately, because of the great importance to God and the king of your reverence's presence here, I am sending the said maese de campo, Pedro de Leiva, with the rest of the men whom he brought so that he may come as escort for your reverence and the wagons or mule-train in which we hope you will bring us some assistance of provisions. Because of the haste which the case demands I do not write at more length, and for the same reason I cannot make a report at present concerning the above to the señor viceroy, because the autos [legal documents] are not verified and there has been no opportunity to conclude them. I shall leave it until your reverence's arrival here. For the rest I refer to the account which will be given to your reverence by the father secretary, Fray Buenaventura de Verganza. I am slowly overtaking the other party, which is sixteen leagues from here, with the view of joining them and discussing whether or not this miserable kingdom can be recovered. For this purpose I shall not spare any means in the service of God and of his Majesty, losing a thousand lives if I had them, as I have lost my estate and part of my health, and shedding my blood for God. May He protect me and permit me to see your reverence in this place at the head of the relief. September 8, 1680. Your servant, countryman, and friend kisses your reverence's hand.

DON ANTONIO DE OTERMÍN

Selection 2: Native American Converts in Seventeenth-Century Canada

Many Native Americans living in Canada encountered Christianity through the work of the Society of Jesus, or Jesuits, an order of Catholic priests who dedicated themselves to missionary work around the globe. Father Claude Chauchetière came to Canada as a Jesuit missionary in 1677 and lived among Native Americans in the mission community of Sault St. Francois Xavier, also known as Kahnawake, near Montreal. Many of its residents were Iroquois converts to Christianity, who moved northward after a prolonged period of warfare and epidemic disease had disrupted their homelands in the Mohawk Valley.

Among these migrants was a young woman Chauchetière identified as Catherine Tegaskouita, but more commonly known today as Kateri Tekakwitha. Tekakwitha was at the center of a group of Native women at Kahnawake who embraced Catholic practices of bodily mortification, including exposing themselves to the elements, fasting, and flagellation. Chauchetière and his fellow Jesuits were impressed by their piety but also struggled with these women over control of their bodies and spiritual lives. After her death in 1680 at the age of 24, Tekakwitha became an object of devotion among French Canadian and Native American Catholics, and she was eventually canonized as a saint in the Catholic Church in 2012. In the letter excerpted below, Chauchetière describes life in Kahnawake and in particular the devotional practices of Tekakwitha and her followers.

Credit: Reuben G. Thwaites, ed., *The Jesuit Relations and Allied Documents: Travels and Explorations of the Jesuit Missionaries in New France, 1610–1791*, 73 vols (Cleveland, OH: Burrows Brothers, 1896–1901), Vol. 62: 175–183.

You will be pleased to hear from me respecting the austerities practiced by certain savage women—Although there may be some indiscretion in their doing so; but it will show you their fervor. More than 5 years ago some of them learned, I know not how, of the pious practices followed by the nuns in Mon[t]real who are hospital sisters. They heard of disciplines, of iron girdles, and of hair shirts. This religious life began to please them very much, and three of them formed an association, in order to commence a sort of Convent; but we stopped them, because we did not Think that The time had yet come for this. However, even if they were not cloistered, they at least observed Chastity; and one of them died with the reputation of sanctity, 3 years Ago next spring. They, and some others who imitated them, would be admired in France, if what they do were known there. The first who began made her first attempt about Christmas in The year 1676, when she divested herself of her clothing, and exposed herself to The air at the foot of a large Cross that stands beside our Cemetery. She did so at a time when the snow was falling, although she was pregnant; and the snow that fell upon her back caused her so much suffering that she nearly died from it—as well as her child, whom the cold chilled in its mother's womb. It was her own idea to do this—to do penance for her sins, she said. She has had four companions in her fervor, who have since imitated her. Two of them made a hole in the ice, in the depth of winter, and Threw themselves into The water, where they remained during the time that it would take to say a Rosary slowly and sedately. One of the two, who Feared that she would be found out, did not venture to Warm herself when she returned to her cabin, but lay down on her mat with lumps of ice adhering to her shoulders. There have been several other Inventions of similar mortifications, which men and women have discovered for the purpose of tormenting themselves, and which constitute their usual exercises of penance.

But we have made them give up whatever was excessive. During the past two years, Their fervor has greatly augmented since God has removed from this world one of these devout savage women who live like Nuns, and she died with the reputation of sanctity. We cease not to say masses to thank God for the graces that we believe we receive, every Day, through her Intercession. Journeys are continually made to her tomb; and the savages, following her example, have become greater Christians than they were. We Daily see wonders worked through her Intercession. Her name was Catherine Tegaskouita. During her lifetime, she had made an agreement with a friend to make each other suffer, because she was too weak to do so by herself, owing to her Continual illness. She begged her companion to do her the Charity of severely chastising her with Blows from a whip. This they did for a year, without anyone knowing it, and for that purpose they withdrew, every Sunday, into a Cabin in the middle of the Cemetery; and there, taking in their hands willow shoots, they mingled prayers with penance. Finally, when one of the two saw that her companion had fallen sick at the end of The year, she was pressed by scruples to reveal The matter, and to ask whether she had not sinned in what she had done. At that time, people here used only willow shoots, or Thorns, which here are very Long; but since they have heard of disciplines, of iron girdles, and of similar Instruments of penance, The use of these Daily becomes more general. And, as The men have found that the women use them, they will not Let themselves be outdone, and ask us to permit them to use these every Day; but we will not allow it. The women, to the number of 8 or 10, Began The practice; and The wife of the dogique—that is to say, of him who Leads the Singing and says the prayers—is among the number. She it is who, in her husband's absence, also causes The prayers to be said aloud, and Leads The Singing; and in this capacity she assembles the devout women of whom we have spoken, who call themselves sisters. They tell One another their faults, and deliberate together upon what must be done for The relief of the poor in the Village—whose number is so great that there are almost as many poor as there are Savages. The sort of monastery that they maintain here has its rules. They have promised God never to put on their gala-dress (for the savage women have some taste, and take pride in adorning themselves with porcelain beads; with vermillion, which they apply to their Cheeks; and with earrings and bracelets). They assist One another in the fields; They meet together to incite one another to virtue; and one of them has been received as a nun in The hospital of monreal [Montreal].

There are married people here who have for a long time lived as brother and sister. There are aged women, veterans in the faith, who Instruct the others as missionaries would do, and God thereby supplies the want of these which we experience. There are women who have shared Their fields,—thus, as it were, taking The bread from their own mouths to give it to the New-comers,—who are not yet in position to do anything for them in return,—in order to win them to God. When There are widows and sick persons, the Captains make their families work, for the love of God, at building Cabins for those who have none. Some live in the woods in the same state of Innocence as do those in the village; and they return with consciences as pure as When they went away. And I may state, without exaggeration, that when they return we do not find in many of them matter for absolution; and yet They are sufficiently enlightened to accuse themselves of the least Imperfections,—Such as Slight distractions during their prayers, petty acts of Impatience, some instance of forgetfulness, and things which, in their case, are often virtues. Modesty is natural to Them. When They pray or Sing in The church, they do so with so much devotion that all the French settlers here who see them are impressed by it, and say that they are more devout than we allege. I was forgetting to tell you that, when They are in the woods, they have the Sundays and feast-days marked by small Lines to the number of seven, one for each Day of the week; we mark Crosses upon the lines that indicate the feast-days and The Sundays, and they observe these very exactly.

There is a savage woman who says the Rosary fully twenty times a Day; and another who says it six times in her day, by dividing It in a very Ingenious fashion … Here is also something very touching. While making My rounds in the Village at eight or nine o'clock, in the evening, I have heard The air resound on all sides with voices issuing from all the Cabins. All were saying their prayers aloud, before retiring to rest; and this is done every night, not a single person failing to do so. Thus have these former man-eaters become lambs through The grace of Jesus Christ, in such a manner as to be examples of Virtue and of Religion in Canada.

We have here no other demon to Contend against than liquor and drunkenness, which make a hell of all the Iroquois villages, wherein life is a continual suffering. The French are the cause of its giving us much trouble here; for, in order to strip the Savages to their Very Shirts, they follow them everywhere, to make them drink and become intoxicated.

It is admirable to see how some of our Christian savages distinguish themselves in repressing this evil. They spill the liquor; they Break the bottles, with incredible courage, exposing themselves to insults and to Blows, of which some still bear the marks. And, in spite of all this, They do not lose Courage. I Know three or four who would endure martyrdom to prevent anything being done to offend God. They are no longer guided by the French, whom they had Hithero considered good Christians, but who They now see very plainly are not such.

Selection 3: A Christian Indian Challenges His Colonial Mentor

David Fowler was a Montauk Indian from eastern Long Island. By the time of his birth in 1735, the Montauks had lived among English colonists for over a century, and many of them had converted to Christianity. At age twenty-four, Fowler attended Moor's Charity School, an Indian school established in Lebanon, Connecticut by Congregational minister Eleazar Wheelock. One of Wheelock's star pupils, Fowler conducted missionary work among the Oneida and Mohawk Indians of New York in the 1760s. He worked there with the Reverend Samuel Kirkland until his falling out with Kirkland and Wheelock led him back to Montauk, where he worked as a schoolmaster. During the Revolutionary Era, he returned to the Oneidas' country as part of a Christian Indian settlement known as Brothertown. He died in 1807.

Wheelock's missionary work, like Fowler's, met with disappointing results. In 1769, he established Dartmouth College in New Hampshire, nominally to serve as a seminary for Christian Indians. Wheelock, however, had grown discontented with his Indian students and shifted Dartmouth's priorities to educating Anglo-Americans.

Fowler's correspondence offers an interesting glimpse inside the relationship between Christian Indians and their European mentors. Note in particular Fowler's descriptions of the non-Christian Indians among whom he labored and his anger at Wheelock's and Kirkland's treatment of his ministry.

The spelling has been modernized.

Credit: James Dow McCallum, ed., *Letters of Eleazar Wheelock's Indians* (Hanover, NH: Dartmouth College Publications, 1932), 87–113.

David Fowler left Eleazar Wheelock's Indian School in Connecticut in the Fall of 1765, and moved to the New York frontier, to work as a schoolmaster and missionary among the Mohawks and Oneidas.

David Fowler to Eleazar Wheelock

Canajoharie [New York], January 21, 1766

Reverend and Honored Sir:

After much Worry and Fatigue about my House and Journeys, after also hungry Belly, I began to keep my School steadily sometime in November. My Scholars learn very well: I find it is impossible to keep the Children steadily to School. Let [Indian] Men labor and work as English do: They are lazy and inhuman pack of Creatures as I ever saw in the World; They have seen me working and tugging Day after Day and never offered to help in the least thing I had to do in my House, only finished covering it and left me. I was obliged to eat with Dogs near two Months. I say with Dogs because they are always licking Water out of the Pails and Kettles we use: Now I live like a Gentleman, I have a plantation of Corn, Flour, Meat and rotten Fish. I applied to Sir William [Johnson, a local Indian agent] for Provision; accordingly, he ordered the Commanding Officer at the Royal Block House to give me out Provision as long as I should want …

I never saw such general Disposition of hearing the Word of God amongst these poor People as I do now: most every one of the adults of this Place, have openly renounced their Liquor and said that they will devote themselves in hearing the Word of God. Now is the time for Ministers to come up whilst they are in such Disposition. Oh, for a Minister whose Heart is full of Love to God and Compassion to poor Sinners, one who is meek and lowly and crafty in winning Souls to Christ, who has a real Sense and worth of Immortal Souls, would greatly weaken the Strong Holds of Satan in this Place. Dear Sir, do all that is in your Power to get up a Minister early in the Spring, for the poor Creatures are really desirous to hear the Word of God; we have no Minister and yet we have a full Assembly every Sabbath. I have nothing New to acquaint you; I enjoy a good State of Health and am contented …

Your affectionate and obedient Servant,
DAVID FOWLER

***

David Fowler to Eleazar Wheelock
    Canajoharie, February 17, 1766
    Reverend Sir,

I received yours 25th of January which offered me much Pleasure, and also warned me against those things which I am so much addicted to. I hope your Admonition will not be entirely lost. I will try to take care to mind what you wrote to me.

I wrote you a large Letter in the Month past which exhausted all the Matter that was in my Head; I now write you but a few Lines. I am pursuing my Business with all Courage and Resolution that lies in my Power or Capacity. Reverend Mr. Chamberlain can inform you what Progress my Scholars have made in learning to read as well as I can.

Sir, I am almost naked, my Cloths are coming all to pieces; I shall be very glad all the Cloth that is intended for me be in readiness against my coming. I design to come down [to Connecticut] the latter End of May or beginning June. I have nothing New to acquaint you, I am well and hearty also contented. I am …

your affectionate Indian Son,
DAVID FOWLER
P.S. Regards to Madam Sir Wheelock and to all the rest.

***

Fowler returned to Connecticut to get supplies for himself and his wife, Hannah. His purchase of some clothing apparently caused Wheelock to reprimand him for being proud, which in turn caused Fowler to vent his anger at Wheelock.

David Fowler to Eleazar Wheelock
    Lebanon [Connecticut], August 26, 1766
    Reverend and Honored Sir,

I think it very hard that I must be blamed so much as I have been since my Return from home, and all for taking up those things at Mr. Breeds [a local trader], When I have Orders from you to get them, for which I am now accounted a Devil or Proud as the Devil, After you have repeatedly and manifestly told me that I should have whatsoever I wanted. If you denied me when I came to ask for them, I should not feel half so bad as I do now, or if you told me in a mild Manner when I got home, "those things which you got were too good and too costly, you must not have them," I should not resist you. You know, Sir, I have always been governed and advised by you with all ease imaginable.

This brings into my mind what Treatment I met since I came here. Yea it is shameful, when I have been so faithful to you as if I was your Negro, yea I have almost killed myself in Laboring. I have done hither to all what laid in my Power to help you; I think I can say and believe you too that I have done more Service to you than all the rest of the Indian Boys. And now I am too bad to live in the House for one of my missteps, therefore I must leave you and your School this very Day and go weeping in the Road homeward.

I am grieved that I have troubled you so much as I have. I am sorry those things were not denied me at first and then it would be all well and easy before now. But assure you, Sir, you shall receive Payment from me yearly till every Farthing be paid, it shall not be said all that Money and Pains which was spent for David Fowler on Indians was for naught. I can get Payment as well as white Man. O Dear me! I can't say no more, I am …

your unworthy Servant,
DAVID FOWLER

***

Wheelock replied to Fowler's letter with his own accusations.
Eleazar Wheelock to David Fowler
Lebanon [Connecticut], August 26, 1766
David Fowler,
I this Minute received Yours and [am] Sorry to find that you are not yet come to your right Temper of Mind. Who has called You a Devil, or Said you are as proud as the Devil since you came here? Who has ever said that you have not behaved well in the Main since you lived with me, or that I have not sat as much by You and expected as much benefit to the grand Design as by any Indian I ever Educated, or [that] there has been any Indian that I have been more friendly to than to you and your Character? Have I ever said you have not done more for my Benefit than all the Indians I ever had, and now you say, "I am too bad to live in the House for one of my missteps, therefore, I must leave you and your School this very day and go weeping in this Road Homeward."

Now, David, consider a little. Is this just, comely, and reasonable Treatment of me? Have I said worse of you or to you than that I was afraid that the Pride of your heart aspired after such Grandeur as was not for the glory of God and could not consist with the good of the general Design in view? That when I had given you leave to get every thing that you wanted for the Design and told you I begrudged you nothing that was necessary for you, that you should effect to clothe yourself and Hannah like Courtiers and that when you knew I had already been reproached through the Country, as I have been, only for letting you Wear an old velvet Coat that was given to you. I told you that the Eyes of all Europe and America were upon you and me too, and the Eyes of thousands who are unfriendly and will not fail to Catch at any occasion to reproach me and the Design. I told you it was no Interest of mine, but only the Honor and Interest of Christ that I was pleading for, and the Success of the Cause which has been so long an [?], and which I have so much labored and Worn out myself, and which certainly so nearly concerns you as me to Labor to promote. Did you not, when I was only Enquiring why it was prudent and best for you to have so many as 4 pairs of shoes at once, rise up and with very unbecoming air go out of the Room and Say "I will have no shoes, I'll wear Indian shoes," and how you and Hannah have Spent your precious Hours yesterday and today I know not. I wish your setting out were more in the Meekness and Humility of Christ.

As for my own part, great as the prospects of your Usefulness are (and they are very great if you will take God with you), I don't at all desire you should return to Oneida with your present

Tempers. Nor am I at all afraid but I can fully vindicate my own Reputation, take what Course you will. I suppose you can't reasonably think it unjust if the Whole and Plain Truth comes to the Light of the World, if I am put upon my own Vindication. Nor do I think you can feel very Easy if you should go till you return to me again, which I promise myself you will do as Soon as you return to God. My heart is the same and as full of Kindness and Good Will toward you as ever it has been, and I am as ready to do any thing that will Honor Christ and promote the Salvation of the Souls of the poor Indians as I ever was, but I have no notion of sending any Man who is aiming to set up himself instead of Christ Jesus as the object of your Worship, and when you will appear the Same as you have heretofore done, you will find me the same. I am ...

Your Sincere Well wisher,
ELEAZAR WHEELOCK

***

David Fowler to Eleazar Wheelock
    Canajoharie, February 26, 1767
    Reverend and Honored Sir:
    I think all that tender Affection which I used to have from you is quite gone: but when I consider my miscarriages I can't say anything for myself, only this: if I am unworthy to be looked upon, I should not be employed. I think it very strange that one who has done most should be forgotten for all those which have been sent into these [parts?], who have not done any thing worth mentioning. All what they have done is only roving abroad and making the Indians angry. I take it very hard that I have not received one Line when others have received Folios after Folios [sheets after sheets of letters]. But since I am forsaken, I now beg the Favor of you to bury my Name entirely and never mention no more to any one abroad, but bury into oblivion though you may hear of my good Behavior, my Managements, and my Prospects and whatsoever you may hear from me that is worthy to be reported, let it never go out of your Doors. But I shall always remember my obligations to you till the Day [of] my Death ...

Your affectionate though unworthy Servant,
DAVID FOWLER

***

One of Fowler's difficulties in New York was his relationship with the Reverend Samuel Kirkland, an associate of Wheelock. Fowler considered himself a partner of Kirkland's mission to the Oneida Indians and grew discontented with Kirkland's treatment of him as a servant and laborer.
    David Fowler to Eleazar Wheelock
    Oneida [New York], March 17, 1767
    Reverend and Honored Sir:
    I suppose you have received my presumptuous Letter; which I believe has given you much Sorrow and Trouble of Mind. For I was in a very bad frame of Mind, occasioned by Mr. Kirkland's resuming too much of greatness before Company; he appeared to me, that he wanted to show what [a] great man he was that he could order us about where and how he pleased; this soon stuck in my Crop; and at this time Mr. Kirkland had letters come to hand and none for me; this increased my anger, and in the midst of my Passion I wrote your Letter. I indeed wrote whatsoever came out first; I hardly knew what I was writing about, nor can I now tell what I wrote, for as soon as I finished writing I sealed it up, but I remember some harsh Word in it.
    ... I now beg a Favor of you which will afford me Comfort and Ease, which is this: whensoever you write to Mr. Kirkland, charge him not to mention one Syllable of [it] to me, for [it] cuts me very much; though I see myself a mean and worthless Fellow and yet I am such [a] foolish Creature as to trouble myself when others receive a Letter.

I speak calmly and sincerely not in ruffle. Another Favor of Mr. Kirkland's Comfort, which is this: Don't try to give him so much authority as that he would persuade or take upon himself to govern me or order me about. As soon as he tries to do that, he won't be so comfortable here; for he can't order me, nor no Missionary that shall come into these parts. As I am an Instructor I am able to act for myself, without having a master over me ...

Your affectionate and unworthy servant,
DAVID FOWLER

***

By 1767, Fowler had grown discontented with his missionary work in New York. He had difficulty keeping Indian students in his school, and the labor of keeping his family housed and fed on the frontier proved too burdensome to continue. He returned to his native Montauk on Long Island to work as a schoolmaster there.

David Fowler to Eleazar Wheelock
Canajoharie, May 28, 1767
Reverend and Honored Sir:

I am really sorry that I have molested you again in my last letter to you, and now I sincerely ask your forgiveness of all my past ungrateful and undutiful behavior to You; I am ashamed of my haughty talk to you; for I have seen the Baseness of [it] since I [have] given you that undutiful treatment. Again, I ask your forgiveness and [that you] no longer think hard of me. I determine to show such Haughtiness to you no more.

I am quite sorry to inform you of my Discouragement here. I can't see what I can do here as long as these Indians don't labor, for they are continually going from Place to Place and when they are at home in some Business [or] another which will take them from the School. I find it too hard to tarry with my wife at my present circumstances, for instead of keeping School, I have been at work almost ever since my arrival here, for I have not kept the School this two Months. I don't know when I have so much to do. The Indians are unwilling to help us in our outward Business [i.e., farming].

I think as soon as my wife gets over her trial [sickness] to come down and go over to Long Island where they are sincerely desirous for a School Master to come amongst them; Jacob [Fowler's younger brother] is too young to manage a School there and our Parents.

Sir, it is too hard for one to carry farming for two Families in a new Country. I can't no more for the Boys are awaiting. Only much Love and Duty from,

Your unworthy Servant,
DAVID FOWLER

Selection 4: An African American's Conversion Experience during the Great Awakening

The most successful preacher of the Great Awakening was George Whitefield, an English minister who toured North America several times between 1738 and his death in 1770. One of the features that distinguished Whitefield and his fellow evangelists was their interest in preaching to all who would listen. Without fixed congregations to attend to, they put little emphasis on doctrinal orthodoxy, and they reached out to socially marginalized men and women who had been ignored or excluded by established churches.

John Marrant was a free black who embraced the New Birth. Born in New York City in 1755, he grew up in the South and lived at various times in Florida, Georgia, and South Carolina. While still in his teens, he proved himself to be a talented musician, but at his family's urging apprenticed himself to learn a trade. His chance encounter with George Whitefield in Charleston, South Carolina led to the kind of life-altering conversion experienced by many other believers during the Great Awakening. He eventually became a Methodist minister who worked among slaves in South Carolina and African-American loyalists who settled in Nova Scotia after the American Revolution.

Credit: John Marrant, *A Narrative of the Lord's Wonderful Dealings with John Marrant, A Black (Now Going to Preach the Gospel in Nova-Scotia) Born in New-York, in North-America*, 2nd edn (London: Gilbert and Plummer, 1785), 9–16.

Unstable as water I returned to town, and wished to go to some trade. My sister's husband being informed of my inclination provided me with a master, on condition that I should serve him one year and a half on trial, and afterwards be bound, if he approved of me. According I went, but every evening I was sent for to play on music, somewhere or another; and I often continued out very late, sometimes all night, so as to render me incapable of attending my master's business the next day; yet in this manner I served him a year and four months, and was much approved of by him. He wrote a letter to my mother to come and have me bound, and whilst my mother was weighing the matter in her own mind, the gracious purposes of God, respecting a perishing sinner, were now to be disclosed.

One evening I was sent for in a very particular manner to go and play for some Gentleman, which I agreed to do, and was on my way to fulfill my promise; and passing by a large meeting house I saw many lights in it, and crowds of people going in. I inquired what it meant, and was answered by my companion, that a crazy man was hallooing [calling loudly] there; this raised my curiosity to go in, that I might hear what he was hallooing about. He persuaded me not to go in, but in vain. He then said, "If you will do one thing I will go in with you." I asked what that was? He replied, "Blow the French horn among them." I liked the proposal well enough, but expressed my fears of being beaten for disturbing them; but upon his promising to stand by and defend me, I agreed. So we went, and with much difficulty got within the doors.

I was pushing the people to make room, to get the horn off my shoulder to blow it, just as Mr. Whitefield was naming his text [the passage from scripture he would preach on], and looking round, and, as I thought, directly upon me, and pointing with his finger, he uttered these words, "PREPARE TO MEET THY GOD, O ISRAEL." The Lord accompanied the word with such power, that I was struck to the ground, and lay both speechless and senseless for twenty-four minutes: When I was come a little too, I found two men attending me, and a woman throwing water in my face, and holding a smelling-bottle to my nose; and when something more recovered, every word I heard from the minister was like a parcel of swords thrust into me, and what added to my distress, I thought I saw the devil on every side of me. I was constrained in the bitterness of my spirit to halloo out in the midst of the congregation, which disturbing them, they took me away; but finding I could neither walk or stand, they carried me as far as the vestry, and there I remained till the service was over.

When the people were dismissed Mr. Whitefield came into the vestry, and being told of my condition he came immediately, and the first word he said to me was, "JESUS CHRIST HAS GOT THEE AT LAST." He asked where I lived, intending to come and see me the next day; but recollecting he was to leave the town the next morning, he said he could not come himself, but would send another minister; he desired them to get me home, and then taking his leave of me, I saw him no more.

When I reached my sister's house, being carried by two men, she was very uneasy to see me in so distressed a condition. She got me to bed, and sent for a doctor, who came immediately, and after looking at me, he went home, and sent me a bottle of mixture, and desired her to give me a spoonful every two hours; but I could not take any thing the doctor sent, nor indeed keep in bed; this distressed my sister very much, and she cried out, "The lad will surely die." She sent for two other doctors, but no medicine they prescribed could I take. No, no; it may be asked, a wounded spirit who can cure? As well as who can bear? In this distress of soul I continued for three days without any food, only a little water now and then. On the fourth day, the minister Mr. Whitefield had desired to visit me came to see me, and being directed upstairs, when he entered the room, I thought he made my distress much worse. He wanted to take hold of my hand, but I durst not give it to him. He insisted upon taking hold of it, and I then got away from him on the other side of the bed; but being very weak I fell down, and before I could recover he came to me and took me by the hand, and lifted me up, and after a few words desired to go to prayer. So he fell upon his knees, and pulled me down also; after he had spent some time in prayer he rose up, and asked me now how I did; I answered, much worse; he then said, "Come, we will have the old thing over again," and so we kneeled down a second time, and after he had prayed earnestly we got up, and he said again, "How do you do now;" I replied worse and worse, and asked him if he intended to kill me? "No, no," said he, "you are worth a thousand dead men, let us try the old thing over again," and so falling upon our knees, he continued in prayer a considerable time, and near the close of his prayer, the Lord was pleased to set my soul at perfect liberty, and being filled with joy I began to praise the Lord immediately; my sorrows were turned into peace, and joy, and love. The minister said, "How is it now?" I answered, all is well, all happy. He then took his leave of me; but called every day for several days afterwards, and the last time he said, "Hold fast that thou hast already obtained, till Jesus Christ come." I now read the Scriptures very much. My master sent often to know how I did, and at last came himself, and finding me well, asked me if I would not come to work again? I answered no. He asked me the reason, but receiving no answer he went away. I continued with my sister about three weeks, during which time she often asked me to play upon the violin for her, which I refused; then she said I was crazy and mad, and so reported it among the neighbours, which opened the mouths of all around against me.

I then resolved to go to my mother, which was eighty-four miles from Charles-Town [Charleston, South Carolina]. I was two days on my journey home, and enjoyed much communion with God on the road, and had occasion to mark the gracious interpositions of his kind providence as I passed along. The third day I arrived at my mother's house, and was well received. At supper they sat down to eat without asking the Lord's blessing, which caused me to burst out into tears. My mother asked me what was the matter? I answered, I wept because they sat down to supper without asking the Lord's blessing. She bid me, with much surprise, to ask a blessing. I remained with her fourteen days without interruption; the Lord pitied me, being a young soldier. Soon, however, Satan began to stir up my two sisters and brother, who were then at home with my mother; they called me every name, but that which was good. The more they persecuted me, the stronger I grew in grace. At length my mother turned against me also, and the neighbours joined her, and there was not a friend to assist me, or that I could speak to; this made me earnest in God. In these circumstances, being the youngest but one of our family, and young in Christian experience, I was tempted so far as to threaten my life; but reading my Bible one day, and finding that if I did destroy myself I could not come where God was, I betook myself to the fields, and some days staid out from morning to night to avoid the persecutors. I stayed one time two days without any food, but seemed to have clearer views into the spiritual things of God. Not long after this I was sharply tried, and reasoned the matter within myself, whether I should turn to my old courses of sin and vice, or serve and cleave to the Lord; after prayer to God, I was fully persuaded in my mind, that if I turned to my old ways, I should perish eternally.

Upon this I went home, and finding them all as hardened or worse than before, and every body saying I was crazy; but a little sister I had, about nine years of age, used to cry when she saw them persecute me; and continuing so about five weeks and three days, I thought it was better for me to die than to live among such people. I rose one morning very early, to get a little quietness and retirement, I went into the woods, and staid till eight o'clock in the morning; upon my return I found them all at breakfast; I passed by them, and went up-stairs without any interruption; I went upon my knees to the Lord, and returned him thanks; then I took up a small pocket Bible and one of Dr. Watt's hymn books, and passing by them went out without one word spoken by any of us. After spending some time in the fields, I was persuaded to go from home altogether. Accordingly I went over the fence, about half a mile from our house, which divided the inhabited and cultivated parts of the country from the wilderness. I continued travelling in the desert [desert] all day without the least inclination of returning back.

Discussion Questions

1. What reasons did Nanboa give to explain the Pueblos' revolt against the Spanish? What evidence can you find in the account of Otermín to support or contradict that explanation?
2. What elements of his converts' religious practices did Father Chauchetière find encouraging and which ones gave him cause for concern? Why do you think the female converts of Kahnawake embraced such extreme forms of bodily mortification?
3. Why did Fowler find his missionary work among the Oneidas so frustrating? What do his letters tell you about the prejudices and ostracism that Christian Indians faced in both the native and colonial worlds?
4. Briefly describe Marrant's conversion experience. How did it differ from that of the other Christian converts described in this chapter?

Suggested Readings

For the religious conversion and resistance in New Mexico, see Andrew L. Knaut, *The Pueblo Revolt of 1680: Conquest and Resistance in Seventeenth-Century New Mexico* (Norman, OK: University of Oklahoma Press, 1995); and Ramón A. Gutiérrez, *When Jesus Came, the Corn Mothers Went Away: Marriage, Sexuality, and Power in New Mexico, 1500–1846* (Stanford, CA: Stanford University Press, 1991). For the spiritual encounter in colonial Canada, see Allan Greer, *Mohawk Saint: Catherine Tekakwitha and the Jesuits* (New York: Oxford University Press, 2005); and James Axtell, *The Invasion Within: The Contest of Cultures in Colonial North America* (New York: Oxford University Press, 1985). For Native American religion during the era of the Great Awakening, see David J. Silverman, *Red Brethren: The Brothertown and Stockbridge Indians and the Problem of Race in Early America* (Ithaca, NY: Cornell University Press, 2010); and Linford D. Fisher, *The Indian Great Awakening: Religion and the Shaping of Native Cultures in Early America* (New York: Oxford University Press, 2012). For African-American religion in early America, see Michael A. Gomez, *Exchanging our Country Marks: The Transformation of African Identities in the Colonial and Antebellum South* (Chapel Hill, NC: University of North Carolina Press, 1998); and Philip D. Morgan, *Slave Counterpoint: Black Culture in the Eighteenth-Century Chesapeake and Lowcountry* (Chapel Hill, NC: University of North Carolina Press, 1998).

5 West Africa and the Atlantic Slave Trade

Figure 5.1 Slave Trading at Fort des Maures, Moyella Island, West Africa.

This engraving from the late eighteenth century depicts Africans and Europeans involved in the slave trade. At the center of the image, a European merchant meets with an African chief, each of whom is accompanied by armed guards. In the background, African and European workers carry goods back and forth from the ships in the harbor. Note the walled fort or "factory" in the background, where slaves would be confined until their departure for the Americas.

Source credit: Corbis Historical/Getty Images.

Introduction

Even before Columbus's voyages to America, Portuguese and Spanish ships were exploring the West African coast, engaging in trade with the people they encountered there, and bringing slaves back to their homeports. Once the Portuguese began cultivating sugar in Brazil, African slaves became an important part of the trans-Atlantic trade with the New World. Between 1492 and 1870, approximately 10 million Africans came to the Americas as a result of the Atlantic Slave Trade, making them the largest immigrant group to the New World during that time. Of those 10 million, about 60 percent went to the Caribbean, 35 percent to Latin America, and 5 percent to North America; the majority arrived between 1700 and 1800, with the peak years of the trade occurring around 1780. African slaves provided labor for plantation colonies that produced sugar, tobacco, rice, cotton, and coffee, and they worked as miners, domestic servants, and urban craftsmen. Regardless of its location, climate, geography, or nationality, each colony in the New World recognized the legitimacy of slavery and used the labor of African slaves.

Throughout the Americas, European colonists came to equate slavery with sub-Saharan Africans and the color of their skin. Slavery had been an important part of the social and economic orders of the ancient Roman and medieval Islamic worlds, but in both of those cases, people of various ethnicities, religions, and races were eligible for enslavement, most typically as a result of warfare and captivity. In the Atlantic World, slavery acquired a distinctive racial designation: it became a lifelong, hereditary status most often justified by the use of racial classifications that defined Africans as inherently unequal and best suited to serve whites. Thus, while using a form of labor as old as history itself, the colonization of the Americas created an entirely new kind of slavery that would have profound ramifications for the intellectual and social development of the Western World.

The Atlantic Slave Trade was also a business involving the exchange of manufactured goods for human beings. The bulk of this trade took place along the West African coast, near the mouths of four major river systems: the Senegal, the Gambia, the Niger, and the Congo (also known as the Zaire) (see Map 5.1). European powers competed against each other to establish diplomatic and commercial relations with African states and kingdoms in these regions. The merchant companies that conducted the trade lacked the manpower and resources to conquer and colonize West Africa. Instead, they entered into agreements with local rulers who allowed them to maintain coastal forts or "factories" from which to conduct their business, in return for tribute and duties paid on their trade. In exchange for slaves, West Africans demanded items of European manufacture, including cloth, iron bars, metal wares, firearms, jewelry, and liquor. Iron bars, which African blacksmiths could work into a variety of goods, became a common means of reckoning prices for slaves in the trade. West Africans had the ability to produce iron and cloth for themselves, but for coastal peoples in the era of the Atlantic Slave Trade, it was cheaper to acquire such items from Europeans. Furthermore, West Africans valued European cloth, swords, and firearms as prestige goods that exhibited the wealth and power of their owners. Europeans did not force this trade upon Africans; nor did they hoodwink Africans into exchanging slaves for trinkets. Rather, Africans participated in the Atlantic Slave Trade because it offered them goods at a lower cost and in greater varieties than they could produce at home.

Of course, describing the Atlantic Slave Trade strictly in terms of economics overlooks the enormous human cost incurred by the slaves themselves. Slavery was not unfamiliar to Africans prior to the Atlantic Slave Trade, but the particular type of slavery bred by this exchange was. In West Africa, a person might be enslaved as a result of war, debt, or criminal behavior, and slaves did all kinds of work, including farming, craft production, and domestic and military service. In short, there were many ways to be enslaved and many types of slavery.

When Europeans began dealing directly with sub-Saharan Africans, the slaves involved in this exchange encountered a type of slavery previously unknown in Africa. They had to endure long journeys from the interior to the coast, moving farther and farther away from familiar people and surroundings. Time spent in coastal forts and on slave ships waiting to depart for America exposed them to malnutrition and diseases that often proved fatal. Slave traders also relied on brutal discipline to maintain order over their human cargoes. The shock of this kind of enslavement was compounded by the difficulties of the Middle Passage, the trans-Atlantic voyage to the Americas, which involved still more physical abuse, malnourishment, and sickness, as well as the deplorable crowding and sanitation of the ship's hold.

The readings in this chapter offer several perspectives on the operation of the Atlantic Slave Trade in West Africa. In the first selection, a Scottish explorer describes how the institution of slavery worked within Africa. In the second, a Danish doctor details the business and personnel involved in maintaining a coastal slave-trading post. The third selection presents a personal account of enslavement from an African who wrote an autobiography after gaining

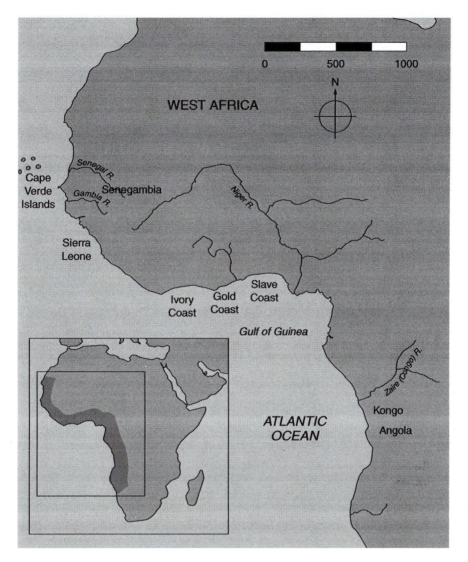

Map 5.1 Coastal West Africa, Showing Major Rivers and Trading Regions.

his freedom in North America. The fourth selection, from the memoir of a British surgeon who served on a slave ship, recounts the horrific conditions endured by slaves during the Middle Passage. As you read these selections, compare and contrast how the slave trade worked from African and European perspectives. Who profited from the human suffering caused by this trade? Where in these selections do you find evidence of cultural exchange and adaptation between the persons involved in trading slaves?

Selection 1: A Scottish Explorer Describes Slavery and the Slave Trade in Africa

A native of Selkirk, Scotland, Mungo Park studied medicine at the University of Edinburgh before undertaking an exploratory expedition along the Gambia and Niger rivers in West Africa. Along with the Senegal River, the Gambia and Niger served as highways for the slave trade, ferrying war captives and other enslaved people out of the interior to the coast, where

African merchants sold them to the captains of European slave ships. Although the Atlantic Slave Trade had been going on for centuries before Park's lifetime, he arrived in Africa not long after its peak, and he became one of the few Europeans to witness the trade's operations within West Africa. Park published his account of this expedition in 1799. A few years later, he returned to West Africa as the head of another expedition, but he reportedly drowned there in 1805.

Credit: Mungo Park, *Travels in the Interior Districts of Africa … in the Years 1795, 1796, and 1797* (London: W. Bulmer, 1799), 287–298.

A state of subordination, and certain inequalities of rank and condition, are inevitable in every stage of civil society; but when this subordination is carried to so great a length, that the person and services of one part of the community are entirely at the disposal of another part, it may then be denominated a state of slavery; and in this condition of life, a great body of the Negro inhabitants of Africa have continued from the most early period of their history; with this aggravation, that their children are born to no other inheritance.

The slaves in Africa, I suppose, are nearly in the proportion of three to one to the freemen. They claim no reward for their services, except food and clothing; and are treated with kindness, or severity, according to the good or bad disposition of their masters. Custom, however, has established certain rules with regard to the treatment of slaves, which it is thought dishonourable to violate. Thus, the domestic slaves, or such as are born in a man's own house, are treated with more lenity than those which are purchased with money. The authority of the master over the domestic slave, as I have elsewhere observed, extends only to reasonable correction; for the master cannot sell his domestic, without having first brought him to a public trial, before the chief men of the place. But these restrictions on the power of the master, extend not to the case of prisoners taken in war, nor to that of slaves purchased with money. All these unfortunate beings are considered as strangers and foreigners, who have no right to the protection of the law, and may be treated with severity, or sold to a stranger, according to the pleasure of their owners. There are, indeed, regular markets, where slaves of this description are bought and sold; and the value of a slave in the eye of an African purchaser, increases in proportion to his distance from his native kingdom: for when slaves are only a few days' journey from the place of their nativity, they frequently effect their escape; but when one or more kingdoms intervene, escape being more difficult, they are more readily reconciled to their situation. On this account, the unhappy slave is frequently transferred from one dealer to another, until he has lost all hope of returning to his native kingdom. The slaves which are purchased by the Europeans on the Coast are chiefly of this description; a few of them are collected in the petty wars, hereafter to be described, which take place near the Coast; but by far the greater number are brought down in large caravans from the inland countries, of which many are unknown, even by name, to the Europeans.

The slaves which are thus brought from the interior, may be divided into two distinct classes; *first*, such as were slaves from their birth, having been born of enslaved mothers; *secondly*, such as were born free, but who afterwards, by whatever means, became slaves. Those of the first description, are by far the most numerous; for prisoners taken in war (at least such as are taken in open and declared war, when one kingdom avows hostilities against another) are generally of this description. The comparatively small proportion of free people, to the enslaved, throughout Africa, has already been noticed; and it must be observed, that men of free condition, have many advantages over the slaves, even in war time. They are in general better armed, and well mounted; and can either fight or escape, with some hopes of success; but the slaves, who have only their spears and bows, and of whom great numbers are loaded with baggage, become an easy prey … when a freeman is taken prisoner, his friends will sometimes ransom him, by giving two slaves in exchange; but when a slave is taken, he has no hopes of such redemption. To these disadvantages, it is to be added, that the Slatees, who purchase slaves in the interior countries, and carry them down the Coast for sale, constantly prefer such as have been in that condition of life from their infancy, well knowing that these have been accustomed to hunger and fatigue, and are better able to sustain the hardships of a long and painful journey, than free men; and on their reaching the Coast, if no opportunity offers of selling them to advantage, they can easily be made to maintain themselves by their labour; neither are they so apt to attempt making their escape, as those who have once tasted the blessings of freedom.

Slaves of the second description, generally become such by one or other of the following causes, 1. *Captivity*. 2. *Famine*. 3. *Insolvency*. 4. *Crimes*. A freeman may, by the established customs of Africa, become a slave, by being taken in war. War, is of all others, the most productive source, and was probably the origin, of slavery; for when one nation had taken from another, a greater number of captives than could be exchanged on equal terms, it is natural to suppose that the conquerors, finding it inconvenient to maintain their prisoners would compel them to labour; at first, perhaps, only for their own support; but afterwards to support their masters. Be this as it may, it is a known fact, that prisoners of war in Africa, are the slaves of the conquerors; and when the weak or unsuccessful warrior, begs for mercy beneath the uplifted spear of his opponent, he gives up at the same time his claim to liberty; and purchases his life at the expense of his freedom.

In a country, divided into a thousand petty states, mostly independent and jealous of each other; where every freeman is accustomed to arms, and fond of military achievements; where the youth who has practised the bow and spear from his infancy, longs for nothing so much as an opportunity to display his valour, it is natural to imagine that wars frequently originate from very frivolous provocation. When one nation is more powerful than another, a pretext is seldom wanting for commencing hostilities. Thus the war between Kajaaga and Kasson was occasioned by the detention of a fugitive slave; that between Bambarra and Kaarta by the loss of a few cattle. Other cases of the same nature perpetually occur, in which the folly or mad ambition of their princes, and the zeal of their religious enthusiasts, give full employment to the scythe of desolation.

The wars of Africa are of two kinds, which are distinguished by different appellations: that species which bears the greatest resemblance to our European contests, is denominated *killi*, a word signifying "to call out," because such wars are openly avowed, and previously declared. Wars of this description in Africa, commonly terminate, however, in the course of a single campaign. A battle is fought; the vanquished seldom think of rallying again; the whole inhabitants become panic struck; and the conquerors have only to bind the slaves, and carry off their plunder and their victims. Such of the prisoners as, through age or infirmity, are unable to endure fatigue, or are found unfit for sale, are considered as useless; and I have no doubt are frequently put to death. The same fate commonly awaits a chief, or any other person who has taken a very distinguished part in the war. And here it may be observed that, notwithstanding this exterminating system, it is surprising to behold how soon an African town is rebuilt and repeopled. The circumstance arises probably from this; that their pitched battles are few; the weakest know their own situation, and seek safety in flight. When their country has been desolated, and their ruined towns and villages deserted by the enemy, such of the inhabitants as have escaped the *sword*, and the *chain*, generally return, though with cautious steps, to the place of their nativity; for it seems to be the universal wish of mankind, to spend the evening of their days where they passed their infancy ...

The other species of African warfare, is distinguished by the appellation of *tegria*, "plundering or stealing." It arises from a sort of heredity feud, which the inhabitants of one nation or district bear towards another. No immediate cause of hostility is assigned, or notice of attack given; but the inhabitants of each, watch every opportunity to plunder and distress the objects of their animosity by predatory excursions. These, are very common, particularly about the beginning of the dry season, when the labour of the harvest is over and provisions are plentiful. Schemes of vengeance are then meditated. The chief man surveys the number and activity of his vassals, as they brandish their spears at festivals; and elated with his own importance, turns his whole thoughts towards revenging some depredation or insult, which either he or his ancestors may have received from a neighbouring state.

Wars of this description are generally conducted with great secrecy. A few resolute individuals, headed by some person of enterprise and courage, march quietly through the woods, surprize in the night some unprotected village, and carry off the inhabitants and their effects, before their neighbours can come to their assistance …

These plundering excursions, always produce speedy retaliation; and when large parties cannot be collected for this purpose, a few friends will combine together, and advance into the enemy's country, with a view to plunder, or carry off the inhabitants. A single individual has been known to take his bow and quiver, and proceed in like manner. Such an attempt is doubtless in him an act of rashness; but when it is considered that, in one of these predatory wars, he had probably been deprived of his child or his nearest relation, his situation will rather call for pity than censure. The poor sufferer, urged on by the feelings of domestic or paternal attachment, and the ardour of revenge, conceals himself among the bushes, until some young or unarmed person passes by. He then, tyger-like, springs upon his prey; drags his victim into the thicket, and in the night carries him off as a slave.

When a Negro has, by means like these, once fallen into the hands of his enemies, he is either retained as the slave of his conqueror, or bartered into a distant kingdom; for an African, when he has once subdued his enemy, will seldom give him an opportunity of lifting up his hand against him at a future period. A conqueror commonly disposes of his captives according to rank which they held in their native kingdom. Such of the domestic slaves as appear to be of a mild disposition, and particularly the young women, are retained as his own slaves. Others that display marks of discontent, are disposed of in a distant country; and such of the freemen or slaves, as have taken an active part in the war, are either sold to the Slatees, or put to death. War, therefore, is certainly the most general, and more productive source of slavery; and the desolations of war often (but not always) produce the second cause of slavery, *famine*, in which case a freeman becomes a slave, to avoid a greater calamity.

Perhaps by a philosophic and reflecting mind, death itself would scarcely be considered a greater calamity than slavery; but the poor Negroes, when fainting with hunger, thinks like Esau of old [a figure from the Old Testament]; *"behold I am at the point to die, and what profit shall this birthright do to me?"* There are many instances of free men voluntarily surrendering up their liberty to save their lives. During a great scarcity which lasted for three years, in the countries of Gambia great numbers of people became slaves in this manner …

The third cause of slavery, is *insolvency*. Of all the offences (if insolvency may be so called), to which the laws of Africa have affixed the punishment of slavery, this is the most common. A Negro trader commonly contracts debts on some mercantile speculation, either from his neighbours, to purchase such articles as will sell to advantage in a distant market, or from the European traders on the Coast; payment to be made in a given time. In both cases, the situation of the adventurer is exactly the same. If he succeeds, he may secure an independency. If he is unsuccessful, his person and services are at the disposal of another; for in Africa, not only the effects of the insolvent, but even the insolvent himself, is sold to satisfy the lawful demands of his creditors.

The fourth cause above enumerated, is *the commission of crimes, on which the laws of the country affix slavery as a punishment*. In Africa, the only offences of this class are murder, adultery, and witchcraft; and I am happy to say, that they did not appear to me to be common. In cases of murder, I was informed, that the nearest relation of the deceased had it in his power, after conviction, either to kill the offender with his own hand, or sell him into slavery. When adultery occurs, it is generally left to the option of the person injured, either to sell the culprit, or accept such a ransom for him, as he may think equivalent to the injury he has sustained. By witchcraft, is meant pretended magic, by which the lives or healths of persons are affected: in other words, it is the administering of poison. No trial for this offence, however, came under my observation while I was in Africa; and I therefore suppose that the crime, and its punishment, occur but very seldom.

When a free man has become a slave by any one of the causes before mentioned, he generally continues so for life, and his children (if they are born of an enslaved mother) are brought up in the same state of servitude. There are however a few instances of slaves obtaining their freedom, and sometimes even with the consent of their masters; as by performing some singular piece of service, or by going to battle, and bringing home two slaves as a ransom; but the common way of regaining freedom is by escape, and when slaves have once set their minds on running away, they often succeed. Some of them will wait for years before an opportunity presents itself, and during that period shew no signs of discontent. In general, it may be remarked, that slaves who come from a hilly country, and have been much accustomed to hunting and travel, are more apt to attempt their escape, than such as are born in a flat country, and have been employed in cultivating the land.

Such are the general outlines of that system of slavery which prevails in Africa; and it is evident, from its nature and extent, that it is a system of no modern date. It probably had its origin in the remote ages of antiquity, before the Mahomedans [Muslims] explored a path across the Desert [Sahara]. How far it is maintained and supported by the slave traffic, which, for two hundred years, the nations of Europe have carried on with the natives of the Coast, it is neither within my province, nor in my power, to explain. If my sentiments should be required concerning the effect which a discontinuance of that commerce would produce on the manners of the natives, I should have no hesitation in observing, that, in the present unenlightened state of their minds, my opinion is, the effect would neither be so extensive or beneficial, as many wise and worthy persons fondly expect.

Selection 2: A European Describes a Slave-Trading Post

All of the European powers involved in the colonization of the Americas participated in the Atlantic Slave Trade. Even the Danes, whose sugar colonies in the Caribbean were among the last established there, engaged in a direct trade with West Africa to supply their New World labor needs. Following precedents established by other European powers, the Danes built coastal forts in the regions where they traded so that they could warehouse goods and the human cargoes destined for slave ships. These posts also housed European traders and laborers, as well as troops charged with protecting them from foreign competitors, pirates, and rebellious slaves. Mortality rates for Europeans living in West Africa during this period were staggering, ranging from 25 to 75 percent per year, and such posts needed to be resupplied constantly with fresh recruits.

Paul Erdmann Isert was a German-born surgeon sent by the Baltic Guinea Company, a Danish slave-trading venture, to work at its West African post Christiansborg in 1783. Isert remained in that position for three years, and then sailed to the West Indies to inspect the plantation colonies there. Upon returning to Copenhagen, he published a narrative based on letters he had written during his African and American sojourn. He was especially interested in the health problems Europeans experienced in West Africa, and his story also sheds light on the social and labor relations between Europeans and Africans working in the slave trade. In 1788, he returned to Africa to establish a plantation colony there, but the plan collapsed shortly after his death in 1789.

Credit: *Letters on West Africa and the Slave Trade: Paul Erdmann Isert's Journey to Guinea and the Caribbean Islands in Columbia* (1788), trans. and ed. Selena Axelrod Winsnes (New York: Oxford University Press, 1992), 147–153, 155–159.

All of the Europeans who are staying in Guinea, regardless of what nation they come from, are in the service of either their king or a company. It was the Portuguese who first sailed along the Guinea Coast, in the mid-fifteenth century. Finding the people on the Gold Coast most courteous they built various fortified places, or forts, there, in which they kept their wares and carried on trade with the inhabitants. At first the articles that they took in barter from the Blacks as payment for their wares were limited principally to gold and ivory. But at the end of the century, after Columbia [America] was discovered, the sumptuousness of the products from there increased in Europe. However, since the Europeans, for their own safety, had exterminated most of the native Columbians, they began to lack workers to provide them with these products, so they turned to Africa which they knew was teeming with people at the time. Even though there were large numbers of people, the difficulty of travel and the climate in Africa would have made conquest too difficult for the Europeans. Thus they got this idea: buy Blacks and take them to their plantations in Columbia.

They had learned by experience that the Blacks were more robust by nature, and more suited to work, than the weaker Indians. For this reason, despite the cost of their transportation—during which many were to die on such a long trip—and other difficulties, they found that the transfer of these unhappy souls, which cost little or nothing at first, was a very profitable business. In this way began the Black slave trade which has been such an important undertaking during these last two centuries—to the shame of mankind.

***

The fifth nation having possessions in Guinea is that of the Danes. At present we have four forts and six lodges, or trading stations. The forts are: Christiansburg, Friedensburg, Kønigstein and Prinzenstein, The lodges are: Labodei, Thessing [Teshi], Temma, Ponny, Aflahu and Popo. These establishments lie within a stretch of fifty miles along the coast. Along this stretch we alone are the masters of trade, except for an English fort, called Prampram, lying between Christiansburg and Friedensburg. Since I have already told you about each of these places, I shall not repeat myself now.

The supreme command over all our possessions is held by the Governor of Christiansburg, who exercises authority over all the other possessions as their Chief. A council made up of the commanders of the other forts has been established for him, without which he cannot treat any matter of importance. The second in rank in the Council is the Chief Trader and Commander of Friedensburg. The other two commanders are Called "Traders" and vote according to their length of service. At the more important lodges, command lies with the factor, and in the less important posts there are assistants, junior officers, or, in some places, only a soldier. The annual salary of the governor is not more than 1,000 *thalers* [silver coins], plus 500 *thalers* for table allowance. The Chief Trader and Commandant of Friedensburg receives 500, and the other commanders 400 *thalers* each.

Commercial posts are held by assistants, under-assistants and reserve assistants. The factors and the two chief assistants, who take care of the bookkeeping and secretarial work, receive 400 *thalers*; the other chief assistants at the lodges and forts, 300; an under-assistant, 250; and a reserve assistant, 10 to 12 *thalers* a month.

The religious staff, when it is complete, consists of a clergyman and a catechist. The former is paid 400 *thalers* and the latter 250 *thalers* annually. The same conditions obtain in the medical service whose Chief Surgeon, stationed at Christiansburg, is paid 400 *thalers*, and the second one, stationed at Friedensburg, 300 *thalers*. But in addition they receive a bonus for each slave shipped out—an amount which can at times equal their salaries. Furthermore, the surgeon at Christiansburg is supplied with a Mulatto who performs bandaging and other surgical tasks, for which he is paid 12 *thalers* monthly.

The military personnel at the main fort consists, at present, of a sergeant, two corporals, two drummers, two pipers, twenty musketeers, one chief gunner, one assistant gunner, two constables, and two assistant constables, the last mentioned being Blacks. The other forts have one sergeant, one corporal, one drummer, one piper, ten musketeers, and, to man the cannon, two constables and a few Company slaves. A gunner is paid 20 *thalers*, a sergeant 16, a corporal 14, and the European soldiers 10 *thalers* monthly. But the Mulatto soldiers receive only 8 *thalers*.

There are also a number of artisans here in the service of the King. The person who is in charge of these and of the Company slaves is called the *Baas*, and receives 20 *thalers* a month. Masons, smiths, joiners and coopers are usually paid 14 *thalers* a month, or more if they are particularly skillful. The total number of Europeans here, at the time of writing this, amounts to not more than 38 people, and the posts are fairly well filled.

In addition there are 200–250 slaves in service who are not sent out of the country. The male slaves are given one *thaler* monthly and the females one-half *thaler*. Indeed, some of the younger girls are paid only one-quarter *thaler*. These wretched souls are most poorly paid for their work, and if they were not able to supplement their pay by one means or another, they could not possibly manage. Admittedly the free Black is not paid any better when his services are hired, but there is this difference, that he has his family in town and they have to feed him. The English have already recognized the drawbacks of the system and give their slaves twice as much as we give ours.

For the administration of all the establishments, the King pays 25,000 *thalers* annually to the Company which, if that is insufficient, is forced to supplement it from its own coffers.

All trade undertaken here is the monopoly of the Company which, to encourage that trade, pays the chiefs of the forts and offices considerable commissions.

On the whole, the Europeans here seldom live in a manner suitable to the nature of the climate. Instead of becoming accustomed to the fruits of the land, they prefer the products of their own lands and do not take into account that they have left their northern stomachs behind in their fatherlands. It is common knowledge that the stomach, as well as all the other organs of the body, becomes sluggish in a hot climate, and thus has not the strength to digest the foods for which it was designed. The extraordinary amount of meat which it is customary to serve at the tables of the rich here is veritable poison to the Europeans, if they do not take it in moderation. They ought to go to the natives of the land and see how four people relish one dish containing not more than one pound of meat or fish, with quantities of grain or other foodstuffs from the plant kingdom. Therefore they are healthy, while the Europeans are constantly plagued by illness.

In fact, it appears that certain northern Europeans, especially Norwegians, are totally unsuited to this climate. When they arrive in this land, even though they have never before in their lives been ill, they are like a fresh-water fish that has been placed in salt water. They become misanthropic, fretful, and do not know why. First they complain of a headache, usually accompanied by vomiting; after 24 hours often follow convulsions; after 36 hours a pustulelike rash appears on the forehead and the calves, and the patient dies—a man who had been perfectly healthy 48 hours earlier.

***

The illness which, for the older Coastmen, usually blazes the trail to Elysium [death] is dysentery. From the heat of the atmosphere, and from eating meat, drinking, and using too much Spanish pepper, they have not rarely weakened their viscera in such a way that if they first get diarrhea it very soon becomes dysentery. The surgeon does himself a disfavour if he is an adversary of astringent medicines. On the contrary, if the fever is not perceptible and the intestines have been cleaned out by a purgative, one might administer a mild astringent mixture (which I tried here) made of a decoction of the bark of a young mangrove in which gum arabic has been dissolved. However, one must be much on one's guard against puddings and meat. The most harmless food is a panada [a flour paste] accompanied by wine. The most important part of the cure is a strict diet, something to which the patient seldom cares to adhere.

***

The Europeans' entertainment in this land is limited. He who has not learned to enjoy his own resources comes off the loser, since society here is so limited that one has not much choice. And because each person is acquainted with all the behaviour or manners of the others, and sees in them, regrettably, so little of merit, one seldom finds another with whom one wishes to keep company. Since public diversions are totally lacking, the refuge of such gentlemen is usually Bacchus [drinking], gaming, and Venus [sex], in all of which a number of our former citizens have so excelled that they have had to pay prematurely with their lives for their debauchery.

One of the most peculiar customs here is the marriage of the Europeans to the daughters of the country. It is called *cassare*, a word which comes from the Portuguese and means to set up house. When a European arrives here one of his first considerations is to acquire one of these bed-fellows, in spite of the fact that I give each one the well-meant advice not to enter into such an arrangement, at least for the first year, since I have often been struck by the harm that results. If he has now chosen one to his taste (a rejection has seldom to be feared) he then sends a humble memorandum to the High Council wherein he announces the name of his chosen future half and asks that he may be given permission to take her as his (*quasi*) wife. The Council, which looks very positively on such a connection, because the European would not then be so easily plagued by homesickness, answers that he is so permitted, but that he must immediately pay one-half month's salary into the Mulatto treasury, and an equal amount when he leaves, as well as four percent monthly during his stay. When this has been acknowledged, the celebration takes place, a celebration which is no different from the one I described to you in an earlier letter about the Blacks, except that the bridegroom in this case usually gives a dinner party where the bride, probably for the first time, eats at table among the Europeans. It is understood here, however, that neither an engagement nor a marriage ceremony has taken place here, and the new husband can send his wife packing the next day if he feels like it.

The children who are born to such a pair are always christened and instructed in Christianity. If the child is a boy he will be employed as a soldier in the king's service as soon as he is ten years old, and thus will enjoy a monthly wage of eight *thalers*. Poor girls and boys, as long as they are not otherwise supported, are given one *thaler* from the Mulatto treasury for their sustenance, a sum which is ample for them.

The property of the man is not held in common with that of the woman, but each keeps his own privately. A Black woman is paid one *thaler* monthly and a Mulatto woman two *thalers* monthly by their husbands, and they are given clothing twice a year. They have the right to demand this, and if the husband refuses they have the right to complain to the Council. In such a case they would be paid the sum, which would then be deducted from the husband's salary. Sometimes there are among the soldiers such ne'er-do-wells that they cannot manage their wages themselves. In such cases the wages are often paid to the Black wife who then has to provide the European with food.

The happiness of all those in service in the country is dependent, for the most part, on the nature of the Governor's temperament. Everyone tries to emulate him, even, indeed, in inconsequential things. If he is excellent, all the others are courteous; miserly, the others will outdo one another in that respect and so it goes through all the ranks. And, "as Heaven is high and Europe far way" (as they say here) at times a governor rules here more despotically than the most absolute monarch in Europe. Unfortunate are those who are in service when a bad man rises to the governorship. And since the mortality rate is usually so high in this country, and everyone gains promotion, it has often happened that people from the lowest ranks, such as soldiers, artisans or cabin boys have risen to the rank of governor. Since these people usually have lacked the opportunity of training their reasoning abilities, their government is often a mixture of petty arrogance and cruelty. This falls not a little tediously on those men (perhaps of greater insight) who because of less seniority in service must be subordinates. It has often cost them their lives. There have been instances where some men to whom it was necessary to give a flogging one day were given the supreme command the next day.

***

The extraordinarily high mortality rate of the Europeans in this land has caused people in Europe to believe that the climate alone is to blame. But they are mistaken in this. From experience alone, one could judge the opposite. In this land from which the Europeans have been able, by a moderate reckoning, to export 60,000 people annually who would never return, the population is still very high, even after 200 years of such export. This fact alone is proof enough that the climate is harmless. According to these calculations, it is clear that during this last hundred years six million people were exported, and one can, without stretching the truth, easily assume that in the preceding centuries, from the beginning of the Black trade, at least twice as many were exported. This makes 18 million in all who were exported. What a figure! In fact, this figure by itself equals the population of a fairly large and populous land, namely, France. It is something other than the climate on the Coast which is unhealthy. It is rather the perverse way of life of those who come to this land that is more the cause of the mortality than is the country itself. Some die from the preconceived idea that it is impossible to live in a land where so many die such a short time after their arrival. Still others become homesick and grieve themselves to death, probably because they have contracted to stay here a certain number of years. As for others, alas! a great many bring such a host of primordial illnesses with them that when these are activated by the hot climate, death is certain.

Those people who, in my experience, are best suited to the climate are young people, of from 25 to 30 years of age. Whoever is over this age should stay away from here since he will seldom reach a higher age. Moreover, the climate is less salubrious for apparently very healthy, sanguine persons than it is for the person who is thin and weak by nature. People who are very sanguine and who come here should not let themselves be deceived by prejudgment. In this hot climate they must not neglect to be well bled, and this should be done immediately upon arrival. They should keep an extremely lean diet during the first year, drink great amounts of cold water, and bathe daily. If all these things are faithfully observed, barring any damage to the character, I can assure them that their bodies will adjust to the climate and even in the unhealthful air of the coast, they can become as old as they would have done in their fatherland.

Selection 3: A Former Slave Remembers His Enslavement in Africa

As a young boy named Broteer, Venture Smith was enslaved in his native West Africa in 1735. He recounted this experience in a narrative he published many years later, after living as a slave and free person in North America. His narrative offers one of the few first-person accounts of the slave trade within West Africa from the perspective of the enslaved.

Broteer was the son of a West African chief whose people were attacked by an enemy army seeking war captives. African slave traders transported him several hundred miles from the interior to the British slave trading post Anamabo (also known as Fort William) on the Gold Coast in modern Ghana. Perhaps because he was only six years old, his captors sold him directly to a crew member on a slave ship, who named him "Venture" and eventually resold him in Rhode Island. Venture worked as a slave in New England and New York, purchasing his freedom in 1765 and that of his wife and children several years later. He took the last name "Smith" from the master with whom he negotiated his self-purchase. He died in Connecticut in 1805, several years after telling his life story to an editor who published it.

Credit: Venture Smith, *A Narrative of the Life and Adventures of Venture, a Native of Africa, But Resident above Sixty Years in the United States of America* (New London, CT: C. Holt, 1798), 9–13.

A detachment from the enemy came to my father and informed him, that the whole army was encamped not far out of his dominions, and would invade the territory and deprive his people of their liberties and rights, if he did not comply with the following terms. These were to pay them a large sum of money, three hundred fat cattle, and a great number of goats, sheep, asses, &c.

My father told the messenger he would comply rather than that his subjects should be deprived of their rights and privileges, which he was not then in circumstances to defend from so sudden an invasion. Upon turning out those articles, the enemy pledged their faith and honor that they would not attack him. On these he relied and therefore thought it unnecessary to be on his guard against the enemy. But their pledges of faith and honor proved no better than those of other unprincipled hostile nations; for a few days after a certain relation of the king came and informed him, that the enemy who sent terms of accommodation to him and received tribute to their satisfaction, yet meditated an attack upon his subjects by surprise, and that probably they would commence their attack in less than one day, and concluded with advising him, as he was not prepared for war, to order a speedy retreat of his family and subjects. He complied with this advice.

The same night which was fixed upon to retreat, my father and his family set off about break of day. The king and his two younger wives went in one company, and my mother and her children in another. We left our dwellings in succession, and my father's company went on first. We directed our course for a large shrub plain, some distance off, where we intended to conceal ourselves from the approaching enemy, until we could refresh and rest ourselves a little. But we presently found that our retreat was not secure. For having struck up a little fire for the purpose of cooking victuals, the enemy who happened to be encamped a little distance off, had sent out a scouting party who discovered us by the smoke of the fire, just as we were extinguishing it, and about to eat. As soon as we had finished eating, my father discovered the party, and immediately began to discharge arrows at them. This was what I first saw, and it alarmed both me and the women, who being unable to make any resistance, immediately betook ourselves to the tall thick reeds not far off, and left the old king to fight alone. For some time I beheld him from the reeds defending himself with great courage and firmness, till at last he was obliged to surrender himself into their hands.

They then came to us in the reeds, and the very first salute I had from them was a violent blow on the head with the fore part of a gun, and at the same time a grasp round the neck. I then had a rope put about my neck, as had all the women in the thicket with me, and were immediately led to my father, who was likewise pinioned and haltered for leading. In this condition we were all led to camp. The women and myself being pretty submissive, had tolerable treatment from the enemy, while my father was closely interrogated respecting his money which they knew he must have. But as he gave them no account of it, he was instantly cut and pounded on his body with great inhumanity, that he might be induced by the torture he suffered to make the discovery. All this availed not in the least to make him give up his money, but he despised all the tortures which they inflicted, until the continued exercise and increase of torment, obliged him to sink and expire. He thus died without informing his enemies of the place where his money lay. I saw him while he was thus tortured to death. The shocking scene is to this day fresh in my mind, and I have often been overcome while thinking on it. He was a man of remarkable stature. I should judge as much as six feet and six or seven inches high, two feet across his shoulders and every way well proportioned. He was a man of remarkable strength and resolution, affable, kind and gentle, ruling with equity and moderation.

The army of the enemy was large, I should suppose consisting of about six thousand men. Their leader was called Baukurre. After destroying the old prince, they decamped and immediately marched towards the sea, lying to the west, taking with them myself and the women prisoners. In the march a scouting party was detached from the main army. To the leader of this party I was made waiter, having to carry his gun, &c.—As we were scouting we came across a heard of fat cattle, consisting of about thirty in number. These we set upon, and immediately wrested from their keepers, and afterwards converted them into food for the army. The enemy had remarkable success in destroying the country wherever they went. For as far as they had penetrated, they laid out the habitations waste and captured the people. The distance they had now brought me was about four hundred miles. All the march I had very hard tasks imposed on me, which I must perform on pain of punishment. I was obliged to carry on my head a large flat stone used for grinding our corn, weighing as I should suppose, as much as 25 pounds; besides victuals, mat and cooking utensils. Though I was pretty large and stout of my age, yet these burthens were very grievous to me, being only about six years and a half old.

We were then come to a place called Malagasco.—When we entered the place we could not see the least appearance of either houses or inhabitants, but upon stricter search found, that instead of houses above ground they had dens in the sides of hillocks, contiguous to ponds and streams of water. In these we perceived they had all hid themselves, as I suppose they usually did upon such occasions. In order to compel them to surrender, the enemy contrived to smoke them out with faggots. These they put to the entrance of the caves and set them on fire. While they were engaged in this business, to their great surprise some of them were desperately wounded with arrows which fell above on them. This mystery they soon found out. They perceived that the enemy discharged these arrows through holes on the top of the dens directly into the air.—Their weight brought them back, point downwards on their enemies heads, whilst they were smoking the inhabitants out. The points of their arrows were poisoned, but their enemy had an antidote for it, which they instantly applied to the wounded part. The smoke at last obliged the people to give themselves up. They came out of their caves, first spatting the palms of their hands together, and immediately after extended their arms, crossed at their wrists, ready to be bound and pinioned. I should judge that the dens above were extended about eight feet horizontally into the earth, six feet in height and as many wide. They were arched over head and lined with earth, which was of the clay kind, and made the surface of their walls firm and smooth.

The invaders then pinioned the prisoners of all ages and sexes indiscriminately, took their flocks and all their effects, and moved on their way towards the sea. On the march the prisoners were treated with clemency, on account of their being submissive and humble. Having come to the next tribe, the enemy laid siege and immediately took men, women, children, flocks, and all their valuable effects. They then went on to the next district which was contiguous to the sea, called in Africa, Anamaboo [Anamabo]. The enemies provisions were then almost spent, as well as their strength. The inhabitants knowing what conduct they had pursued, and what were their present intentions, improved the favorable opportunity, attacked them, and took enemy prisoners, flocks and all their effects. I was then taken a second time. All of us were then put into the castle, and kept for market. On a certain time I and other prisoners were put on a canoe, under our master, and rowed away to a vessel belonging to Rhode-Island, commanded by capt. Collingwood, and the mate Thomas Mumford. While we were going to the vessel, our master told us all to appear to the best possible advantage for sale. I was bought on board by one Robertson Mumford, steward of said vessel, for four gallons of rum, and a piece of calico, and called VENTURE, on account of his having purchased me with his own private venture. Thus I came by my name. All the slaves that were bought for that vessels cargo, were two hundred and sixty.

Selection 4: A Surgeon Describes Conditions on a Slave Ship

Alexander Falconbridge served as a surgeon on four British slaving voyages to West Africa during the 1780s, at a time when the Atlantic Slave Trade was at its peak. He was shocked by the conditions he encountered during these voyages, and this experience led him to join the British abolitionist movement. His memoir, published in 1788, became an important exposé of the slave trade, and it led to him serving as an expert witness during Parliamentary hearings on the issue. Falconbridge returned to West Africa as part of the Sierra Leone colony in 1791, and he died there a year later. In the passages below, he describes the impact that overcrowding, poor ventilation, and unsanitary conditions had on the slaves' physical and mental health during their confinement aboard slave ships.

Credit: Alexander Falconbridge, *An Account of the Slave Trade on the Coast of Africa*, 2nd edn (London: James Phillips, 1788), 25–27, 29–32, 35–37, 38–39, 41–42.

The men negroes, on being brought aboard the ship are immediately fastened together, two and two, by hand-cuffs on their wrists, and by irons rivetted on their legs. They are then sent down between the decks, and placed in an apartment partitioned off for that purpose. The women likewise are placed in a separate apartment between decks, but without being ironed. And an adjoining room, on the same deck, is besides appointed for the boys. Thus are they all placed in different apartments.

But at the same time, they are frequently stowed so close, as to admit of no other posture than lying on their sides. Neither will the height between decks, unless directly under the grating, permit them the indulgence of an erect posture; especially where there are platforms, which is generally the case. These platforms are a kind of shelf, about eight or nine feet in breadth, extending from the side of the ship towards the centre. They are placed nearly midway between the decks, at the distance of two or three feet from each deck. Upon these the negroes are stowed in the same manner as they are on the deck underneath.

In each of the apartments are placed three or four large buckets, of a conical form, being near two feet in diameter at the bottom, and only one foot at the top, and in depth about twenty-eight inches; to which, when necessary, the negroes have recourse. It often happens, that those who are placed at a distance from the buckets, in endeavoring to get to them, tumble over their companions, in consequence of their being shackled. These accidents, although unavoidable, are productive of continual quarrels, in which some of them are always bruised. In this distressed situation, unable to proceed, and prevented from getting to the tubs, they desist from the attempt; and, as the necessities of nature are not to be repelled, ease themselves as they lie. This becomes a fresh source of broils and disturbances, and tends to render the condition of the poor captive wretches still more uncomfortable. The nuisance arising from these circumstances, is not unfrequently increased by the tubs being much too small for the purpose intended, and their being usually emptied but once every day. The rules for doing this, however, varies in different ships, according to the attention paid to the health and convenience to the slaves by the captain.

About eight o'clock in the morning the negroes are generally brought upon deck. Their irons being examined, a long chain, which is locked to a ring-bolt, fixed in the deck, is run through the rings of shackles of the men, and then locked to another ring-bolt, fixed also in the deck. By this means fifty or sixty, and sometimes more, are fastened to one chain, in order to prevent them from rising or endeavoring to escape. If the weather proves favorable, they are permitted to remain in that situation till four or five in the afternoon, when they are disengaged from the chain, and sent down.

***

Upon the negroes refusing to take sustenance, I have seen coals of fire, glowing hot, put on a shovel, and placed so near their lips, as to scorch and burn them. And this has been accompanied with threats, of forcing them to swallow the coals, if they any longer persisted in refusing to eat. These means have generally had the desired effect. I have also been credibly informed, that a certain captain in the slave trade poured melted lead on such of the negroes as obstinately refused their food.

Exercise being deemed necessary for the preservation of their health, they are sometimes obliged to dance, when the weather will permit their coming on deck. If they go about it reluctantly, or do not move with agility, they are flogged; a person standing by them all the time with a cat-o'-nine-tails in his hand for that purpose. Their musick, upon these occasions, consists of a drum, sometimes with only one head; and when that is worn out, they do not scruple to make use of the bottom of one of the tubs before described. The poor wretches are frequently compelled to sing also; but when they do, their songs are generally, as may naturally be expected, melancholy lamentations of their exile from their native country ...

On board some ships, the common sailors are allowed to have intercourse with such of the black women whose consent they can procure. And some of them have been known to take the inconstancy of their paramours so much to heart, as to leap overboard and drown themselves. The officers are permitted to indulge their passions among them at pleasure, and sometimes are guilty of such brutal excesses, as disgrace human nature.

The hardships and inconvenience suffered by the negroes during the passage, are scarcely to be enumerated or conceived. They are far more violently affected by the sea-sickness, than the Europeans. It frequently terminates in death, especially among the women. But the exclusion of the fresh air is among the most intolerable. For the purpose of admitting this needful refreshment, most of the ships in the slave-trade are provided, between the decks, with five or six air-ports on each side of the ship, of about six inches in length, and four in breadth; in addition to which, some few ships, but not one in twenty, have what they denominate *wind-sails*. But whenever the sea is rough, and the rain heavy, it becomes necessary to shut these, and every other conveyance by which the air is admitted. The fresh air being thus excluded, the negroes rooms very soon grow intolerably hot. The confined air, rendered noxious by the effluvia exhaled from their bodies, and by being repeatedly breathed, soon produces fevers and fluxes, which generally carries off great numbers of them.

During the voyages I made, I was frequently a witness to the fatal effects of this exclusion of the fresh air. I will give one instance, as it serves to convey some idea, though a very faint one, of the sufferings of those unhappy beings whom we wantonly drag from their native country, and doom to perpetual labour and captivity. Some wet and blowing weather having occasioned the port-holes to be shut, and the grating to be covered, fluxes and fevers among the negroes ensued. While they were in this situation, my profession requiring it, I frequently went down among them, till at length their apartments became so extremely hot, as to be only sufferable for a very short time. But the excessive heat was not the only thing that rendered their situation intolerable. The deck, that is, the floor of their rooms, was so covered with the blood and mucus which had proceeded from them in consequence of the flux, that it resembled a slaughter-house. It is not in the power of the human imagination to picture itself a situation more dreadful or disgusting. Numbers of the slaves having fainted, they were carried upon deck, where several of them died, and the rest were with great difficulty, restored. It had nearly proved fatal to me also. The climate was too warm to admit the wearing of any clothing but a shirt, and that I had pulled off before I went down; notwithstanding which, by only continuing among them for about a quarter of an hour, I was so overcome with the heat, stench, and foul air, I had nearly fainted; and it was not without assistance, that I could get upon deck. The consequence was, that I soon after fell sick of the same disorder, from which I did not recover for several months.

***

The place allotted for the sick negroes is under the half deck, where they lie on the bare planks. By this means, those who are emaciated, frequently have their skin, and even their flesh, entirely rubbed off, by the motion of the ship, from the prominent parts of the shoulders, elbows, and hips, so as to render the bones in those parts quite bare. And some of them, by constantly lying in the blood and mucus, that had flowed from those afflicted with the flux, and which, as before observed is generally so violent as to prevent their being kept clean, have their flesh much sooner rubbed off, than those who have only to contend with the mere friction of the ship. The excruciating pain which the poor sufferers feel from being obliged to continue in such a dreadful situation, frequently for several weeks, in case they happen to live so long, is not to be conceived or described. Few, indeed, are ever able to withstand the fatal effects of it. The utmost skill of the surgeon is here ineffectual. If plaisters [dressings] be applied, they are very soon displaced by the friction of the ship; and when bandages are used, the negroes very soon take them off, and appropriate them to other purposes.

The surgeon, upon going between decks, in the morning, to examine the situation of the slaves, frequently finds several dead; and among the men, sometimes a dead and living negroe fastened by their irons together. When this is the case, they are brought upon the deck, and being laid on the grating, the living negroe is disengaged, and the dead are thrown overboard.

It may not be improper here to remark, that the surgeons employed in the Guinea trade, are generally driven to engage in so disagreeable an employ by the confined state of their finances. An exertion of the greatest skill and attention could afford the diseased negroes little relief, so long as the causes of their diseases, namely, the breathing of a putrid atmosphere, and wallowing in their own excrements, remain. When once the fever and dysentery get to any height at sea, a cure is scarcely ever effected.

***

As very few of the negroes can so far brook the loss of their liberty, and the hardships they endure, as to bear them with any degree of patience, they are ever upon the watch to take advantage of the least negligence in their oppressors. Insurrections are frequently the consequence; which are seldom suppressed without much bloodshed. Sometimes these are successful, and the whole ship's company is cut off. They are likewise always ready to seize every opportunity for committing some act of desperation to free themselves from their miserable state; and notwithstanding the restraints under which they are laid, they often succeed.

While a ship, to which I belonged, lay in Bonny River [part of the Niger River delta], one evening, a short time before our departure, a lot of negroes, consisting of about ten, was brought on board; when one of them, in a favourable moment, forced his way through the network on the larboard side of the vessel, jumped overboard, and was supposed to have been devoured by the sharks.

During the time we were there, fifteen negroes belonging to a vessel from Liverpool, found means to throw themselves into the river; very few were saved; and the residue fell a sacrifice to the sharks. A similar instance took place in a French ship while we lay there.

***

One morning, upon examining the place allotted for the sick negroes, I perceived that one of them, who was so emaciated as scarcely to be able to walk, was missing, and was convinced that he must have gone overboard in the night, probably to put a more expeditious period to his sufferings. And, to conclude on this subject, I could not help being sensibly affected, on a former voyage, at observing with what apparent eagerness a black woman seized some dirt from off an African yam, and put it into her mouth; seeming to rejoice at the opportunity of possessing some of her native earth.

From these instances I think it may be clearly deduced that the unhappy Africans are not bereft of the finer feelings, but have a strong attachment to their native country, together with a just sense of the value of liberty. And the situation of the miserable beings above described, more forcibly urges the necessity of abolishing a trade which is the source of such evils, than the most eloquent harangue, or persuasive arguments could do.

Discussion Questions

1. Using Park's account, briefly summarize the ways in which a West African could be enslaved. How did the manner in which a person was enslaved affect the likelihood that he or she would end up on a slave ship bound for the Americas?
2. What do you find most interesting about Isert's description of a coastal slave factory? What evidence does he present of European and African cooperation in the day-to-day operation of these posts?
3. Compare Smith's account of his boyhood enslavement with what you learned about slavery in West Africa from Selection 1: does Smith's personal experience confirm or contradict Park's analysis of African slavery?
4. According to Falconbridge, what were the chief factors contributing to shipboard mortality of slaves during the Middle Passage? How does his analysis of the human costs of the slave trade compare to that of Isert in Selection 2?

Suggested Readings

For the distinctive nature of New World slavery and its significance in the intellectual development of the West, see David Brion Davis, *Slavery and Human Progress* (New York: Oxford University Press, 1984). For estimates of the numbers involved in the Atlantic Slave Trade, see Philip D. Curtin, *The Atlantic Slave Trade: A Census* (Madison, WI: University of Wisconsin Press, 1969); and Paul E. Lovejoy, "The Volume of the Atlantic Slave Trade: A Synthesis," *Journal of African History* 23 (1982): 365–394. On the nature of slavery in Africa, see Paul E. Lovejoy, *Transformations in Slavery: A History of Slavery in Africa* (Cambridge: Cambridge University Press, 1983); and Patrick Manning, *Slavery and African Life: Occidental, Oriental, and African Slave Trades* (Cambridge: Cambridge University Press, 1990). For African perspectives on the operation of the Atlantic Slave Trade, see Randy J. Sparks, *Where the Negroes Are Masters: An African Port in the Era of the Slave Trade* (Cambridge, MA: Harvard University Press, 2014); and Pernille Ipsen, *Daughters of the Trade: Atlantic Slavers and Interracial Marriage on the Gold Coast* (Philadelphia, PA: University of Pennsylvania Press, 2017). The economics of the Atlantic Slave Trade are addressed in Joseph C. Miller, *The Way of Death: Merchant Capitalism and the Angolan Slave Trade, 1730–1830* (Madison, WI: University of Wisconsin Press, 1988).

Studies of the Atlantic Slave Trade that emphasize its role in shaping the Atlantic World include David Eltis, *The Rise of African Slavery in the Americas* (Cambridge: Cambridge University Press, 1999); Ira Berlin, *Many Thousands Gone: The First Two Centuries of Slavery in North America* (Cambridge, MA: Harvard University Press, 1998); Michael A. Gomez, *Reversing Sail: A History of the African Diaspora* (Cambridge: Cambridge University Press, 2004); and John Thornton, *Africa and Africans in the Making of the Atlantic World, 1400–1800* (Cambridge: Cambridge University Press, 1998). The human toll exacted by the Middle Passage is described in Marcus Rediker, *The Slave Ship: A Human History* (New York: Viking, 2007); and Sean M. Kelley, *The Voyage of the Slave Ship Hare: A Journey into Captivity from Sierra Leone to South Carolina* (Chapel Hill, NC: University of North Carolina Press, 2016).

6　The Plantation Complex in the Caribbean

Figure 6.1 Sugar Making on a Caribbean Plantation.

This early depiction of a sugar mill illustrates the steps involved in processing sugar cane. The three-roll mill (or ingenio), powered by oxen, crushes the cane and extracts the juice, which flows into a cistern and is then transferred into copper kettles, where it is boiled until it crystallizes. Byproducts of this process included the "trash," or crushed cane, which became fuel for the boiling fires; and molasses, which could be distilled into rum, also known as "kill-devil." What does this image tell you about the nature of labor relations on the sugar plantation? What hazards did slaves face in this process and what role did planters play in it?

Source credit: De Agostini Picture Library/Getty Images. From Charles de Rochefort, *Historie Naturelle et Morale des Iles Antilles de l'Amerique* (Rotterdam, 1665).

Introduction

The islands of the Caribbean stretch in an eastern arc from the tip of Florida to the coast of South America. The four largest—Cuba, Hispaniola (modern Haiti and the Dominican Republic), Puerto Rico, and Jamaica, known as the Greater Antilles—were colonized by the Spanish in the wake of Columbus. The Lesser Antilles are a string of much smaller islands that were colonized by the Dutch, French, and English during the seventeenth century, in part to serve as naval bases for raiding Spanish shipping and in part to cultivate cash crops that flourished in the tropical climate and rich volcanic soil these islands provided (see Map 6.1).

By far, the most significant of those crops was sugar. Sugar cultivation originated in India and was carried westward into the Mediterranean World by Arabic traders and colonizers.

Europeans' taste for it increased during the Crusades, when the Mediterranean island of Cyprus became its chief supplier. Landowners there relied on a mixed labor force of servants and slaves from Eastern Europe, the Near East, and Africa to grow sugar cane and refine it. Gradually, sugar moved west, as Venetian merchants bankrolled plantations in Crete, Sicily, North Africa, and the southern Iberian Peninsula. In the fifteenth century, Spanish and Portuguese colonizers brought sugar to the Atlantic's Canary and Madeira Islands, respectively. In all of these places, the cultivation of sugar encouraged the development of what historians call the plantation complex: a method of cash crop production for international markets that relies on unfree labor controlled by a small, landowning elite. The profits from this trade motivated Columbus to carry sugar plants with him on his first voyage across the Atlantic, in hopes that he would find new regions suitable for this crop's cultivation.

Spanish attention in the Americas was quickly diverted by the pursuit of gold and silver, but the Portuguese successfully transplanted sugar along with their African Slave Trade to Brazil. The Dutch briefly conquered Brazil in the early seventeenth century, but when the Portuguese regained control there, Dutch merchants and planters brought their capital, expertise, and African slaves for sugar planting into the Caribbean. So began a sugar revolution that transformed the Lesser Antilles. The French and English had colonized a number of small islands, relying on white indentured servants to cultivate tobacco and subsistence crops. Within a generation, the economy of these islands shifted to sugar production, and the plantation complex took root. European immigration fell as a small planter class engrossed the arable land and imported enslaved Africans to work it. Caught in this land squeeze, former servants and other propertyless whites migrated elsewhere in search of opportunity.

Caribbean planters profited handsomely from the high demand for sugar in Europe, and many became absentee landlords, living off their fortunes in Paris or London. A typical plantation had fifty or more slaves working in gangs under a handful of white managers and overseers. On these sugar islands, Africans outnumbered Europeans by ratios ranging from 3:1 to 25:1. For both races, men far outnumbered women and tropical diseases took a heavy toll on new arrivals. Imbalanced sex ratios and high mortality rates meant that these colonies had to rely on a constant influx of new workers to sustain their sugar production.

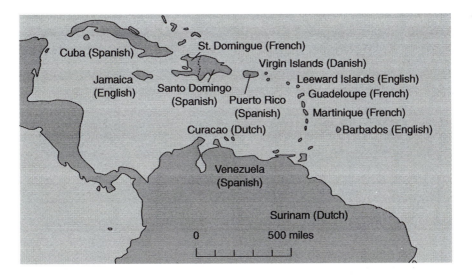

Map 6.1 The Caribbean Islands, *c*.1780.

The major sugar islands of the Caribbean with northern coast of South America, noting European possession.

By the mid-eighteenth century, the Caribbean sugar economy was in full flower. English production centered in Barbados and Jamaica, the latter of which had been won from Spain in 1655. The French produced sugar on the islands of Martinique and Guadeloupe, but their most profitable Caribbean possession was St. Domingue, a colony established on the western half of Hispaniola, wrestled from the Spanish in the seventeenth century. Dutch sugar colonies included the islands of St. Maarten and St. Eustatius, as well as Surinam and Demerara on the northern coast of South America. The Spanish developed sugar plantations in Venezuela and Cuba, the latter of which would dominate the Caribbean's sugar industry in the nineteenth century. Even the Danes, latecomers to the scramble for empire, had established sugar colonies in the Lesser Antilles by the late eighteenth century. White and black migrants from the English and French sugar islands transplanted the plantation complex to the North American mainland, settling in the coastal lowlands of South Carolina and Georgia and in the lower Mississippi Valley of French Louisiana. In North America, tobacco and rice were the cash crops of the colonial era, but cotton and sugar production increased significantly as the plantation complex expanded west in the nineteenth century.

Plantation societies became cauldrons of adaptation and resistance by the slaves who lived and worked in them. African-American cultural patterns emerged in the slaves' language, diet, music, and religion, combining precedents from their African past with influences from the European and Native American peoples among whom they lived. Whenever possible, slave runaways established their own communities independent of white authority, often by retreating to mountainous interiors or dense jungles beyond the fringe of white settlement. These maroon communities, as they were known, varied in size and duration from region to region. One of the largest was Palmares, home to thousands of Africans in Brazil during the sixteenth and seventeenth centuries; in North America, runaway slaves from Georgia and South Carolina established a maroon settlement near the Spanish fortress of St. Augustine in Florida; maroon communities in Jamaica proved so difficult to defeat in battle that English planters negotiated peace treaties with them instead.

The plantation complex, embraced by every European colonial power in the Caribbean, became a model for colonization throughout the Americas, creating immense wealth for the European planters who owned the land and untold miseries for the African slaves who worked it. By 1776, there were 2.5 million slaves in the New World, most of them living on plantations that produced sugar, tobacco, coffee, cacao, rice, or cotton for export to the Old World. The plantation complex linked the fate of those slaves to the international market for the goods they produced. Indeed, the last New World society to abolish African slavery, Brazil, had been the first to use slaves for sugar production.

The readings in this chapter present three different perspectives on the Caribbean plantation complex. In the first selection, an English colonist describes Barbados as it was undergoing the shift from European servant labor to African slave labor in the mid-seventeenth century. In the second selection, a mercenary in Dutch Surinam describes a sugar colony of the late eighteenth century, with its white planter class dwarfed by a much larger population of rebellious slaves. In the third selection, a former slave uses his experiences in Barbados and Montserrat to argue for the abolition of the Atlantic Slave Trade. As you read these passages, think about how they depict the colonization of the Caribbean over time. How did the social order that emerged in Barbados in the mid-seventeenth century anticipate the world of the Caribbean more than one hundred years later? What were the long-term costs of producing sugar in the New World?

Selection 1: Servants, Slaves, and Masters in Barbados

The English colony of Barbados was one of the first Caribbean islands to develop a plantation complex based on sugar cultivation. The English, who colonized the island in the 1620s, initially relied on a mixture of tobacco planting and subsistence agriculture to support them-selves, and their labor force was made up mostly of European indentured servants. Between 1640 and 1660, they switched to sugar production, a transition that was accompanied by a shift in the labor force from white indentured servants to African slaves. By the latter part of the seventeenth century, Barbados was a prototypical sugar colony: Africans outnumbered Euro-peans by a ratio of 4:1, a small planter class controlled the land, and the island's population concentrated so much on producing sugar that it had to import foodstuffs from North America to feed itself.

Richard Ligon was a royalist exile from the English Civil Wars when he emigrated to Barba-dos in 1647. He lived there for several years before returning to England and publishing his description of the island in 1657. In addition to providing a detailed description of the social and economic order of Barbados, *A True & Exact History of the Island of Barbadoes* included a map of the island identifying the major plantations. The excerpt below is from the book's second edition, published in 1673. In it, Ligon describes the living and working conditions of the island's indentured servants, slaves, and planters.

The spelling has been modernized.

Credit: Richard Ligon, *A True & Exact History of the Island of Barbadoes*, 2nd edn (London: Peter Parker and Thomas Guy, 1673), 43–51, 53–56.

The Island is divided into three sorts of men, viz. Masters, Servants, and Slaves. The slaves and their posterity, being subject to their Masters forever, are kept and preserved with greater care than the servants, who are theirs but for five years, according to the law of the Island. So that for the time, the servants have the worser lives, for they are put to very hard labor, ill lodging, and their diet very slight. When we came first on the Island, some Planters themselves did not eat bone meat, above twice a week: the rest of the seven days, Potatoes, Loblolly [thick gruel], and Bonavist [a type of bean]. But the servants no bone meat at all, unless an Ox died: and then they were feasted, as long as that lasted. And till they had planted good store of Plantains, the *Negroes* were fed with this kind of food; but most of it Bonavist, and Loblolly, with some ears of Maize toasted, which food (especially Loblolly,) gave them much discontent: But when they had Plantains enough to serve them, they were heard no more to complain; for tis a food they take great delight in, and their manner of dressing, and eating it, is this: 'tis gathered for them (somewhat before it be ripe, for so they desire to have it,) upon *Saturday*, by the keeper of the Plantain grove; who is an able *Negro*, and knows well the number of those that are to be fed with this fruit; and as he gathers, lays them all together, till they fetch them away, which is about five a clock in the afternoon, for that day they break off work sooner by an hour: partly for this purpose, and partly for that the fire in the furnaces is to be put out, and the Ingenio [cylin-ders for crushing sugar cane] and the rooms made clean; besides they are to wash, shave and trim themselves against *Sunday*. But 'tis a lovely sight to see a hundred handsome *Negroes*, men and women, with every one a grass-green bunch of these fruits on their heads, every bunch twice as big as their heads, all coming in a train one after another, the black and green so well becoming one another. Having brought this fruit home to their own houses, and pilling off the skin of so much as they will use, they boil it in water, making it into balls, and so they eat it. One bunch a week is a *Negro's* allowance. To this, no bread nor drink, but water. Their lodging at night a board, with nothing under, nor any thing a top of them. They are happy people, whom so little contents. Very good servants, if they be not spoiled by the *English*. But more of them hereafter.

As for the usage of the Servants, it is much as the Master is, merciful or cruel. Those that are merciful, treat their Servants well, both in their meat, drink, and lodging, and give them such work, as is not unfit for Christians to do. But if the Masters be cruel, the Servants have very wearisome and miserable lives. Upon the arrival of any ship, that brings servants to the Island, the Planters go aboard; and having bought such of them as they like, send them with a guide to his Plantation; and being come, commands them instantly to make their Cabins, which they not knowing how to do, are to be advised by other of their servants, that are their Seniors; but, if they be churlish, and will not show them, or if materials be wanting, to make them Cabins, then they are to lye on the ground that night. These Cabins are to be made of sticks, withes [twigs], and Plantain leaves, under some little shade that may keep the rain off; Their suppers being a few Potatoes for meat, and water or Mobbie [an alcoholic beverage made from sweet potatoes] for drink. The next day they are rung out with a Bell to work, at six a clock in the morning, with a severe Overseer to command them, till the Bell ring again, which is at eleven a clock; and then they return, and are set to dinner, either with a mess of Loblolly, Bonavist, or Potatoes. At one a clock, they are rung out again to the field, there to work till six, and then home again, to a supper of the same. And if it chance to rain, and wet them through, they have no shift, but must lie so all night. If they put off their cloths, the cold of the night will strike into them; and if they be not strong men, this ill lodging will put them into a sickness: if they complain, they are beaten by the Overseer; if they resist, their time is doubled, I have seen an Overseer beat a Servant with a cane about the head, till the blood has followed, for a fault that is not worth the speaking of, and yet he must have patience, or worse will follow. Truly, I have seen such cruelty there done to Servants, as I did not think one Christian could have done to another. But, as discreeter and better natured men have come to rule there, the servants lives have been much bettered; for now, most of the servants lie in Hammocks, and in warm rooms, and when they come in wet, have shift of shirts and drawers, which is all the cloths they wear, and are fed with bone meat twice or thrice a week.

***

A little before I came from thence, there was such a combination amongst them [servants], as the like was never seen there before. Their sufferings being grown to a great height, and their daily complainings to one another (of the intolerable burdens they labored under) being spread throughout the Island; at the last, some amongst them, whose spirits were not able to endure such slavery, resolved to break through it, or die in the act; and so conspired with some others of their acquaintance, whose sufferings were equal, if not above theirs; and their spirits no way inferior, resolved to draw as many of the discontented party into this plot, as possibly they could; and those of this persuasion, were the greatest numbers of Servants in the Island. So that a day was appointed to fall upon their Masters, and cut all their throats, and by that means, to make themselves not only freemen, but Masters of the Island. And so closely was this plot carried, as no discovery was made, till the day before they were to put it in act: And then one of them, either by the failing of his courage, or some new obligation from the love of his Master, revealed this long plotted conspiracy; and so by this timely advertisement, the Masters were saved: Justice *Hetersall* (whose servant this was) sending Letters to all his friends, and they to theirs, and so to one another, till they were all secured; and by, examination, found out the greatest part of them; whereof eighteen of the principal men in the conspiracy, and they the first leaders and contrivers of the plot, were put to death, for example to the rest. And the reason why they made examples of so many, was, they found these so haughty in their resolutions, and so incorrigible, as they were like enough to become Actors in a second plot, and so they thought good to secure them; and for the rest, to have a special eye over them.

It has been accounted a strange thing, that the *Negroes*, being more than double the numbers of the Christians that are there, and they accounted a bloody people, where they think they have power or advantages; and the more bloody, by how much they are more fearful than others: that these should not commit some horrid massacre upon the Christians, thereby to enfranchise themselves, and become Masters of the Island. But there are three reasons that take away this wonder; the one is, They are not suffered to touch or handle any weapons: The other, That they are held in such awe and slavery, as they are fearful to appear in any daring act; and seeing the mustering of our men, and hearing their Gun-shot, (than which nothing is more terrible to them) their spirits are subjugated to so low a condition, as they dare not look up to any bold attempt. Besides these, there is a third reason, which stops all designs of that kind, and that is, They are fetched from several parts of *Africa*, who speak several languages, and by that means, one of them understands not another: For, some of them are fetched from *Guinny* [Guinea] and *Binny* [Benin], some from *Cutchew* [?], some from *Angola*, and some from the River of *Gambia*. And in some of these places where petty Kingdoms are, they sell their Subjects, and such as they take in Battle, whom they make slaves; and some mean men sell their Servants, their Children, and sometimes their Wives; and think all good traffic, for such commodities as our Merchants send them.

When they are brought to us, the Planters buy them out of the Ship, where they find them stark naked, and therefore cannot be deceived in any outward infirmity. They choose them as they do Horses in a Market; the strongest, youthfullest, and most beautiful, yield the greatest prices. Thirty pound sterling is a price for the best man *Negroe*; and twenty-five, twenty-six, or twenty-seven pound for a Woman; the Children are at easier rates. And we buy them so, as the sexes may be equal; for, if they have more Men than Women, the men who are unmarried will come to their Masters, and complain, that they cannot live without Wives, and desire him, they may have them Wives, which satisfies them for the present; and so they expect the good time: which the Master performing with them, the bravest fellow is to choose first, and so in order, as they are in place, and every one of them knows his better, and gives him the precedence, as Cows do one another, in passing through a narrow gate; for, the most of them are as near beasts as may be, setting their souls aside. Religion they know none; yet most of them acknowledge a God, as appears by their motions and gestures: For, if one of them do another wrong, and he cannot revenge himself, he looks up to Heaven for vengeance, and holds up both his hands, as if the power must come from thence, that must do him right.

***

On *Sunday* they [slaves] rest, and have the whole day at their pleasure; and the most of them use it as a day of rest and pleasure; but some of them who will make benefit of that days liberty, go where the Mangrove trees grow, and gather the bark, of which they make ropes, which they truck away for other Commodities, as Shirts and Drawers.

In the afternoons on *Sundays*, they have their Music, which is of kettle drums, and those of several sizes; upon the smallest the best Musician plays, and the other come in as Choruses: the drum all men know, has but one tone; and therefore variety of tunes have little to do in this music; and yet so strangely they vary their time, as 'tis a pleasure to the most curious ears, and it was to me one of the strangest noises that ever I heard made of one tone; and if they had the variety of tune, which gives the greater scope in Music, as they have of time, they would do wonders in that Arts. And if I had not fallen sick before my coming away, at least seven months in one sickness, I had given them some hints of tunes, which being understood, would have served as a great addition to their harmony; time without tune, is not an eighth part of the Science of Music.

I found *Macow* [a slave Ligon knew] very apt for it of himself, and one day coming into the house, (which none of the *Negroes* use to do, unless an Officer, as he was,) he found me playing on a Theorbo [a large stringed instrument], and singing to it, which he hearkened very attentively to; and when I had done, he took the Theorbo in his hand, and stroked one string, stopping it by degrees upon every fret, and finding the notes to vary, till it came to the body of the instrument; and that the nearer the body of the instrument he stopped, the smaller or higher the sound was, which he found was by the shortening of the string, considered with himself, how he might make some trial of this experiment upon such an instrument as he could come by; having no hope ever to have any instrument of this kind to practice on. In a day or two after, walking in the Plantain grove ... I found this *Negro* (whose office it was to attend there) being the keeper of that grove, sitting on the ground, and before him a piece of large timber, upon which he had laid cross, six Billets, and having a handsaw and a hatchet by him, would cut the billets by little and little, till he had brought them to the tunes, he would fit them to; for the shorter they were, the higher the Notes, which he tried by knocking upon the ends of them with a stick, which he had in his hand. When I found him at it, I took the stick out of his hand, and tried the sound, finding the six billets to have six distinct notes, one above another, which put me in a wonder, how he of himself, should without teaching do so much. I then showed him the difference between flats and sharps, which he presently apprehended, as between *Fa*, and *Mi*: and he would have cut two more billets to those tunes, but I had then no time to see it done, and so left him to his own enquiries. I say thus much to let you see that some of these people are capable of learning Arts.

***

On *Sundays* in the afternoon, their Music plays, and to dancing they go, the men by themselves, and the women by themselves, no mixed dancing. Their motions are rather what they aim at, than what they do; and by that means, transgress the less upon the *Sunday*; their hands having more of motion than their feet, and their heads more than their hands. They may dance a whole day, and never heat themselves; yet, now and then, one of the activest amongst them will leap bolt upright, and fall in his place again, but without cutting a caper. When they have danced an hour or two, the men fall to wrestle, (the Music playing all the while) and their manner of wrestling is, to stand like two Cocks, with heads as low as their hips; and thrusting their heads one against another, hoping to catch one another by the leg, which sometimes they do: But if both parties be weary, and that they cannot get that advantage, then they raise their heads, by pressing hard one against another, and so having nothing to take hold of but their bare flesh, they close, and grasp one another about the middle, and have one another in the hug, and then a fair fell is given on the back. And thus two or three couples of them are engaged at once, for an hour together, the women leave off their dancing, and come to be spectators of the sport.

When any of them die, they dig a grave, and at evening they bury him, clapping and wringing their hands, and making a doleful sound with their voices. They are a people of a timorous and fearful disposition, and consequently bloody, when they find advantages. If any of them commit a fault, give him present punishment, but do not threaten him; for it you do, it is an even lay, he will go hang himself, to avoid punishment.

What their other opinions are in the matter of Religion, I know not; but certainly, they are not altogether of the sect of the *Sadduces* [Jewish priests of ancient times]. For, they believe a Resurrection, and that they shall go into their own Country again, and have their youth renewed. And lodging this opinion in their hearts, they make it an ordinary practice, upon any great fright, or threatening of their Masters, to hang themselves.

But Colonel *Walrond* [a sugar planter] having lost three or four of his best *Negroes* this way, and in a very little time, caused one of their heads to be cut off, and set upon a pole a dozen foot high; and having done that, caused all his *Negroes* to come forth, and march round about this head, and bid them look on it, whether this were not the head of such an one that hanged himself. Which they acknowledging, he then told them, that they were in a main error, in thinking they went into their own Countries, after they were dead; for, this man's head was here, as they all were witnesses of; and how was it possible, the body could go without a head. Being convinced by this sad, yet lively spectacle, they changed their opinions; and after that, no more hanged themselves.

***

Though there be a mark set upon these people [slaves], which will hardly ever be wiped off, as of their cruelties when they have advantages, and of their fearfulness and falseness; yet no rule so general but has its exception: for I believe, and I have strong motives to cause me to be of that persuasion, that there are as honest, faithful, and conscionable people amongst them, as amongst those of *Europe*, or any other part of the world.

A hint of this, I will give you in a lively example; and it was in a time when Victuals were scarce, and Plantains were not then so frequently planted, as to afford them enough. So that some of the high spirited and turbulent amongst them, began to mutiny, and had a plot, secretly to be revenged on their Master; and one or two of these were Firemen that made the fires in the furnaces, who were never without store of dry wood by them. These villains, were resolved to make fire to such part of the boiling-house [for refining sugar], as they were sure would fire the rest, and so burn all, and yet seem ignorant of the fact, as a thing done by accident. But this plot was discovered, by some of the others who hated mischief, as much as they loved it; and so traduced them, as they were forced to confess, what they meant should have been put in act the next night: so giving them condign [deserved] punishment, the Master gave order to the overseer that the rest should have a day's liberty to themselves and their wives, to do what they would; and withal to allow them a double proportion of victual for three days, both which they refused: which we all wondered at, knowing well how much they loved their liberties, and their meat, having been lately pinched of the one, and not having overmuch of the other; and therefore being doubtful what their meaning was in this, suspecting some discontent amongst them, sent for three or four of the best of them, and desired to know why they refused this favor that was offered them, but received such an answer: as we little expected; for they told us, it was not sullenness, or slighting the gratuity their Master bestowed on them, but they would not accept any thing as a recompense for doing that which became them in their duties to do, nor would they have him think, it was hope of reward, that made them to accuse their fellow servants, but an act of Justice, which they thought themselves bound in duty to do, and they thought themselves sufficiently rewarded in the Act. The substance of this, in such language as they had, they delivered, and poor *Sambo* [a slave leader] was the Orator; by whose example the others were led both in the discovery of the Plot, and refusal of the gratuity. And withal they said, that if it pleased their Master, at any time, to bestow a voluntary boon upon them, be it never so slight, they would willingly and thankfully accept it: and this act might have beseemed the best Christians, though some of them were denied Christianity, when they earnestly sought it. Let others have what opinion they please, yet I am of this belief; that there are to be found amongst them, some who are as morally honest, as Conscionable, as humble, as loving to their friends, and as loyal to their Masters, as any that live under the Sun; and one reason they have to be so, is, they set on great value upon their lives: And this is all I can remember concerning the *Negroes*, except of their games, which I could never learn, because they wanted language to teach me.

***

Now for the Masters, I have yet said but little, nor am able to say half of what they deserve. They are men of great abilities and parts, otherwise they could not go through, with such great works as they undertake; the managing of one of their Plantations, being a work of such a latitude, as will require a very good head-piece, to put in order, and continue it so.

I can name a Planter there, that feeds daily two hundred mouths, and keeps them in such order, as there are no mutinies amongst them; and yet of several nations. All these are to be employed in their several abilities, so as no one be idle. The first work to be considered, is Weeding, for unless that be done, all else (and the Planter too) will be undone, and if that be neglected but a little time, it will be a hard matter to recover it again, so fast will the weeds grow there. But the ground being kept clean, 'tis fit to bear any thing that Country will afford.

After weeding comes Planting, and they account two seasons in the year best, and that is, *May* and *November*; but Canes are to be planted at all times, that they may come in, one field after another; otherwise, the work will stand still. And commonly they have in a field that is planted together, at one time, ten or a dozen acres. This work of planting and weeding, the Master himself is to see done; unless he have a very trusty and able Overseer; and without such a one, he will have too much to do. The next thing he is to consider, is the Ingenio [sugar mill], and what belongs to that; as, the Ingenio itself, which is the *Primum Mobile* of the whole work, the Boiling-House, with the Coppers and Furnaces, the Filling room, the Still-House, and Curing-House; and in all these, there are great casualties. If any thing in the Rollers, as the Gouges, Sockets, Sweeps, Cogs, or Braytrees, be at fault, the whole work stands still; or in the Boiling-House, if the Frame which holds the Coppers, (and is made of Clinkers, fastened with plaster of *Paris*) if by the violence of the heat from the Furnaces, these Frames crack or break, there is a stop in the work, till that be mended. Or if any of the Coppers have a mischance, and be burnt, a new one must presently be had, or there is a stay in the work. Or if the mouths of the Furnaces, (which are made of a sort of stone, which we have from *England*, and we call it there, high gate stone) if that, by the violence of the fire, be softened, that it molder away, there must new be provided, and laid in with much art, or it will not be. Or if the bars of Iron, which are in the floor of the Furnace, when they are red hot (as continually they are) the fire-man, throw great sides of wood in the mouths of the Furnace, hard and carelessly, the weight of those logs, will bend or break those bars, (though strongly made) and there is no repairing them, without the work stand still; for all these depend upon one another, as wheels in a Clock. Or if the Stills be at fault, the *kill-devil* [rum] cannot be made. But the main impediment and stop of all, is the loss of our Cattle, and amongst them there are such diseases, as I have known in one Plantation, thirty that have died in two days. And I have heard, that a Planter, an eminent man there, that cleared a dozen acres of ground, and railed it about for pasture, with intention, as soon as the grass was grown to a great height, to put in his working Oxen; which accordingly he did, and in one night fifty of them died; so that such a loss as this, is able to undo a Planter, that is not very well grounded. What it is that breeds these diseases, we cannot find, unless some of the Plants have a poisonous quality; nor have we yet found out cures for these diseases; Chickens guts being the best remedy was then known, and those being chopped or minced, and given them in a horn, with some liquor mixed to moisten it, was thought the best remedy: yet it recovered very few.

Selection 2: A Description of African Maroon Communities

Surinam, a colony on the northeastern shore of South America, was infamous for its slave rebellions and maroon communities. The English ceded Surinam to the Dutch in the 1660s in exchange for New Netherland (renamed New York by its new owners). Surinam's proximity to the Lesser Antilles and its sugar economy made it a part of the Caribbean plantation complex. The average sugar estate there was home to more than 200 slaves, and Africans outnumbered Europeans twenty-five to one. Maroon communities spawned by rebels and runaways from these plantations constantly harassed the colony's Dutch proprietors.

John Gabriel Stedman was a Scottish military officer who served in the Netherlands during the latter eighteenth century. Between 1773 and 1777, he lived in Surinam as part of an expeditionary force sent by the Dutch to fight rebellious slaves and to disperse the maroon communities that sheltered them. That Stedman lived to tell his tale was no small feat; less than 15 percent of the European soldiers involved in this war returned home. Stedman eventually settled in England, where he published his narrative of the Surinam expedition in 1796. In the excerpts that follow, he describes the maroon communities he was sent to subdue and the system of sugar production they were rebelling against.

Credit: John Gabriel Stedman, *Stedman's Surinam: Life in an Eighteenth-Century Slave Society*, eds. Richard Price and Sally Price (Baltimore, MD: Johns Hopkins University Press, 1992), 25–32.

No sooner was this unfortunate colony delivered from its outward enemies than it was attacked by inward ones of a more fierce and desperate nature. In former times, the Carib and other Indians had often disturbed this settlement, but ever since a peace was established after the arrival of Governor Sommelsdyck in this colony, they have inviolably kept it, living in the greatest harmony and friendship with the Europeans.

The revolted Negro slaves are the foes I now intend to speak of, who may with truth be called the terror of this settlement, if not the total loss of it. From the earliest remembrance, some runaway Negroes had skulked in the woods of Surinam, but these were of very small consideration till about the year 1726 or 1728, when with their hostile numbers increasing, and mostly being armed with (in addition to bows and arrows) lances and firelocks which they had pillaged from the estates, they committed continual outrages and depredations upon the coffee and sugar plantations. These they did both from a spirit of revenge for the barbarous and inhuman treatment which they had formerly received from their masters and with a view toward carrying away plunder such as gunpowder, balls, hatchets, etc., in order to provide for their subsistence and defense. These Negroes were mostly settled in the upper parts of the rivers Coppename and Saramacca, from which last they take the name of the Saramaka Rebels, which distinguishes them from other gangs that have since revolted.

Several commands of military and plantation people were now sent out against them but were of very small effect in bringing them to reason by promises, or in getting them rooted out by blows. In 1730, a most shocking execution of eleven poor captives was experimented—to terrify, if possible, their companions, and thus to make them return to their duty. One man was hanged alive upon a gibbet with an iron hook struck through his ribs, and two others, being chained to stakes, were burnt to death by slow fire. Six women were broken alive upon the rack, and two girls were decapitated, through which tortures they went without uttering a sigh. In 1733, three Indians were also decapitated, for having killed three French deserters, which shows how far the civil law now extends in this country.

But I must return to the Negroes, on whom it appears the inhuman carnage that I have mentioned above had very little effect, indeed quite the reverse, since it enraged the Saramaka Rebels to such a degree that they became dreadful to the colonists. This lasted for several years successively until the colonists—no longer being able to support the expense and fatigue of sallying out against them in the woods, besides the great losses and terrors which they so frequently sustained by their invasions—at last resolved to treat for peace with their sable enemies.

Governor Mauricius, who was at this period at the head of the Colony, accordingly sent out a strong detachment to the rebel settlement on the Saramacca River for the purpose of effecting, if possible, the so much wished-for peace. After some skirmishing with the struggling Rebel parties, the detachment at last arrived at their headquarters, where they demanded and obtained a parley. At this time, in 1749, a treaty of peace consisting of ten or twelve articles was actually concluded between them, as had been done before in 1739 with the rebels on the island of Jamaica.

The chief of the Saramaka Rebels was a Creole Negro called Captain Adu, who now received from the Governor as a present a fine large cane with a massive silver pommel, on which were engraved the arms of Surinam, as a mark of their further independence and as preliminary to the other presents that were to be sent out the following year, as stipulated by the treaty, particularly arms and ammunition, once the peace was finally concluded. To the Governor, Adu then returned a handsome bow with a complete case of arrows, which had been manufactured by his own hands, as a token that during that time, on his side, all enmity was ceased and at an end.

This affair gave great satisfaction to some, indeed to most of the inhabitants of Surinam, who now thought themselves and their effects perfectly secure, while others looked on this treaty as a most hazardous resource, nay, as a sure step to the Colony's inevitable ruin. Be that as it may, I cannot help thinking, with the latter, that regardless of Governor Mauricius' good intentions, nothing can be more dangerous than making a forced friendship with people who, by the most abject slavery and bad usage, were provoked to break their chains and shake off the yoke to seek revenge and liberty, and who by this trust being put in them have it in their power to become from day to day more formidable. Nor can I help thinking, on the contrary, that the insurrection having already risen to such a pitch, the colonists ought to have continued fighting against it while they had a nerve to strain, or a hand left to draw a trigger—not from a motive of cruelty, but for the political good of so fine a settlement. After all, if taken at the worst, it is still better to lose one's life with one's fortune, sword in hand, than to live in the perpetual dread of losing both by one general massacre.

That the best of all would be never to have driven these poor creatures to such extremities by constant ill treatment speaks for itself. At the same time, it is certainly true that to govern the Coast-of-Guinea Negroes well, nay, even for their own benefit, the strictest discipline is absolutely necessary. But I ask: Why in the name of humanity should they undergo the most cruel racks and tortures, entirely depending upon the despotic caprice of their proprietors and overseers, which it is well known is too generally the case throughout the West Indies? And why should their bitter complaints be never heard by the magistrate that has it in his power to redress them? Because His Worship himself is a planter and scorns to be against his own interest. Such is most truly the case, and such is no less truly lamentable, not only for the sake of the master and the man, but also and chiefly for that of one of the finest colonies in the West Indies being, by such unfair proceedings, put in the utmost danger and difficulty. However, it is to be supposed that exceptions do here take place, as they do in all other circumstances—God forbid they should not—and I myself have seen and even at different times been eyewitness where plantation slaves were treated with the utmost humanity, where the hand of the master was seldom lifted but to caress them, and where the eye of the slave sparkled with gratitude and affection.

Let us now step forward and see what were the fruits of making peace with the Saramaka Rebels. In 1750, which was the year thereafter, the promised presents were dispatched to Captain Adu, but the detachment that carried them was attacked on their march and every soul of them murdered on the spot by a desperate Negro called Zamzam who, not having been consulted at the peacemaking, had since put himself at the head of a strong party. He now carried off the whole stock (consisting of arms and ammunition, checked linens, canvas cloth, hatchets, saws and other carpenter's tools, besides salt beef, pork, spirits, etc.) as his own private property. Moreover, Adu, not having received his presents, suspected that the delay was intended to cut their throats, by means of a new supply of troops which he was told was coming from Europe.

By this accident the peace was immediately broken, cruelties and ravages increased more than ever, and death and destruction once more raged throughout the Colony. In 1757, things were come from bad to worse (while one Mr. Crommelin was Governor of this colony), a new revolt having broken out in the Tempaty Creek among the Negroes, owing to nothing but their being so cruelly treated by their masters. This fresh insurrection was of such serious consequence—they having joined themselves to 1600 other runaway Negroes already settled in eight different villages between the Tempaty and the River Marawina, along the banks of the Djuka Creek—that after repeated battles and skirmishes (they being all well armed, as I have mentioned) without much success for the colonists or any hopes of quelling it, they saw themselves once more reduced to suing for peace with their own slaves, as they had done in 1749 with the Rebels of Saramaka (but which peace was, as I have said, broken in 1750 by the irascible conduct of the Rebel Negro Zamzam).

To let the whole world now see that black men are not such brutes as the generality of white ones imagine, I must beg leave to mention a few of the principal ceremonies that attended the ratification of this peace. In 1760, the first thing was another parley, proposed by the colonists. This was, to be sure, agreed to by the Rebels, and these latter not only desired but absolutely insisted that the Dutch should send them yearly (among a great variety of other articles) a handsome quantity of firearms and ammunition, as specified in a long list made up in broken English by a Negro whose name was Boston and who was one of their captains.

Next, Governor Crommelin sent two commissioners, Mr. Sober and Mr. Abercrombie, who marched through the woods escorted by a few military etc., to carry some presents to the Rebels preliminary to the ratification of the peace. At the arrival of the above gentlemen in the Rebel camp at the Djuka Creek, they were introduced to a very handsome Negro called Araby who was the chief of them all, and born in the forest among the last 1600 that I have mentioned. He received them very politely, and taking them by the hand, desired they would sit down by his side upon the green, at the same time assuring them they needed not be under any apprehensions of evil, since coming in so good a cause, no one intended or even dared to hurt them.

But when the above-mentioned Captain Boston perceived that they had brought a parcel of trinkets—such as knives, scissors, combs, and small looking-glasses—and had forgotten the principal articles in question, viz., gunpowder, firearms, and ammunition, he resolutely stepped up to the commissioners and asked in a thundering voice if the Europeans imagined that the Negroes could live on combs and looking-glasses, adding that one of each was fully sufficient to let them all see their faces with satisfaction, while a single gallon of *mansanny*, viz., gunpowder, should have been accepted as a proof of their trust. But since that had been omitted, they should, with his will, never more return to their countrymen till every article of his list should be fulfilled. A Negro captain called Quacoo now interfered, saying that these gentlemen were only the messengers of their Governor and Court, and as they could not be answerable for their masters' proceedings they should certainly go back to where they came from without hurt or molestation, and not even he, Captain Boston, should dare to oppose them.

The chief of the Rebels then ordered silence and desired Mr. Abercrombie to make up a list himself of such articles as he, Araby, should name him, which that gentleman having done, the Rebels not only gave him and his companions leave peaceably to return with it to town, but their Governor and Court a whole year to deliberate on what they were to choose—peace or war. They swore unanimously that during that interval all animosity should cease on their side, after which, having entertained them in the best manner their situation in the woods afforded, they wished them a happy journey to Paramaribo.

Upon this occasion, one of the Rebel officers represented to Mr. Sober and to Mr. Abercrombie what a pity it was that the Europeans, who pretend to be a civilized nation, should be so much the occasion of their own ruin by their inhuman cruelties towards their slaves.

We desire you (continued this Negro) to tell your Governor and your Court that in case they want to raise no new gangs of Rebels, they ought to take care that the planters keep a more watchful eye over their own property and not so often trust them to the hands of a parcel of drunken managers and overseers, who by wrongfully whipping the Negroes, debauching their wives and children, neglecting the sick, etc., are the ruin of the Colony and willfully drive to the woods such quantities of stout, handsome people who by their sweat got your subsistence and without whose hands your colony must drop to nothing, and to whom at last in this pitiful manner you are glad to come and ply for friendship.

Mr. Abercrombie now begged of them to be accompanied with one or two of their principal officers to Paramaribo, where he promised they should be vastly well treated etc., but the chief, Araby, answered him with a smile that there would be sufficient time a year thereafter, once the peace was thoroughly concluded, and that then even his youngest son should be at their service to receive his education among them. And as for his subsistence and even for that of his descendants, he should take the sole care upon himself without ever giving the Christians the smallest trouble. After this, the commissioners left the Rebels and all arrived safe and sound at Paramaribo.

The year of deliberation being ended, the Governor and Court sent out two fresh commissioners to the Negro camp to bring the so much wished-for peace to a thorough conclusion. After a great deal of canvassing and ceremonies on both sides, with the presents being promised to the Negroes according to their wishes (as some nations pay tribute to the Emperor of Morocco), at last it was finally agreed on. And as a proof of their affection for the Europeans, the Negroes indiscriminately insisted that, during their remaining stay in the Rebel camp, each of the commissioners should take for his constant companion one of their handsomest young women. They also treated them with game, fish, fruit, and the best of all that the forest afforded, entertaining them without intermission with music, dancing, and cheering, besides firing one volley after another, after which they returned contented to town.

This done, the above presents were sent to the Negroes near the River Marawina by Mr. Mayer, escorted by six hundred men, soldiers and slaves, and which gentleman had nearly baffled the whole business by—contrary to his orders and from a pusillanimous principle— delivering all the presents to the Rebels without receiving the hostages in return. Fortunately, however, Araby kept his word and sent down four of his best officers as pledges to Paramaribo. By this the peace was perfectly accomplished, when a treaty of twelve or fourteen articles was signed by two white commissioners and sixteen of Araby's black captains in 1761, which ceremony took place on the Plantation Auka on the River Surinam where all the parties met—this being the spot of rendezvous appointed for the purpose, after four different embassies had been sent by the Europeans to the Negroes.

But signing this treaty alone was still not looked on as sufficient by the Rebel chief Araby and his people, who all immediately swore an oath, and insisted on the commissioners doing the same, after the manner in practice by themselves, not trusting entirely, they said, in that made use of by the Christians, which they had seen too often broken, whereas for a Negro to break his oath is absolutely without example (of this, at least, I never saw or heard of an instance during all the time that I lived in the Colony), which plainly argues that the Africans are not so entirely destitute of morality and even religion as a number of ignorant Europeans imagine, and which I hope still more clearly to demonstrate on other occasions.

The solemnity made use of on this day consisted in both parties, with a lance or penknife, letting themselves a few drops of blood from the arm into a calabash or cup with clean spring water, into which were also mixed a few particles of dry earth, and of which all present were obliged to drink a draught upon the spot, Europeans and Africans without exception, which they call drinking each other's blood. This was done after having first scattered a few drops upon the ground, when their *gadoman* or priest, with upcast eyes and outstretched arms, took Heaven and Earth as witness, and with a most audible voice and awful manner, invoked God's curse and malediction on all such as should first break this sacred treaty made between them, from that moment henceforth to all eternity, to which the multitude answered "*Da so*," which signifies in their language "Amen." The solemnity being ended, Araby and each captain was presented with a fine large cane and silver pommel on which were engraved the arms of the Colony (to distinguish them from other Negroes, as had already been done with the Saramaka captain, Adu, in 1749).

The above-mentioned Negroes are called Aukas [Ndjukas], after the name of the plantation where the peace articles were signed, by which name they are distinguished from the Saramakas, whom I have already described.

The Auka Negroes have indeed behaved indifferently well ever since the foregoing treaty— fortunately for the Colony of Surinam, from which they must yearly receive (as I have said, among a number of other articles) a handsome quantity of ball and gunpowder …

By their capitulation to the Dutch, the above Auka and Saramaka Rebels must yearly receive, as I have mentioned, a handsome quantity of arms and ammunition from the Colony, for which those have received in return the Negroes' promises of being their faithful allies, to deliver up all deserters (for which they receive proper bounties), never to appear armed at Paramaribo above five or six at a time, and also to keep their settlements at a proper distance from the town or plantations—the Saramaka Negroes at the River Saramacca, and the Auka Negroes near the River Marawina, where one or two white men called Postholders were to reside among them as a species of envoy. Both these tribes were now supposed to be in all some three thousand people. However, only several years later their numbers were computed by those who were sent to visit their settlements to be no less than fifteen or twenty thousand people (including wives and children). They have already become overbearing and even insolent, brandishing their silverheaded canes under the noses of the inhabitants by way of derision and independence, forcing from them liquors and very often money and, if they refuse, putting them in mind how (when they were their slaves) they murdered their parents and their husbands. From what I have just mentioned, and with their numbers increasing from day to day, I must conclude that should ever the peace be once more broken, the above new allies will become the most dreadful foes that ever the Colony of Surinam will have to deal with. I would mention besides the example and encouragement these treaties give other slaves to revolt even without provocation against their masters, and obstinately fight for the same privileges. At the same time, those planters who dare so inhumanely to persecute their slaves without a cause deserve, in my opinion, no better treatment, and this, most assuredly, too often is the consequence.

Selection 3: A Former Slave Condemns the Inhumanity of Caribbean Slavery

Olaudah Equiano, who was also known as Gustavus Vassa during his lifetime, wrote the most widely read slave narrative of the eighteenth century. He claimed that he had been born in Africa and sold into the slave trade as a child, but a baptismal record and naval muster book indicate that he may have in fact been born into slavery in South Carolina. Regardless of his origins, he worked as a slave on several different naval and merchant vessels in the Atlantic World until purchasing his freedom in 1766. He continued his life at sea as a free man, until settling in Britain and becoming a leading voice in the abolitionist cause during the 1780s. He published the first edition of his narrative in 1789 and died in 1797.

Equiano's extensive travels as an enslaved and free sailor gave him the opportunity to observe slaves living and working in a variety of ways, and he was appalled by the conditions he witnessed in the Caribbean. In the passages below, he describes the cruelties that he saw Caribbean slave traders, planters, and overseers inflicting on their fellow human beings.

Credit: Olaudah Equiano, *The Interesting Narrative of the Life of Olaudah Equiano, or Gustavus Vassa, the African, Written by Himself* (New York: W. Durell, 1791), 145–150, 157–161.

While I was thus employed by my master I was often a witness to cruelties of every kind, which were exercised on my unhappy fellow slaves. I used frequently to have different cargoes of new negroes in my care for sale; and it was almost a constant practice with our clerks, and other whites, to commit violent depredations on the chastity of the female slaves; and these I was, though with reluctance, obliged to submit to at all times, being unable to help them. When we have had some of these slaves on board my master's vessels to carry them to other islands, or to America, I have known our mates to commit these acts most shamefully, to the disgrace, not of Christians only, but of men. I have even known them to gratify their brutal passion with females not ten years old; and these abominations some of them practiced to such scandalous excess, that one of our captains discharged the mate and others on the account. And yet in Montserrat I have seen a negro man staked to the ground, and cut most shockingly, and then his ears cut off bit by bit, because he had been connected with a white woman who was a common prostitute:

as if it were no crime in the whites to rob an innocent African girl of her virtue; but most heinous in a black man only to gratify a passion of nature, where the temptation was offered by one of a different colour, though the most abandoned woman of her species. One Mr. D—told me that he had sold 41,000 negroes, and that he once cut off a negro-man's leg for running away. I asked him if the man had died in the operation, how he as a Christian could answer for the horrid act before God? and he told me, answering was a thing of another world; what he thought and did were policy. I told him that the Christian doctrine taught us to do unto others as we would that others should do unto us. He then said that his scheme had the desired effect—it cured that man and some others of running away. Another negro man was half hanged, and then burnt, for attempting to poison a cruel overseer. Thus by repeated cruelties are the wretched first urged to despair, and then murdered, because they still retain so much of human nature about them as to wish to put an end to their misery, and retaliate on their tyrants!

These overseers are indeed for the most part persons of the worst character of any denomination of men in the West Indies. Unfortunately, many humane gentlemen, by not residing on their estates, are obliged to leave the management of them in the hands of these human butchers, who cut and mangle the slaves in a shocking manner on the most trifling of occasions, and altogether treat them in every respect like brutes: They pay no regard to the situation of pregnant women, nor the least attention to the lodging of the field negroes. Their huts, which ought to be well covered, and the place dry where they take their little repose, are often open sheds, built in damp places; so that, when the poor creatures return tired from the toils of the field, they contract many disorders, from being exposed to the damp air in this uncomfortable state, while they are heated, and their pores are open. This neglect certainly conspires with many others to cause a decrease in the births as well as in the lives of the grown negroes.

I can quote many instances of gentlemen who reside on their estates in the West Indies, and then the scene is quite changed; the negroes are treated with lenity and proper care, by which their lives are prolonged, and their masters are profited. To the honor of humanity, I knew several gentlemen who managed their estates in this manner; and they found that benevolence was their true interest. And, among many I could mention in several of the islands, I knew one in Montserrat whose slaves looked remarkably well, and never needed any fresh supplies of negroes; and there are many other estates, especially in Barbadoes, which, from such judicious treatment, need no fresh stock of negroes at any time. I have the honour of knowing a most worthy and humane gentleman, who is a native of Barbadoes, and has estates there. This gentleman has written a treatise on the usage of his own slaves. He allows them two hours for refreshment at mid-day; and many other indulgencies and comforts, particularly in their lying; and besides this, he raises more provisions on his estate than they can destroy; so that by these attentions he saves the lives of his negroes, and keeps them happy as the conditions of slavery can admit. I myself, as shall appear in the sequel, managed an estate, where, by those attentions, the negroes were uncommonly cheerful and healthy, and did more work by half than by the common mode of treatment they usually do. For want, therefore, of such care and attention to the poor negroes; and otherwise oppressed as they are, it is no wonder that the decrease should require 20,000 new negroes annually to fill up the vacant places of the dead.

Even in Barbadoes, notwithstanding those humane exceptions, which I have mentioned, and others I am acquainted with, which justly make it quoted as a place where slaves meet with the best treatment and need fewest recruits of any in the West Indies, yet this island requires 1,000 negroes annually to keep up the original stock, which is only 80,000. So that the whole term of a negro's life may be said to be there but sixteen years! And yet the climate here is in every respect the same as that from which they are taken, except in being more wholesome. Do the British colonies decrease in this manner? And yet what a prodigious difference is there between an English and West India climate?

***

I have often seen slaves, particularly those who were meagre, in different islands, put into scales and weighed; and then sold from three pence to six pence or nine pence a pound. My master, however, whose humanity was shocked at this mode, used to sell such by the lump. And at or after a sale it was not uncommon to see negroes taken from their wives, wives taken from their husbands, and children from their parents, and sent off to other islands, and wherever else their merciless lords chose; and probably never more during life to see each other! Oftentimes my heart had bled at these partings; when the friends of the departed have been at the water side, and, with sighs and tears, have kept their eyes fixed on the vessel till it went out of sight.

A poor Creole negro I knew well, who, after having been often thus transported from island to island, at last resided in Montserrat. This man used to tell me many melancholy tales of himself. Generally, after he had done working for his master, he used to employ his few leisure moments to go a fishing. When he had caught any fish, his master would frequently take them from him without paying him; and at other times some other white people would serve him in the same manner. One day he said to me, very movingly, "Sometimes when a white man take away my fish I go to my maser, and he get me my right; and when my master by strength take away my fishes, what me must do? I can't go to anybody to be righted: then" said the poor man, looking up above "I must look up to God Mighty in the top for right." ...

Nor was such usage as this confined to particular places or individuals; for, in all the different islands in which I have been (and I have visited no less than fifteen) the treatment of slaves was nearly the same; so nearly indeed, that the history of an island, or even a plantation, with few such exceptions as I have mentioned, might serve for a history of the whole. Such a tendency has the slave-trade to debauch men's minds, and harden them to every feeling of humanity! For I will not suppose that the dealers in slaves are born worse than other men. No, it is the fatality of this mistaken avarice, that it corrupts the milk of human kindness and turns it to gall. And, had the pursuits of those men been different, they might have been as generous, as tender-hearted and just, as they are unfeeling, rapacious and cruel. Surely this traffic cannot be good, which spreads like a pestilence, and taints what it touches! which violates the first natural right of mankind, equality and independency, and gives one man a dominion over his fellows which God could never intend! For it raises the owner to a state far above man as it depresses the slave below it; and, which all the presumption of human pride, sets a distinction between them, immeasurable in extent, and endless in duration! Yet how mistaken is the avarice even of the planters? Are slaves more useful by being thus humbled to the condition of brutes, than they would be if suffered to enjoy the privileges of men? The freedom which diffuses health and prosperity throughout Britain answers you, No. When you make men slaves you deprive them of half their virtue, you set them in your own conduct an example of fraud, rapine, and cruelty, and compel them to live with you in a state of war; and yet you complain that they are not honest or faithful! You stupefy them with stripes, and think it necessary to keep them in a state of ignorance; and yet you assert that they are incapable of learning; that their minds are such barren soil or moor, that culture would be lost on them; and that they come from a climate, where nature, though prodigal of her bounties in a degree unknown to yourselves, has left man alone scant and unfinished, and incapable of enjoying the treasures she has poured out for him!—An assertion at once impious and absurd. Why do you use those instruments of torture? Are they fit to be applied by one rational being to another? And are ye not struck with shame and mortification, to see the partakers of your nature reduced so low? But, above all, are there no dangers attending this mode of treatment? Are you not hourly in dread of an insurrection?

Discussion Questions

1. How does Ligon compare the working life of servants and slaves in Barbados? How does he compare these two groups in terms of their motivations and methods of resistance to their masters' authority?
2. Where in Ligon's account of Barbados do you see evidence of cultural adaptations made between the island's European and African inhabitants? How do the slaves express their African cultural heritage in their music, religion, and recreation?
3. According to Stedman, why were slaves in Surinam in a constant state of rebellion? Why did planters there find it necessary to negotiate with such rebels? Where do you see evidence in these diplomatic negotiations of cultural exchange and adaptation between Europeans and Africans? Why do you suppose slave rebellion was far more prevalent in Stedman's Surinam than Ligon's Barbados?
4. How does Equiano's analysis of Caribbean slavery compare to that of Ligon and Stedman? On what grounds does he argue for improving the living and working conditions of slaves, and what impact does he think the Atlantic Slave Trade is having on Europeans?

Suggested Readings

For the origins and nature of the Caribbean plantation complex, see Philip D. Curtin, *The Rise and Fall of the Plantation Complex: Essays in Atlantic History* (Cambridge: Cambridge University Press, 1990); and Robin Blackburn, *The Making of New World Slavery* (London: Verso Press, 1997). The links between slavery and sugar production are explored in Sidney Mintz's *Sweetness and Power: The Place of Sugar in Modern History* (New York: Penguin Books, 1985); and Stuart B. Schwartz, ed., *Tropical Babylons: Sugar and the Making of the Atlantic World, 1450–1680* (Chapel Hill, NC: University of North Carolina Press, 2004). For a comparative study of plantation slavery in the Caribbean and North America, see Richard S. Dunn, *A Tale of Two Plantations: Slave Life and Labor in Jamaica and Virginia* (Philadelphia, PA: University of Pennsylvania Press, 2014). For the slaves' efforts to build lives and families in the plantation complex, see Randy M. Browne, *Surviving Slavery in the British Caribbean* (Philadelphia, PA: University of Pennsylvania Press, 2017). Slave resistance, rebellion, and marronage have received much attention in histories of the plantation complex. For the maroons encountered by Stedman, see Richard Price, *The Guiana Maroons* (Baltimore, MD: Johns Hopkins University Press, 1976). For other New World maroon communities, see Mavis C. Campbell, *The Maroons of Jamaica, 1655–1796: A History of Resistance, Collaboration, and Betrayal* (Granby, MA: Bergin and Garvey, 1988); and Jane Landers, *Black Society in Spanish Florida* (Urbana, IL: University of Illinois Press, 1999).

For more on Ligon's Barbados, see Richard S. Dunn, *Sugar and Slaves: The Rise of the Planter Class in the English West Indies, 1624–1713* (Chapel Hill, NC: University of North Carolina Press, 1972). The operation of the Caribbean plantation complex at the time of John Stedman's sojourn in Surinam is described in Arthur L. Stinchcombe, *Sugar Island Slavery in the Age of Enlightenment: The Political Economy of the Caribbean World* (Princeton, NJ: Princeton University Press, 1995). Vincent Carretta's *Equiano, the African: Biography of a Self-Made Man* (New York: Penguin Books, 2005) reconstructs the life and travels of the famous abolitionist.

7 The Spanish and Portuguese in the Americas

Figure 7.1 Spanish Missionaries and Indian Converts in Mexico.

These images from Mexico tell the viewer much about how Spanish missionaries approached their work. In the upper left, two missionaries convert the village's leading families, who bow in submission to their new spiritual overlords. The scene below them depicts the sins that the Spanish associated with unconverted Indians: indolence, superstition, murder, lasciviousness, and disobedience. The scene on the right depicts the missionaries attending to their converts so as to protect them from the evils of backsliding and paganism, represented by the winged demonic figures in the background. How does this scene of conversion compare with Figure 4.1?

Source credit: Converting the Indians. From Pablo Beaumont, *Cronica de Michoacan* (Rare Manuscript Division, New York Public Library).

Introduction

Columbus's voyage of 1492 sparked a European competition for New World empire that lasted for over 300 years. Spain and Portugal led this scramble, and for most of the sixteenth century, the Old World's invasion of the New was shaped by these two powers. The Iberian Peninsula's position as a gateway between the Mediterranean Sea and the Atlantic Ocean helps explain this development. Spain and Portugal had strong maritime industries that enjoyed the patronage of their rulers and investment from merchants in Italian city-states such as Genoa and Venice. Also, the Iberian Peninsula had been a crossroads for peoples from Europe, North Africa, and the Near East for centuries—fertile ground for the exchange of the geographic and technical knowledge necessary to support oceanic navigation. Lastly, the Peninsula's southwestern orientation into the Atlantic gave its inhabitants a natural advantage in exploring sea routes to sub-Saharan Africa, Asia, and eventually America. For a century prior to Columbus's voyage, the Spanish and Portuguese were conquering and colonizing islands in the eastern Atlantic, and that experience provided important precedents for their forays into the Americas.

Thus, there are many good reasons to consider the Spanish and Portuguese together when studying the Atlantic World, but important differences did exist in their approaches to colonization. The Spanish organized their American enterprise on a model inherited from their centuries-long *Reconquista* of the Iberian Peninsula from Islamic Moors. Treating Native Americans in much the same way as they had the Moors and native peoples of the Canary Islands, the Spanish subjugated them militarily, planted colonists to occupy the new territory, and then incorporated the conquered people into Spanish society through a combination of forced labor and religious conversion. The Portuguese, on the other hand, modeled their invasion of America after commercial enterprises they pursued elsewhere in the world, trading with the natives and eventually transplanting the plantation complex from their eastern Atlantic colonies to Brazil.

In 1494, before the Spanish and Portuguese even comprehended the geographic extent of the Americas, they agreed in the Treaty of Tordesillas to a north-to-south boundary line through the Atlantic Ocean that would divide their overseas dominions. As subsequent voyages of exploration would discover, the bulk of the Americas fell west of this line and therefore into Spanish hands. The exception was Brazil, which jutted far enough eastward to fall under Portuguese jurisdiction, which also included West Africa and the trade routes around the Cape of Good Hope into the Indian Ocean. This artificial border had important ramifications for peoples throughout the Atlantic World. The Spanish found themselves nominal lords over a dominion populated by millions of Indians and containing untold wealth; within a generation, a lethal combination of Spanish germs and military power subdued the mighty Aztecs and Incas and turned their homelands into the center of Spain's overseas empire. The Portuguese, on the other hand, concentrated their energies as much in the East as in the West, creating a global trading empire in which Brazil played a role as an exporter of sugar and importer of African slaves (see Map 7.1).

Spanish expansion in the Americas was motivated by the pursuit of mineral wealth. Spanish adventurers flocked to the Caribbean in the wake of Columbus looking for the source of the gold they found in jewelry worn by the natives. They joined small expeditionary forces known as *entradas*, usually organized under the leadership of a single man and financed privately by investors and participants. The most spectacular successes for such enterprises occurred in Mexico from 1519 to 1521, when Hernando Cortés conquered the Aztecs, and in Peru from 1532 to 1533, when Francisco Pizarro conquered the Incas, but many others ended disastrously, as hostile Indians and unfamiliar terrain put an end to the fortune seekers.

After the initial wave of conquest, mining became the central economic activity of Spain's New World empire. To meet the insatiable demand for workers in Peruvian and Mexican mines, the Spanish transplanted to America the *encomienda*, a system of tribute labor they had imposed on conquered peoples in Iberia and the Canary Islands. Typically, Indian villages paid this tribute by sending individuals to work for the Spanish on a rotating basis during the course of the year. While Spanish mines demanded the most labor, Indians also worked on Spanish rural estates (*haciendas*) and in the workshops of Spanish towns. The Church helped maintain this system by converting Indians to Christianity and encouraging them to submit to Spanish authority. Indians resisted these impositions, sometimes in organized rebellions that cost many lives, but more often in less obvious ways, such as continuing to practice their native rituals and beliefs in secret or under the guise of observing Christian ceremonies.

The Spanish reliance on Indian labor led to a close association between invaders and natives that produced a sizable population of *mestizos*, the offspring of Spanish men and

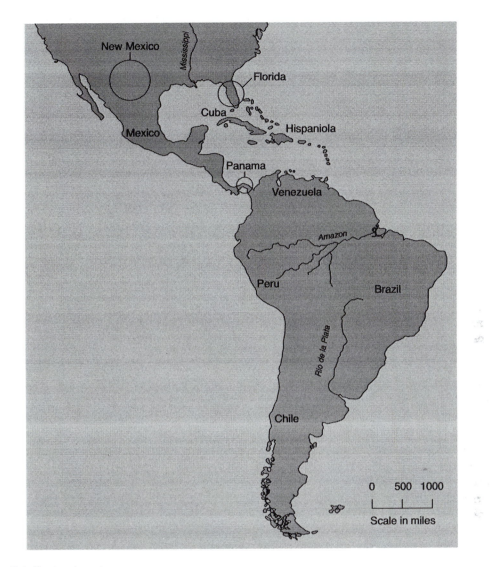

Map 7.1 Iberian America.

Spanish and Portuguese possessions in Central and South America.

Native women. The Spanish also brought African slaves with them to the Americas, and a smaller population of mulattoes, free blacks, and enslaved Africans found a place in Spanish American society, chiefly as domestic servants, retainers, and urban workers. By 1700, Spanish America featured an amalgam of European, Indian, and African peoples, with a small Spanish population on top, a much larger free *mestizo* population in the middle, and bottom rungs occupied by mulattoes, Indians, and Africans living in varying degrees of submission to their Spanish rulers.

The Portuguese took a very different approach to New World colonization. With no native empires to plunder for gold and silver, Brazil seemed to offer little more than a place to cut wood and resupply ships. In keeping with their methods in Africa and Asia, the Portuguese built coastal forts in Brazil to trade with the natives and keep out European rivals, but their presence in Brazil was negligible until colonists began planting sugar there in the mid-sixteenth century. Faced with the same labor shortage as the Spanish, the Portuguese carried African slaves across the Atlantic to work their plantations, and by the seventeenth century, they had created the first slave society in the Western Hemisphere. Intermarriage and sexual relations between the Portuguese and Africans in Brazil created new social categories. These groups were dominated by the offspring of Portuguese men and African women, who were known collectively as *pardos*. Like Spanish America's *mestizos*, *pardos* occupied an important place in Brazilian society, often working as producers of subsistence crops and as urban craftsmen. They represented the middling status between freedom and slavery made possible by intermarriage and cultural assimilation.

As the Atlantic economy expanded and diversified, the Spanish and Portuguese experiences in the Americas tended to converge. Mining, for example, became a central part of the economy of southern Brazil after the discovery of gold in the interior region of Minas Gerais in the 1690s. Likewise, in the late colonial period, Cuban sugar plantations became an important source of Spanish wealth. Perhaps the most significant point of convergence was the role that peoples of mixed-race descent came to play in Spanish and Portuguese colonies. The Spanish and Portuguese shared a legal tradition that encouraged the incorporation of strangers and former enemies into society by religious conversion, and in the case of slaves, by allowing them to negotiate terms of self-purchase with their owners. In Iberian America, this practice meant that a non-European's skin color or other physical features could never definitively fix his or her status in either freedom or slavery. While full equality with their European rulers was an impossibility, *mestizos*, *pardos*, Indians, and Africans could—by way of marriage, conversion, and emancipation—gain a legal and social status suspended somewhere between unconditional freedom and abject enslavement.

The readings in this chapter examine how race and labor relations intersected in the colonization of Iberian America. In the first selection, an English traveler in seventeenth-century Mexico and Guatemala describes the system of tribute labor the Spanish forced on Native Americans there. In the second selection, an Italian priest details the wealth and racial caste system in eighteenth-century Mexico City, as well as an episode of labor unrest in the mining industry. The third selection looks at plantation society in Brazil and dissects the social hierarchy there. As you read these sources, look for similarities between them that illustrate the Iberian approach to overseas expansion. How do the Spanish and Portuguese regard Africans and Native Americans? How do they create new social groups out of their encounters with them? What are the points of tension within those social orders?

Selection 1: An English Traveler Explains the *Repartimiento* System in Spanish America

One of the distinguishing features of the Spanish colonial order in America was the *repartimiento*, a system of forced labor imposed on Native Americans. The Spanish Crown intended for the *repartimiento* to correct abuses associated with the earlier *economienda* system, which resulted in the enslavement of many Natives by the conquistadors and their followers in the sixteenth century. The *repartimiento* gave more oversight to civil officials and required the payment of wages to Indian workers, but it still relied on forced drafts of laborers from local Indian populations to serve the needs of public and private parties. Indians working in this system faced malnutrition, exposure to disease, physical abuse, and dangerous working conditions in mines and other industries.

Thomas Gage was an Englishman who joined the Catholic priesthood and worked in Mexico and Guatemala as a missionary in the early seventeenth century. After returning to Britain, he converted to Protestantism, and during the English Civil Wars (1641–1649), he turned vehemently against his former faith. In 1648, he published the first edition of his travels in Spanish America. His description of the *repartimiento* system in Guatemala reflects the overall anti-Spanish tone of this work, but it is also a valuable account of how the system worked from an outside observer. Gage died in 1656, taking part in the English expedition that wrested control of Jamaica from Spain.

Credit: Thomas Gage, A *Survey of the Spanish-West-Indies* (London: Thomas Horne, 1702), 313–316.

… The *Indians* of the several Towns are to have in a readiness so many Labourers as the Court of *Guatemala* hath appointed to be weekly taken out of such a Town, who are conducted by an *Indian* officer to the Town of general meeting; and when they come with their Tools, their Spades, Shovels, Bills, or Axes, with their provision of Victuals for a Week (which are commonly some dry cakes of Maiz[e], puddings of Frixoles, or *French* beans, and a little Chile or biting long Pepper, or a bit of cold meat for the first day or two) and with Beds on their backs (which is only a coarse woollen Mantle to wrap about them when they lie on the bare ground) then they are shut up in the Town-House, some with Blows, some with Spurnings, some with Boxes on the ear, if presently they go not in.

Now all being gathered together, and the house filled with them, the *Juez Repartidor*, or Officer, calls by the order of the List such and such a *Spaniard*, and also calls out of the house so many *Indians* as by the Court are commanded to be given to him (some are allowed three, some four, some ten, some fifteen, some twenty, according to their Employments) and delivereth to the *Spaniard* his *Indians*, and so to all the rest, till they be all served, who when they receive their *Indians*, take from them a Tool, or their Mantles, to secure them that they run not away, and for every *Indian* delivered unto them, they give unto the *Juez Repartidor*, or Officer half a *Rial* (a Spanish coin), which is three pence an *Indian* for his Fees, which amounts yearly to him to a great deal of Mon[e]y; for some Officers make a partition or distribution of four hundred, some of two hundred, some of three hundred *Indians* every week, and carries home with him so many half hundred Rials for one or half a days work.

If Complaint be made by any *Spaniard* that such and such an *Indian* ran away from him and served him not the Week past, the *Indian* must be brought and surely tied to a post by his hands in the Market place, and there be whipt upon his bare back. But if the poor *Indian* complain that the *Spaniard* cozened and cheated him of his Shovel, Ax, Bill, Mantle, or Wages, no Justice shall be executed against the cheating *Spaniard*, neither shall the *Indian* be righted, though it is true the Order [law] runs equally in favour of both *Indian* and *Spaniard*.

Thus the poor *Indians* are sold for three pence apiece for a whole weeks slavery, not permitted to go home at nights to their wives, though their Work lie not above a mile from the Town where they live; nay, some are carried ten or twelve miles from their home, who must not return till Saturday night late, and must that Week do whatsoever their Master pleased to command them. The Wages appointed them will scarce find them Meat and Drink, for they are not allowed a Rial a day, which is but six pence, and with that they are to find themselves, but for six days work and diet they are to have five Rials, which is half a Crown. This same Order is observed in the city of *Guatemala*, and Towns of *Spaniards*, where every family that wants the Service of an *Indian* or *Indians*, though it be but to fetch Water and Wood on their backs or to go of errands, is allowed the like Service from the nearest *Indian* Towns.

It would grieve a Christians heart to see how by some cruel *Spaniards* in that Weeks service the poor wretches are wrong'd and abused; some visit their Wives at home, whilst their poor Husbands are digging and delving; others whipping them for their slow working; others wounding them with their Swords, or breaking their heads for some reasonable and well-grounded Answer in their own behalf; others stealing from them their tools; others cheating them of half, others of all their wages, alleging that their service cost them half a Rial, and yet their Work not well performed. I knew some who made a common practice of this, when their Wheat was sown, and they had little to do for the *Indians*; yet they would have home as many as were due to their Farm, and on *Monday* and *Tuesday* would make them cut and bring on their backs as much wood as they needed all that Week, and then on Wednesday at noon (knowing the great desire of the *Indians* to go home to their Wives, for which they would give any thing), would say to them, What will you give me now, if I let you go home to do your own Work? Whereto the *Indians* would joyfully reply and answer, some that they would give a Rial, others two Rials, which they would take and send them home, and so would have much Work done, Wood to serve their house a week, and Mon[e]y as much as would buy them meat, and Cacao for Chocolate two weeks together; and thus from the poor *Indians* do those unconscionable *Spaniards* practice a cheap and lassie [lazy] way of living. Others will sell them away for that week to a Neighbour that hath present need of Work, Demanding Rials apiece for every *Indian*, which he that buys them will be sure to defray out of their wages.

So likewise are they in Slavish Bondage and Readiness for all Passengers and Travellers, who in any Town may demand to the next Town as many *Indians* to go with his Mules, or to carry on their backs a heavy Burthen as he shall need, who at the Journeys end shall pick some quarrel with them, and so send them back with Blows and Stripes without any Pay at all. A *Petaca*, or leathern trunk, and chest of above a hundred weight they will make these Wretches to carry on their backs a whole day, nay, some two or three days together, which they do by tying the Chest on each side with Ropes, having a broad leather in the middle, which they cross over the forepart of their Head, or their Forehead, hanging thus the Weight on their heads and brows, which at their journeys end hath made the Blood stick in the foreheads of some, galling and pulling off the skin, and marking them in the fore-top of their heads, who as they are called *Tamemez*, so are easily known in a Town by their Baldness, that leather girt having worn off all their hair.

With these hard usages, yet those poor people make shift to live amongst the *Spaniards*, but so that with anguish of heart they are still crying out to God for Justice, and for Liberty, whose only comfort is in their Priests and Fryers [friars], who many times quiet them when they would rise up in mutiny, and for their own ends often prevail over them with fair and cunning persuasions, to bear and suffer for Gods sake, and for the good of the Common-wealth, that hard Task and Service which is laid upon them. And though in all Seasons, wet and dry, cold and hot, and Ways, plain and mountainous, green and dirty, dusty and stony, they must perform this hard Service to their commanding Masters, their Apparel and Cloathing is but such as may cover the Nakedness of their Body, nay, in some it is such torn Rags as will not cover half their Nakedness.

Selection 2: An Italian Priest Describes Social Relations in Mexico City

Mexico City was the capital city of the Viceroyalty of New Spain and one of the largest cities in Spanish America. Its architecture featured large public plazas, fountains, and churches, and it was the seat of power for bureaucracies of church and state that dominated public life in colonial Mexico. In 1770, when Philadelphia, then the largest city in British North America, had about 30,000 people, Mexico City was more than three times as big, with a population approaching 100,000.

Ilarione de Bergamo was an Italian priest sent by his religious order to Mexico in 1761 to solicit donations for missionary work in Tibet. The fact that a friar in Italy would travel all the way across the Atlantic to seek financial support for a mission in Central Asia is testimony to New Spain's reputation for wealth and opulence. Bergamo spent five years in Mexico, and shortly after returning home, he recorded his impressions of its people and landscape in a manuscript intended for friends and family. Bergamo, like many visitors to New Spain, was intrigued by the social order that developed around the intermarriage of Native Americans, Africans, and Europeans. As a priest, he was also interested in how the Mexican Inquisition enforced orthodoxy on such a diverse population and in the tense labor relations between Spanish owners and Indian laborers in Mexico's mines.

Credit: Robert Ryal Miller and William J. Orr, eds., *Daily Life in Colonial Mexico: The Journey of Friar Ilarione da Bergamo, 1761–1768* (Norman, OK: University of Oklahoma Press, 2000), 88–89, 90–92, 115–116, 151–152, 161–163.

The city of Mexico has more than one hundred and thirty thousand inhabitants [in Bergamo's time, it was likely closer to 100,000]. Moreover, such is the daily concourse of other people from the city and other surrounding towns that there is a continual ebb and flow of people in the streets and plazas, providing the semblance of a continual fair. There are numerous plazas, and in practically all of them there is a fountain in the middle spurting water. The principal plaza, though, is the one with the cathedral and viceroy's palace, where people primarily gather to carry on their trade. And the immense variety of things sold here—for food, clothing, and every other human use—and the mechanic arts are a sight to behold. Indeed, any kind of item for whatever use a person might deem necessary can be found here. This huge plaza is filled with shops made of boards, which, if need be, can be quickly lifted [and removed]. In the middle of this plaza is a very lovely fountain, with jets of water soaring to a considerable height. Here, too, a gallows consisting of four columns is invariably erected off to the side. There are various districts with their arcades all lined with stores full of merchandise. Various canals from the lake, which they call *acequias*, enter the city. Through them the Indian folk from nearby places convey in their canoes items of all kinds like vegetables, lumber, wheat, flour, charcoal, fruits, and many other things, which are consumed daily in Mexico City.

In the districts where there is no canal or acequia there are subterranean water conduits, which perennially supply not only public fountains but many houses as well, these benefitting from a well-constructed receptacle in their courtyard. This water, which fills the need of the entire city, is conveyed in a canal [i.e., an aqueduct] seven leagues from the city, built entirely of arches and rather elevated in some places.

***

For the quality of its buildings, ornaments, and wealth of its churches, it [Mexico City] can be said to vie with the finest cities of Italy. It is true that there are no grand palaces, as in Rome and its outskirts, because they cannot erect massive buildings since the foundations are not completely solid. But in their interior, perhaps, they are richer for the sumptuousness of their ornamentation. All the houses of this city are of stone and brick and whitewashed. Viewed in perspective, they are of fine architecture, with well-ordered balconies, windows and soffits in Chinese style, magnificent gates, courtyards with marble columns, and spacious and commodious entrance stairways painted between one step and the next in checkered fashion so that, viewed from a certain distance, the entire stairwell looks as though it were covered with cloth. The only defect the houses have is that they are not proportionate in height, though I have seen various ones five stories high. Most, though, have three. The rooms located on the floor by the door are where the serving people dwell. Above them are the rooms they call *entresuelo*, where there are stores of merchandise, because here practically everyone is a merchant. Finally, there are the masters' quarters. Though not very wealthy, all have their forloni [vans or hauling carts] or coaches because these Mexican gentlemen are so dainty that they would not go on any outing unless they went by coach …

As for the women, it is true that they are very beautiful and of a fine disposition, spirited, pretty, and with considerable rhetorical talent, so that they far surpass out Italian women. But they are ambitious (as in every other country), proud, dainty, and indolent. Many favor the Europeans (who are called *gachupines*), and they more willingly marry them, even though impoverished, than their own compatriots called creoles, even though wealthy. They view them—that is, the creoles—as lovers of mulatto women, from whom they have imbibed bad customs with their milk. Consequently, the creole men hate the Europeans.

The women adopt the Spanish style of dress—that is, the ladies as well as the merchant and artisan women who can [afford to]. The rest are attired as their status permits. Because there are different castes of people, each person thus dresses not only on a level with her wealth but also according to her caste. If a woman is an Indian, though wealthy, she dresses in accordance with Indian custom, however opulently; if she is mulatta, according to mulatto custom, etc. I regret having lacked familiarity with the design so that I could provide an illustration of those women's dresses, which certainly are a matter of curiosity in some cases, perhaps more so than in the case of Greek women.

The mulattos are born of white and blacks and vice versa. The mestizos are those who are born of Spaniards with Indian or creole women, and vice versa, so that they have a varied physiognomy. Thus, there are six castes of people in this realm: Europeans, creoles, mulattos, mestizos, Indians, and blacks.

***

Generally speaking, the creoles, Indians, and mestizos, along with mulattos, are sluggards, drunkards, thieves, swindlers, and lechers—and that is also true of the women. Nevertheless, it cannot be denied that there are people of every status, sex, and condition who are very good Christians, are generally charitable, and give alms. They are cordial, though somewhat averse to foreigners. Though they have an inherent esteem for the Spaniards, they confuse them with other Europeans, whom they all call gachupines, using another term for the others. In view of the affection and esteem for them, it is generally appropriate to pass as gachupín, but not particularly as Italian, French, or German, et cetera.

Ordinarily their songs are quite shameless, but still worse are their dances, which include rather indecent gestures. Three kinds of fiestas are conventional in the realm. The first is the festivity, properly speaking, where they dance French-style. Here aristocratic and polite society is involved, and there are no disorders or scandals. The second they call *saroas* [i.e., *soirées*], in which there is a medley of songs, music, dancing, drunkenness, and other ills. The third, finally, is the so-called *fandango*, which is the most universal one among the common people and where, for the most part, they perform the dances they call the *chuchumbe, bamba*, and *guesito*, which are all quite indecent.

The climate of this country is more hot than temperate. Brandy consumption, foods heavily seasoned with pepper, and popular custom (introduced, in my opinion, by the first conquistadors, as the historical accounts make clear) have resulted in a universal epidemic as far as women are concerned. For it has been attested to me many times by various people of probity that the majority of young people who marry (referring here to the common people) are not virgins. The main evidence of this is the great abuse prevalent in those lands of living *amancebao* [i.e., *amancebado*], as they put it, which in Italian means living in concubinage. Great are the numbers of those who pass through life in such a wretched state, including quite decent people, too, whom their superiors, both spiritual and temporal, are unable to reform. And very frequently these people, wretched in spirit after having been together awhile, separate, not out of a sense of obligation but due to a change in fortune or inclination. And thus so many women marry having children without having had a husband, and hence the country is rife with illegitimate progeny.

***

... I do not want to overlook a minor episode, which occurred in March 1768. On a certain predetermined day, in the church of Santo Domingo eight live relics were exposed, not to communal veneration but to public derision. They were a heretical blasphemer, an obdurate Calvinist, an idolatrous Indian woman, a witch, a bigamist, a secular cleric with only minor orders who had celebrated some masses, a lay brother of a certain order who had said mass, and an obdurate Jew. All of them were then exposed all day long to public view in the presbytery of the spacious church of Santo Domingo. To this end, the main altar with some other accessories had been removed to allow a good view of these culprits. The reason for their condemnation was publicized by a placard on their chests. All day long they suffered the scorn, derision, and gossiping of the people. Nevertheless, some of them endured this with great composure, as though it meant nothing. Moreover, such were the alcoholic drinks administered to them (because on such occasion they are given all they ask for) that some of them were partially intoxicated.

The following day they were all led through the open streets of the city, accompanied by police and escorted by soldiers and all the officials of the Inquisition, both priests and regular clergy, and laypersons, too, all of them on horseback. The throng of people was beyond number. Riding a young donkey, each culprit was wearing on his or her head a long cap shaped like a horn, formed of cardboard, except for the two who had celebrated mass, who went with their heads uncovered. On his chest each one wore a sign listing his or her offense. Around the neck of the idolatrous woman they hung a tiny idol, and each person was accompanied by an Indian in the guise of an executioner, who, with a wooden stick in hand, dealt each one light blows on the back from time to time. After this event they were all returned to the prisons of the Inquisition. I do not know what happened afterward because a few days later I left Mexico City for Italy. According to the laws of Spain, some them ought to have been burned alive.

***

I will conclude the subject of mining with a brief account of an uprising that occurred in 1766 in Real del Monte [a mining town northeast of Mexico City], where I was living. There were some dissensions, the reason for which I do not know, that erupted between the mineworkers and officials acting on behalf of the owner, Don Pedro Romero de Terreros. Before long, on a certain day, a large number of Indians gathered in this mining camp. All of them were mineworkers, not just from this location but from other nearby areas as well. The intention of these people (as was later determined) was to kill the owner, i.e., Señor Terreros, and all of his officials and burn down the mines. Had this occurred, it would have been their own ruination and that of the whole country as well. But God did not permit such ravaging to occur.

So, on August 15, [1766,] this day set by that rabble for the total destruction of Real del Monte, many of them gathered in the mine of San Cayetano. There, after some quarrels between them and a miner, or mine official, they stoned him so that he died a few hours later. When the alcalde mayor or *podestà* of Pachuca, a young man recently arrived from Spain who happened to be there, attempted to bring these people to a halt by drawing his sword, they flung themselves on him with such ferocity and cruelty that they left him there dead, completely crushed by stones.

Señor Terreros, having heard about the uprising and the two fatalities that had already occurred, hid in a room where he kept plenty of fodder for the horses, burying himself up to his neck in this. However much the rebel Indians tried to hunt him down and kill him, they could not find him. It was necessary for the parish priest to lead a procession with the Blessed Sacrament, which I also accompanied, so as to convey Señor Romero de Terreros from his hiding place and guide him into the church, underneath the baldachin [canopy over an altar], as a sanctuary for himself and his general foreman. It was a gratifying sight arriving in certain places with the Blessed Sacrament. There were many women and children, [and] listening to their wailing and weeping one would have thought it was the final day [of judgment].

While all this was going on, other women, enraged like their husbands, were going about tossing lighted embers onto the piles of straw of the mines to set them ablaze. There was no damage, thanks to the diligence of a few individuals. The insurgents moved on to a house where they believed a certain mine official was hidden, whom they had vowed to kill. They smashed in the door and windows and went inside, but they did not find the one they were looking for. They moved on to the jails, ecclesiastical as well as secular, forced them open, and removed all the prisoners, their accomplices.

Then they passed on to Pachuca, where they did the same thing, i.e., forcibly liberated all the prisoners. They then headed to the home of the foremen of the mines to burn it down. Those estranged individuals only desisted from their design because some Reformed fathers, who have a monastery in that town, had promptly arrived on the scene, loudly threatening to bring down the wrath of God, while hoisting a crucifix above their heads.

The matter ended with the mines being closed down for some time, and the first to experience the devastation were the instigators of the uprising. As day laborers in the mines with no other means of livelihood, they were compelled to suffer from the damage they themselves had wrought.

Some troops were sent up from Mexico City with orders to put down the revolt. Some [instigators] were hanged in Mexico City; others less culpable were sent to labor in the garrison. And finally I made my little rounds, not finding alms at this time except by happenstance.

I have mentioned a few things about the mines, but there is a lot more that could be written about them ... I will only say that, after these lands were conquered by the Spaniards, such was the quantity of gold, silver, and other precious articles coming from there that all Europe has felt the effects and still feels the benefit.

Selection 3: A Description of Plantation Society in Portuguese Brazil

The Portuguese pioneered sugar cultivation in the New World in Pernambuco, a region in northeastern Brazil. Between 1816 and 1818, a French businessman named L. F. de Tollenare toured this region and its plantations. His report perceptively explains how access to land and labor combined with race to create a distinctive social hierarchy in Brazil. The planters who owned land, slaves, and sugar mills sat on top of this pyramid. Free whites, blacks, *pardos*, and Indians fell into subsequent levels depending upon whether they cultivated sugar or subsistence crops and whether they worked for themselves or others. Slaves were the foundation of this order, their labor absolutely necessary to the colony's economy.

Credit: *Children of God's Fire: A Documentary History of Black Slavery in Brazil*, ed. Robert Edgar Conrad (University Park, PA: Pennsylvania State University Press, 1994), 63–71.

I will divide the inhabitants of these regions into three classes (I am not speaking of the slaves, who are nothing but cattle). These three classes are:

1.   The owners of sugar mills [*senhores de engenho*], the great landowners.
2.   The *lavradores*, a type of tenant farmer.
3.   The *moradores*, squatters or small cultivators.

The sugar-mill owners are those who early received land grants from the crown, by donation or transfer. These subdivided grants constitute considerable properties even today, as can be seen from the expanses of 7,000 and 10,000 acres of which I spoke earlier; the crown does not have more lands to grant; foreigners should be made aware of this.

There are some sugar-mill owners who interest themselves in the theoretical aspects of agriculture and who make some effort to improve the methods of cultivation and production. I was conscious of their existence, at least, because of the derision of which they were the object. I visited six mills and encountered few notable men.

With bare legs, clad in a shirt and drawers or a dressing gown of printed calico, the sugar-mill owner, armed with a whip and visiting the dependencies of his estate, is a king who has only animals about him: his blacks; his squatters or *moradores*, slaves whom he mistreats; and some hostile vassals who are his tenants or *lavradores*.

The great distances and lack of security on the roads do not encourage contacts with neighbors. Not even in the church are there opportunities to meet, because each mill either has its own chapel, or, what is more frequently the case, there isn't any church and no religious worship is carried on at all. The Portuguese government, which requires that a chaplain sail aboard merchant ships, would perhaps promote the progress of civilization by ordering that a priest be maintained at mills which have a certain number of blacks.

When a sugar-mill owner visits another one, the ladies do not make their appearance. I spent two days in the house of one of them, a very charming man who overwhelmed me with kindness, and I did not see his family either in the living room or at the dinner table. On a different occasion I arrived unexpectedly after supper at the house of another of them, the splendor of which promised better taste; I noticed on the floor a piece of embroidery which seemed to have been tossed there suddenly. I asked for a glass of water in order to have a chance to go into the next room, but they made me wait for a long time. The lady of the house prepared a choice meal, but I did not see her. Furthermore, the same thing happened to me in a country house near Recife that belonged to a native of Lisbon.

In these houses, where the owners reside for the whole year, one does not observe anything fashioned to make them comfortable; one does not even find the avenue which among [the French] adorn both the simple property and the sumptuous chateau, neither parks, nor gardens, nor walks, nor pavilions. Living in the midst of forests, the inhabitants seem to fear shadows; or, more precisely stated, up to the edge of the forest around the mill everything is denuded and scorched to a distance of a quarter of a league. I witnessed at Salgado [a sugar plantation near the town of Cabo] the cutting down for firewood of orange groves which the previous owner had planted near the house, either for his pleasure or his profit.

Generally the residences are elevated on pillars; the cellar serves as a stable or as a dwelling place for the blacks; a long stairway provides access to the main floor, and it is on this level, or terrace, where one can enjoy the cool air. The rooms do not have ceilings; instead the timber-work of the roof is exposed and, between its extremities and the walls that hold it up, there is a free space of five inches to increase the air currents. The interior divisions are made with simple lath partitions measuring nine to ten feet in height, so that all the rooms have the roof as a common ceiling.

Luxury consists of a great variety of silverware. When a foreigner is entertained, in order to wash himself, he is given splendid vessels made of this metal, of which also the coffee trays used at table, the bridles and stirrups for the horses, and knife hilts are made. Some sugar-mill owners showed me luxurious and expensive English firearms, and I also saw porcelain tea sets from England of the most beautiful type.

I ought to say a few words about meals. Supper consists of an abundant and thick soup, in which garlic abounds, or some other plant of a very pronounced and disagreeable taste which I did not recognize. The first plate is boiled meat which is not very succulent, the tastelessness of which they try to conceal with bacon, which is always a little rancid, and with manioc flour, which each serves himself with his fingers. For a second plate, they serve a chicken ragout and rice with pepper. Bread is not seen, although it is much appreciated; they could manufacture it from foreign flour, which Recife is well supplied with, but it is not the custom. The black men or mulatto women (I saw many of the latter serving at table) fill the glasses with wine as soon as they are emptied, but people do not persist in drinking; liqueurs are not served with dessert.

***

The sugar-mill owners are the only landholders. The only exceptions I know of are some chapels erected 100 or 150 years ago by the piety of the Portuguese and endowed with 50 to 60 uncultivated acres ... The extension of the lands owned by the mills is therefore immense, and the capital invested in them is much less considerable than it was in the French [Caribbean] islands. Only the most important establishments have 140 to 150 blacks. One could estimate the importance of the mills by the number of slaves, if it were not for the existence of the *lavradores*.

The *lavradores* are tenants without leases. They plant cane, but do not own mills. They send the harvested cane to the mill that they are dependent upon, where it is transformed into sugar. Half of it belongs to the *lavrador* and half to the sugar-mill owner. The latter keeps the molasses, but furnishes the cases for the sugar. Each one pays his tithe separately. The *lavradores* normally possess from six to ten blacks and themselves wield the hoe. They are Brazilians of European descent, little mixed with mulattoes. I counted from two to three *lavradores* per mill.

This class is truly worthy of interest since it possesses some capital and performs some labor. Nevertheless, the law protects it less than it does the mill owners. Since they do not make contracts, once a piece of land becomes productive, the mill owner has the right to expel them without paying compensation. It should be recognized that leases of only a year are not very favorable to agriculture. The *lavrador* builds only a miserable hut, does not try to improve the soil, and makes only temporary fences, because from one year to the next he can be expelled, and then all his labor is lost. He invests his capital in slaves and cattle, which he can always take with him ...

***

If I estimate an average of eight blacks for each *lavrador*, and sugar production at fifty *arrobas* [about 1,600 pounds] per slave, which is not too much considering the vigilance and labor of the master himself, I can calculate the annual income of each *lavrador* at four hundred *arrobas* of sugar [about 12,800 pounds], which six or seven years ago was sold for about 3,000 francs. Now, this income is clear, since the *lavrador* does not buy anything at all to feed his blacks, and he lives very frugally from the manioc he plants.

Therefore, this class of capitalists, if favored by the government, is destined some day to exercise a major role in the political economy of Brazil. Consider the influence that they would have if the government would guarantee leases for nine years, and especially if an agrarian law were adopted that would obligate the present owners to make concessions, at stipulated prices, of certain parts of their uncultivated lands to anyone who might wish to buy them. Yet today everything remains exactly the opposite. I was witness to a rich mill owner's expulsion from his property of *all* the *lavradores* and squatters whom his less wealthy predecessors had allowed to establish themselves there. The number of exiles reached almost 600 persons, the property measuring two square leagues in size [about thirty square miles].

***

The *lavradores* are quite proud to receive on a basis of equality the foreigner who comes to visit them. Under the pretext of seeking shelter, I entered the houses of several to speak with them. The women disappeared as in the homes of ladies, though I was always offered sweets. I never managed to get them to accept the little presents of cheap jewelry which I had supplied myself with for the trip. This noble pride caused me to respect the hard-working *lavradores*, a class intermediate between the haughty mill owner and the lazy, subservient, and humble squatter. The *lavrador* has a miserable house, for the reasons I have already mentioned. However, when he abandons the hoe to go to Serinhaem [a nearby town] or to church, he dresses himself up like a city man, rides a good horse, and has stirrups and spurs made of silver.

The *moradores* or squatters are small settlers to whom the sugar-mill owners grant permission to erect a hut in the middle of the forest and to farm a small piece of land. The rent they pay is very small, worth at the most a tenth part of their gross product, without an obligation to pay the royal tithe. Like the *lavradores*, they do not have a contract, and the master can send them away whenever he wishes. As a general rule, they are mixtures of mulattoes, free blacks, and Indians, but Indians and pure blacks are rarely encountered among them. This free class comprises the true Brazilian population, an impoverished people because they perform little labor. It would seem logical that from this class a number of salaried workers would emerge, but this does not happen. The squatter refuses work, he plants a little manioc, and lives in idleness. His wife has a small income because, if the manioc crop is good, she can sell a bit of it and buy some clothing. This comprises their entire expense, because their furniture consists of only a few mats and clay pots. Not even a manioc scraper is found in all their houses.

The squatters live isolated, far from civil and religious authority, without comprehending, so to speak, the value of property. They replaced the Brazilian savages but have less value, since the latter at least had some political and national affiliation. The squatters know only their surroundings, and look upon all outsiders practically as enemies. The sugar-mill owners court their women for their pleasure; they flatter them greatly, but from these seductions acts of vengeance as well as stabbings result. Generally speaking, this class is hated and feared. Because they pay them little or badly and often rob them, the sugar-mill owners who have the right to dismiss the squatters fear taking this dangerous step in a country that lacks police. Assassinations are common, but do not result in any pursuit whatsoever. I knew a certain mill owner who did not travel alone a quarter of a league from his house, because of the hostility and treachery of his squatters. He had incurred their wrath, and I had similar reasons to fear them when I entered their huts.

***

I promised to make a quick survey of the black population. I am not in possession, however, of enough information about the laws that govern them to be able to deal with the matter adequately. Here is what I can say at the moment in respect to them.

The Salgrado mill contains about 130 to 140 slaves, including those of all ages, but there is no written list of them. Deducting the children, the sick, and the people employed in domestic service and in the infirmary, there remain only about a hundred people who are fit for agricultural labor. During the four or five months that the sugar harvest lasts, the toil of the mill blacks is most violent; they alternate so as to be able to stay on their feet for eighteen hours. I said earlier that they received for food a pound of manioc flour and seven ounces of meat. Here it is distributed already cooked. There are few properties on which slaves are allowed to plant something for themselves. Passing through the forests, I sometimes came upon small clearings where the blacks had come secretly to plant a little manioc. These were certainly not the lazy ones. Nevertheless, Gonçalo [a slave] told me not to speak about it to their master, because this could expose them to punishment.

Upon arrival from Africa, the blacks who have not been baptized in Angola, Mozambique, or another place where there are Portuguese governors, receive baptism upon disembarking; this is nothing but a pointless formality, because they are not given any instruction whatsoever. At certain mills, I saw the blacks being married by the priest, but in others they are united only by their whims or inclinations. In either case the master may sell separately the husband and the wife and the children to another buyer, regardless of how young they may be. A black baby is worth 200 francs at birth. Some masters make their slaves hear mass, but others save the cost of a chaplain, claiming that the sacrifice of the mass is a matter too grand for such people. Finally, there are mill owners who are more or less formalistic in matters of religion, and more or less able to appreciate its influence upon the conduct and habits of their slaves. It seems to me that it is in the interest of the masters to maintain family ties.

At the Salgado mill, I saw only good slave quarters; everywhere, for that matter, they are of stone and lime and well roofed. Those of Salgado are ten feet wide and fifteen feet in depth, with a small interior division forming almost two rooms. It has a door which can be locked with a key, and a round opening toward the field to provide ventilation. The brick floor is two feet above the level of the adjacent ground, which makes such houses much more healthful than those of many French peasants. Each black is supposed to have his own private room, but love and friendship generally prevent them from living alone.

A mat, a clay cup or a gourd, sometimes a few claypots, and some tatters and rags make up the furnishings of the home of a black couple. All have permission to light a fire in their rooms and they take advantage of it. Their food is furnished to them already prepared, so that they have no need to cook. However, the fire is a distraction for them and serves for preparing fish or other food which they manage to acquire, lawfully or not. I observed that they were very careful to lock their doors and that when they were barred inside their houses they opened them with great reluctance. Although I was rather friendly with them in Salgado, I had some difficulty in satisfying my curiosity regarding the interior of their huts. I also saw some of the latter that were made of mud and covered with cocoa leaves.

***

The black women generally have a flexible and elegant figure, the shoulders and arms very well formed. Many are seen who could qualify as pretty women if their necks were longer, giving more freedom to their heads. Their breasts are firm and fleshy, and they seem to understand their value, proving themselves very wise by concealing them, since this, in fact, is the way they commit terrible sins. It is unusual to see a black woman, even seventeen or eighteen years of age, whose neck has retained the shape which we prize so much and which European art imitates more or less badly. Nevertheless, they are not without a certain ability to hide its flaccidness [goiter?] with a piece of blue or red cloth. They tie these under their armpits, arrange the draping nicely over their waists and thighs, and make a large knot over the bosom, which hides the deformity I have just mentioned. The shoulders remain naked and the knees nearly uncovered, the scantiness of the cloth, which is made even tinier because of the part reserved for creating the knot, betraying all the body's movements, and I must say that they are all attractive and very graceful ... Their legs are normal, but their feet are damaged by hard work and the lack of footwear. They habitually have their heads uncovered, though some are given round hats which are not very becoming to them. They are happy when they can adorn themselves with a necklace or some bits of jewelry. Many of them, lacking such ornaments, attach a feather or a small round stick of wood to their ears. A tobacco pipe a foot long is usually thrust through the knotted cloth over the breast, and there it figures majestically like the dagger belonging to a leading lady of the theater.

This is the portrait of the black women who fix themselves up a bit. One sees others in a state of abandonment which is much less picturesque, dressed in a tattered shirt and an old petticoat which leaves the part beneath the breasts uncovered. Always, however, when they wrap their bodies or heads with a piece of cloth, the result is quite agreeable.

***

The men have a better appearance when they are naked than the women, because of the flabbiness of the breasts that disfigures the latter. They are less robust than our porters, but the habit of going about without clothing makes their movements less wooden. What they possess that is better are their arched chests and their sinewy thighs. It is rare to see gray and wrinkled persons among them. Their black, shiny-smooth skin, destitute of hair, allows one to observe the entire play of their very active muscles. The arms and especially the legs are usually weak, but I saw some blacks with Apollo-like physiques.

Those coming from Africa have their shoulders, arms, and chests covered with symmetrical marks, which seem to be made with a hot iron, and the women also display these marks. For clothing the men are given a shirt and some breeches, but these garments evidently make them uncomfortable, and few preserve them, particularly the shirts. Most of the time they are satisfied with tying a rope around their loins from which hangs, both in front and behind, a small piece of cloth with which they try to hide that which modesty does not permit them to display.

The children also get clothing, but they make quick work of it so that they can go about naked. When they reach fourteen or fifteen years of age, they are beaten with switches to make them more careful. At that time some are seen wearing their shirts hung over one shoulder in the fashion of Roman patricians, and, seen thus, they are reminiscent of Greek statues.

The blacks employed in domestic service, or close to their masters, dress with less elegance and more in the European manner. They take care of their breeches and shirts and sometimes even possess a waistcoat. Gonçalo had an embroidered shirt, and when he wore his lace hat and small trinkets which I had given him his pride was greater than that of any dandy; but when we went out hunting, his greatest pleasure was to leave at both his necessary and unnecessary items of clothing.

Discussion Questions

1. According to Gage, what abuses did Indian workers suffer as a result of the *repartimiento* system? In what ways did this labor system serve as a kind of enslavement?
2. Briefly describe the different racial castes Bergamo finds in Mexican society. What different habits and attitudes does he attribute to each of these castes? How do you think his racial attitudes shaped his description of the labor unrest he witnessed in Real del Monte?
3. In Tollenare's description of Brazil's social order, what groups occupy positions between white planters and African slaves? How does the type of work a person does in this society help define his or her place within it?
4. Religion and race were key factors in shaping the hierarchy of colonial societies in Iberian America. Compare and contrast how these readings describe the spiritual condition of non-Europeans; what motives did the Spanish and Portuguese have for converting the Indians and Africans who worked for them?

Suggested Readings

For works that consider the colonization of Iberian America in a trans-Atlantic context, see J. H. Elliott, *Spain and Its World, 1500–1700: Selected Essays* (New Haven, CT: Yale University Press, 1989); and A. J. R. Russell-Wood, *The Portuguese Empire, 1415–1808: A World on the Move* (Baltimore, MD: Johns Hopkins University Press, 1998). For works that compare the development of the Iberian empires with the British Empire, see J. H. Elliott, *Empires of the Atlantic World: Britain and Spain in America, 1492–1830* (New Haven, CT: Yale University Press, 2006); and Jorge Cañizares-Esguerra, ed., *Entangled Empires: The Anglo-Iberian Atlantic, 1500–1830* (Philadelphia, PA: University of Pennsylvania Press, 2018). The best overview of Iberian America that treats both the Spanish and Portuguese is James Lockhart and Stuart B. Schwartz, *Early Latin America: A History of Colonial Spanish America and Brazil* (Cambridge: Cambridge University Press, 1983).

For the Spanish Conquest and the colonial societies that developed in its wake, see Matthew Restall, *Seven Myths of the Spanish Conquest* (New York: Oxford University Press,

2003); Nancy M. Farriss, *Maya Society under Colonial Rule: The Collective Enterprise of Survival* (Princeton, NJ: Princeton University Press, 1984); and Inga Clendinnen, *Ambivalent Conquests: Maya and Spaniard in Yucatan, 1517–1570* (Cambridge: Cambridge University Press, 1987). Useful studies of how racial intermarriage shaped Spanish America's social order include R. Douglas Cope, *The Limits of Racial Domination: Plebian Society in Colonial Mexico City, 1660–1720* (Madison, WI: University of Wisconsin Press, 1994); and Rebecca Earle, "The Pleasures of Taxonomy: Casta Paintings, Classification, and Colonialism," *William and Mary Quarterly*, third series, 73 (July 2016): 479–520. A classic study of intermarriage in Brazil and its effects on the slave system and social order there is Carl N. Degler, *Neither Black Nor White: Slavery and Race Relations in Brazil and the United States* (Madison, WI: University of Wisconsin Press, 1971). For Brazil, see also James H. Sweet, *Recreating Africa: Culture, Kinship, and Religion in the African-Portuguese World, 1441–1770* (Chapel Hill, NC: University of North Carolina Press, 2003).

8 The Dutch, French, and English in North America

Figure 8.1 Cityscape of New Amsterdam in 1655.

New Amsterdam was renowned for its multi-ethnic character and commercial orientation (see Selection 1). It played a central role in shipping furs from the interior of North America to Europe and was part of the Dutch trading network in the Atlantic World. This illustration from a map of New Netherland shows the city of New Amsterdam (modern New York City) at the southern tip of Manhattan Island. Note the images of Native Americans surrounding the cityscape. What information do you think the artist was trying to convey about New Netherland by including these figures on this map?

Source credit: Courtesy of the New York State Library, Manuscripts and Special Collections.

Introduction

Europeans colonized North America at a much slower pace than South America or the Caribbean, but not because they were unaware of it. The problem was that they could find none of the gold and silver enriching the Spanish *conquistadors* in Mexico and Peru. For more than a century after Columbus, European encounters with North America were motivated not so much by a desire to exploit the continent as to get around it. Merchants and mapmakers imagined a Northwest Passage that would carry ships into the Pacific and westward to Japan and China. Such dreams did not die easily, even as they claimed the lives and fortunes of those who pursued them.

The first Europeans to draw a profit from North America were fishing crews that set up seasonal camps in Nova Scotia and Newfoundland to catch and dry the cod that swam offshore in the Grand Banks. These expeditions occasionally included contact with the native inhabitants of the region, in which the visitors exchanged manufactured goods such as cloth, kettles, and liquor for the pelts of furbearing animals. In the Southeast, the Chesapeake Bay region attracted pirates seeking a refuge from which they could launch raids against the Spanish treasure fleets in the Caribbean.

Fish, furs, and a place to hide: hardly as enticing as gold and silver. Yet the Dutch, French, and English gradually warmed to the idea of colonizing North America and in doing so, integrated it into the Atlantic World. These powers pioneered the use of joint-stock companies, which worked much like modern corporations, raising money by selling shares to investors and splitting any profits among them. Indian relations figured prominently in the success or failure of these ventures, and the Dutch, French, and English competed fiercely with each other for the native alliances that would ensure a profitable fur trade. From the start, their colonies developed close economic ties to the plantation complex in the Caribbean, opening a conduit for trade and migration from that region by which African slavery gained footholds in North America.

In describing North American colonization, it is helpful to call to mind the different models followed by the Spanish and Portuguese (see Chapter 7). While there were distinctive elements to the Dutch, French, and English endeavors, each also represented a variation on practices first pursued by the Iberian powers. The Dutch regarded North America in much the same way as the Portuguese did Brazil, as one outpost in a global trading network. Indeed, the Dutch entered the race for empire in the late sixteenth century on the heels of the Portuguese, successfully challenging their monopoly on trade with India and the Spice Islands of Southeast Asia, and then briefly controlling Portuguese possessions in Africa and Brazil in the 1630s and 1640s.

During this period of rapid overseas expansion, Amsterdam merchants formed the West India Company to oversee their commercial interests in the New World. This joint-stock venture established the colony of New Netherland in North America. The Dutch claimed a broad expanse of territory between the Delaware and Connecticut Rivers, but the heart of New Netherland was the Hudson River Valley. At the northern end, 150 miles into the continent's interior, traders at Fort Orange (modern Albany) collected furs from the Indians. They shipped them downriver to New Amsterdam (modern New York City), a seaport that attracted a diverse group of merchants and mariners. When the French missionary Isaac Jogues visited the city in 1643, he noted that its inhabitants spoke eighteen different languages and professed six different faiths. Dutch ships sailing between Africa, Brazil, the Caribbean, and New Netherland carried much of seventeenth-century North America's international trade, including the first African slaves brought to the continent. The West India Company tried to recruit settlers for New Netherland, but as long as the fur trade dominated the colony's economy, its population remained small and transient. Squeezed by more populous colonies to the north and south, New Netherland capitulated to the English in 1664, who renamed it New York. Many Dutch mercantile families chose to remain there under English rule, and they continued to influence the cultural and economic development of this region well into the eighteenth century.

The French colonization of North America curiously blended Spanish and Portuguese precedents. As with the Spanish, missionary work among Native Americans was a central prop of French colonial power. Religious orders dedicated solely to this task made converts in Indian villages along the St. Lawrence and Great Lakes waterways; when they achieved a critical mass, they resettled the Christian Indians in *reserves* closer to French settlements (see Chapter 4), where they formed a bulwark against the French colonists' Native and European enemies. Unlike the Spanish, the French did not forcibly convert Natives, nor did they demand tributary labor from them. Instead, their missionary work went hand in hand with the extension of their trade. Following tactics reminiscent of the Portuguese in West Africa, French missionaries converted natives while traders intermarried with them, creating a cooperative relationship by which the newcomers extracted a valuable commodity from the continent's interior, in this case furs rather than slaves.

The French empire in North America consisted primarily of allied Indian villages, inland forts, and the canoes that ferried people and goods between them. French colonists known as *habitants* worked farms in the St. Lawrence River Valley and the eastern Canadian province known as Acadia (modern Nova Scotia). French traders, soldiers, and missionaries followed the Great Lakes westward and built forts at portages between these waterways, such as Niagara, Detroit, and Michilimackinac. By the early eighteenth century, the French had navigated the Mississippi and established posts in the Illinois country and Louisiana. Yet, for all their skillful navigation of the continent's interior, the French never achieved a stable rate of population growth in North America. The Crown encouraged and sometimes even compelled emigration to Canada, but most would-be settlers found the French sugar colonies in the Caribbean more enticing. When France and Britain went to war in 1754 for control of North America, French influence extended over far more territory, but their colonial population of 80,000 was dwarfed by the one million inhabitants of the British colonies. The French found the defense of their North American dominions untenable, and in 1763, they ceded Canada to Britain and Louisiana to Spain.

As has already been hinted at, the great advantage the English enjoyed over their imperial rivals in North America was the rapid growth of their colonial population. This would suggest that the English followed the example of the Spanish, conquering native peoples and planting settlers in their place. Early English incursions into the Chesapeake Bay did resemble Spanish *entradas*: small expeditions of privately financed adventurers searched for gold and silver and dealt harshly with any natives who resisted them. But unlike the Spanish, the English were reluctant to intermarry with Indians, and no equivalent of Spanish America's *mestizo* population emerged in the English colonies. Instead, English migration to North America in the seventeenth century was marked by more balanced sex ratios between male and female colonists than anywhere else in the Atlantic World. The religious groups that populated New England (Puritans) and New Jersey and Pennsylvania (Quakers) tended to migrate as families, and in the temperate climate of those northern colonies, they enjoyed lower mortality rates and higher birth rates than colonists in the tropics. In the Chesapeake Bay region, early English emigration had a more skewed sex ratio, roughly six males to every female, but one that was still considerably more balanced than in Spanish America (10:1) or Brazil (20:1).

African slaves made up another significant portion of British North America's colonial population. While every English colony recognized and sanctioned the institution of slavery, only those south of Pennsylvania developed into slave societies on the model of the plantation complex. In the Chesapeake, slaves cultivated tobacco and accounted for 40 percent of the colonial population. In South Carolina, a colony that was initially settled by planters and slaves from Barbados, slaves accounted for 60 percent of the population, making it the only colony in North America with a black majority. Like their European counterparts, Africans living in North America generally found a healthier climate than in other regions of the New World, and they achieved a positive rate of reproduction by the mid-eighteenth century, a demographic feat unmatched in any other Atlantic zone of colonization at that time.

North America's most striking difference with the other zones of New World colonization was its failure to develop an interracial population similar to Spanish America's *mestizos* or Brazil's *pardos*. Only the French exhibited anything like the Iberian penchant for incorporating strangers into their colonial society by intermarriage, and sexual unions between French traders and Indian women produced a significant *métis* population in western Canada. The English, on the other hand, avoided such practices. In their plantation colonies, they prohibited marriage between blacks and whites, and the English colonial social order afforded little room or opportunity to people of multiracial heritage. Whereas the meeting of Africans, Indians, and Europeans in Iberian America created new interracial groups and social orders, the same encounter in North America had by 1750 produced a population sharply divided into racial categories of black, red, and white.

The readings in this chapter describe the colonization of North America from the Dutch, French, and English perspectives. In the first selection, a Dutch traveler in the late seventeenth

Map 8.1 The Dutch, French, and English in North America.

Dutch, French, and English zones of colonization in North America.

century comments on the ethnic diversity of New Amsterdam/New York City and its inhabitants' relations with the local Indians. In the second, a French military officer during the 1750s compares the Christian Indians and non-Christian Indians of New France. In the third, an inhabitant of Philadelphia discusses English colonial population growth and what he sees as the future of Indians, Africans, and Europeans in North America. As you read these sources, compare them to each other and what you learned about the Spanish and Portuguese in Chapter 7. How did the Dutch, French, and English experiences parallel and diverge from each other? What factors best explain the very different ways in which Africans, Indians, and Europeans interacted with each other in North America and South America?

Selection 1: A Dutch Traveler in New Netherland/New York, 1679–1680

Jasper Danckaerts was a native of the Netherlands who belonged to a Protestant sect known as the Labadists. From 1679 to 1680, he traveled in North America with a fellow believer to investigate moving their church across the Atlantic (they eventually settled in Maryland). Although the Dutch had ceded New Netherland to the English in the 1660s, the society Danckaerts encountered in the Hudson Valley was still predominantly Dutch in character, and he quickly felt at home. The diary he kept during his American sojourn provides an interesting look at New Netherland's population as it moved from Dutch to English rule. In the passages that follow, Danckaerts describes his visit to Staten Island and his negative impressions of the Dutch fur trade (see Figure 8.1).

Credit: *Journal of Jasper Danckaerts, 1679–1680*, eds. Bartlett Burleigh James and J. Franklin Jameson (New York: C. Scribner's Sons, 1913), 69–70, 76–80.

11th, Wednesday. We embarked early this morning in his boat and rowed over to Staten Island, where we arrived about eight o'clock. He [a ferryman] left us there, and we went on our way. This island is about thirty-two miles long and four broad. Its sides are very irregular, with projecting points and indented bays, and creeks running deep into the country. It lies for the most part east and west, and is somewhat triangular. The most prominent point is to the west. On the east side is the narrow passage which they call the channel, by which it is separated from the high point of Long Island. On the south is the great bay which is inclosed by Nayaq, Conijnen Island, Rentselaer's Hook, Nevesinck, etc. On the west is the Raritans. On the north or northwest is New Garnisee [Jersey], from which it is separated by a large creek or arm of the river, called Kil van Kol. The eastern part is high and steep, and has few inhabitants. It is the usual place where ships, ready for sea, stop to take in water, while the captain and passengers are engaged in making their own arrangements and writing letters previous to their departure. The whole south side is a large plain, with much salt meadow or marsh, and several creeks. The west point is flat, and on or around it is a large creek with much marsh; but to the north of this creek it is high and hilly, and beyond that it begins to be more level, but not so low as on the other side, and is well populated. On the northwest it is well provided with creeks and marshes, and the land is generally better than on the south side, although there is a good parcel of land in the middle of the latter. As regards the middle or most hilly part of the island, it is uninhabited, although the soil is better than the land around it; but, in consequence of its being away from the water, and lying so high, no one will live there, the creeks and rivers being so serviceable to them in enabling them to go to the city, and for fishing and catching oysters, and for being near the salt meadows. The woods are used for pasturing horses and cattle, for being an island, none of them can get off. Each person has marks upon his own by which he can find them when he wants them. When the population of the country shall increase, these places will be taken up. Game of all kinds is plenty, and twenty-five and thirty deer are sometimes seen in a herd. A boy who came into a house where we were, told us he had shot ten the last winter himself, and more than forty in his life, and in the same manner other game. We tasted here the best grapes. There are now about a hundred families on the island, of which the English constitute the least portion, and the Dutch and French divide between them about equally the greater portion. They have neither church nor minister, and live rather far from each other, and inconveniently to meet together. The English are less disposed to religion, and inquire little after it, but in case there were a minister, would contribute to his support. The French and Dutch are very desirous and eager for one, for they spoke of it wherever we went, and said, in the event of not obtaining Domine Tessemaker, they would send, or had sent, to France for another. The French are good Reformed churchmen, and some of them are Walloons [Protestants from modern Belgium]. The Dutch are also from different quarters.

***

16th, Monday. I was occupied to-day in copying my journal. In the morning there came an Indian to our house, a man about eighty years of age, whom our people called Jasper, who lived at Ahakinsack or at Ackinon [Hackensack]. Concerning this Indian our old people related that when they lived on Long Island, it was once a very dear time; no provisions could be obtained, and they suffered great want, so that they were reduced to the last extremity; that God the Lord then raised up this Indian, who went out fishing daily in order to bring fish to them every day when he caught a good mess, which he always did. If, when he came to the house, he found it alone, and they were out working in the fields, he did not fail, but opened the door, laid the fish on the floor, and proceeded on his way. For this reason these people possess great affection for him and have given him the name of Jasper, and also my *nitap*, that is, my great friend. He never comes to the Manhatans without visiting them and eating with them, as he now did, as among his old friends. We asked him why he had done so much kindness to these people. "I have always been inclined," he answered, "from my youth up to do good, especially to good people known to me. I took the fish to them because Maneto [the spirit] said to me, you must take fish to these people, whispering ever in my ear 'You must take fish to them.' I had to do it, or Maneto would have killed me." Our old woman telling us he sometimes got drunk, we said to him he should not do so any more, that the Great Sakemacker [God] who is above, was offended at such conduct and would kill him. "No," said he, laughing as if that were a mistake of ours, "it is Maneto who kills those who do evil, and leaves those who do good at peace." "That is only," we replied, "because Maneto is the slave and executioner of the Great Sakemacker above," and we then asked him if he believed there was such a great and good *sakemacker* there? "Undoubtedly," he said, "but he remains above, and does not trouble himself with the earth or earthly things, because he does nothing except what is good; but Maneto, who also is a *sakemacker*, is here below, and governs all, and punishes and torments those men who do evil and drink themselves drunk." Hereupon we inquired of him why he did so then. "Yes," he said, "I had rather not, but my heart is so inclined that it causes me to do it, although I know it is wrong. The Christians taught it to us, and give us or sell us the drink, and drink themselves drunk." We said to him: "Listen! if we came to live near you, you would never see us drunk, nor would we give or sell you or your people any rum." "That," he replied, "would be good." We told him he must not make such a difference between himself and a Christian, because one was white and the other red, and one wore clothes and the other went almost naked, or one was called a Christian and the other an Indian, that this great and good Sakemacker was the father of us all, and had made us all, and that all who did not do good would be killed by Maneto whether they were called Christians or Indians; but that all who should do good would go to this good *sakemacker* above. "Yes," said he, "we do not know or speak to this *sakemacker*, but Maneto we know and speak to, but you people, who can read and write, know and converse with this *sakemacker*."

We asked him, where he believed he came from? He answered from his father. "And where did your father come from?" we said, "and your grandfather and great-grandfather, and so on to the first of the race?" He was silent for a little while, either as if unable to climb up at once so high with his thoughts, or to express them without help, and then took a piece of coal out of the fire where he sat, and began to write upon the floor. He first drew a circle, a little oval, to which he made four paws or feet, a head and a tail. "This," said he, "is a tortoise, lying in the water around it," and he moved his hand round the figure, continuing, "This was or is all water, and so at first was the world or the earth, when the tortoise gradually raised its round back up high, and the water ran off of it, and thus the earth became dry." He then took a little straw and placed it on end in the middle of the figure, and proceeded, "The earth was now dry, and there grew a tree in the middle of the earth, and the root of this tree sent forth a sprout beside it and there grew upon it a man, who was the first male. This man was then alone, and would have remained alone; but the tree bent over until its top touched the earth, and there shot therein another root, from which came forth another sprout, and there grew upon it the woman, and from these two are all men produced." We gave him four fishhooks with which he was much pleased, and immediately calculated how much in money he had obtained. "I have got twenty-four stivers' [Dutch coins] worth," he said. He then inquired our names, which we gave him, and wished to know why he asked for them? "Well," he replied, "because you are good people and are true *nitaps*; and in case you should come into the woods and fall into the hands of the Indians, and they should wish to kill or harm you, if I know or hear of it I might help you, for they will do you no injury when they know me." For he was the brother of a *sakemacker*. We told him that we did not give them to him on that account, but only from regard because he was a good person, although the good will or thankfulness which he wished to show thereby was good. "Well," he said, "that is good, that is good," with which, after eating something, he departed.

But at noon he returned with a young Indian, both of them so drunk they could not speak, and having a calabash [bowl] of liquor with them. We chided him, but to no purpose, for he could neither use his reason nor speak so as to be understood. The young Indian with him was a *sakemacker*'s son, and was bold. He wanted to have a piece of meat that was on the table, and on which we all had to make our dinner, when we told him it was not for him. "Yes," said he, "I see it is so;" nevertheless, and although we offered him something else to eat, he was evilly disposed and dissatisfied, and would take nothing except the piece of meat alone; but that was not given to him. Whereupon Jasper told him he must be quiet, that the old people and we were all his *nitaps*, and by degrees quieted him, they sitting together by the fire and drinking their rum. They left afterwards for Long Island.

17th, Tuesday. Nothing transpired to-day.

18th, Wednesday. In the afternoon Jasper, the Indian, came back again, and proceeded confidently to our room in the rear of the house, but sober and in his senses. He told us how he had been with his nephew, the *sakemacker*'s son, to Long Island, among the other Indians; and that he had given away, not only his fish-hooks, but also his shoes and stockings. We found fault with him at first for having become so drunk, contrary to his promise, and when he well knew it was wrong. To which he said he had to buy some nails for an Englishman who lived near him, from another Englishman here, who had sold and given him the rum.

I must here remark, in passing, that the people in this city, who are almost all traders in small articles, whenever they see an Indian enter the house, who they know has any money, they immediately set about getting hold of him, giving him rum to drink, whereby he is soon caught and becomes half a fool. If he should then buy any thing, he is doubly cheated, in the wares, and in the price. He is then urged to buy more drink, which they now make half water, and if he cannot drink it, they drink it themselves. They do not rest until they have cajoled him out of all his money, or most of it; and if that cannot be done in one day, they keep him, and let him lodge and sleep there, but in some out of the way place, down on the ground, guarding their merchandise and other property in the meantime, and always managing it so that the poor creature does not go away before he has given them all they want. And these miserable Christians are so much the more eager in this respect, because no money circulates among themselves, and they pay each other in wares, in which they are constantly cheating and defrauding each other. Although it is forbidden to sell the drink to the Indians, yet every one does it, and so much the more earnestly, and with so much greater and burning avarice, that it is done in secret. To this extent and further, reaches the damnable and insatiable covetousness of most of those who here call themselves Christians. Truly, our hearts grieved when we heard of these things, which call so grievously upon the Supreme Judge for vengeance. He will not always let His name be so profaned and exposed to reproach and execration.

Selection 2: A French Military Officer Describes the Indians of Canada, 1757

Louis Antoine de Bougainville was an officer who served in the French army during the Seven Years' War (also known as the French and Indian War), the climactic struggle in the long Anglo-French rivalry for dominion in North America. As an aide-de-camp to the famous general the Marquis de Montcalm, Bougainville traveled extensively in Canada and witnessed first hand the symbiotic relationship between Indians and colonists that was the hallmark of French colonization there. At the end of the war, Bougainville returned to Europe and joined an exploratory voyage to the South Pacific. During the American Revolution, he visited America again, this time as a French naval officer.

As his globetrotting would indicate, Bougainville was a man of considerable curiosity, and his journal from the Seven Years' War is full of insights about the strengths and weaknesses of the French regime in North America. In the passages that follow, he describes Montcalm's recruitment of Indian allies for his 1757 campaign against the British in New York. During Montcalm's frequent diplomatic councils with the Indians, Bougainville learned to distinguish between the "domesticated Indians" who lived in French missionary villages and those Indians from the "Far West" (i.e., western Great Lakes region) who were considerably more autonomous.

Credit: *Adventure in the Wilderness: The American Journals of Louis Antoine de Bougainville, 1756–1760*, trans. and ed. Edward P. Hamilton (1964; Norman, OK: University of Oklahoma Press, 1990), 122–125, 146–148, 150.

July 9: The Marquis de Montcalm left today with MM. de Rigaud, St. Luc, de Longueil, Junior, and Abbé Piquet to go and sing the war song at the Lake and at Sault St. Louis. We have first been to the Lac Des Deux Montagnes, which is twelve or thirteen leagues from Montreal and is formed by the Ottawa River. North of this lake is an Indian village. Indians of three different nations live there, Nipissings, Algonkins, and Iroquois. They have three separate groups of houses, although all united in the same village. They have a common church, which is attractive and properly ornamented. Two Sulpician missionaries are in charge, one for the Nipissings and the Algonkins, the other for the Iroquois.

The Indians go to pray in the church three times a day, each in his own tongue, and they attend with exemplary devotion. They serve as choir boys and chanters. The men sit on one side and the women on the other, and the choir formed by the latter is very melodious.

The cabins are well enough built but very filthy. There is a special council house for each nation and a large one, which must be three hundred feet long, for the general councils of the three nations.

Upon our arrival we were saluted by a triple discharge of two swivels and of musketry from Indians lined up on the river bank, the missionaries at their head. They led us to the church and from there to the parsonage, where the principal chiefs came to compliment the Marquis de Montcalm. In the afternoon they held a council in which the Marquis de Montcalm told the Indians that he had come to see them and to give them through this visit marks of his friendship and esteem. Then he revealed to them the project planned against Fort George [Fort William Henry in New York], the union of all the Indians in order to co-operate in its execution, and the hope that the Marquis de Vaudreuil [governor-general of Canada] had that they, his children, and children of the true Faith, would help him with all their strength to destroy the common enemy. He ended by saying that he would give them three oxen for a feast and that he planned to sing the war song with them in the great council house. The Indians thanked the Marquis de Montcalm for his visit, assured him that they would follow his wishes and that in the evening they would tell him the number of warriors who would march with him.

We then visited the chiefs in their cabins. In the course of this we saw a Nipissing Indian, dishonored in the eyes of his brothers and of the Canadians because he wore breeches, covered his head, ate, dressed, and slept like a Frenchman. He goes neither to the hunt nor to war. He keeps a shop in his house filled especially with contraband goods, and he has a very lucrative business. The Indians scorn him, but do not reproach him or treat him badly. For in this place of complete liberty, *Trahit sua quemque voluptas* ["His own liking leads each on"]. This man reminds me of that thought that it is trade which most of all civilizes man.

In the evening we went to the council house, the Indians were sitting there on the floor, ranged by tribes. In the middle were hung at intervals pots filled with meat destined for the war feast. A few candles lighted up this place which seemed like a witches' cavern. Kisensik spoke first. After the ordinary compliments, he asked the Marquis de Montcalm for permission to give his advice on war when the occasion offered. He then outlined his tribe's requests and the number of warriors it would furnish. The chiefs of the other two nations then spoke on the same subjects. After the Marquis de Montcalm had replied to their proposals, Aoussik, seizing a bullock's head by the horns and stalking around with it, sang his war song. The other chiefs of the three nations followed him with the same ceremony, and I sang it in the name of M. de Montcalm and was much applauded. My song was nothing else but these words: "Trample the English underfoot" cadenced to the movement of Indian cries. They then presented the Marquis de Montcalm with the first morsel, and the war feast having started, we withdrew.

The next day, the tenth, we went to Sault St. Louis. Two canoes, each with ten naked Indians, the finest men of all the villages, painted for war in red and blue, adorned with bracelets of silver and of wampum, came before us on the river a quarter league from the Sault. They brought to the Marquis de Montcalm a letter from Father la Neuville, a Jesuit, who heads this mission, in which he advised him of the ceremony about to be observed. The two canoe loads, in truth a charming sight, held the attention of all the Europeans. On the river bank we found the missionary, who received the Marquis de Montcalm upon his stepping ashore, made a short speech and led him to the church between two rows of Indians who saluted him, the chiefs with their spears and the rest with a triple discharge from their guns. They sang the *Te Deum* [a Latin hymn] in the Iroquois tongue, after which the Marquis de Montcalm was led to the council chamber, where the chiefs joined him. The same propositions, the same answers, the same ceremonies as at the Lac Des Deux Montagnes, and moreover, that of covering, in the name of the Marquis de Vaudreuil, two dead Iroquois chiefs, and of presenting me to the nation as a candidate for adoption. Three oxen given for the war feast, which went off just like that of last night. The Iroquois adopted me during this feast and gave me the name of "Garionatsigoa," which means "Great Angry Sky." Behold me then, an Iroquois war chief! My clan is that of the Turtle, first for eloquence in council, but second for war, that of the Bear being first. They exhibited me to all the nation, gave me the first morsel of the war feast, and I sang my war song, in part with their first war chief. The others dedicated theirs to me.

I paid calls on all my clan and gave the wherewithall for feasts in all the cabins. As for the rest of it, the village at the Sault is attractive, laid out in regular form with a parade ground which divides it and serves as a riding field, for they have many horses and exercise them continually. The church is pretty and well decorated. The Indians have, as do those at the Lake, fields cultivated by their women, fowl and cattle, all individually owned. They sell, buy, and trade just like Frenchmen.

***

July 27: Today the Marquis de Montcalm went to camp at the Portage, where his presence was necessary to speed the arrangements for the colony troops, the brigading of the militia, the necessary distributions, and the assignment of bateaux [flat-bottomed boats for carrying supplies], etc. •

A grand council was held to reunite and bind together by a belt of six thousand beads the 40 nations who are here. The chiefs and orators of these nations composed the council.

Kisensik, famous Nipissing chief, opened it. "My brothers," he said to the nations of the Far West, "we domesticated Indians thank you for having come to help us defend our lands against the English who wish to usurp them. Our cause is good and the Master of Life favors it. Can you doubt it, my brothers, after the fine deed you have just accomplished. We admired it, we pay you our compliments. It covers you with glory, and Lake St. Sacrement [Lake George], stained red with the blood of Englishmen, will forever attest this exploit. Let me say that it also covers us with glory, we, your brothers, and we are proud of it. Our joy should be still greater than thine, my Father," said he, addressing the Marquis de Montcalm, "thou who hast passed over the great ocean, not for thine own interest, for it is not thy cause that thou hast come to defend, it is that of the great King who said: 'Go, cross the great ocean and go and defend my children.' He will reunite you, my brothers, and bind you together with the most solemn of ties. Accept this sacred bond with joy and let nothing ever break it."

This harangue was translated by the various interpreters and received with applause.

The Marquis de Montcalm then said to them, "My children, I am delighted to see you all reunited for the good work. So long as your union lasts the English will never be able to resist you. I cannot speak better to you than your brother, Kisensik, who has just spoken. The great King has without doubt sent me to protect and defend you, but he has above all charged me to see that you are made happy and invincible by establishing among you this friendship, this unity, this joining together to carry on the good work, which should exist among brothers, children of the same father, of the great Ononthio [Indian's name for the French governor-general]. I give you this belt as a sacred pledge of his word, symbol of good understanding and strength through the conjunction of the different beads which compose it. I bind you all together so that nothing can separate you before the defeat of the English and the destruction of Fort George."

This speech was then reported by the different interpreters and the belt thrown into the midst of the assembly.

It [the belt] was picked up by the orators of the different nations, who exhorted them to accept it, and Pennahouel, on presenting it to those of the Far West, said to them, "Behold a circle is drawn around you by the great Ononthio which none of us can leave. So long as we remain within its embrace the Master of Life will be our guide, will inspire us as to what we shall do and will favor all our enterprises. If some nation quits before the time, the Master of Life is not accountable for the evils that could hit them, but its misfortune will be its own and will not fall upon the nations who here promised an indissoluble union and complete obedience to their father's will." Once the orators had spoken in raising up the belt they put it down again in the midst of the assembly. The belt, following the custom of the nations, belongs to that one which has the greatest number of warriors in the army. It was without question granted to the Iroquois, who were and who almost always are the most numerous, and whose former victories over almost all of the nations of North America have given them a superior standing, which they continue to hold. They took the belt and their orator, addressing himself to the nations of the Far West, told them that, charmed by seeing their brothers reunited with them, and recognizing the help that they had just brought them for the defense of their lands, they begged them to accept this belt, pledge of their union, and to take it into their villages where it would be an eternal symbol of their friendship, of their common success, a witness which would keep in front of their eyes the happy results accomplished in this campaign, and would remind them to maintain forever this bond, the source of power of their warriors.

The Nipissing orator arose to tell the Iroquois: "My brothers, we are most thankful for this mark of respect you have shown to our brothers from the West. It was also our intention, and you have only anticipated us." One must note this procedure of the Nipissing. Its objective was to make the Iroquois realize that the Nipissings were the friends of all the Indians, and not to allow them to prescribe the right of precedence which their seniority gave them.

Pennahouel, in the name of the western Indians, thanked the Iroquois and accepted the belt. The different nations held a council that night to determine which one of them should keep it.

***

July 28: The Indians have turned in the sticks showing the number of men they expect to go on foot. The Nipissings wished to keep their people out of this division, claiming that it was needlessly tiring; they did not succeed.

The Miamis, to the number of eight, left without telling anyone. A Potawatomi chief told the Marquis de Montcalm of it and offered to try to bring them back. He was given a belt and strings [of wampum] to help him succeed.

An English corpse came floating by the Indians' camp. They crowded around it with loud cries, drank its blood, and put its pieces in the kettle. However, it was only the western Indians who committed these cruelties. Our domesticated ones took no part in it; they spent all day in confession.

Selection 3: Benjamin Franklin Calculates the Population of British North America

Benjamin Franklin had recently retired from his printing business when he wrote this famous essay, in which he tried to explain the causes of the rapid population growth in England's North American colonies. As an inhabitant of Philadelphia, Franklin was well positioned to observe the eighteenth-century influx of immigrants to the mid-Atlantic colonies, and his remarks on colonial marriage patterns and birth rates indicate his awareness of the unique environmental and demographic factors that shaped English colonization in North America. The most significant part of Franklin's argument, however, was the criticism it levied at the traditional European approach to colonization, including its reliance on African slave labor and restrictions on colonial economic development. Franklin offered instead a vision of empire in which prolific English farmers would create a captive market for England's manufactured goods. His remarks about Germans, Africans, and Indians and the roles they would play in the future of North America also reflect the English reluctance to incorporate strangers into their colonial social order via intermarriage and religious conversion.

Credit: Benjamin Franklin, "Observations Concerning the Increase of Mankind," in William Clark, *Observations on the Late and Present Conduct of the French with Regard to their Encroachments on the British Colonies in North America … to Which Is Added … Observations Concerning the Increase of Mankind* (Boston, MA: S. Kneeland, 1755), 2–15.

Europe is generally full settled with Husbandmen [farmers], Manufacturers, etc. and therefore cannot now much increase in People: America is chiefly occupied by Indians, who subsist mostly by Hunting. But as the Hunter, of all Men, requires the greatest Quantity of Land from whence to draw his Subsistence, (the Husbandman subsisting on much less, the Gardner on still less, and the Manufacturer requiring least of all), The Europeans found America as fully settled as it well could be by Hunters; yet these having large Tracks, were easily prevail'd on to part with Portions of Territory to the new Comers, who did not much interfere with the Natives in Hunting, and furnish'd them with many Things they wanted.

Land being thus plenty in America, and so cheap as that a labouring Man, that understands Husbandry, can in a short Time save Money enough to purchase a Piece of new Land sufficient for a Plantation, whereon he may subsist a Family; such are not afraid to marry; for if they even look far enough forward to consider how their Children when grown up are to be provided for, they see that more Land is to be had at Rates equally easy, all Circumstances considered.

Hence Marriages in America are more general, and more generally early, than in Europe. And if it is reckoned there, that there is but one Marriage per Annum [year] among 100 Persons, perhaps we may here reckon two; and if in Europe they have but 4 Births to a Marriage (many of their Marriages being late) we may here reckon 8, of which if one half grow up, and our Marriages are made, reckoning one with another at 20 Years of Age, our People must at least be doubled every 20 Years.

But notwithstanding this Increase, so vast is the Territory of North-America, that it will require many Ages to settle it fully; and till it is fully settled, Labour will never be cheap here, where no Man continues long a Labourer for others, but gets a Plantation of his own, no Man continues long a Journeyman to a Trade, but goes among those new Settlers, and sets up for himself, etc. Hence Labour is no cheaper now, in Pennsylvania, than it was 30 Years ago, tho' so many Thousand labouring People have been imported.

The Danger therefore of these Colonies interfering with their Mother Country in Trades that depend on Labour, Manufactures, etc. is too remote to require the Attention of Great-Britain.

But in Proportion to the Increase of the Colonies, a vast Demand is growing for British Manufactures, a glorious Market wholly in the Power of Britain, in which Foreigners cannot interfere, which will increase in a short Time even beyond her Power of supplying, tho' her whole Trade should be to her Colonies: Therefore Britain should not too much restrain Manufactures in her Colonies. A wise and good Mother will not do it. To distress, is to weaken, and weakening the Children, weakens the whole Family.

Besides if the Manufactures of Britain (by Reason of the American Demands) should rise too high in Price, Foreigners who can sell cheaper will drive her Merchants out of Foreign Markets; Foreign Manufactures will thereby be encouraged and increased, and consequently foreign Nations, perhaps her Rivals in Power, grow more populous and more powerful; while her own Colonies, kept too low, are unable to assist her, or add to her Strength.

'Tis an ill-grounded Opinion that by the Labour of Slaves, America may possibly vie in Cheapness of Manufactures with Britain. The Labour of Slaves can never be so cheap here as the Labour of working Men is in Britain. Any one may compute it. Interest of Money is in the Colonies from 6 to 10 per Cent. Slaves one with another cost £30 Sterling per Head. Reckon then the Interest of the first Purchase of a Slave, the Insurance or Risque on his Life, his Cloathing and Diet, Expences in his Sickness and Loss of Time, Loss by his Neglect of Business (Neglect is natural to the Man who is not to be benefited by his own Care or Diligence), Expence of a Driver to keep him at Work, and his Pilfering from Time to Time, almost every Slave being *by Nature* a Thief, and compare the whole Amount with the Wages of a Manufacturer of Iron or Wool in England, you will see that Labour is much cheaper there than it ever can be by Negroes here. Why then will Americans purchase Slaves? Because Slaves may be kept as long as a Man pleases, or has Occasion for their Labour; while hired Men are continually leaving their Master (often in the midst of his Business,) and setting up for themselves.

As the Increase of People depends on the Encouragement of Marriages, the following Things must diminish a Nation, viz. 1. The being conquered; for the Conquerors will engross as many Offices, and exact as much Tribute or Profit on the Labour of the conquered, as will maintain them in their new Establishment, and this diminishing the Subsistence of the Natives discourages their Marriages, and so gradually diminishes them, while the Foreigners increase. 2. Loss of Territory. Thus the Britons being driven into Wales, and crowded together in a barren Country insufficient to support such great Numbers, diminished 'till the People bore a Proportion to the Produce, while the Saxons increas'd on their abandoned Lands; 'till the Island became full of English. And were the English now driven into Wales by some foreign Nation, there would in a few Years be no more Englishmen in Britain, than there are now People in Wales. 3. Loss of Trade. Manufactures exported, draw Subsistence from Foreign Countries for Numbers; who are thereby enabled to marry and raise Families. If the Nation be deprived of any Branch of Trade, and no new Employment is found for the People occupy'd in that Branch, it will also be soon deprived of so many People. 4. Loss of Food. Suppose a Nation has a Fishery, which not only employs great Numbers, but makes the Food and Subsistence of the People cheaper; If another Nation becomes Master of the Seas, and prevents the Fishery, the People will diminish in Proportion as the Loss of Employ, and Dearness of Provision, makes it more difficult to subsist a Family. 5. Bad Government and insecure Property. People not only leave such a Country, and settling Abroad incorporate with other Nations, lose their native Language, and become Foreigners; but the Industry of those that remain being discourag'd, the Quantity of Subsistence in the Country is lessen'd, and the Support of a Family becomes more difficult. So heavy Taxes tend to diminish a People. 6. The Introduction of Slaves. The Negroes brought into the English Sugar Islands, have greatly diminish'd the Whites there; the Poor are by this Means depriv'd of Employment, while a few Families acquire vast Estates; which they spend on Foreign Luxuries, and educating their Children in the Habit of those Luxuries; the same Income is needed for the Support of one that might have maintain'd 100. The Whites who have Slaves, not labouring, are enfeebled, and therefore not so generally prolific; the Slaves being work'd too hard, and ill fed, their Constitutions are broken, and the Deaths among them are more than the Births; so that a continual Supply is needed from Africa. The Northern Colonies having few Slaves increase in Whites. Slaves also pejorate [weaken] the Families that use them; the white Children become proud, disgusted with Labour, and being educated in Idleness, are rendered unfit to get a Living by Industry.

Hence the Prince that acquires new Territory, if he finds it vacant, or removes the Natives to give his own People Room; the Legislator that makes effectual Laws for promoting of Trade, increasing Employment, improving Land by more or better Tillage; providing more Food by Fisheries; securing Property, etc. and the Man that invents new Trades, Arts or Manufactures, or new Improvements in Husbandry, may be properly called *Fathers* of their Nation, as they are the Cause of the Generation of Multitudes, by the Encouragement they afford to Marriage.

As to Privileges granted to the married, (such as the *Justrium Liberorum* [special liberties granted to mothers of three or more children] among the Romans), they may hasten the filling of a Country that has been thinned by War or Pestilence, or that has otherwise vacant Territory; but cannot increase a People beyond the Means provided for their Subsistence.

Foreign Luxuries and needless Manufactures imported and used in a Nation, do, by the same Reasoning, increase the People of the Nation that furnishes them, and diminish the People of the Nation that uses them. Laws therefore that prevent such Importations, and on the contrary promote the Exportation of Manufactures to be consumed in Foreign Countries, may be called (with Respect to the People that make them) *generative Laws*, as by increasing Subsistence they encourage Marriage. Such Laws likewise strengthen a Country, doubly, by increasing its own People and diminishing its Neighbours.

Some European Nations prudently refuse to consume the Manufactures of East-India. They should likewise forbid them to their Colonies; for the Gain to the Merchant, is not to be compar'd with the Loss by this Means of People to the Nation.

Home Luxury in the Great, increases the Nation's Manufacturers employ'd by it, who are many, and only tends to diminish the Families that indulge in it, who are few. The greater the common fashionable Expence of any Rank of People, the more cautious they are of Marriage. Therefore Luxury should never be suffer'd to become common.

The great Increase of Offspring in particular Families, is not always owing to greater Fecundity of Nature, but sometimes to Examples of Industry in the Heads, and industrious Education; by which the Children are enabled to provide better for themselves, and their marrying early, is encouraged from the Prospect of good Subsistence.

If there be a Sect therefore, in our Nation, that regard Frugality and Industry as religious Duties, and educate their Children therein, more than others commonly do; such Sect must consequently increase more by natural Generation, than any other Sect in Britain.

The Importation of Foreigners into a Country that has as many Inhabitants as the present Employments and Provisions for Subsistence will bear; will be in the End no Increase of People; unless the New Comers have more Industry and Frugality than the Natives, and then they will provide more Subsistence, and increase in the Country; but they will gradually eat the Natives out. Nor is it necessary to bring in Foreigners to fill up any occasional Vacancy in a Country; for such Vacancy ... will soon be filled by natural Generation. Who can now find the Vacancy made in Sweden, France or other Warlike Nations, by the Plague of Heroism 40 Years ago; in France, by the Expulsion of the Protestants; in England, by the Settlement of her Colonies; or in Guinea, by 100 Years Exportation of Slaves, that has blacken'd half America?

The thinness of Inhabitants in Spain is owing to National Pride and Idleness, and other Causes, rather than to the Expulsion of the Moors, or to the making of new Settlements.

There is in short, no Bound to the prolific Nature of Plants or Animals, but what is made by their crowding and interfering with each others' Means of Subsistence. Was the Face of the Earth vacant of other Plants, it might be gradually sowed and overspread with one Kind only; as, for Instance, with Fennel; and were it empty of other Inhabitants, it might in a few Ages be replenish'd from one Nation only; as, for Instance, with Englishmen. Thus there are suppos'd to be now upwards of One Million English Souls in North-America, (tho' 'tis thought scarce 80,000 have been brought over Sea) and yet perhaps there is not one the fewer in Britain, but rather many more, on Account of the Employment the Colonies afford to Manufacturers at Home. This Million doubling, suppose but once in 25 Years, will in another Century be more than the People of England, and the greatest Number of Englishmen will be on this Side the Water. What an Accession of Power to the British Empire by Sea as well as Land! What Increase of Trade and Navigation! What Numbers of Ships and Seamen! We have been here but little more than 100 Years, and yet the Force of our Privateers in the late War, united, was greater, both in Men and Guns, than that of the whole British Navy in Queen Elizabeth's Time. How important an Affair then to Britain, is the present Treaty for settling the Bounds between her Colonies and the French, and how careful should she be to secure Room enough, since on the Room depends so much the Increase of her People?

In fine, A Nation well regulated is like a Polypus; take away a Limb, its Place is soon supply'd; cut it in two, and each deficient Part shall speedily grow out of the Part remaining. Thus if you have Room and Subsistence enough, as you may by dividing, make ten Polypes out of one, you may of one make ten Nations, equally populous and powerful; or rather, increase a Nation ten fold in Numbers and Strength.

And since Detachments of English from Britain sent to America, will have their Places at Home so soon supply'd and increase so largely here; why should the Palatine Boors [Germans] be suffered to swarm into our Settlements, and by herding together establish their Language and Manners to the Exclusion of ours? Why should Pennsylvania, founded by the English, become a Colony of *Aliens*, who will shortly be so numerous as to Germanize us instead of our Anglifying them, and will never adopt our Language or Customs, any more than they can acquire our Complexion.

Which leads me to add one Remark: That the Number of purely white People in the World is proportionally very small. All Africa is black or tawny. Asia chiefly tawny. America (exclusive of the new Comers) wholly so. And in Europe, the Spaniards, Italians, French, Russians and Swedes, are generally of what we call a swarthy Complexion; as are the Germans also, the Saxons only excepted, who with the English, make the principal Body of White People on the Face of the Earth. I could wish their Numbers were increased. And while we are, as I may call it, *Scouring* our Planet, by clearing America of Woods, and so making this Side of our Globe reflect a brighter Light to the Eyes of Inhabitants in Mars or Venus, why should we in the Sight of Superior Beings, darken its People? why increase the Sons of Africa, by Planting them in America, where we have so fair an Opportunity, by excluding all Blacks and Tawneys, of increasing the lovely White and Red? But perhaps I am partial to the Complexion of my Country, for such Kind of Partiality is natural to Mankind.

Discussion Questions

1. What evidence does Danckaerts present of ethnic and religious diversity on Staten Island? Describe the tone of his encounter with the old Indian: What effects does Danckaerts think the Dutch fur trade has had on the Indians' welfare?

2. How does Bougainville compare those Indians who live under the supervision of missionaries with those from the western Great Lakes? What evidence do you find in this source

of the ways in which the French and Indians influenced and altered each other's way of conducting diplomacy and warfare? How does it illustrate the linkage between trade, religion, and war in the French colonial endeavor?

3. To what causes does Franklin attribute the rapid population growth in British North America, and how does he think the British should adapt their colonial policy to take advantage of it? How might Franklin's argument be used to justify seizing land from its native owners, and why is he opposed to expanding slavery in North America?

4. All of these sources comment in one way or another on the colonizers' interaction with the native inhabitants of North America. What assumptions and prejudices about Indians did the Dutch, French, and English share? What other factors (e.g., geography, climate, economy) might explain the different course that the European-Indian encounter took in their respective zones of colonization?

Suggested Readings

Historians have typically taken a regional approach to studying the colonization of North America, but rising interest in the Atlantic World has led to several studies that compare this process across ethnic, national, and geographic borders. For a comprehensive account that includes Spanish Florida and New Mexico as well as the French, Dutch, and English experiences addressed in this chapter, see D. W. Meinig, *The Shaping of America: A Geographical Perspective on 500 Years of History Volume I: Atlantic America, 1492–1800* (New Haven, CT: Yale University Press, 1986). Ian K. Steele's *Warpaths: Invasions of North America* (New York: Oxford University Press, 1994) compares and contrasts the Dutch, French, English, and Spanish experiences in warfare against each other and Native Americans. The Anglo-French rivalry for dominion over the interior of the continent is described in Eric Hinderaker, *Elusive Empires: Constructing Colonialism in the Ohio Valley, 1673–1800* (Cambridge: Cambridge University Press, 1997); and Paul W. Mapp, *The Elusive West and the Contest for Empire, 1713–1763* (Chapel Hill, NC: University of North Carolina Press, 2011).

For the founding and operation of New Netherland in an Atlantic context, see Jaap Jacobs, *The Colony of New Netherland: A Dutch Settlement in Seventeenth-Century America* (Ithaca, NY: Cornell University Press, 2009); Wim Klooster, *The Dutch Moment: War, Trade, and Settlement in the Seventeenth-Century Atlantic World* (Ithaca, NY: Cornell University Press, 2016); and Susanah Shaw Romney, *New Netherland Connections: Intimate Networks and Atlantic Ties in Seventeenth-Century America* (Chapel Hill, NC: University of North Carolina Press, 2017). For overviews of French colonization in North America, see James Pritchard, *In Search of Empire: The French in the Americas, 1670–1730* (Cambridge: Cambridge University Press, 2004); and Allan Greer, *The People of New France* (Toronto: University of Toronto Press, 1997). For the interplay of warfare, diplomacy, and slavery in New France, see Brett Rushforth, *Bonds of Alliance: Indigenous and Atlantic Slaveries in New France* (Chapel Hill, NC: University of North Carolina Press, 2012). Overviews of English colonization in North America noteworthy for their Atlantic context include Jack P. Greene, *Pursuits of Happiness: The Social Development of Early Modern British Colonies and the Formation of American Culture* (Chapel Hill, NC: University of North Carolina Press, 1988); and David Hackett Fischer, *Albion's Seed: Four British Folkways in America* (New York: Oxford University Press, 1989).

9 The Wooden World
Maritime Labor and Piracy

Figure 9.1 A Seventeenth-Century Buccaneer.

Pirate crews often included escaped servants and slaves who lived in maroon communities scattered throughout the Caribbean (see Selection 1). These multi-ethnic and multiracial communities survived through a combination of cutting wood and hunting feral pigs and cattle, the meat and hides of which they sold to plantations and passing ships. The name "buccaneer" has its root in "boucan," meaning to roast or dry meat over an open fire, as is illustrated here in the bottom left inset. How does this image contradict the popular image of Caribbean pirates?

Source credit: Alexander Exquemelin, *Histoire des Advanturiers* (Paris). Roger-Viollet/Getty Images.

Introduction

Dr. Samuel Johnson, the great eighteenth-century English writer, once said of maritime work,

> no man will be a sailor who has contrivance enough to get himself into jail; for being in a ship is being in jail only with the chance of being drowned … A man in jail has more room, better food, and commonly better company.

Johnson's opinion of a sailor's life is indicative of the contempt in which the upper classes typically held those men who earned their livings on the high seas. A wealthy London gentleman such as Johnson may have regarded the sailors crowding his city's wharves and taverns as little better than common criminals, but he could not have enjoyed his high style of living without them, for it was their labor that brought the fruits of overseas commerce—silks, china, tobacco, coffee, tea, sugar—to his door.

The Atlantic empires described in Chapters 7 and 8 were bound together by ships and the crews that sailed them. Mercantilism, an economic theory that shaped the colonial policy of all European powers in the Atlantic World, calculated a nation's wealth in terms of its international trade; nations grew rich by exporting more than they imported and by monopolizing their colonies' commerce with the rest of the world. Ships and seamen were national assets in this equation. Empire was something intangible—a claim to dominion over a foreign place or people—until maritime laborers made it profitable by loading, transporting, and unloading their cargoes.

Contemporaries referred to shipboard life as the "wooden world," and the men who inhabited it experienced extremes of personal autonomy and subordination. At a time when the vast majority of people labored on a specific plot of land to which they were tied by leases and local custom for a lifetime, sailors were remarkably mobile. They worked according to contracts that bound them to a ship's master only for the duration of a voyage. They could range among continents in their search for employment and easily abandon one captain for another by jumping ship. Time spent at sea freed them from the supervision of traditional social authorities at home, such as family and church. Of course, a sailor's life could be equally circumscribed on both land and sea. Onboard ship, he lived in close quarters with his shipmates and under the absolute authority of his captain. Discipline was swift and violent, including floggings, beatings, and confinement. At home, a sailor lacked political representation and social status. He typically lived among the other urban poor and shared their sub-standard housing, sanitation, and diets. A sailor's geographic mobility should not be confused with social mobility. Regardless of the city or nation, maritime workers in the Atlantic World occupied one of the lowest rungs on the social ladder.

The risks of a seafaring life encouraged sailors to develop particular attitudes and values that were expressed in their appearance, habits, and politics. Contemporaries recognized sailors by their body and dress. Exposure to the elements, shipboard accidents, and diseases associated with tropical climates weathered sailors' faces and disfigured their bodies. Tattoos visually set them apart from other urban laborers, and often featured nautical images such as anchors and mermaids to denote pride of profession. Sailors wore distinctive clothing as well: canvas jackets and tarred pants (to insulate them from wind and water), which earned them the nickname "Jack Tar" in the English-speaking world. The stereotype of the sailor as a rootless, godless, and drunken ruffian was a product of the fatalism and liberality that seafaring encouraged. Well aware of the high mortality rates involved in their work, sailors preferred to part with their money rather than save it. Their spendthrift ways included generous support of other sailors and their kin whenever the death or injury of a shipmate called for charity. While locked out of the traditional channels of political power, sailors were by no means apolitical. Like the rest of the working poor, they practiced their politics "out-of-doors" by rioting against authorities who violated their notions of customary rights and social justice. In particular, sailors targeted press gangs that forced men into service aboard naval vessels, notorious for their low pay and harsh discipline. Anti-impressment riots were some of the most violent episodes of civil unrest in the Atlantic World, and the issue remained a politically charged one for seafarers into the nineteenth century.

Another distinctive element of maritime labor in the Atlantic World was its multi-ethnic and multiracial quality. Ship crews were a composite of Europeans, Africans, and Americans and mirrored the international nature of the profession. Portuguese pilots could be found on vessels from all nations; African and African-American sailors helped European ships navigate coastal waters on both sides of the Atlantic; Native Americans participated in northern New England's whalefishery. Sailors also engaged in and in some cases were the offspring of inter-racial sexual relations. Diego el Mulato was born a slave of European-African parents in Havana, but achieved notoriety as the leader of Dutch pirates in the seventeenth-century Caribbean. For some maritime slaves, such as Olaudah Equiano (see Chapter 6, Selection 3), petty trading from port to port enabled them to purchase their freedom. Other slaves found seafaring a welcome break from the monotony of work on land. Free blacks were drawn to maritime work for the relative independence it provided from white authority and the links it offered to other African-American communities. While black sailors earned less than their white counterparts and still faced racism on the high seas, they nonetheless helped shape an African-American consciousness by founding churches and mutual aid societies in their seaport communities and by transmitting anti-slavery ideology throughout the Atlantic World.

By its very nature, international seafaring encouraged the erosion of established identities and the creation of new ones. Nowhere was this tendency more evident than in the experience of pirates. Piracy came to the New World on the heels of Columbus. French, Dutch, and English privateers, adventurers licensed by their governments to seize enemy ships during wartime, hunted their fortunes by attacking the Spanish treasure fleets that carried American gold and silver to Europe. Favorite pirate haunts included Tortuga, a French-controlled island just east of the passage between Cuba and Hispaniola, and the Bahamas, from which pirates preyed upon ships navigating the straits between Florida and Cuba. In addition to hijacking Spanish silver, pirates plundered coastal cities and engaged in contraband slave trading.

The complexion of Atlantic piracy changed as the nationalist privateers of the early colonial period gave way to seafaring adventurers of no fixed political allegiance. In the seventeenth century, communities of *buccaneers* developed in the Caribbean; made up of runaway slaves, Native Americans, and European sailors and servants who had deserted their masters, they lived autonomously by cutting wood, hunting feral pigs and cattle, and exporting meat and hides to the sugar islands. By 1700, with British naval power commanding much of the Atlantic, a new breed of pirates known as freebooters emerged, sailing under no particular flag and attacking ships and seaboard settlements indiscriminately. In the last great wave of Atlantic piracy, about 5,000 such freebooters preyed on transoceanic trade between 1716 and 1726. As the British Navy pursued them, freebooters fanned out into the Carolinas of North America, Sierra Leone in West Africa, and even Madagascar in the Indian Ocean. Approximately 500 of them were executed in colonial and British ports, their bodies left to rot in the gallows as testimony to the new rule of law on the high seas.

The readings in this chapter offer several perspectives on seafaring in the Atlantic World. In the first selection, a former Dutch servant in the Caribbean explains the protocol pirates used when organizing their crews and voyages. In the second selection, a Puritan minister uses the execution of a pirate to admonish both sailors and ship captains for deviating from Christian values. The third selection relates the story of an American sailor forced into service in the British Navy during the Napoleonic Wars. In the final selection, a New York woman who joined her husband on a whaling voyage comments on the physical and spiritual condition of sailors on her ship. As you read these sources, consider what they have to say about the attractions and risks of a seafaring life in the Atlantic World. What drew sailors to this employment, and what deprivations did they endure because of it? Where do you see evidence in these narratives of particular cultural values or identities rooted in life at sea?

Selection 1: A Dutch Pirate in the Seventeenth-Century Caribbean

Alexander Olivier Exquemelin was a native of the Netherlands who came to the Caribbean in the 1660s as an indentured servant of the French West India Company. Upon gaining his freedom, he went to sea as a buccaneer. Exquemelin told the tale of his exploits in a book first published in the Netherlands; an English translation appeared in 1684 with the author's name anglicized as John Esquemeling. *The Buccaneers of America* is an important eyewitness account of Caribbean piracy. While it is filled with lurid accounts of pillage and torture, it also includes details on the "nuts and bolts" of how this profession operated. In the passages that follow, Exquemelin describes the recruitment and organization of a pirate crew, and the economic and sexual relations between pirates and Indian women.

Credit: John Esquemeling, *The Buccaneers of America*, ed. William Stallybrass, 2nd edn (London: William Crooke, 1684), 20–22, 59–61, 233–234.

Before the Pirates go out to sea, they give notice unto everyone that goes upon the voyage, of the day on which they ought precisely to embark, intimating also unto them their obligation of bringing each man in particular so many pounds of powder and bullets as they think necessary for that expedition. Being all come on board, they join together in council, concerning what place they ought first to go unto wherein to get provisions—especially of flesh, seeing they scarce eat anything else. And of this the most common sort among them is pork. The next food is tortoises, which they use to salt a little. Sometimes they resolve to rob such or such hog-yards, wherein the Spaniards often have a thousand head of swine together. They come unto these places in the dark of the night, and, having beset the keeper's lodge, they force him to rise and give them as many heads as they desire, threatening withal to kill him in case he disobeys their commands or makes any noise. Yea, these menaces are oftentimes put in execution, without giving any quarter unto the miserable swinekeepers or any other person that endeavours to hinder their robberies.

Having gotten provisions of flesh sufficient for their voyage, they return unto their ship. Here their allowance, twice a day to every one, is as much as he can eat, without either weight or measure. Neither does the steward of the vessel give any greater proportion of flesh, or anything else, unto the Captain than unto the meanest mariner. The ship being well victualled, they call another council, to deliberate towards what place they shall go to seek their desperate fortunes. In this council, likewise, they agree upon certain articles, which are put in writing, by way of bond or obligation, which every one is bound to observe, and all of them, or the chiefest, do set their hands unto. Herein they specify, and set down very distinctly, what sums of money each particular person ought to have for that voyage, the fund of all the payments being the common stock of what is gotten by the whole expedition; for otherwise it is the same law, among these people as with other Pirates: *No prey, no pay*. In the first place, therefore, they mention how much the Captain ought to have for his ship. Next the salary of the carpenter, or shipwright, who careened, mended, and rigged the vessel. This commonly amounts unto 100 or 150 pieces-of-eight; being, according to the agreement, more or less. Afterwards for provisions and victualling they draw out of the same common stock about 200 pieces-of-eight. Also a competent salary for the surgeon and his chest of medicaments, which usually is rated at 200 or 250 pieces-of-eight. Lastly, they stipulate in writing what recompense or reward each one ought to have that is either wounded or maimed in his body, suffering the loss of any limb, by that voyage. Thus they order for the loss of a right arm 600 pieces-of-eight, or 6 slaves; for the loss of a left arm 500 pieces-of-eight, or 5 slaves; for a right leg 500 pieces-of-eight, or 5 slaves; for a left leg 400 pieces-of-eight, or 4 slaves; for an eye 100 pieces-of-eight, or one slave; for a finger of the hand the same reward as for the eye. All which sums of money, as I have said before, are taken out of the capital sum or common stock of what is gotten by their piracy. For a very exact and equal dividend is made of the remainder among them all. Yet herein they have also regard unto qualities and places. Thus the Captain, or chief Commander, is allotted five or six portions to what the ordinary seamen have; the Master's Mate only two; and other Officers proportionable to their employment. After whom they draw equal parts from the highest even to the lowest mariner, the boys not being omitted. For even these draw half a share, by reason that, when they happen to take a better vessel than their own, it is the duty of the boys to set fire unto the ship or boat wherein they are, and then retire unto the prize which they have taken.

They observe among themselves very good orders. For in the prizes they take, it is severely prohibited unto every one to usurp anything in particular unto themselves. Hence all they take is equally divided, according to what has been said before. Yea, they make a solemn oath to each other not to abscond, or conceal the least thing they find amongst the prey. If afterwards any one is found unfaithful, and has contravened the said oath, immediately he is separated and turned out of the society. Among themselves they are very civil and charitable to each other. Insomuch that, if any wants what another has, with great liberality they give it one to another. As soon as these Pirates have taken any prize of ship or boat, the first thing they endeavour is to set on shore the prisoners, detaining only some few for their own help and service, unto whom also they give their liberty after the space of two or three years. They put in very frequently for refreshment at one island or another, but more especially into those which lie on the Southern side of the isle of Cuba. Here they careen their vessels, and in the meanwhile some of them go to hunt, others to cruize upon the seas in canoes, seeking their fortune. Many times they take the poor fishermen of tortoises, and, carrying them to their habitations, they make them work so long as the Pirates are pleased.

***

The custom of this island is such that, when any Pirates arrive there, every one has the liberty to buy for himself an Indian woman, at the price of a knife or any old axe, wood-bill, or hatchet. By this contract the woman is obliged to remain in the custody of the Pirate all the time he stays there. She serves him in the meanwhile, and brings him victuals of all sorts that the country affords. The Pirate, moreover, has liberty to go when he pleases, either to hunt, or fish, or about any other divertisements of his pleasure; but withal is not to commit any hostility, or depredation upon the inhabitants, seeing the Indians bring him in all that he stands in need of, or that he desires.

Through the frequent converse and familiarity these Indians have with the Pirates, they sometimes use to go to sea with them, and remain among them for whole years, without returning home. Whence it comes that many of them can speak English and French, and some of the Pirates their Indian language. They are very dexterous at darting with the javelin, whereby they are very useful to the Pirates towards the victualling their ships, by the fishery of tortoises, and *manitas*, a sort of fish so called by the Spaniards. For one of these Indians is alone sufficient to victual a vessel of an hundred persons. We had among our crew two Pirates who could speak very well the Indian language.

Selection 2: A Pirate Faces Execution in Boston

As the British Navy cracked down on piracy in the Atlantic during the early eighteenth century, many pirates were tried and executed in colonial seaports, where their corpses were left to hang as a warning to other sailors. In Puritan New England, ministers commonly delivered sermons at public executions, using the spectacle to drive home spiritual lessons about the consequences of sin and the importance of repentance. Cotton Mather delivered such an execution sermon in Boston in July 1726, when several pirates were hanged after being convicted of crimes on the high seas. Mather's reference to sailors as "our *Sea-faring Tribe*" indicates how much he saw members of this occupation as a breed apart from regular society. His description of the pirate William Fly's refusal to engage in the penitent behavior expected of a convicted criminal also suggests how much disdain pirates had for Mather and other symbols of civil authority on land.

Credit: [Cotton Mather], *The Vial Poured Out Upon the Sea* (Boston, MA: T. Fleet and N. Belknap, 1726), 42–45, 47–48.

And now, The Great GOD has ordered it, that a Number of *Dying Men* appear among us, in some Tragical and peculiar Circumstances. Another Company of PIRATES under *Sentence of Death* appear among us, and are within a few Hours to be Executed.

Certainly, It will be the *Wisdom* of us all, but especially of our *Sea-faring Tribe* [sailors], to learn from these *Dying Men*, some things which the *living* that *see the End* of these Men must *lay to Heart*, if they would not with an *Hard Heart* lay up for themselves *Treasures of Wrath*, to be poured out upon them, in the *Righteous Judgment* of GOD.

Learn from these poor Men, the Mischief of those *Two Vices*, wherein so many of the *Sea-Faring Tribe* suffer the doleful *Shipwreck* of their Souls, and are *drowned in Perdition*. The first, that of *Drunkenness*; And then, that of profane *Swearing* and *Cursing*, These poor Men do, with unutterable Anguish cry out, under the heavy Load of *Guilt*, which these Two Vices have laid and left upon them. The former Vice, *resigns* the Sinner up to the *Possession* of the *Devil*; and by Consequence, to all manner of Wickedness. The latter Vice, *declares* that the *Devil* has taken an horrible *Possession* of the Sinner, and the Wretch cannot now so truly say, what he use to do, *My Tongue is my own*; as he may say, *'Tis the Devils*: And being *Set on Fire of Hell*, 'tis plain, what and where a *Torment* is intended for it. Being thus *Warned* of them, Oh! *Steer clear of the Rocks*, where you see the *Breakers* before you!

At the same time, when Oh! when, will the *Sea* no longer have cause to say of *Wisdom*, *It is not in me*! And complain that they who follow the *Sea*, will so *Madly* as they do, abandon themselves, and let their Souls *drive* to the Courses of *Self-Destruction*! Poor Sailours, Will you never hearken to the *Voice of Wisdom*? Always be *Madmen*, and with the *Madness in your Hearts* go to the Dead? Never become a Pious, a Sober, a Serious, and a Prudent Generation? Let the Condition of these Poor Men help you to *receive Instruction* and *acquaint your Hearts with Wisdom*. In their Condition you see, that if you *go on still in your Trespasses* a Provoked GOD can by the Hands of *Sea-Monsters*, which thro' His *Curse* upon you do *Increase and Multiply*, & become the *Terror of them that haunt the Sea*, bring sore plagues upon you: And ever one of these *Leviathans* have a permission to pillage no less than Four Hundred Vessels of you. Yea, and what is infinitely worse; In *their* Condition you see what *you* may be left unto: And how far, if you remain Incorrigible in your evil ways, the Justice of GOD may give you up to the *Lusts of your own Hearts*, and leave you to do those things, which may bring a *fearful End* upon you, that once you little imagined. *Oh! What may you come to!*

My Friends; *Be Admonished by these things*; And, *Be wise.*

But while I am addressing the poor *Sailours*, and beseeching them, that they would not let the *Devil*, who is the worst of *Masters*, enslave them, nor have their *Names* in the *Book* of, *The Wicked one*, I would presume upon an Address to the *Masters* of our Vessels, that they would not be too like the *Devil*, in their *Barbarous Usage* of the *Men* that are under them, and lay them under *Temptations* to do *Desperate Things*. We allow, Sirs, That you must be *Commanders* aboard, and you must keep a *Strict Hand* over your Men; and you may, *as Times go*, too often have occasions for *Severities*; But still, there must be no room for *Barbarities*. Our best *Commanders* find they can do without such Things. The *Men* must be used as *Rational Creatures*. Yea, *Masters*, you must Remember your MEN,—Don't you call 'em so?—They are your *Brethren*. And you would certainly find it so, that with a *Merciful Usage* of your *Men*, if you wisely maintain the *Exercises* of PIETY aboard your Vessels, and be yourselves bright *Examples* of it, your GOD, and the *Conscience* that speaks from and for Him in your *Men*, would be on *your side*, and your *Authority* would be sufficiently Established.

***

The EXECUTION.

And now, *speedily*, that is to say, On *Tuesday*, the *Sentence against the Evil Works* of these Men, must be executed. One of the Four, namely, [George] *Condick*, was Reprieved. As for [William] *Fly*, he had been all along, a most uncommon and amazing Instance of Impenitency and Stupidity, and what *Spectacles of Obduration* the Wicked will be, when they have by a course of Wickedness under and against Warnings, provoked the GOD of Heaven to withhold His Influences from them. The Sullen and Raging Mood, into which he fell, upon his being first *Imprison'd*, caused him to break forth into furious Execrations, and Blasphemies too hideous to be mention'd; and not eat one morsel of any thing, but subsist only upon a little Drinking, for almost all of the remaining part of his Life. He declined appearing in the Public Assemblies, on the *Lords-day*, with the other Prisoners, to be under the appointed means of Grace, because, forsooth, *he would not have the Mob to gaze upon him*. He seem'd all along ambitious to have it said, *That he died a brave fellow!* He pass'd along to the place of Execution, with a *Nosegay* in his hand, and making his *Complements*, where he *thought he saw occasion*. Arriving there, he nimbly mounted the Stage, and would fain have put on a Smiling Aspect. He reproached the Hangman, for not understanding his Trade, and with his own Hands rectified matters, to render all things more Convenient and Effectual.

When he was called upon, to *Speak* what he should judge proper to be spoken on that sad occasion, at least for the Warning of Survivors, he only said, That *he would advise the Masters of Vessels to carry it well to their Men, lest they Should be put upon doing as he had done*.

At the same time, he declared his obstinate Refusal, to *Forgive* the Person that had been the Instrument of bringing him to Justice. When the Necessity of that *Charity* was urgently press'd upon him; and advantage taken from a Recital of the *Lords-Prayer* used among the Devotions of the Criminals on the present Occasion, to urge it; he still persisted in his *Unrelenting Frame*; and an Expression of that Importance was in the last words, he Expired withal. But it was observed and is affirm'd, by some Spectators, that in the Midst of all his affected *Bravery*, a very sensible *Trembling* attended him; His hands and his *Knees* were plainly seen to *Tremble*. And so we must leave him for the *Judgment to come*.

Selection 3: An American Sailor Experiences Impressment in the British Navy

The British practice of impressment had its roots in laws that allowed naval officers to force civilians into service on their ships during times of national emergency. Between 1790 and 1815, as Great Britain fought a series of wars with Revolutionary and Napoleonic France, the British Navy extended this practice to American sailors, claiming that they were British subjects who had deserted from British ships. American sailors often carried Seaman's Protection Certificates issued by the US government to prove their citizenship, but British press gangs had little regard for such documents.

Joshua Penny was one of several thousand American seamen pressed into service with the British Navy during this era. A native of Long Island, he went to sea as a fifteen year old in

1788. His impressment in Jamaica in 1794 led to eleven years of unwilling service on a number of British ships sailing in the Atlantic and Indian Oceans. He returned home to Long Island in 1805, but during the War of 1812, he went back to sea and was captured again by the British, this time enduring nine months of imprisonment. He published his story in 1815.

Credit: Joshua Penny, *The Life and Adventures of Joshua Penny, a Native of Southold, Long Island, Suffolk County, New York* (New York: Alden Spooner, 1815), 10–13, 25–27, 29–30.

Not many days had passed after our arrival [in Jamaica], ere [before] we were again haunted by press-gangs, and our whole crew impressed. We were put into the *Alligator* frigate of 28 guns, under the command of captain Africk. Four of us were Americans; the others chiefly Danes and Swedes. A fever raged in this ship, and out of forty men, there were eleven corpses to be interred on the first morning.

No sooner was the captain on the deck in the morning, than we were ready with our American protections [certificates proving their American citizenship]. He said, "men I will not look at your protections—my ship is in distress, and I will have men to carry me to England." He refused to hear a word on the subject of liberating any one of our number. The ship got under way, and the next morning went into Montego Bay [Jamaica], and anchored in the harbour at 8 o'clock in the evening; her boats were manned to board the merchants' ships lying there; and impressed from them without discrimination. This business of kidnapping continued until day-break, when they got underway in season to prevent applications for relief. There were forty men impressed that night, some of whom were American mates and supercargoes [agents charged with overseeing a ship's cargo]—some had been taken out of their beds on shore, without liberty to dress themselves. We ran down to the fleet in the offing, of 114 sail merchantmen waiting for this ship to join the convoy of two ships of the line and the brig *Jack Tar*. The next day however, our ship was dispatched by order of the admiral, on a commission to Havanna [Cuba]; we lay twenty-four hours at the Moro-Castle then went to sea and rejoined the fleet.

The next day I was taken sick of a fever—was soon deprived of my sense, and when I first recollected myself, was out of my hammock and attempting to walk on deck; sudden blindness prostrated my feeble frame, when I heard a general shout, "there goes another dead yankee." I was returned into my hammock; the doctor shortly after came along, and on finding a corpse next to me, he called his lob-lolly boy [assistant] and chid[ed] him for not seeing that dead man's hammock cut down; adding, "that other man (meaning me) will be dead before 12 o'clock; and you ought to have the dead removed immediately, to make room for me." My fever was broken, so that the doctor's prophetic sentence was entirely harmless ...

The sick had recovered after reaching the English Channel, and all the impressed seamen taken from Jamaica, were ordered on the quarter deck. The captain then addressing himself to us, said, "I want to know who of you impressed in Jamaica, are willing to take his majesty's bounty [a cash bonus paid for enlisting]: it is customary to allow impressed men twenty-four hours to consider whether they will accept this privilege; if not, they are on arriving at the Spithead [Portsmouth, England], to be put on board some vessel bound to foreign parts, where they shall not have opportunities to write to the d_____d [damned] consul [the U.S. consulate]." He called me singly and said, "You have been the sickest, and I have been a father to you: do you refuse the king's bounty?" I answered (pointing to an arm chest) if he would give me that chest full of guineas and a lieutenant's commission, he could not tempt me. He replied, "you had every day for two months, a dish from my own table, which no other man in the ship has had, and now you refuse to take the king's bounty! You are a d_____d yankee rebellious rascal!" At Spithead we were called on deck with our baggage: What was next to be done with us we were left to conjecture. A part of our company expected to be set on shore—others had previously written letters to be sent to the consuls of their respective nations; but all were disappointed. A launch conveyed us along side of the *Stately* 64 [guns], captain Douglass. In two hours our squadron was ordered to sea. This squadron consisted of the *American* 64, commodore Blanket, *Ruby* 64, *Rattlesnake* sloop of war, and two frigates, beside the *Stately* whose names I have forgotten. We had put our letters on board of a passage boat; and were sailing to some unknown part of the world. The officers, alike ignorant with the men, bet on our destination. Bets were laid on Batavia [modern Jakarta], Botany Bay [Australia], &c. but after being at sea ten weeks, we made the *Table Mountain* [a mountain overlooking the Dutch colony of Cape Town, South Africa]; and every preparation was made for action. The next morning at daybreak we were joined by admiral Elphinstone, with three 74's, three frigates, two sloops of war, and a gun brig. At 8 o'clock, the signal to clear away for action was hoisted on board the admiral's ship, and repeated by the commodore. We entered False Bay, where the Dutch had one fort of 8 guns, and another of four. Fifty men, who composed the whole force there, spiked their cannon and retreated to Cape Town, leaving our fleet to take possession of every thing. A frigate and man of war brig lay in the harbour. We pillaged the East-India stores [supplies of the Dutch East India Company] on the shore—stove the casks of wine and spirits, which ran like rivulets towards the sea. The liquor was said to be poisoned by the Dutch. English sailors would have drank the spirits, with permission, if they had really believed it to be poisoned; provided they could have got fairly drunk before they died. Our land forces were on shore the next day.

***

… I was drafted to the *Sphinx*, a ship of 20 guns, bound to cruise off St. Helena [a British post in the Southern Atlantic]. An American whaling ship lay near us at St. Helena, and four of us who messed together, all Americans, agreed to escape to the whaler; and after bribing the sentinel, plunged into the water. The others succeeded; but not being a good swimmer, I rested on our buoy and got with difficulty into the ship's head by climbing on the cable.

One of the three who effected their escape was James Hall. He attempted to escape from on board of the *Sceptre*, before our draft from that ship, by swimming to an English Indiaman [merchant ship]. He stowed himself away on board the Indiaman, but when the watch list was called the next morning, he was missed. The captain of the *Sceptre*, on receiving the report of Hall's absconding, ordered all boats out to search the ships in port. He was found in the first ship they searched, and was of course to be punished. All hands were called to see the culprit flogged; and stood as usual with their hats off. Hall was young, with thin skin; and on receiving three strokes of the *cat* [cat-o-nine tails, a whip used for flogging sailors] cried out "Oh captain! For God's sake forgive me!" The captain then suspending the punishment, asked the unfortunate young man "if he would now promise to attempt no more to runaway?" To which Hall answered, "No, by G_____d [God] *captain, I will never give it up for one bad job.*" As often this solemnity occurs, the surgeon stands by the captain, to give notice of the man's fainting. After three strokes more were given, the surgeon communicated the danger of the patient; upon which the cat was again arrested. Hall, scarcely able to articulate; addressing himself to the captain, said "*Captain, we Americans can't bear flogging like you Englishmen, we are not used to it.*" The captain turned, and walking off, with difficulty refrained from laughing aloud; but the whole ship's company smiled, though they dared not laugh. Hall was released, because this captain did not happen to be a barbarian. I have always noticed, that when an American was whipped, he fainted.

A few days after my unsuccessful attempt to reach the American ship, in St. Helena, all hands were called to get our ship underway, and on calling the fore-top-men [crewmen], the three yankees were missing. The captain then called the purser's steward to ascertain the missing yankees' mess. I was then called upon to relate what I knew of their running off. I told the captain, as a number of men had been on shore watering the ship, I thought they had been there on duty. That was a falsehood, but *was not malicious*. He asked me if I could swim? No, I answered. He then took a book out of his pocket and said, "You are a yankee, sir, and have been seven years in the navy without ever being flogged, and *now I'll flog you if you are God Almighty's first lieutenant!!!*"

All hands were now called up on deck to witness my punishment; and I was immediately seized up. My senses left me when I had received three strokes of the *cat*. I fell (so I was afterwards informed) hanging by the wrists, with my head on one shoulder, until the whole number of stripes had been applied. The surgeon informed the captain of my condition, when the captain said, "*he shall take his dozen, dead or alive!*" I was cut down, and at first recollection of myself, they were washing my face with a tub of water.

***

Not long after this the 4th of June came, when the seamen are allowed to get drunk because this is their king's birth day; and when the 4th of July came, I applied to Lt. Pingally [an officer of the ship] for liberty to get drunk. He said, "go along forward, you yankee rascal." The captain then spoke to him, when he, as I suppose, informed him of my request. He called me to him, and asked—What do you mean, sir, by asking permission to do what you know is contrary to the regulations of this ship? I recollect, sir, said I, that about a month ago you gave the English liberty to get drunk because it was their king's birth day; and now I want the liberty to rejoice on my nation's birth day. The captain laughing heartily, ordered that two gallons of wine and one of brandy be procured from the shore for me and my *yankee mess* to rejoice. We all liked this captain. The glass passed merrily round in our *yankee mess*, of thirty in number, and they began to sing *Hail Columbia, happy land!* A north countryman [from the north of England], who called himself the bully of the ship, came along for the purpose of fomenting a quarrel, and told us, "get out of the way, you d_____d yankee buggers." This was, consequently, taken as an insult. I gave him an unceremonious box on the ear, and asked if that was what he meant. Yes, he answered, it is exactly what I want. A few blows were passed between us, when the officer between decks coming up, ordered *fair play*—he had observed that several others were aiding my antagonist by pelting me. A few more passes were made at each other; at last I struck him with the left hand, and in drawing back found two of the bully's teeth sticking in the joint of one of my fingers. My antagonist, on losing his front teeth, yielded immediately.

Selection 4: A Woman's Perception of Life on a Whaling Ship

Within the maritime world, a clear division of labor separated men and women. Men went to sea while women stayed behind to maintain family, home, and community in port towns and cities. Only rarely did women accompany male partners who worked on overseas voyages, and rarer still is the woman who left behind a written account of the experience. At the peak of the North American whalefishery in the mid-nineteenth century, some women did join their husbands at sea. They tended to be ship captains' wives, who chose to endure the rigors of a whaling expedition rather than the long-term absence of their spouses, whose work often took them away from home for a year or two at a time.

Martha Smith Brewer Brown joined her husband Captain Edwin Peter Brown on a whaling voyage out of Long Island, New York in 1847. The Browns circumnavigated the globe, hunting whales primarily in the Pacific and Arctic Oceans. Martha kept a journal while at sea, in which she recorded her impressions of life and work aboard ship. A pious woman, she expressed concern for the state of the sailors' souls and described how shipboard life ran counter to good Christian habits and morals. Through her eyes, we see in sharp relief the contrast between the values of seafarers and landed society.

Credit: *She Went A-Whaling: The Journal of Martha Smith Brewer Brown from Orient, Long Island, New York, Around the World on the Whaling Ship Lucy Ann, 1847–1849*, transcribed and edited by Anne MacKay (Orient, NY: Oysterponds Historical Society, 1993), 47–52.

MONDAY 10 [DECEMBER 1847] [*in margin: "John died"*]

This morning about 7 we were called in the stereage to witness the departure of an immortal soul. He died very suden. The Capt. went in imediately and he gasped but once. He never strugled, nor groned nor to appearance mooved a musle. He said last evening he felt that he must die, felt prepared, and was willing to go this morning. At 6 he told Steward he thought he could stand it to get to New Holland [Australia]—he did not have his reason all the time. A short time before he died the boy said [he] heard him singing and laughing. He is Portugee and could not understand him. We think he might have been happy, but we do not know. It is not probile he knew he was dying. He never left a message for his friends although the Capt. often asked him if he had not something he wished to say to them. I heardly think he would have given us the names of his parents or friends of his own accord. He was young, only 15. I hope he has gone to a brighter and happyer world, but that we can not know. We will leave him in the hands of a just God who doeth all things well. He was buried this afternoon at 4 oclock. It was a sollemn sight to see his body launched into the deep. I think nearly every one wept. Oh that they may lay it to heart and realized their turn will soon come. They are far from being what we would wish them to be. They have looked rather thoughtfull today and I pray the impressions may not be banished as soon as his body is out of our sight. Poor boy, I cannot realize he is gone. Poor in the world estimate, but if he had sincerely repented of his sins and was truly a child of grace, how much richer far than we who remain behind. Whether he felt any dred of being buried in the sea or not, I do not know. He did not say any thing about it, and we did not mention the subject to him, but it matters not where the body is if the soul is prepared for heaven, prepared to meet its God.

THURSDAY 13 [*in margin: "ate porpossis"*]

Today I have the unspeakable pleasure of seeing a whale brought along side. The second mate struck him. I was on deck most of the time they were off, notwithstanding it was somewhat rainy. It was past 7 when they came on board, and after getting dinner it was to late to cut him in. Like wise it was blowing pretty strong so we were obliged to lay by him all night. It [is] quite encourageing to think we have got one of the thirty of forty we have got to get, ere we can anticipate returning home. It looks like a long day I can assure you to look ahead to the time when this ship shall be full of oil and we homeward bound.

FRIDAY 14

Morning rather unpleasent but commenced cutting in about 10 AM. And of cours the Capt. worked hard. Evry time the ship roaled, the whail went nearly all under water, but they succeeded in getting him in at 9 pm. Weather quite good. Got supper, cleared up, but have not commenced boiling yet.

SATURDAY 15

Called the Capt. between 5 and 6. Lowered for whale—no success. Commenced boiling before breakfast but have not made very grate headway. Will be under the necesity of boiling tomorow, Sunday, but I do not see how whaleman can in evry way keep the Sabath. They can truly not go off in the boats and take them, but if they have one alongside or in the bluber room, it appears necessary they should take care of it.

MONDAY 17

Today hands imployed brakeing out the fore peek and stowing down 42 barrels of oil. Merely a nest egg. Hope they will have the good luck to get the nest full soon and set the sails for home. Finished boiling this morning about day light. It has been very pleasent all day. I have been making my blue dress after supper. They caught two nice large porposses—now for a feast on fresh meet agane. By the bye it goes well.

WEDNESDAY 19

Another pleasent day and I have improved it washing. Had a good time. Got my cloths dry before night, but lost one apron overboard—the first time I have had the bad luck to loos anything. Got through little, afternoon. Had fried parters [potatoes?] as turnovers for dinner.

JANUARY 23, 1848, *Indian Ocian, Ship Lucy Ann*

To day has been a lovely day, a good breeze and a compleet day for whaleing. The Capt., I think, has been quite anxous to see whale. The first time he has been to the masthead [on] Sunday, but he who know all things saw best not to tempt them. And here I will add we have not seen a whale on Sunday since we have been out. How kind is Almighty God to withhold temptation when there is not strength of mind sufficient to resist it. I fear and tremble evry week that we shall see them but it is my earnest prayer that God will be gracious and tempt us no further than we are able to bare.

The 23 of Jan was my dear Father's bearth day. If he was living to day he would be 68 years old. But as our heavenly Father saw fit 8 years ago to remove him from this world of trouble, sorow and pain, of which he always had his share, to one we trust of perfect bliss, happyness. He can never more come to us, but we can go to him. Then let us strive to meet him in heaven, dear brothers and sisters, for that is our privalage.

MONDAY 31

Nothing in particular to day. Strong brizes from the west. In the morning at 2 am raised Vandieman's land [Tasmania], but at so grate a distance it appeared like a cloud. Nothing was visable and of course we were not much interested. I think I should be nearly intoxicated with delight if I could once more get ashore where I could feel at home, and go as I was a mind to—for instance on Long Island. But let me get ashore any where, I anticipate I should enjoy it some.

TUESDAY, FEB 1ST [in margin: "man flogged"]

Ship Lucy Ann Between New Holland & New Zealand Feb 1848

Today has been quite pleasent, and it is very acceptable to think that we may now have some good weather, for it has been nothing but a succession of gales and bad weather since we left the cape of Good Hope. But if it is not one thing is another. Sunday morn when the Capt. first got up, he went on deck and caught to [two] of the foremast hands fighting, in direct oposition to the rules and regulation of the ship. He sent one out on the bowsprit and the other to the mizenmast and kept them there untill 10 oc [o'clock] without their breakfast. It was their watch below. This morning, or before noon, he appeared at the fore castle—lo and behold there were four gambling for tobacco. Two managed to get rid of their cards so that he could not know certainly they were playing, but the others said they were. Seaman he sent out on the bowsprit agane, for he was the one sent there for fiting [fighting], and Rider to the mizenmast head. Kept them there all the forenoon, their watch below agane. In the afternoon he called them of [off] aft, read to them apiece on the results of gambling and lectured them full a half hour, threw their cards overboard. Agane, at 8 bels in the evening Baldwin, one of the boatsteerers, came with a complaint that Seaman had been calling him a horred name—the third offence three days a runing. The Capt.'s patienes was clear gone—he went on deck and gave him 5 or 6 lashes with the end of the topgalent bowlin [rope used to tie a sail]. Then for the first time I learned he had floged a man several weeks before. What will come next I do not know. You who live on land do not know half the trials a sea Capt. is subject to. If you do not like a man's conduct you can pay him and let him go, or you can flee to the law. But here there is no such thing. Of course there must be some rules and regulation on board ship. When a man is made acquainted with them in the first of it, what can he expect but abide the conciquences if he does not abide by the rules. So Mother, you see I have very little influence so far.

FRIDAY 11

This morning at daylight raised two Ships, one of them cutting in. At 8 PM raised three Kings [island off of New Zealand] steered for them. About 2 PM sent two boats ashore to see if any-thing was to be got in the way of provision. The third mate soon returned with the chief, said there was plenty of potatoes and that was what we wanted. He came abord [aboard] to make the bargain with the Capt. but more expressly to get some Rum. They could not land that side of the Island we was, but this kanacker [a Polynesian man] came down the rocks some way. The Capt. made a trade with him, sent them back. But by this the current was runing so strong and the wind ahead, the second boat could not get around, and was obliged to land the Chief where they took him. So the third mate walked across the land to the other boat, or the landing place, to have Mr. Sisen take the potatoes. But mean time he had come around, thinking the Capt. had not sent him back. When they got on board nothing had been seen of the other boat, and of course we imagined the boat had swamped and all were drowned. But alass [at last] they come and brought 10 little pon fish. This ends our tour of the three Kings.

SATURDAY EVE FEBRUARY 12

And so we are spared to enjoy the privalages of another Saturday night, and if we cannot meet with our friends at the temperance meeting nor in social prayer, we know that our Savior is present to hear our feeble petiton if offered in faith. What a blessed privalage. I think at times what could we do here without the Bible and the family alter [altar]. I long to live nearer to God and enjoy more of that love. It is our privalage to do. I have to mourn daily my coldness of heart, ant [and it] appears the more I strive the more I see my imperfection—and short comeings. Today has been very pleasent. Very little wind, some of the time almost a calm. It is warm and I spend most of my time on deck. The Capt. is aloft a grate deal of the time and it is lonely below. I have just come from the deck where we have been jumping the rope for exersize—The Capt., my self, and the mates—nice sport.

SUNDAY 13

This has been a lovely day. A pretty little brieze with three studen sails out, and we have been moving at a midling rate. But with all this pleasentness we could not enjoy the privalage of hearing the sound of the church going bell, nor of assembling ourselves together without it in the house of God, to hear dispensed the words of truth and life. And if we were like many or most of our crew, would not read a word for ourselvs. Methinks our condition would be a deplorable one. What better are they than the poor heathen, especially hear at sea? They have appeared very well so far on the Sabath, they make but little noise. But what they do in the fore castle I can not say. The Capt. has not had to reprimand them once, I believe. I have proposed reading to them. Some of them say they would like to hear good reading. I desire to put it of [off] no longer than next Sabath if it is pleasent. The Capt. thinks he cannot take up his cross for he says he has no one to help him, which is very true. But I trust the Lord will help him, then surely he will be helped. The mate tries not to believe in anything, but still he has a heart, and I trust one that is susceptible of right and wrong, and a Wife that is a professer of religeon. And I hope he will ere long join her heart and hand in her heavenward journey.

Discussion Questions

1. According to Exquemelin, how did pirates determine their leadership and rates of pay? Does he present any evidence of a particular ethic or set of values that bound pirates together? Why would piracy appeal to sailors used to working in merchant or naval ships?

2. What sins does Mather associate with sailors and life at sea? What does he find remarkable about Fly's conduct before his execution, and what does that conduct tell you about Fly's impressions of civil and religious authorities on land?

3. What does Penny's story about his impressment tell you about shipboard life for sailors on naval ships? How did the treatment of sailors on naval ships differ from that on pirate ships? Where in Penny's story do you see evidence of the distinctive political values or identities of sailors?

4. What elements of shipboard work, leisure, and discipline does Brown find contrary to Christian habits and morals? How do you think the crew responded to her concern for their spiritual and physical welfare? What do her impressions of shipboard life tell you about gender roles in the maritime world?

Suggested Readings

Marcus Rediker's *Between the Devil and the Deep Blue Sea: Merchant Seamen, Pirates, and the Anglo-American World, 1700–1750* (Cambridge: Cambridge University Press, 1987) offers an engaging account of the working life of British seamen in the eighteenth century. Marcus Rediker and Peter Linebaugh link sailors to the wider experience of laboring peoples in the Atlantic World in *The Many-Headed Hydra: Sailors, Slaves, Commoners, and the Hidden History of the Revolutionary Atlantic* (Boston, MA: Beacon Press, 2000). Other books that address the politics and culture of Anglo-American seafarers include Daniel Vickers, *Young Men and the Sea: Yankee Seafarers in the Age of Sail* (New Haven, CT: Yale University Press, 2005); Nathan Perl-Rosenthal, *Citizen Sailors: Becoming American in the Age of Revolution* (Cambridge, MA: Harvard University Press, 2015); and Paul Gilje, *"To Swear Like a Sailor": Maritime Culture in Early America, 1750–1850* (New York: Cambridge University Press, 2016). Simon P. Newman analyzes the unique physical appearance of sailors, especially their tattoos, in "Reading the Bodies of Early American Seafarers," *William and Mary Quarterly*, third series, 55 (1998): 59–82. For the impressment of sailors by the British Navy, see Denver Brunsman, *The Evil Necessity: British Naval Impressment in the Eighteenth-Century Atlantic World* (Charlottesville, VA: University of Virginia Press, 2013).

Two good comprehensive accounts of Atlantic World piracy are Kris Lane, *Pillaging the Empire: Piracy in the Americas, 1500–1750* (Armonk, NY: M. E. Sharpe, 1998); and Marcus Rediker, *Villains of All Nations: Atlantic Pirates in the Golden Age* (Boston, MA: Beacon Press, 2004). For a look at the contest in the Caribbean from the Spanish perspective, see Carla Rahn Phillips, *Six Galleons for the King of Spain: Imperial Defense in the Early Seventeenth Century* (Baltimore, MD: Johns Hopkins University Press, 1992). Works that explore Atlantic seafaring through the lenses of gender and sexuality include Lisa Norling, *Captain Ahab had a Wife: New England Women and the Whalefishery, 1720–1870* (Chapel Hill, NC: University of North Carolina Press, 2000); B. R. Burg, *Sodomy and the Perception of Evil: English Sea Rovers in the Seventeenth Century Caribbean* (New York: New York University Press, 1983); and *Iron Men, Wooden Women: Gender and Seafaring, 1700–1920*, eds. Margaret Creighton and Lisa Norling (Baltimore, MD: Johns Hopkins University Press, 1996); and Joan Druett, *Petticoat Whalers: Whaling Wives at Sea, 1820–1920* (Hanover, NH: University Press of New England, 2001).

10 The Atlantic Highway

European Migrations

Figure 10.1 Contract of Indenture, 1766.

Thousands of European migrants came to America during the eighteenth century as indentured servants (see Selections 1 and 2), signing contracts in which they agreed to serve their masters for several years in exchange for passage across the Atlantic Ocean. In this indenture, signed in Dublin, Ireland in 1766, Patrick Larkin bound himself to Thomas Blood, who was likely a ship captain assembling a cargo of servants for a trans-Atlantic voyage. Upon arrival in America, Blood would have sold Larkin and the other servants to local residents. Note that the indenture states that Larkin is "ordered to be transported." That language indicates that he was a convicted felon sentenced to "transportation," or seven years of labor in the colonies.

Source credit: Private Papers Collection, Library of Virginia.

Introduction

For thousands of years of human history, the Atlantic Ocean was a barrier, the edge of the known world for peoples living on both sides of it. Columbus changed all that with his voyage of 1492, turning the Atlantic into a highway connecting two previously isolated worlds. All sorts of goods passed back and forth across this highway, and of course, people did too. By far, the largest component of this human exchange was the 10 million Africans who crossed the ocean in the Atlantic Slave Trade (see Chapter 5). The colonization of the Americas set Europeans in motion as well, and about 1.4 million of them crossed the Atlantic between 1500 and 1800.

This human tide ebbed and flowed from region to region depending upon a variety of circumstances, and many of these people stayed only temporarily in the Western Hemisphere. When we label them as *immigrants* (meaning *coming to*), we romanticize them as brave souls who bid farewell to friends and families, never looked back, and made new lives for themselves in a strange land. But the Atlantic Ocean was a highway with eastbound as well as westbound lanes. Emigrants (meaning *coming from*) left Europe for the Americas but could and occasionally did return home. Even if they settled permanently in the new land, they maintained contact with family, neighbors, and business partners in the Old World by sending letters and messengers back along the same routes they had traveled. If we were to observe this movement from a midpoint in the Atlantic, it would not resemble a group of individuals scrambling over some natural barrier separating east from west. Rather, we would see people constantly moving back and forth, creating networks of communication and exchange that bound the continents closer together in a web of interdependence.

The European states that built empires in the New World tried as much as possible to regulate this trans-Atlantic movement. On the one hand, they wanted to populate their overseas dominions with loyal subjects who could defend the territory from hostile natives, rebellious slaves, or foreign enemies. In the race for empire, whichever state populated a territory first had the surest claim to it. On the other hand, governments wanted to control who went overseas. Some states, such as Spain and France, did not want religious nonconformists in their colonies. Others, such as England and the Netherlands, were more tolerant of religious differences, but tried to recruit settlers for specific economic purposes. All European states wanted to keep track of who was going, so that emigrants would not leave without paying debts or taxes owed at home, and many policy makers believed that too much emigration would hurt a nation by draining it of its most important resource: people.

The state's attempt to supervise migration from above was countered by the initiative of emigrants from below. Historians often use a "push–pull" model to describe the motives for human migration: certain conditions push people out of their homeland, while others pull them toward a new destination. Emigrants in early modern Europe responded to a variety of pushes and pulls that the state could not, or in some cases did not wish to, control. For example, the conversion of farmland into pasturage in Britain between 1500 and 1850 uprooted thousands of rural workers; the state abetted this displacement by allowing landlords to enclose lands previously used in common by rural villagers. Families dispossessed by this change fed the stream of British emigration to the New World. Explosive population growth in Europe also contributed to the pool of emigrants, as did the religious wars of the Protestant Reformation. In the Rhine River Valley, aristocrats strengthened laws designed to tie peasants to the land, but when famine and warfare made life there unbearable, the inhabitants ignored such restrictions and sought passage to Eastern Europe or North America. When a state tried to take advantage of such a push by directing emigrants to certain destinations or purposes, its efforts could easily go awry. In 1710, England's Queen Anne sponsored the emigration of 3,000 Germans to New York, where she expected them to work in the pine forests of the Hudson Valley making naval stores. Once in America, the Germans abandoned their overseers and settled their own farming communities on a remote frontier, collectively thumbing their noses at the colonial governor who tried to stop them. Thus could the best-laid plans fall apart when emigrants slipped the grasp of state officials.

Most Europeans who came to the Americas prior to 1800 did so in some form of bondage, typically indentured servitude. In exchange for signing a contract, or indenture, promising their labor to a master for a fixed number of years, emigrants secured trans-Atlantic passage and the necessaries of life while they served their time. English servants typically agreed to terms of service lasting four to five years. French *engagés* served three years, but the Crown later halved that term in an effort to increase white emigration to its sugar colonies. German-speaking redemptioners, who often traveled as families, negotiated the length of their service based upon the balance they owed for their passage once they landed in America. Those who had their debt paid or "redeemed" by relatives or friends walked off the ship free people; those not so fortunate sold themselves or family members into servitude to make up the difference.

Soldiers, sailors, and convicts also arrived in America in a form of servitude. Men who enlisted in the army or navy faced long terms of service that exposed them to disease, bodily danger, and brutal discipline. It is no wonder that many deserted when in America to look for more comfortable circumstances elsewhere. Potential emigrants from Spain, for example, had to go through a licensing process designed to weed out non-Catholics, debtors, and criminals. Many Spaniards circumvented this system by enlisting in the convoys that guarded the Atlantic treasure fleets and then jumping ship in America. In the first half of the seventeenth century, this tactic accounted for 50 percent of Spanish emigration to the New World. The British Transportation Act of 1718 gave convicted felons the choice between servitude in America or the noose at home. During the eighteenth century, this policy brought an estimated 50,000 English, Irish, and Scots to North America, accounting for about 25 percent of the emigration from the British Isles to America in that period. Orphans, vagrants, and other socially marginal folk faced similar types of state-sanctioned emigration throughout the colonial era.

Servitude and military service were occupations that attracted young, single, male emigrants from urban seaports. Another component of the Atlantic migration consisted of people from rural communities who maintained contact with families and friends back home after the Atlantic crossing, thereby creating private networks that publicized and sponsored emigration from one region to another. Rather than reflecting a breakdown of traditional community and kinship ties, this type of emigration, in which religious ties figured prominently, transplanted local identities and values in a wholesale fashion from one side of the ocean to the other. English Puritans and Quakers migrated to New England and Pennsylvania respectively, forming their American communities in ways that imitated distinctive regional patterns back home. French-speaking Protestants known as Huguenots were barred from French colonies, but they found an open door in British North America, where they named settlements such as New Rochelle and New Paltz after their European hometowns. German-speaking sects such as the Mennonites, Moravians, and Dunkers came to Pennsylvania because freedom from a state-sponsored church allowed them to recreate their spiritual and social communities with little interference. Many of the Jews expelled from Portugal in the early sixteenth century moved to Brazil. From there, some were drawn to the religiously tolerant Dutch colonies in the Caribbean and New Netherland, creating a network of Jewish communities that spanned the Americas.

The long-term trend in Atlantic migration was away from state control and in favor of individual initiative. Most state-supervised efforts to encourage or limit emigration to certain groups or regions crumbled in the face of the New World's insatiable demand for human labor and the Old World's surplus of population. The Atlantic highway beckoned the disenfranchised, the desperate, and the ambitious, who paid much less attention to national borders and identities than government officials would have liked. In the eighteenth and nineteenth centuries, the tide of European emigration swelled with peoples such as Germans, Scots-Irish (descendants of Scottish colonizers of Northern Ireland), and Scandinavians whose home states had no American empires of their own. Their migration further eroded the state's power to tie people to the land and helped shape the modern notion of a universal human right to freedom of movement across national borders.

The readings in this chapter focus on Atlantic migrations in the eighteenth century. They offer a look at emigration from German, French, and Scottish perspectives and express a range of emotions about it. It is important to remember that the vast majority of emigrants in this era did not leave texts describing their experiences. Literacy rates were low, and those emigrants who went as servants were the least likely to write about it. Thus, each of the sources presented below has its own bias, evident in the tone and style of the piece. As you read them, compare and contrast these biases: Does one source ring truer than the others? Is it possible to derive an accurate composite of the emigration experience from these sources?

Selection 1: An Englishman Enters into an Indenture

Like many indentured servants who came to colonial America, William Moraley was from a middle-class background but had difficulty finding employment in his native land. He learned his father's trade of watchmaking, but then the two had a falling out and the son found himself disinherited. Faced with mounting debts and no means to pay them, Moraley left Newcastle in the north of England for London, where he hoped to find work. When his situation there became desperate, he moved to America as an alternative to being imprisoned for debt.

Moraley lived in Pennsylvania and New Jersey as a servant and free man for five years, but he never found economic security. His inclinations toward drink and debt, which had plagued him at home, did not help his situation in America either. He returned to Newcastle and resumed the watchmaking trade, dying there in 1762. The account he published of his American travels offers one of the few first-hand accounts of how ship captains and their agents recruited individuals for the trans-Atlantic servant trade.

Credit: William Moraley, *The Infortunate: The Voyage and Adventures of William Moraley, an Indentured Servant*, eds. Susan E. Klepp and Billy G. Smith (University Park, PA: Pennsylvania State University Press, 1992), 49–54.

… I being resolute, as not caring what became of me, it enter'd into my Head to leave *England*, and sell myself for a Term of Years into the *American* Plantations. Accordingly I repair'd to the *Royal Exchange* [a commercial building in London], to inform myself, by the printed Advertisements fix'd against the Walls, of the Ships bound to *America*; where musing by myself, a Man accosted me in the following Manner. Sir, said he, I have for some time observed you, and fancy your Condition of Life is alter'd for the worse, and guess you have been in better Circumstances; but if you will take my Advice, I'll make it my Business to find out some way which may be of Service to you. Perhaps you may imagine I have a Design to inveigle you, but I assure you I have none; and if you will accept to a Mug of Beer, I will impart what I have to propose to you. The Man appearing sincere, I gave Ear to him.

I was dress'd at that Time in a very odd Manner. I had on a Red Rug Coat, with Black Lining, Black Buttons and Button Holes, and Black Lace upon the Pockets and facing; an old worn out Tye Wig, which had not been comb'd out for above a Fortnight; an unshaven Beard; a torn Shirt, that had not been wash'd for above a Month; bad Shoes; and Stockings all full of Holes.

After he had shav'd me, he proposed to me an *American* Voyage, and said there was a Ship at *Limehouse* Dock, that would sail for *Pensilvania* in three or four Days. Sir, said I, a Person like me, oppress'd by Dame Fortune, need not care where he goes. All Places are alike to me; and I am very willing to accept of your Offer, if I could have some View of bettering my Condition of Life, though I might have expected a better Fate than to be forc'd to leave my Native Country; But adverse Fortune is become familiar to me, by a Series of Misfortunes; so had rather leave a Place where I have no Prospect of advancing myself, than to continue here where I have no Friends to relieve me. Besides, in a distant Place, not being known, no Person can reflect on me for any ill Management, which oftentimes discourages one's Friends from supporting one, knowing the ill Use that is made of their Support.

Sir, says the Person, I'm entirely of your Way of Thinking, and believe you will better yourself by following my Advice. I will recommend you to the Captain, who is bound for *Philadelphia*, in *Pensilvania*, a Country producing everything necessary for the Support of Life; and when your Time is expir'd, you will be free to live in any of the Provinces of *America*.

Then he ask'd me, if I was bred to any Business. I told him, Watch-making was my Occupation. He said, he was afraid I would not do for any other Business, that being of little Service to the *Americans;* the useful Trades being, Bricklayers, Shoemakers, Barbers, Carpenters, Joiners, Smiths, Weavers, Bakers, Tanners, and Husbandmen more useful than all the rest. They bind themselves for four Years; but if I would consent to bind myself for five, he said he would undertake to get me admitted. Those Men Brokers have generally for their Pains Three Half Crowns, given them by the Masters of those Vessels which they are employ'd for.

After we had drank two Pints of Beer, he paid the Reck[o]ning. I absolutely agreed to go, and to that Intent we went before Sir *Robert Bailis*, Lord Mayor, where I was sworn as not being a married Person, or an Apprentice by Indenture. He paid for my Oath one Shilling, a Prerequisite of his Clerk. From thence we went to *London-Bridge*, to a Stationer's Shop, and there an Indenture of Servitude was drawn, which I sign'd. After this we took [a] Boat at *Billingsgate*, steer'd our Course for *Limehouse*, where we arriv'd about Eleven o'Clock in the Forenoon. The Ship was named the *Bonetta*, of about 200 Tons; the Owner *Charles Hankin*, [and] *James Reed*, Commander. There were on board 20 Persons, all Men, bound to the same Place, and on the same Account. As soon as I enter'd, my Friend left me to think better on it, and wish'd me a prosperous Voyage, and a good Wife.

I observ'd several of my Brother Adventurers seem'd very dejected, from whence I guess'd they repented of their Rashness. Soon after, Dinner was brought on the Table, which consisted of stew'd Mutton Chops. I was very glad I had an Opportunity of trying the Temper of my Tusks, for I had not eaten any Meat for four Days. I eat very heartily, and wash'd down the mutton with about two Quarts of Small Beer. I began to think myself happy, in being in a Way to eat; and on this Account, became insensible of the Condition I had brought myself to. In the Afternoon, the Master and Mate being absent, I ventur'd into the Cabin, and peeping into a Chest, discover'd a large Quantity of Raisins, of which I made free with about two Pound, and pocketed them for my own Use: Besides, the Small Beer stood upon Deck and was free for us at all times; so that laying all Reflections [aside], I comforted myself with the Hopes of living well all the Voyage, but was soon made sensible to the contrary when we set out to Sea …

Three Days after, being under Sail, a Boat hail'd us, and the Boatman ask'd if there was not one *Moraley* on board. The Mate denied I was there; but was answer'd that there was an Order from the Lord Mayor to bring him back again. To which he replied, I was gone, the Captain having discharg'd me. So the Boatman was satisfied, and return'd. I was then fast asleep below, and the rest of the People were kept under Deck, to prevent their Knowle[d]ge of this Enquiry; which when I was made acquainted with, I curs'd my Fate ten thousand times.

That Evening we sail'd down the River for the *Nore*, and arriv'd at *Eriff*, where we took in fresh Provisions, and the next Morning anchor'd close to *Gravesend*. A Custom House Officer came on board, and demanded of us, one by one, whether we were forced against our Wills, or if we went voluntarily. There every Adventurer had his Apparel given him for the Voyage, which was, a Sea Jacket, two coarse chequ'd Shirts, a Woollen Waistcoat, two coarse Handkerchiefs, one Pair of Hose, a Woollen Cap, and a pair of bad new Shoes. Thus accoutr'd, we set Sail for *America*, with a fair Wind, on the 7th day of *September*, in the Year 1729.

Selection 2: A German Migrant's Passage to America

John Frederick Whitehead was born in Pomerania (a region split between modern Germany and Poland) in 1757. In his early teens, he left home in search of employment, traveling to the cities of Hamburg and Amsterdam, and eventually falling in with "soulsellers," who were recruiting servants for overseas colonies. Whitehead initially planned to go to Batavia in the Dutch East Indies, but his recruiters placed him instead on a ship headed for Philadelphia, where he arrived in 1773. Whitehead spent his term of indenture as a farmhand in Berks County, Pennsylvania. After gaining his freedom, he worked as a laborer and weaver, eventually marrying and raising a family in humble circumstances. He dictated a narrative of his life to family and friends in 1795 and died twenty years later. In the passages below, he describes the difficulties he endured during his Atlantic crossing and the process by which he was sold to his new master in America.

Credit: Susan E. Klepp, Farley Grubb, and Anne Pfaelzer de Ortiz, eds., *Souls for Sale: Two German Redemptioners Come to Revolutionary America. The Life Stories of John Frederick Whitehead and Johann Carl Büttner* (University Park, PA: Pennsylvania State University Press, 2006), 128–129, 132–133.

[B]ut before I proceed any further I shall detain the Reader with an account of our Disasters and affliction which we Suffered in this Voyage. it was not above two Weeks after we left the Coast of England that we were visited by a mortal Disease which soon swept away all such as were any ways infected with the Venereal Disease. but although it seemed to begin upon them first, it seized likewise such as were known to lead an inoffensive Life. our Doctor seemed to be unacquainted with it; he scarcely knew what to call it, but it was generally believed to by a branch of the Scurvy or Yaws. the first Simtoms of it was a violent itching round the Fundement [buttocks] which soon generated into a Number of Pustels which were small in the beginning but soon grew to the size and shape of a small Pea attended with a constant burning and itching. the Patient also was afflicted with a constant Fever and loss of Senses and exceeding weak and fainty, especially when exposed to the Air. and I have seen some to crawl upon Deck who seemed pretty chearful while they remained beneath but as soon as they came in the Air they would fall into a swoon, if not expire. the Mariners themselves, from the Captain down to the Shipswab did not escape the Disorder. the Mate and Cabbin Boy, with near half the Sailers, were interred in the Liquid Tomb and our Doctor with nearly forty Passengers and Servants shared the same fate. and I think I may venture to say a Vessel never crossed the Atlantic in a more feeble condition than we, for scarcely ever more than two or three sailers were capable of Duty so that there was frequent occasion for some of the Servants to exert themselves in assisting the Sailers, especially in the Time of a Storm and what is most to be wondered at is that never any were canted overboard. now as for the burial of our Dead, I can assure the Reader that we made as little solemnity as ever any People in the World did that profess themselves Christians, for as the Grave was always ready to receive the Corpse and we had nothing to do but sew them up in a piece of sail cloth with a Bag that contained nearly two Quarts of Sand across their feet and so plunged them in. but towards the latter part of July they seemed to die apace and there was scarcely a Morning when we arose without finding two and sometimes three dead amongst us. this roused us, as it were, from a State of slumber and not knowing whose turn might be next, we thought it Time to begin a reformation. we choosed our Surgeon, who was pretty far advanced in Years and of a tolerable good Character, as also a Scholar, for to be our Priest and we began not only to inter our Dead decently [with] Prayers and singing Hymns but also met on the Sabbath together on Deck [with those] that were capable of coming in order to worship. this was greatly recommended by our Captain who ordered us further to read Morning and Evening Prayers and sing an Hymn or two which we did and continued it even while we were lying before the City of Philadelphia.

***

Now although the Disease raged amongst us to a great degree, I kept in a good State of Health till near the beginning of August and then it seemed as if not only the Disease attacked me with all its Fury but I was also afflicted with, as I called it, an Elephantic Itch, for I never have seen such an Itch to my Memory in my Life. for my Arms and Hands, both within and without, were almost covered with Pustels nearly as big as a Spanish Fivepence, filled with yellow offensive matter. my Thighs and Hams were in the same condition and the rest of my Body was nearly covered with small red Pustels resembling the Seeds of a Fish. but my Hips and Seat were greatly afflicted with the aforesaid intolerable Disease which spread with such rapidity that in a little Time my whole Seat was in one intire Scab. and although I greatly suffered in those parts, It seemed tolerable easy to what extreme pain I underwent in a part which Modesty forbids me to mention and had I not been well assured I had no reason to think of being infected with the Venereal Disease, I should have concluded I had been in a State of peutrifaction. I many Times [was made] to think on Job and I thought I could truly say with him that I was lothesome to myself. and my Garments did cleave to my Flesh and its colour changed by the violence of my Disease and what added greatly to my affliction was the inability of cleansing myself by which I became almost covered with filth and Lice. my Head also was full of sores and Scabs full of Lice and Nits till one of my Messmates was moved with compassion towards me and undertook to cleanse me. it was also my ill fortune to be destitute to the help of a Doctor or Surgeon for the first being buried in the deep and [as for] the latter his Salves and Ointments were all spent so there was [no] visible help for me. but the Invisible Lord and Supreme Physician was graciously pleased to deliver me, as it were, out of the Jaws of Death. for whilst I was standing, as it were, on the Brink of the Grave and expecting nothing else every moment than for to be plunged in the abys of Eternity. I was relieved and began to recover beyond all expectation, so as to crall about and I gathered Strength pretty fast so that I was in a State capable of cleansing myself. I often had to think on the vast difference there seemed to be between us poor infirm Mortals on Shipboard and them on Shore: where they [on land] may lie on their Beds of Down and their Friends and Relations administering all the help and relief in their power to make the situation as easy as possible—to turn him with a Sheet from Side to Side and sometimes raise him high or low according as he finds the most ease and if any thing might please his palate he enjoys it as soon as possible. but alas! the hard Oak Plank had to serve us instead of a downy Bed and the violent motion of the Vessel, especially in the Time of a Storm, was the Sheet that shifted us from Side to Side.

Selection 3: A French Account of a Passage to Canada

"Jolicoeur" Charles Bonin, or J. C. B. as he identified himself in his narrative, was a well-educated eighteen year old when he set out from his home in Paris, in 1751, to seek work with an uncle in the port city of La Rochelle. His uncle's death forced him to reconsider his options, and he decided to head for Canada, where he enlisted in the army and served in the Seven Years' War. Like many French emigrants to America, Bonin was young, single, and transient; at no time did he seem to consider his move permanent, and he returned to France in 1761. He wrote his narrative many years later, in a style that combines an old soldier's war stories with history and travelogue. In the passages that follow, he provides a colorful account of his trans-Atlantic passage, as well as explanations for his decisions to emigrate and enlist in the army.

Credit: *Travels in New France by J. C. B.*, eds. Sylvester K. Stevens, Donald H. Kent, and Emma Edith Woods (Harrisburg, PA: Pennsylvania Historical Commission, 1941), 1–5, 10, 15–17.

Year 1751:—I left Paris on the 15th of March to go to La Rochelle, with my father's permission. I was then eighteen years old. While I was walking along the road, I came upon a detachment of one hundred and twenty recruits led by an officer. He was taking them to the Isle of Rhée, the place of their departure. This officer hailed me, and questioned me about the purpose of my trip, my affairs and financial resources. I replied that I was going, with my father's permission, to join my uncle who was captain of the posts at La Rochelle, and had been awaiting me for six months. As for my financial resources, they were not large but sufficient for me until my arrival. Then my uncle would put me in the way of earning more. After this reply, the officer proposed that I travel with him to my destination, where he was going to stay, but on condition that I take care of his things on the way. To this I consented willingly. By my behavior I gained his confidence, and was lodged and fed with him.

When we arrived at La Rochelle, I thanked him and took leave of him in order to go and join my uncle. But when I arrived at his place, I was indeed surprised to learn that the latter had been buried a week before. Because of this misfortune, together with the smallness of my resources for returning to Paris, I decided to find the officer I had just left, and tell him what had happened. This man offered to take me with him to the Isle of Rhée, where he hoped to get me a job from the governor of the citadel. I accepted his offer.

The next day, April 2nd, we crossed in two small sailboats to the Isle of Rhée. As soon as we arrived, I followed the officer, who led his recruits to the citadel and turned them over to the governor. He recommended me so highly that I was at once employed in his office. The pay was small; but in my position I dared not hesitate.

When I had worked about twelve months, I was tormented with a desire to travel. I sought information about the best country to live in; about Louisiana and Canada, the only places to which recruits were then taken from the Isle of Rhée. The sailors told me that Canada was more healthy, although its climate was colder. I decided to take their advice, and to take advantage of the first sailing, which was not far off. This I did despite the offers made by the governor, which I refused, expecting that the voyage would be more profitable. The orders had come to have a number of select recruits embark for the colonies of Louisiana and Canada. The first sailing was to Louisiana, and included two hundred men. Some of these had been companions of mine on the road. The second sailing was not delayed, and I took advantage of it.

The 12th of June, I left the Isle of Rhée, five leagues from La Rochelle, in one of two small boats which took three hundred recruits down the Charente River, which is two leagues from Rochefort. There a vessel was waiting to take us to Canada. This vessel was called the *Chariot Royal*. It was a frigate used as a transport, and although pierced for thirty-six cannon, it carried only eight. It was commanded by a naval captain named Salabéry.

The 27th of the same month of June, we set sail by a good wind from the northeast, which in two days carried us from the coast of France, setting our course to the west-northwest.

The 31st, the wind became so contrary that we had to use the bowline and tack about for several days. The sea was so rough that we experienced a bad tempest which made us put on the spencer [a low sail]. On this occasion I paid tribute to the sea with a sickness which lasted as long as the bad weather, nearly five days. All this time I could not eat. At last the wind went down, and the sea became calm. I then recovered my appetite, but, the wind falling completely, the ship stood still, and we were becalmed for two days.

July 15th, a light easterly breeze came up and helped us on our way, but not for long. For, two days later, another storm struck and made us keep on the spencer four more days. In spite of myself, I renewed the tribute to the sea that I had thought paid in full. A rough sea has a disagreeable effect on my stomach.

At last the wind began to shift, the sea became placid, and we could continue our journey, but for only twenty-four hours. A contrary wind then became so strong that we had to tack for three days. After that, the wind shifted to the south, and we went on our way to the Jacquet Bank, some distance from the Grand Banks of Newfoundland. There, a contrary wind forced us to luff for several days. Then a fierce tempest, also from the west, drove us back about eighty leagues. In these circumstances the rudder line happened to break, and the compass was put out of order. Repairs were quickly made, and four days later we could continue on our way.

August 15th, the wind was again contrary, and we had about three weeks of continual tacking.

The 14th of September, we arrived at the Grand Banks of Newfoundland, in eighty fathoms of water. Immediately the sailors cried, "Long live the King." This is a custom among the sailors when they find bottom.

The Banks of Newfoundland are nine hundred leagues west of France. They are thought to be one hundred and fifty leagues long by about ninety wide, and from fifteen to eighty fathoms deep. They are really a mountain under water. We had much to suffer on these banks from rain and contrary winds, which held us up for several days in spite of all our efforts. This is the most disagreeable and most uncomfortable place in the ocean. The sun seldom appears, and the air is filled with a cold dense fog.

The nearest land is Cape Rouge, which stretches for thirty-five leagues from east to west, and is part of the island of Newfoundland, which will be described later.

The wind had just fallen when we arrived on the Grand Banks, and since there was a beautiful calm, the sailors wanted to catch some codfish. But as it was late, they put off the party until the next day, provided the weather was favorable. Unfortunately, there was a heavy rain during the night, along with thunder and lightning. The whole sky seemed to be cracking open. There was one crash of thunder after another, and the lightning alone threw momentarily the light of day into the darkness. The thunderbolts fell near the vessel with a racket like cannon-fire. We were all terrified. During the hour and a half that the storm continued we seemed to be in the trenches. I was ready at any moment to become food for the codfish on which we had planned to feast the next day.

After two hours of worry and anxiety, between life and death, the light of day appeared; the thunder and lightning stopped; the wind ceased; and the sea became calm. The sailors repaired the damaged rigging, and we were then able, about noon, to catch some fish. In three days' fishing we took enough cod to feed us for several days.

***

As the weather continued calm, the crew amused themselves with a baptismal ceremony that the sailors practice on those who cross the banks for the first time. For this ceremony, they disguise an old sailor with a large fur cap, a pair of high boots, a white wig on his head, a helmet, and a large white false beard. The sailor thus costumed descends from the maintopmast where he dressed. With the aid of cords and pulleys he slides to the foot of the foremast, where the other sailors receive and conduct him to the foot of the mainmast. Near this they hold the new member to a seat on the edge of a tub filled with water. There Father Terreneuve [Newfoundland] makes the new member swear to keep the secret from those who have not yet passed this latitude, with a promise never to touch the wife of another sailor. This he must promise at once. If the new member has not taken the precaution of buying drinks, he is immediately tipped into the water by the two men holding him. He then emerges to change his clothes. During this time Father Terreneuve goes away, takes off his costume, and reappears, so that the man who was ducked will not recognize him. This is the end of the ceremony, which is quite disagreeable in cold weather, and is only a game played by the sailors to get money.

***

On the fourth [of November], taking advantage of the tide, we rounded a point of land on our left, which extended somewhat above Orleans Island and to the north. This is called Point Lévis. Then only can the city of Quebec be seen, opposite the channel by the island, and about a league to the west. We entered the roadstead and anchored at four o'clock in the afternoon, after a difficult voyage of nearly five months. As it was too late to land, we waited until the next day.

On the morning of the fifth we landed. The recruits were taken to the barracks, and I was given lodgings with a wholesale merchant named Samson, who lived in the lower town. I was very well lodged. I remained five days with this honest merchant, who treated me with kindness. In this time I roamed the city and its surroundings, getting from my host any information that I desired.

***

In five days, I had visited the most interesting places. I was then forced to give up my life of needy idleness. I therefore determined to take up the military profession, which, though seeming severe, would nevertheless relieve me at once from my difficulties.

This decision was compelled by circumstances. I felt an inclination for a more lucrative occupation. But I made up my mind and of my own free will left the merchant with whom I had been boarding, going at once to the artillery commander to enlist in that company, because, after making inquiries, that branch of the service seemed more to my liking. They were paid sixteen to eighteen francs a month.

When I informed this officer of my wish to enlist, he said I was unfit and not tall enough to enter the artillery service. Fortunately for me, three women were there, who were willing to take an interest in my welfare, because of my well-bred air. After he had asked me various questions, which I answered frankly to the best of my ability, the officer decided to enlist me as a gunner, at the request of these ladies. They thanked him, and to show their satisfaction, proceeded to give me the nickname of "Jolicoeur [sweet-heart]." A louis [a French gold coin] of provincial paper money accompanied it, which one of them gave me. I accepted it very willingly, for I was penniless. At the same time I received the commander's orders to be present at the review by the Governor General, which was to be held the next day, November the 12th, on the Place d'Armes. The recruits were to be incorporated into the various companies of troops garrisoned in the city and not yet formed in regiments, because they were reckoned free companies of the marine. I was present at the review. All the troops were under arms in three lines, which included eighteen companies. The recruits opposite were unarmed and formed two lines.

The governor, accompanied by the staff officer, arrived about noon. When they had assigned me my place at the end of the two artillery companies, which perform the duties of grenadiers, the inspection began. When the commander spoke of me to the governor, he looked me over. That was all, as far as I was concerned. He went on to the other companies and finally to the recruits. There, each captain, according to his age, beginning with the gunners, took the number of men assigned to him. The commander of the gunners chose ten without counting me, and the other captains did the same. When the selection of men was finished, each company retired with its recruits. I was one of five taken into the second company, which was lodged over the Gate St. Jean. The next day we were given our clothing and equipment.

As usual during a review, a great many persons, even the most distinguished people of the city, were attracted by curiosity. I saw there with pleasure my three patronesses, who made much of me and gave me eighteen francs in silver. Their generosity was a happy omen for me. When I joined the company, I gave the eighteen francs I had just received to pay my initiation fee, as was the usual custom. It secured me friends in the usual soldier way, but I valued them only as far as they could serve my interest, and without making a habit of frequenting taverns with them.

They gave me as a bedfellow (for they slept double) a Parisian with a handsome and pleasing face, who had the vices of gambling and drink. He was also quarrelsome and ill-natured, often drawing his sword without the slightest provocation. In time, however, I began to acquire so much influence over him, that I subdued his fits of passion by my very presence. In the morning he was good-natured and amiable, especially toward women, whom he studied to deceive. He was extremely fond of dancing, at which he was an expert. He gave me a liking for it, by taking me with him to balls and teaching me its principles. At the end of three months I became, under his supervision, almost as proficient in that art, which helped at least for a time to turn him from his vices. Later, when I neglected him somewhat, he took up his old habits. He took advantage of my kindness to him by wearing my clothes and helping himself to my money, to a point where I was often unable to go out. This conduct cooled my friendship, and I decided to break with him.

During the month of December, a merchant offered me a place in his store to keep books and learn his business. I took it without hesitation because I had vowed, viewing the uncertainty of the future, that I would learn everything possible that I might need to use. I knew that a man who has but one aim might find himself embarrassed if that should fail him. I then began work with the merchant, who, finding me full of zeal for his interests, became my friend. I pleased him so much that he worked for my discharge from the army. This benevolent act encouraged me to show him my great gratitude, which I did with all my heart. He took all the steps he thought necessary for my discharge, but they were fruitless. I was told, indirectly, that this good man intended to take me into his business as soon as he had procured my discharge, and to give me the store, and his only daughter in marriage. She was a beautiful, well-educated young girl. On this occasion fortune was unkind, and I regretted then that I had enlisted.

Selection 4: Two Scottish Opinions on the Emigration Experience

In the fifteen years prior to the American Revolution, a new tide of emigration spilled out of the British Isles and into North America. A considerable number of these emigrants came from Scotland, seeking cheap lands and settling on a backcountry frontier that stretched from New York to Georgia. Promotional and support networks made up of kin and neighbors sprung up on both sides of the Atlantic to sustain this migration, and correspondence between Scotland and America provided the primary channel for exchanging information. Alexander Thomson was a farmer from near Glasgow, who moved his large family to the Pennsylvania frontier in 1771. He prospered quickly on his own land and had the letter that follows published back home to inform others of the opportunity waiting for them in America.

Baikia Harvey, a sixteen-year-old indentured servant from the Orkney Islands, had a much different experience. He arrived in Georgia on the eve of the American Revolution and quickly found himself embroiled in guerilla warfare between patriots and loyalists. His letter to his godfather conveys a sense of the terror that his new surroundings caused him. He was killed in battle in 1779, while serving in a patriot unit attacking a British post.

Credit: Alexander Thomson, "Franklin County One Hundred Years Ago," *Pennsylvania Magazine of History and Biography* 8 (October 1884): 315–321, 326–327; and "[To] Thomas Baikie, Esq., in Burnass in the Parish of Firth the Orkineys North Britin," December 30, 1775, document reference number D3/385, Orkney Library and Archive, Kirkwall, Orkney, Scotland.

Corkerhill [Thomson's farm, near Shippensburg] in Pensilvania, August 16th, 1773.
   Dear Sir,
   I know well that after the promises I made you, you could not have thought that so much time would pass, before you had any letter from me. Indeed I did not forget my promise, but after I had got an agreeable settlement to myself, I was desirous to have some particular knowledge of this country, before I should undertake to write any account of it to you.
   In July 1771, I and my wife and twelve of our children went aboard the Friendship in the harbour of Greenock: It was after the middle of that month when we set sail for

North-America, and happily we arrived at the city Boston on the tenth of September, all in perfect health.

I believe that some of my neighbours and acquaintance thought it strange, that one of my age should forsake his native country: but I thought I had but too much reason to do as I have done: as I was blessed with a numerous family, (and I have had another child since I left Scotland) I was very desirous to provide for them: All my sons who were able to work were brought up to the business of farming, and it was by their labour that I was assisted to gain any money I have: I therefore endeavoured to have one or two of the eldest of my sons settled in farms at home; and with that view I employed myself for the space of five years, in looking out for such farms as might answer my purpose. I travelled through the country for twenty miles round the place where I lived; but tho' I found plenty of vacant farms, I told you before, and I declare it again on the word of an honest man, that I could see no farm for which the laird [landlord] did not ask more than double the rent it was worth; so that if I had meddled with any of them I say well that my sons would never be able to pay the rent, and that in three or four years I would not have had one shilling to rub upon another.

After I had spent so much time and labour to no purpose, I confess that at length I conceived a sort of distaste for the lairds: I imagined that as they knew I had a little money, they wanted to get it from me as fast as they could; and in truth some of my neighbours observed a change in my temper, and alleged that I was turned so obstinate that I would not stay in the country, even though some laird should offer me a farm or two on reasonable terms: and I dare not say they were altogether in the wrong.

As I was going to America not for merchandizing but as a farmer; several of my acquaintance and well-wishers told me that I would save both time and money by landing at New York or Philadelphia, but I had a great curiosity to see Boston, especially as I understood that some of my father's friends had settled there long ago, and some from Paisley very lately. However I stayed at Boston but a few days; for I made all the haste I could to wait on Dr. Witherspoon [a fellow Scot and President of Princeton College] at Princeton in West-Jersey, and when I had gone there, I was sorry to hear that he had gone away a day or two before, to convey some of his pupils home to their parents who lived in Virginia; but I had the good luck to come up with him in the city of Philadelphia. I delivered to him the letters I had from Scotland, and he received me very kindly: When he understood my errand he was very earnest to assist me to get a right farm. He advised me to take patience, and that I should not be hasty in making a bargain. But that as he was upon a journey, I should wait at Princeton till his return, when he would do all he could to get me settled in a comfortable manner: He also advised me to rent a farm for some time, but as I had so great a family with me, I was desirous to have a house of my own as soon as I could conveniently get it: and I also thought it would be better for me to improve land that was my own than any rented farm; and as I had heard so much said about the goodness of land upon the Ohio, both at home and since I had come here, I would fain have settled there at first, but as I could not conveniently do so, I bargained for the plantation on which I now live, before Dr. Witherspoon returned from Virginia; and if it had not been for the reason I have told you, I would have conducted myself entirely by his advice. But I have much cause to rejoice and none to repent that I made this purchase.

***

It was in April 1772, that I settled on this plantation: It is situated at the distance of 150 miles from Philadelphia, and it is just as far from Fort-pit [modern Pittsburgh]; it lies in a large and beautiful valley which runs thro' all Pensylvania, Maryland, and Virginia it consists of about 430 acres, and there was a house of two stories high, and office-houses upon it: The house is built of square blocks of wood nocked or indented into one another; it is well plaistered, so that it is warm enough, and I have six convenient rooms in it.

My plantation which I have called Corkerhill, after the name of the farm where my father lived and died, and where I lived so long; My plantation consists wholly of limestone-land, and in general limestone-land is reckoned the best in this country. There is plenty of limestone for manure in every field, and it doth not cost much labour or expence to come at it; and it can be burned with the wood which we grub out when we clear the ground. Our greatest labour is to cut the wood into small pieces when we are to burn the lime.

Dear Sir, I do assure you I am well pleased with the country, and with my situation in it. I bless God that I came here, and I heartily thank every man who encouraged me and helped me to get the better of that fear which a man is under when he is to venture over so wide a sea, and indeed when, excepting my eldest son, I was to carry along with me all that was dear to me in the word, I could not but be anxious about them; but I was determined in my mind, and providence hath been very favourable to us. We are all at present in good health; and blessed be God, we have always been so since we came into this country. They say here, that the air and climate of Pensilvania agrees better with European constitutions, than even the air of Europe itself, and I am inclined to think that this is true, from that constant health which my family have enjoyed.

***

We who are country people used always to think it a great matter, that the gentlemen in Scotland had orchards, we thought this a fine thing; but here, almost every farmer hath a good orchard, and indeed squashes, pimpkins [sic], gourds, cucumbers, melons, and all other garden-stuff grow in the open fields: But unluckily through the slothfulness of my predecessor, there was no orchard on the plantation when I came to it; To supply this defect, I have already planted two hundred fruit trees, and I was pleased to see that one of the trees had three apples upon it this year, though it was not planted till march last.

Dear Sir, I have said so much about my industry and labour upon the plantation, but I have said it on purpose, because I know that a vile and false report hath been published at home, that it is only lazy persons who come over here. Now you know well, and I need not tell you that the very contrary is true; the lazy are motionless, and like snails abide on the spot where they are, till they either starve, or are compelled by hunger to go a begging: whereas the industrious strive to maintain themselves by their labour without being troublesome to any body, and many of them finding it difficult to live by their labour at home, they are so far from being lazy, that they have activity and spirit to venture over to America: but I pity many of your poor people who are indeed very lazy; and it is impossible but they must be lazy, because they have found by long experience that by all their labour they can make no profit to themselves.

***

Dear Sir, notwithstanding my promise, I am yet very unfit to write you a description of the country; and indeed it is needless, as you know so much and so well about it already: but for the sake of my promise, and for your satisfaction, I will tell you the truth about it as far as I can, and I shall begin with the climate.

Till I came into this country I did not, I could not imagine the climate was so fine and so healthy: The air is sweet and clear, and we find an agreeable smell; one would think that the sky is much farther distant from us than it seems to be at home. The south-west wind rules the summer seasons, and the north-west the winter. The winters which are very agreeable continue from December till March; and we have no such black foul weather as at home, but a fine pure sky and bright heavens; no storms as at home, but fine small breezes; no winds to shake or rains to rot the corn.

Sir, I cannot express the beauty of the summer season, it is so fine, so pleasing, and healthy. While I and my sons are clearing ground, and go for a while to walk, or rest ourselves in the forest among the tall oaks on a summer day, the sight of the heavens and the smell of the air give me a pleasure which I cannot tell you how great it is. When we sit down to rest, the breezes of the south-west wind, and the whispering noise it makes on the top of the trees, together with the fine smell of the plants and flowers pleases us so exceedingly, that we are almost enchanted and unwilling to part with such a pleasure. If my dear countrymen knew the beauty and healthiness of the climate, they would not be so afraid to come to North-America. There are a good number of old people just about where I live, some sixty, some seventy, and some eighty years of age. I thought it right to tell you all this, because I know that much pains have been taken to spread abroad a bad opinion of the country and climate, as if it were unhealthy: I will not say why this hath been done, but I suspect it hath taken its rise from some designing men among you, who though they saw many people in great straits, and many next door to starving, have for some views of their own, endeavoured to terrify them from coming here.

In truth, I am sorry to hear of the great distress of farmers and tradesmen in your country. You mention this in your letter, but I have heard much more from some folks I lately met with when I was at Philadelphia; and so far as I understand, the weavers and other tradesmen, as also many farmers are in a far worse condition than they were when I came away in the year 1771, for it seems the tradesmen cannot get employment, and the meal continues to be as dear as it was. If the tradesmen and farmers would come here, they would soon find themselves in a better condition; and there is plenty of room for them all, yea for all the people that are in the three kingdoms. And this is the best poor man's country in the world, for the price of provisions is cheap, and the price of labour is dear; and there are many people in Pensilvania and the neighbouring provinces, who had to work here to pay their freight, who have good plantations and are in wealthy circumstances: But this country is chiefly profitable to those farmers who bring along with them one, two, or three hundred pounds; such farmers can afford to eat good pork, beef, or mutton, as often as those who have one, two, or three hundred pounds of yearly rent in Scotland; that is to say, if they have some tolerable skill in farming, and live upon the land they take up here; and I believe there are no farmers in the world who live on so coarse and so poor food as do the generality of farmers in poor Scotland.

***

I had almost forgot to tell you, That when I was at Philadelphia, I saw some Scotch newspapers in which a great deal was said about the death of emigrants by sea and their wretched state after they have come to the American towns. As I have said already, I never heard of any ill happening to emigrants by sea, and if they suffer any harm here, it will be rather from the hospitality than from the cruelty of this people; no doubt those who are forced to indent must be in a state of dependance till they have served out their time, and I pity their case. But as I have told you, I know several people here who served to pay their freight, who have now good plantations. However, our opinion here is, That both your farmers and tradesmen should come away before they grow so poor that they will have nothing to bring with them, or even to pay their freight ...

I am, ...

Alexander Thomson

***

Dear Godfather

I am very sorry that I did not take your Advise and stay at home with you as I have found to my sad Experence that I ought not to have slighting your Advise Mr Gordon was vere good to me but Mr Brown us'd me vere ill and I Runaway from them & wint to the Armey that was mar[c]hing up to the Back parts of South Carolina against a sett of people they call Torrys in this Country and when I cam back I went to One Mr LeRoy Hammond a Merchant in So. Carolina & he Bought my time which I am vere glad of for he & his Lady uses me vere will & gives me Cloaths & I Ride with my Master & Loves them Both You'l Please to send me all the Money you can Colect that is my Due by the first safe oppertunity that I may be enabled to Buy my time & Put myself to some Tradesman to Learn his calling for a Tradsman has good Wages in this Country I beg that none of my Relation[s] may come to this Country Except they are able to pay their passage thir Selves and then they may come as soon as they like this is a good poor mans Country when a man once getts into a way of Liveing but our Country people knows Nothing when they come hear the Americans are Smart Industours hardy people & fears Nothing our people is only Like the New Negros that comes out of the ships at first whin they come amongst them[.] I am Just Returnd from the Back parts Where I seed Eight Thousand Men in Arms all with Riffel'd Barrill Guns which they can kill the Bigness of a Dollar Betwixt Two & three hundreds yards Distance the Little Boys not Bigger then my self has all their Guns & marshes with their Fathers & all thir Cry is Liberty or Death Dear God-father tell all my Country people not to come hear for the Americans will Kill them Like Deer in the Woods & they will never see them they can lie on their Backs & Load & fire & every time they Draw sight at any thing they are sure to kill or Criple & they Run in the Woods Like Horses I seed the Liberty Boys take Between Two & three hundred Torrys & one Liberty man would take & Drive four or five before him Just as the Shepards do the sheep in our Country & they have taken all their Arms from them and putt the Headmen in Gail [jail]—so that they will never be able to make head against them any more—Pray Remember me to my Dear freind Mr. James Riddoh Mrs. Gordon Madam Allin Madam Young My Uncle & Aunt & all their Femily & in perticular Mr. John Gordon—I am Dear Godfather Your Most Obident and Huml. Godson

Snowhill Near Augusta in Georgia
Baikia Harvey
Decemr. 30th 1775
P.S. Please to write me the first Oppertunity to the Care of Mr. John Houston in Savannah Georgia Province etc.

Discussion Questions

1. How does Moraley describe the process of indenture? What evidence do you find in his account of ways recruitment agents coerced or cajoled people into agreeing to emigrate as servants?
2. According to Whitehead and Bonin, what were some of the perils faced by emigrants during the trans-Atlantic passage? How do you think those perils compared to those faced by slaves coming from Africa in the Middle Passage (see Chapter 5, Selection 4)?
3. According to Thomson, what were the keys to succeeding in America? Why does he describe Pennsylvania as "the best poor man's country in the world"?
4. Both Bonin and Harvey ended up in military service after they emigrated to America. Why do you think this occupation attracted recent emigrants? What reasons do Bonin and Harvey give for enlisting?

Suggested Readings

Human migration is one of the most important unifying themes in Atlantic World history, enabling scholars to compare and contrast the experiences of different peoples, nations, and regions at different times during the colonization of the Americas. Two useful overviews are

Europeans on the Move: Studies on European Migration, 1500–1800, ed. Nicholas Canny (Oxford: Clarendon Press, 1994), and *"To Make America": European Emigration in the Early Modern Period*, eds. Ida Altman and James Horn (Berkeley, CA: University of California Press, 1991). Noteworthy for their comparative approach are Marianne S. Wokeck, *Trade in Strangers: The Beginnings of Mass Migration to North America* (University Park, PA: Pennsylvania State University Press, 1999), which analyzes eighteenth-century German and Irish emigration to Pennsylvania, and Alan L. Karras, *Sojourners in the Sun: Scottish Migrants in Jamaica and the Chesapeake, 1740–1800* (Ithaca, NY: Cornell University Press, 1992), which compares the Scottish experiences in North America and the Caribbean. For the perils migrants faced during their Atlantic passage, see Stephen R. Berry, *A Path in the Mighty Waters: Shipboard Life and Atlantic Crossings to the New World* (New Haven, CT: Yale University Press, 2015).

Several important studies focus on emigration from the British Isles to North America. For the seventeenth century, see Alison Games, *Migration and the Origins of the English Atlantic World* (Cambridge, MA: Harvard University Press, 1999). For the eighteenth century, see Bernard Bailyn, *Voyagers to the West: A Passage in the Peopling of America on the Eve of the Revolution* (New York: Random House, 1986). A. Roger Ekirch discusses British convict migration to North America in *Bound for America: The Transportation of British Convicts to the Colonies, 1718–1775* (New York: Oxford University Press, 1987). For convicts and other forced migrants, see also Gwenda Morgan and Peter Rushton, *Eighteenth-Century Criminal Transportation: The Formation of the Criminal Atlantic* (New York: Palgrave Macmillan, 2004); and Morgan and Rushton, *Banishment in the Early Atlantic World: Convicts, Rebels, and Slaves* (London: Bloomsbury, 2013).

For eighteenth-century German migration, see Aaron Spencer Fogleman, *Hopeful Journeys: German Immigration, Settlement, and Political Culture in Colonial America, 1717–1775* (Philadelphia, PA: University of Pennsylvania Press, 1996); and Philip Otterness, *Becoming German: The 1709 Palatine Migration to New York* (Ithaca, NY: Cornell University Press, 2004). Ida Altman analyzes Spanish emigration to the New World in *Emigrants and Society: Extremadura and America in the Sixteenth Century* (Berkeley, CA: University of California Press, 1989). For an examination of the disease and mortality involved in European migration to the Caribbean, see Philip D. Curtin, *Death by Migration: Europe's Encounter with the Tropical World in the Nineteenth Century* (Cambridge: Cambridge University Press, 1989); and Pierre Force, *Wealth and Disaster: Atlantic Migrations from a Pyrenean Town in the Eighteenth and Nineteenth Centuries* (Baltimore, MD: Johns Hopkins University Press, 2016).

11 Interracial Marriage and Sexuality in the Atlantic World

Figure 11.1 Native Women and the Fur Trade.

This map depicts the Ohio country, the region visited by fur trader Nicholas Cresswell during the 1770s (see Selection 3). Note the Native American women included in the lower right and lower left illustrations. Native women played an important role as go-betweens in the fur trade, as noted in Cresswell's journal. What message do you think the artist was trying to convey to the viewer by including these scenes on this map?

Source credit: Thomas Hutchins, *A General Map of the Country on the Ohio and Muskingham* … (1765). Library of Congress Prints and Photographs Division, LC-USZC4-4809.

Introduction

Of the many ways in which Europeans, Africans, and Native Americans interacted in the Atlantic World, perhaps none was more consequential for the formation of colonial societies than interracial sexual relations. Sexual violence was a part of the colonization process wherever Europeans tried to establish their authority over other peoples. But interracial sexuality also took the form of consensual unions that established the foundations for marriages and families, which in turn shaped new colonial social orders and legal systems for raising children and owning and transmitting property. In other words, investigating interracial marriage and sexuality enables the historian to see the human relationships that shaped the Atlantic World at their most intimate level.

All human societies construct gender roles—the ideas and behaviors associated with being male or female—to help order social relationships. Each society defines its own standards for masculinity and femininity, for sexual conduct and expression, for a division of labor between men and women, and as with any other social category, gender roles adapt to changing historical circumstances. The Atlantic World offers an interesting theater for studying the historical construction of gender because it brought together peoples with vastly different notions of how the two sexes ought to interact. Each group involved in this collision tried to preserve its own gender roles, but each also found those roles challenged by exposure to new people, environments, and ideas. Like any other aspect of human culture, gender had to be reconstructed in the crucible of the Atlantic World to reflect the new societies that emerged there.

Early European emigration to the Americas tended to be overwhelmingly male, leading many male colonists to pursue economic and sexual partnerships with women who came from societies that constructed gender very differently. In Canada, for example, European fur traders found marriage to Native American women a profitable way of gaining entry to Native communities. The Indians of New France came from a society in which kinship was determined matrilineally and much of daily life was matrifocal: family and clan membership passed through the mother, and clan matrons—the elder women of different lineages—held considerable influence over village politics. Women also were the primary agricultural laborers and managed the planting and harvesting of crops, while men took responsibility for hunting, trade, and diplomacy with outsiders. Missionaries tried to impose a European gender division of labor on their Christian converts, encouraging men to work in the fields and women to learn domestic tasks such as spinning and dairying, but they met with limited success. The extension of the fur trade and preservation of Indian friendship demanded that the French not push the imposition of their gender roles too far, lest marriage alliances fail and converts abandon the faith.

By the eighteenth century, there emerged in North America a type of interracial marriage that French fur traders called "marriage *à la façon du pays.*" In such unions, a male European fur trader took a Native American wife in a ceremony that involved asking the permission of her family and presenting them a gift of trade goods. These women contributed to the labor of the fur trade by continuing such traditional work as stringing snowshoes and making canoes, but they also served as interpreters and negotiators between Indians and Europeans. Missionaries frowned upon such marriages because they followed Native rather than Christian custom, were often temporary, and in some cases were even polygamous. Nevertheless, the custom remained an important part of the fur trade well into the nineteenth century and gave Indian women an influence in the marketplace and diplomatic councils that their European counterparts could not rival.

The intersection of sex, race, and labor in plantation colonies had very different ramifications. In early plantation societies, European men and women often worked side by side in the fields, and female servants were particularly susceptible to the sexual and physical abuse of their masters. As the slave population of a plantation colony increased, masters preferred to put African women to work in the fields alongside their male counterparts, so that white women could cease fieldwork and resume their traditional domestic duties. In this manner, plantation societies associated slavery with a feminized dependence and servility, while creating a standard of female respectability that was limited to whites only. This racial construction of gender is evident in the changing meaning of the word "wench" in colonial Virginia. The English who colonized Virginia initially used "wench" as a derogatory term for women of lower-class status, applying it interchangeably to white servants and black slaves. By the early eighteenth century, when slavery had displaced servitude as the colony's chief form of labor, white colonists used "wench" only in reference to women of African descent.

In Iberian America, the construction of gender roles reflected the distinctive heritage of Spanish and Portuguese colonists as well as their close contact with Native American and African populations. The confluence of Islamic and Christian faiths on the Iberian Peninsula during the medieval era had produced an ideal of femininity that emphasized seclusion and sexual purity. A family's honor depended in a large part upon how well its female members met social standards of piety and modesty, and marriage and female religious orders developed as the appropriate institutions for making sure women met these expectations. In the New World, the offspring of sexual unions between Iberian men and Native American or African women violated Iberian notions of "purity of blood," or the absence of non-Christian ancestry necessary for social and legal legitimacy. Elites placed great value in legal marriage (as recognized by the state and church), because it provided the basis for separating a father's rightful heirs from his illegitimate ones. People of mixed-race ancestry (see Chapter 7) lacked such "purity of blood" and often lived in a state of concubinage, or informal marriage, which the clergy frowned upon but society nevertheless tolerated. Thus, a correlation developed between race, social status, and illegitimacy in Iberian colonies: non-whites, who occupied the lower rungs of the social ladder, were more likely to bear illegitimate children than property-owning whites. Family honor and female chastity became values linked specifically to an elite exhibiting "purity of blood," while the lower orders of society lacked access to the legal recognition and property necessary to achieve such status.

The readings in this chapter offer differing perspectives on interracial sexuality and colonial gender roles from the seventeenth century to the mid-nineteenth century. During this era, women generally had lower literacy rates than men, and thus, left far fewer first-person accounts of their lives. African and Native American women were even less likely to leave behind such records, but their experiences can be glimpsed in the selections below. As you read them, think about how you might use these sources to describe how interracial sexuality shaped gender roles in colonial societies. How did religion and labor influence the way men and women entered into marriages and formed families across racial lines?

Selection 1: A French Nun Remarks on Native American Women

Marie de L'Incarnation was a French nun of the Ursuline order, founded in the sixteenth century to educate girls in the Catholic faith. The Ursulines extended their mission to North America when they established a convent school for Indian girls in Quebec in 1639. L'Incarnation was one of the founders of this convent, and she lived there until her death in 1672. In many ways, she led a remarkable life: a wife at age eighteen and a mother and widow by twenty, she became a nun and emigrated to America in her late thirties. Her writings provide a detailed record of the Ursuline mission in New France as well as a fascinating portrait of seventeenth-century Quebec society. Her letters are also indispensable to the study of gender relations in New France because she worked closely with Native girls and women and because hers is one of the few female voices in a record dominated by male priests. In the following excerpted letters, she describes some of the Indians who came under her tutelage. The praise she heaps upon her converts is indicative of the gendered values and sexuality she expected Native women to adopt as Christians, but her descriptions of Indians who resisted conversion also tells us about how Christianity upset traditional gender relations within Native communities.

Credit: *Word from New France: The Selected Letters of Marie de L'Incarnation*, trans. and ed. Joyce Marshall (Toronto: Oxford University Press, 1967), 71–75, 104–107.

There is talk of giving us two girls of this nation [Huron] and two Algonkins, these in addition to the eighteen that have filled our seminary, not to speak of the day-girls that come here continually. I assure you, Madame, that in France it will be hard to believe the benedictions God continually pours upon our little seminary. I shall give you a few particulars so as to acquaint you with our consolation.

The first Savage seminarian that was given to us, Marie Negabamat by name, was so used to running in the woods that we lost all hope of keeping her in the seminary. The Reverend

Father Le Jeune, who had persuaded her father [Noel Negabamat] to give her to us, sent two older Christian girls with her. These remained with her for some time in order to settle her, but to no avail, for she fled into the woods four days later, after tearing a dress we had given her to pieces. Her father, who is an excellent Christian and lives like a saint, ordered her to return to the seminary, which she did. She had not been here two days when there was a wonderful change. She seemed no longer to be herself, so disposed was she to prayer and the practices of Christian piety, so that today she is an example to the girls of Quebec, although they are all very well brought-up. As soon as she has committed a fault, she comes to ask pardon on her knees and she does the penances she is given with incredible submissiveness and amiability. In a word, it is impossible to look at her without being touched by devotion, so marked is her face by innocence and inner grace.

At the same time we were given a big girl of seventeen years whose name is Marie Amisk-ouevan. One could not see anything more tractable, more innocent, or more candid even than this girl, for we have never surprised her in a lie, which is a great virtue among the Savages. If her companions accuse her, she never excuses herself. She is so ardent in praying to God that it is never necessary to advise her to do so; she even leads the others, and it seems as if she were their mother, so much charity has she towards them. She has great intelligence for retaining what is taught her, especially the mysteries of our holy Faith, which makes us hope she will do great good when she returns to the Savages. She is sought in marriage by a Frenchman, but it is intended to give her to a man of her own nation because of the example it is hoped she will give the other Savages. If God would give someone in France the devoutness to help her build a little house, this would undoubtedly be a work of very great merit. This girl has helped us greatly in the study of her tongue because she speaks French well. In a word, she wins every-one's heart by her great sweetness and her fine qualities.

Your god-daughter, Marie-Magdeleine Abatenau, was given to us entirely covered with smallpox and still only six years old. She had at that age cared alone for her father and mother during the malady from which they died and with such skill that she was the wonder of everyone that saw her. No one more obedient than this child could be seen—she even antici-pates obedience, for she is skillful at taking up her position in those places where she foresees we might be able to employ her—and she does everything she is told with such good behaviour and good grace one would take her for a girl of rank. This, then, is your god-daughter, I should gladly say your daughter in Jesus Christ. I shall add for your consolation that she knows her catechism by heart, as well as the Christian prayers, which she recites with a devoutness capable of inspiring like feelings in those that see her.

Marie-Ursule Gamitiens, the god-daughter of Mademoiselle de Luynes, is only five or six years old. Small though she is, we have no trouble getting her to make her Christian devotions, for she is no sooner awake than she prepares herself to pray to God. She says her rosary during Mass and sings hymns in her Savage tongue.

Agnès Chabdikouechich was given to us at the same time. The name Agnès suits her very well, for she is a lamb in gentleness and simplicity. Some time before she entered the seminary she met the Reverend Father de Quen in the woods where she was cutting her provision. She had no sooner seen him than she threw her hatchet aside and said, "Teach me." She did this with such good grace that he was sensibly touched by it and, to satisfy her fervour, brought her and one of her companions to the seminary, where in a short time they were fitted for Holy Baptism. She has made very great progress with us in the knowledge of the mysteries and, as well, in good manners, embroidery, reading, playing the viol, and a thousand other little skills. She is only twelve years old and made her First Communion at Easter with three of her companions.

Nicole Assepanse was given to us the same day at the age of seven. Her parents, who are among the most prominent of the Savages, begged us to receive her for a time because she could not accompany them to the hunt. This girl has a mind so open that she is as capable of instruction as a girl of twenty. She was only five months in the seminary and was able to recount the principal points of our Faith and knew the catechism and Christian practices perfectly. When her mother came to fetch her on her return from the hunt, the innocent had her pray. I admired the simplicity of the mother, who was not yet baptized, in receiving instruction from her daughter with so much ardour and docility.

Overjoyed at hearing her daughter pray and respond to the catechism, she said, "My daughter, you will instruct your father and me. If you wish to remain longer in the seminary where you are so much loved, you will become even better fitted to do it."

The girl nevertheless could not leave her mother whose only child she was, but she said, "Though I wish to go, it is not because I lack for anything. I eat as much as I wish, the virgins give me fine clothes and love me very much, but I cannot leave you."

As she said these words, she was taken away to be brought back to the cabins, where she is admired by all the Savages.

It would take me too long to speak to you separately of them all but I shall tell you in general that these girls love us more than they love their parents, showing no desire to accompany them, which is most extraordinary in the Savages. They model themselves upon us as much as their age and their condition can permit. When we make our spiritual exercises, they keep a continual silence. They dare not even raise their eyes or look at us, thinking that this would interrupt us. But when we are finished, I could not express the caresses they give us, a thing they never do with their natural mothers.

Four of them received communion at Easter. They performed this act with such purity that the slightest shadow of sin frightened them, and with so much ardour and desire for union with Our Lord that, as they waited to receive it, they cried out, "Ah, when will Jesus come to kiss our hearts?"

When the Reverend Father [Claude] Pijart, who had baptized and instructed them for communion, saw them behave with angelic modesty, he could not restrain his tears.

***

In our seminary we have persons great and small, girls and women, that are given to us for a number of reasons as determined in the council of the Savages. We have had two this year, one of whom was removed from a pagan that had taken her as his wife—unknown to her kinsmen, who are Christians, though she was also a pagan. These good converts, who wanted her to be instructed in the Faith so they could give her in marriage to a Christian, could not suffer this injury and gave the man to understand that, if he wished to marry their kinswoman, he must give up another wife he had and also become a Christian. He promised to do so but, as there is no honour among the infidels, he broke his word, which forced the woman's kinsmen to take her from him and give her to us.

The Reverend Father de Quen told us that she would cause us great trouble and that he believed she would break out of the enclosure in a very short time and do her best to return to the pagan, whom she loved. We received her nevertheless with affection. She was sad for two or three days and then suddenly became as gentle as a child. She wished earnestly to be instructed and receive Holy Baptism. Her kinsmen could not believe in so great and sudden a change, for she wished not to see her husband again unless he became a Christian and her kinsmen agreed. Nevertheless, as the Savages are fickle and do not trust each other willingly except after a long proof of fidelity, they took her back to their cabin.

Some time later, when this poor woman was going somewhere, she met her husband. She took flight; he ran after her. She went into the house of a Frenchman; he went in with her. She hid herself for fear of having to speak to him; he declared that he would not leave without speaking to her. At last he did speak to her and did not neglect any sort of flattery that might persuade her to go back to him—but in vain. He grew angry, he shouted, he threatened to kill them all if his wife were not restored to him. But while he was carrying on in this way, she took a little turning without his noticing, made her way to the cabin of her kinsmen and in this way escaped the importunate man. While he was urging her thus, she had been saying in her heart: I wish to believe in earnest. I wish to be baptized. I love obedience.

She said she loved obedience because she had been forbidden to speak to the pagan and not to obey on such occasions is a crime among our new Christians. She recounted everything that had happened but no one would believe her, and all maintained that she had accompanied the pagan willingly and disobeyed the commandment she had been given. She repeated that she wished to be baptized but, despite her protestations, council was held to decide how her offence should be punished. Some said she should be condemned to death as a perpetual example and that if this offence remained unpunished the women and girls would imitate her disobedience. Others, who were not so ardent, replied that for the first time they should proceed more gently and that it would be sufficient to condemn her to be publicly whipped. So it was decided, and nothing remained but to find someone to execute the sentence.

The most zealous of the company rose, saying, "I shall do it."

Meanwhile the poor innocent woman did not say a word but thought in her heart that this humiliating punishment would be a preparation for baptism. All the women and girls were now greatly ashamed, for by the sentence they had to be present at its execution, which was to take place at the door of the church. The Savages did not wish, however, to execute the sentence without informing Father de Quen, who was then very occupied in the confessional. When he was able to listen, he was told of the evil the woman was believed to have committed and of the resolution to punish her. Without knowing what had happened or how far the matter was to go, he replied that she deserved to be punished and withdrew.

The executioner then led the woman to the door of the church, ordered her to place her hands on the railing of the bridge and uncovered her shoulders. Without complaint and with matchless submissiveness and graciousness, she did everything that was wished of her.

Then the executioner raised his voice, saying, "Harken, harken, Frenchmen. Know that we love obedience. Here is one of our daughters that has disobeyed. So we are going to punish her as you punish your children. And you, women and girls of the Savages—the same will be done to you if you disobey." With these words, he gave her a great lash with the whip. "Count," he said to the woman, "and remember well."

He said this because he was to give her five lashes. When he reached the third, Father de Quen, hearing that it was not coming to an end and that the lashes were being delivered very roughly, came out and called halt to the zealous executioner. The woman dressed herself again with great sweetness and tranquillity and went to see the Father to beg him to baptize her.

But as he did not know of her innocence, he sent her away very roughly, saying, "If you wish me to believe you, go to the Ursulines tomorrow after sunrise and I shall baptize you with your companions if you persevere."

We knew nothing of what had taken place, but the Reverend Father came to see us and gave us the details of the whole story. I must confess, my very dear Mother, that I thought to be angry with him for letting that poor innocent woman be whipped without checking the ill-considered zeal of the Savages, but at last, as the whole thing took place innocently on one side and the other, we had to laugh at the simplicity of the Savages while remaining edified by the patience of the woman.

She anticipated the time and came to see me at daybreak with a group of girls, saying she had come to wait for the Father so she could be baptized. I asked her if she wished earnestly to be numbered among God's children, and she replied that she had come only for that.

"But," I asked her, "what do you say about being whipped? Are you quite content with that?"

"Yes," she said. "I wished to suffer that indignity to prepare myself for baptism and I endured it in peace, since Jesus endured and paid for me."

I confess, my very dear Mother, that I was overjoyed to hear her and to see her so inclined towards grace. I instructed her and sent for the Father. He baptized her, and throughout the ceremony she showed a modesty that gave sufficient evidence that her entreaties had been without pretense. I had her given the name of our first mother, St Angéle, feeling that this was her due since God had converted her in a house of our holy mother's daughter …

Selection 2: A Scottish Woman's Impressions of Gender and Sexual Relations in the British West Indies and North Carolina

Janet Schaw accompanied her brother Alexander on a trip from Edinburgh, Scotland to the Caribbean, North America, and Portugal from 1774 to 1776. The Schaws were middle-aged siblings from a wealthy mercantile family with business connections in the places they visited. They traveled in high style, including female and male servants. Janet's journal reads like the travelogue from what today might be called an "adventure vacation": a trip to an exotic place taken by a wealthy person who likes the idea of roughing it for awhile but never intends to stray too far from the lap of luxury.

In her journal, Schaw recorded her impression of gender relations in the colonial societies she visited. She expressed concern for the ability of European men and women to maintain a proper level of gentility and refinement in the New World, and the evidence she saw of sexual relations between male slave owners and female slaves violated her sense of propriety. In the passages that follow, her descriptions of colonial men, their wives, and their slaves reveal some of the ways in which gender, sexuality, and race intersected in the Atlantic World.

Credit: *Journal of a Lady of Quality, Being the Narrative of a Journey from Scotland to the West Indies, North Carolina, and Portugal, in the Years 1774 to 1776*, eds. Evangeline Walker Andrews and Charles McLean Andrews (London: Oxford University Press, 1923), 111–115, 153–155.

As I am now about to leave them, you, no doubt, will expect me, to give my opinion as fully on the Inhabitants, as I have done on their Island [Antigua] and manners, but I am afraid you will suspect me of partiality, and were I to speak of Individuals, perhaps you might have reason, but as to the characters in general I can promise to write without prejudice, and if I only tell truth, they have nothing to fear from my pen. I think the men the most agreeable creatures I ever met with, frank, open, generous, and I dare say brave; even in advanced life they retain the Vivacity and Spirit of Youth; they are in general handsome, and all of them have that sort of air, that will ever attend a man of fashion. Their address is at once soft and manly; they have a kind of gallantry in their manner, which exceeds mere politeness, and in some countries, we know, would be easily mistaken for something more interesting than civility, yet you must not suppose this the politeness of French manners, merely words of course. No, what they say, they really mean; their whole intention is to make you happy, and this they endeavour to do without any other view or motive than what they are prompted to by the natural goodness of their own natures. In short, my friend, the woman that *brings a heart here* will have little sensibility if she carry it away.

I hear you ask me, if there is no alloy to this fine character, no reverse to this beautiful picture. Alas! my friend, tho' children of the Sun, they are mortals, and as such must have their share of failings, the most conspicuous of which is, the indulgence they give themselves in their licentious and even unnatural amours, which appears too plainly from the crowds of Mullatoes, which you meet in the streets, houses and indeed every where; a crime that seems to have gained sanction from custom, tho' attended with the greatest inconveniences not only to Individuals, but to the publick in general. The young black wenches lay themselves out for white lovers, in which they are but too successful. This prevents their marrying with their natural mates, and hence a spurious and degenerate breed, neither so fit for the field, nor indeed any work, as the true bred Negro. Besides these wenches become licentious and inso-lent past all bearing, and as even a mulattoe child interrupts their pleasures and is troublesome, they have certain herbs and medicines, that free them from such an incumbrance, but which seldom fails to cut short their own lives, as well as that of their offspring. By this many of them perish every year. I would have gladly drawn a veil over this part of a character, which in every thing else is most estimable.

As to the women, they are in general the most amiable creatures in the world, and either I have been remarkably fortunate in my acquaintance, or they are more than commonly sens-ible, even those who have never been off the Island are amazingly intelligent and able to con-verse with you on any subject. They make excellent wives, fond attentive mothers and the best house wives I have ever met with. Those of the first fortune and fashion keep their own keys and look after every thing within doors; the domestick Economy is entirely left to them; as the husband finds enough to do abroad. A fine house, an elegant table, handsome carriage, and a crowd of mullatoe servants are what they all seem very fond of. The sun appears to affect the sexes very differently. While the men are gay, luxurious and amorous, the women are modest, genteel, reserved and temperate. This last virtue they have indeed in the extreme; they drink nothing stronger in general than Sherbet, and never eat above one or two things at table, and these the lightest and plainest. The truth is, I can observe no indulgence they allow themselves in, not so much as in scandal [gossip], and if I stay long in this country, I will lose the very idea of that innocent amusement; for since I resided amongst them, I have never heard one woman say a wrong thing of another. This is so unnatural, that I suppose you will (good naturedly) call it cunning; but if it is so, it is the most commendable cunning I ever met with, as nothing can give them a better appearance in the eyes of a stranger.

As we became better acquainted, their reserve wore off, and I now find them most agreeable companions. Jealousy is a passion with which they are entirely unacquainted, and a jealous wife would be here a most ridiculous character indeed. Let me conclude this by assuring you, that I never admired my own sex more than in these amiable creoles. Their Sentiments are just and virtuous; in religion they are serious without ostentation, and perform every duty with pleasure from no other motive but the consciousness of doing right. In their persons they are very genteel, rather too thin till past thirty, after that they grow plump and look much the better for it. Their features are in general high and very regular, they have charming eyes, fine teeth, and the greatest quantity of hair I ever saw, which they dress with taste, and wear a great deal of powder. In short, they want only colour to be termed beautiful, but the sun who bestows such rich taints on every other flower, gives none to his lovely daughters; the tincture of whose skin is as pure as lily, and as pale. Yet this I am convinced is owing to the way in which they live, entirely excluded from proper air and exercise. From childhood they never suffer the sun to have a peep at them, and to prevent him are covered with masks and bonnets, that abso-lutely make them look as if they were stewed. Fanny who just now is blooming as a new blown rose, was prevailed on to wear a mask, while we were on our Tour, which in a week changed her colour, and if she had persevered I am sure a few months would have made her as pale as any of them. As to your humble Servant, I have always set my face to the weather; wherever I have been. I hope you have no quarrel at brown beauty.

***

WILMINGTOWN [NORTH CAROLINA]

I have been in town a few days, and have had an opportunity to make some little observa-tions on the manners of a people so new to me. The ball I mentioned was intended as a civil-ity, therefore I will not criticize it, and tho' I have not the same reason to spare the company, yet I will not fatigue you with a description, which however lively or just, would at best resemble a Dutch picture, where the injudicious choice of the subject destroys the merit of the painting. Let it suffice to say that a ball we had, where were dresses, dancing and ceremonies laughable enough, but there was no object on which my own ridicule fixed equal to myself and the figure I made, dressed out in all my British airs with a high head and a hoop and trudging thro' the unpaved streets in embroidered shoes by the light of a lanthorn [lantern] carried by a black wench half naked. No chair, no carriage—good leather shoes need none. The ridicule was the silk shoes in such a place. I have however gained some most amiable and agreeable acquaintances amongst the Ladies; many of whom would make a figure in any part of the world, and I will not fail to cultivate their esteem, as they appear worthy of mine.

I am sorry to say, however, that I have met with few of the men who are natives of the country [male colonists born in America], who rise much above my former description, and as their natural ferocity is now inflamed by the fury of an ignorant zeal, they are of that sort of figure, that I cannot look at them without connecting the idea of tar and feather. Tho' they have fine women and such as might inspire any man with sentiments that do honour to humanity, yet they know no such nice distinctions, and in this at least are real patriots. As the population of the country is all the view they have in what they call love, and tho' they often honour their black wenches with their attention, I sincerely believe they are excited to that crime by no other desire or motive but that of adding to the number of their slaves.

The difference between the men and the women surprised me, but a sensible man, who has long resided here, in some degrees accounted for it. In the infancy of this province, said he, many families from Britain came over, and of these the wives and daughters were people of education. The mothers took the care of the girls, they were train'd up under them, and not only instructed in the family duties necessary to the sex, but in those accomplishments and genteel manners that are still so visible amongst them, and this descended from Mother to daughter. As the father found the labours of his boys necessary to him, he led them therefore to the woods, and taught the sturdy lad to glory in the stroke he could give with his Ax, in the trees he felled, and the deer he shot; to conjure the wolfe, the bear and the Alligator; and to guard his habitition from Indian inroads was most justly his pride, and he had reason to boast of it. But a few generations this way lost every art or science, which their fathers might have brought out, and tho' necessity no longer prescribed these severe occupations, custom has established it as still necessary for the men to spend their time abroad in the fields; and to be a good marksman is the highest ambition of the youth, while to those enervated by age or infirmity drinking grog remained a last consolation.

Selection 3: Interracial Intimacy in the Fur Trade

Accounts of the fur trade typically present it as a masculine pursuit: male Indian hunters killed the animals, whose hides and pelts were purchased by male colonial traders. Such descriptions, however, overlook the central role Native women played in this business. They processed the hides and pelts brought to them by their male family members, scraping and stretching them so that they would be marketable to traders. The tastes and preferences of Native women also shaped the types and quality of goods that traders brought into Indian country. Most important, Native women helped acculturate colonial traders to the social norms of Indian communities, and they helped clothe, feed, and shelter traders who were hundreds of miles from home. Marrying Native women, even temporarily, gave traders kinship ties that could protect and provide for them during times of danger and want in Indian country. Native women benefited from these relationships by cultivating bonds of reciprocity and obligation with traders that went well beyond trading and selling goods.

The role of interracial sexuality in building these intercultural bonds usually went unrecorded. Missionaries decried such relationships as licentious and complained that they tended to encourage savagery in the traders rather than civility among the Indians. Thus, traders were not inclined to record or publicize their Indian marriages, but Nicholas Cresswell wrote about his in his journal. Cresswell came to North America from England in 1774, intending to invest in western lands. While traveling in the Ohio country, he took up the fur trade under the guidance of a mentor named John Anderson. In summer 1775, Cresswell and Anderson visited Delaware Indian towns along the Muskingum River, using Fort Pitt (modern Pittsburgh) as their base. Following Anderson's example, Cresswell took an Indian wife whom he referred to as "Nancy," who helped the novice trader adapt to his new profession.

Credit: Nicholas Cresswell, *The Journal of Nicholas Cresswell, 1774–1777* (New York: Dial Press, 1924), 107–110, 111–114, 116, 122.

Tuesday August 29th, 1775. Left White-Eye's [a Delaware chief's] town. Saw the bones of one Mr. Cammel, a White man, that had been killed by the Indians. Got to Co-a-shoking [another Delaware town] about noon. It is at the forks of the Muskingham. The Indians have removed from Newcomer Town to this place. King Newcomer [a Delaware chief] lives here. Sold part of my goods here to good advantage. Crossed a Branch of Muskingham and went to Old Hundy, this is a scattering Indian settlement. Lodged at a Mohawk Indian's house who offered me his Sister and Mr. Anderson his Daughter to sleep with us, which we were obliged to accept.

Wednesday August 30th, 1775. My bedfellow very fond of me this morning and wants to go with me. Find I must often meet with such encounters as these if I do not take a Squaw to myself. She is young and sprightly, tolerably handsome, and can speak a little English. Agreed to take her. She saddled her horse and went with us to New Hundy about 3 Miles off, where she had several relations who made me very welcome to such as they had. From there to Coashoskis where we lodged in my Squaw's Brother's [home], made me a Compliment [gift] of a young wolf, but I could not take it with me.

Thursday, August 31st, 1775. At Coashoskis. Mr. Anderson could not find his horse. Sold all my goods for Furs. In the afternoon rambled about the Town, smoking Tobacco with the Indians and did everything in my power to make myself agreeable to them. Went to see the King. He lives in a poor house, as he is as poor in dress as any of them, no emblem of Royalty or Majesty about him. He is an old man, treated me very kindly, called me his good friend and hoped I would be kind to my Squaw. Gave me a small string of Wampum as a token of friendship. My Squaw uneasy to see me write so much.

Friday September 1st, 1775. At Coashoskin Mr. Anderson found his horse. Saw an Indian Dance in which I bore a part. Painted by my Squaw in the most elegant manner. Divested of all my clothes, except my Calico short breech clout, leggings, and Mockesons. A fire was made which we danced round with little order, whooping and hallooing in a most frightful manner. I was but a novice at the diversion and by endeavouring to act as they did made them a great deal of sport, and ingratiated me much in their esteem. This is the most violent exercise, to the adepts in the art I ever saw. No regular figure, but violent distortion of features, writhing and twisting the body in the most uncouth and antic postures imaginable. Their music is an old Keg with one head knocked out and covered with a skin and beat with sticks which regulates their times. The men have strings of Deer's hoofs tied round their ankles and knees, and gourds with shot or pebble stones in them in their hands which they continually rattle. The women have Morris bells or Thimbles with holes in the bottom and strung upon a leathern thong tied round their ankles, knees, and waists. The jingling of these Bells and Thimbles, the rattling of the Deer's hoofs and gourds, beating of the drum and kettle, with the horrid yells of the Indians, render it the most unharmonious concert, that human idea can possibly conceive. It is a favourite diversion in which I am informed they spend great part of their time in Winter. Saw an Indian Conjuror dressed in a Coat of Bearskin with a Visor mask made of wood, frightful enough to scare the Devil. The Indians believe in conjuration and Witchcraft. Left the Town, went about two miles. Camped by the side of a run. A young Indian boy, son of one

Baubee a Frenchman, came after us and insists on going with us to Fort Pitt. Find myself very unwell this evening, pains in my Head and Back. Nancy [Cresswell's Indian wife] seems very uneasy about my welfare. Afraid of the Ague [fever].

…

Sunday September 3rd, 1775. Last night, Nancy brought an Indian Squaw which called me her Nilum, i.e. Nephew, as Mr. Anderson told me, and behaved very kindly to me. She put her hand on my head for some time, then took a small brown root, out of her pocket and with her knife chopped part of it small, then mixed it with water, which she gave me to drink, or rather swallow, being about a spoonful, but this I evaded by keeping it in my mouth till I found an opportunity to spit it out. She then took some in her mouth and chewed it and spit on the top of my head, rubbing my head well at the same time. Then she unbuttoned my shirt collar and spat another mouthful down my back. This was uncomfortable but I bore it with patience. She lent me her Matchcoat [trade blanket] and told me to go sleep. Nancy was ordered not to give me any water till morning, however, I prevailed on the good-natured creature to let me take a vomit that Mr. Anderson had with him as soon as the old woman was gone, which has cured me tho' the old woman believes her nostrum did it. Obliged to stay here. This day, somebody had stolen one of Mr. A[nderson]'s Horses.

Monday, September 4th, 1775. Saw an Indian Scalp. Heard an Indian play upon a Tin Violin and make tolerable good musick. Went to Kanaughtonhead [a Christian Delaware town], walked all the way, my horse loaded with skins. Camped close by the Town. Nancy's kindness to be remembered.

Tuesday, September 5th, 1775. At Kanaughtonhead. Went to the meeting where Divine service was performed in Dutch and English with great solemnity. This Chapel is much neater than that at Wale-hack-tap-poke. Adorned with basket work in varrious colours all round, with a Spinet made by Mr. Smith the Parson, and played by an Indian. Drank Tea with Captn. White-Eyes and Captn. Wingenund [two Delaware chiefs] at an Indian house in Town. This Tea is made of the tops of Ginsing and I think it very like Bohea Tea. The leaves are put into a tin canister made water tight, and boiled till it is dry, by this means the juices to not evaporate. N[ancy] did not chuse to go into the town, but employed herself in making me a pair of Mockesons.

…

Sunday September 10th, 1775. Rambled till noon when we found ourselves at Boquet's old Fort [built during a military expedition in 1764] now demolished. Went to an Indian Camp, where Mr. Anderson met with an old Wife of his, who would go with him, which he agreed to. We have each of us a Girl. It is an odd way of travelling but we are obliged to submit to it …

Monday September 11th, 1775. Mr. Anderson and I with our Ladies proceeded, and left the people to bring the skins and cattle which he had purchased. Travelled over a great deal of bad land. About sundown Mr. A[nderson] called out, "A Panther." I looked about and saw it set in a tree about twenty yards from me. Fired at it on horseback and shot it through the neck. It is of a Brown colour and shaped like a cat, but much larger. It measured five foot nine inches from Nose end to Tail end. Camped and skinned the Panther. This exploit has raised me in N[ancy's] esteem exceedingly, tho' I claim no merit from it, being merely accidental.

Tuesday, September 12th, 1775. Our Squaws are very necessary, fetching our horses to the Camp and saddling them, making our fire at night and cooking our victuals, and every other thing they think will please us. Travelled over several barren mountains, some of them produce great plenty of wild Grapes. Lodged in an old Indian Camp. Bad water.

…

Saturday, September 30th, 1775. Went over the River and bought a Porcupine Skin of an Indian. It is something like our Hedgehog at home, only the quills are longer. The Indians dye them of various colours and work them on their trinkets … N[ancy] very uneasy. She weeps plentifully. I am unhappy that this honest creature has taken such a fancy to me.

Sunday, October 1st, 1775. Took leave of most of my acquaintances in town [Fort Pitt]. Mr. Douglas [another trader] gave me an Indian Tobacco pouch made of a Mink Skin adorned with porcupine quills. He is desirous of keeping a correspondence with me, which in all probability will be for the interest of us both. I have conceived a great regard for the Indians and really feel a most sensible regret in parting from them, however contemptible opinion others may entertain of these honest poor Creatures ...

Monday, October 2nd, 1775 ... Settled my affairs with Mr. John Anderson, who has behaved more like a father than a common acquaintance. Made him a compliment of my silver buckles and agreed to keep up a correspondence. Parting with N[ancy] was the most affecting thing I have ever experienced since I left home. The poor creature wept most plentifully. However base it may appear to conscientious people, it is absolutely necessary to take a temporary wife if they have to travel amongst the Indians. Left Fort Pitt.

Selection 4: An Interracial Marriage Causes Controversy in New England

During the early nineteenth century, several Protestant churches based in New England formed missionary societies aimed at converting Native Americans to Christianity and speeding their assimilation into white society. They focused their efforts on Indian nations in the American Southeast, particularly the Cherokees of Georgia, establishing missions in their homelands and in some cases, sponsoring the education of Cherokee youth in boarding schools. One such institution was the Foreign Mission School, commonly known as the "Heathen School," founded in Cornwall, Connecticut in 1819. Local townspeople generally supported the Foreign Mission School until two of its Cherokee students, John Ridge and Elias Boudinot, became engaged to marry Sarah Bird Northrup and Harriett Gold respectively, daughters of two prominent local families. The controversy that erupted over these two interracial marriages turned many supporters against the Mission School, and it closed in 1828. Despite the opposition they faced, Ridge and Northrup married, as did Boudinot and Gold, and the couples moved back to the Cherokee nation in Georgia, where they became embroiled in events leading to the forced removal of the Cherokees and other Indian nations west of the Mississippi River during the 1830s.

When Elias Boudinot and Harriett Gold announced their engagement, various members of the Gold family tried to convince Harriett to reconsider. The letters in which they carried on this dispute offer a rare and intimate glimpse inside one family's efforts to reconcile its religious beliefs with the racial prejudices then evident in American society. People referenced in the letters excerpted below include Harriett's brother Stephen, her sister Catharine, her sister Flora and Flora's husband Herman Vaill, and her sister Mary and Mary's husband Daniel Brinsmade.

Credit: Theresa Strouth Gaul, ed., *To Marry an Indian: The Marriage of Harriett Gold and Elias Boudinot in Letters, 1823–1839* (Chapel Hill, NC: University of North Carolina Press, 2005), 83–86, 89–90, 92–93, 99–100, 141–142.

Harriet Gold to Herman and Flora Gold Vaill and Catherine Gold, 25 June 1825

Dear Brother and Sisters,
   ... Yes it is so—the time has come when your Sister Harriet is already published [engaged] to an Indian ... Pen cannot describe nor language express the numerous & trying scenes through which I have passed since you left us. But I trust I have had that support through them all, which the world could not give. Never before did I so much realize the worth of religion & so much pity those, who, in time of trouble were without this inestimable treasure. I have seen the time when I could close my eyes upon every earthly object & look up to God as my only supporter, my only hope—when I could say with emotions I have never felt before, to my

heavenly Father, "other refuge I have none, So I helpless hang on thee." I still have the consolation of feeling that I have not acted contrary to duty & that what I have done as respects forming a connexion [marriage] is not adverse to divine approbation. I know that I appear at present to stand alone, the publick, "good people & bad," are against me. I cannot say that all are against me—there are many who are still my friends, but the excitement at present is such that they dare not have it known that they are on my side. You can have no idea of the scenes we have witnessed the week past ... I will give you a brief description ... wednesday last was appointed for the day when great things were to be and [illegible] were effected. It being thought unsafe for me to stay at home I left the night before & was kept in a chamber at Capt. Clarks where I had a full prospect of the solemn transactions in our Valley. In the evening our respectable young people Ladies & Gentlemen convened on the plain to witness and approve the scene and express their indignation. A painting had been prepared representing a beautiful young Lady & an Indian; also on the same, a woman, as an instigator of Indian marriages. Evening came on. The church Bell began to toll one could conclude, speaking the departure of a soul. Mr. John C. Lewis and Mr. Rufus Payne [two local men] carried the corpses [effigies] & Brother Stephen [Harriett's brother Stephen Gold] set fire to the barrel of Tar or rather the funeral pile—the flames rose high, & the smoke ascended—some said it reminded them of the smoke of their torment which they feared would ascend forever. My heart truly sung with anguish at the dreadful scene. The Bell continued to toll till 10. or 11 O'c[lock] ... There is a great division of feeling among many but especially in our family. It appears as though a house divided could not stand. Ma is almost worn out she feels as though her children had not tenderness for her & instead of comforting her were ready to fill her cup of affliction till it is more than running over ... Many of the good people of this place do feel greatly [wounded?] by the proceedings of last Wednesday eve. I fear Brother Stephen has, to prevent scandal brought real scandal upon himself that cannot easily be wiped off. Even the most unprincipled say, they never heard of any thing so low even amongst the heathen as that of burning a Sister in effigy ...

Could I see you I could say many things to you. I cannot by one letter give you any idea of my feelings or circumstances. Brother Vaill[,] you doubtless well remember the morning of my birthday when I was 18. We walked in the garden, A thick, dubious cloud o'ercast the sky. Do you not recollect our conversation? The time has come & I see a thick cloud & although you then said you would sympathise with me, as you so little expected such things—I do not expect that sympathy. The few friends I now have are dearer to me than ever—many delight in showing disrespect, others take uncommon pains to notice & respect me. I feel as though I had wronged no one. I have done nothing but what I had a perfect and lawful right to do.

Daniel Brinsmade to Herman and Flora Gold Vaill, 29 June 1825

D[ea]r Br[other] & Sister,

You have doubtless ere [before] this heard that the Cornwall business is all before the publick ... The excitement is very great in Cornwall. the young men burnt them [Harriett Gold and Elias Boudinot] in effigy and tolled the bell nearly the whole night ... I shall do all in my power to prevent her [Harriett] getting away but expect it will be in vain. I shall know more particulars when Mary [Harriett's sister and Daniel's wife] returns and will write. [I] hope you will let us hear from you often.

June 30th—Mary has returned and I am now more distressed than ever our parents have long since given their written consent to the union. thro Harrietts craftiness by making them believe that she should die if she did not have her Indian last winter. I have not words to express my indignation at the whole proceeding—the whole family are to be sacrificed to gratify if I may so express it the animal feeling of one of its members—and lo! The whole is clothed under the garb of religion they could not fight against God—is the reply. I think the brothers & sisters are in duty bound to address their parents on this subject with suitable but decided disapprobation of the transaction. They at first gave a decided negative to it but for fear H[arriett] would die in love for the Indian they wrote again and said yes ... I wish I could see you for one blessed minute I could tell you more than I can convey in two letters. They already have business enough in Cornwall—this marriage (O forbid it), has already brought about difficulty ...

Cornwall is in great turmoil and if the disturbers of the peace could be disposed of and had in safe keeping—it would rejoice the Christian publick.

Herman Vaill to Harriett Gold, 29 June 1825

Dear Sister Harriett,

...

I suppose you are not in doubt as to the nature of the intelligence that has reached us concerning you. And after having given the subject in question, a deliberate, & I trust, a prayerful consideration; after having looked at it in all its probable bearings, & viewed it in connexion with what I deem its inevitable consequences; I am prepared to advise; & my dear Sister, I do, most affectionately advise, that you give up all present intentions, & all thoughts, of becoming united in marriage with an Indian.

I do not give you this advice because I feel no interest in the welfare of the Indians. I trust I love the cause which is operating to raise them from their degraded condition. I rejoice that success has so far attended the efforts of Christians in their behalf; & one of the great reasons why I advise you to abandon your intention of marrying among them, is, that under existing circumstance, such a step will probably do far more to hinder than to promote, the measures which are in operation for their welfare.

Nor do I advise you thus, because I view such a connexion, as unlawful, in itself. On this point my opinion has always been, That there is nothing in the nature of such a connexion, merely, that can stamp it with criminality.

Nor do I give you this advice because I have any personal objections against [the] man. I have always respected him for his talents, for his diligence in [study?] & the proficiency he made in learning, while at the F.M. [Foreign Mission] school; & for his hopeful piety. I know nothing personally against him as to his disposition; & I would even hope that he may not be one of those who return to their former sins, but that he may prove himself faithful to Christ; & grateful to his Christian benefactors; & of great good to his Nation. But to become thus useful, & to prove himself thus grateful to his friends, & faithful to Christ, it is not necessary that he should marry a white woman ... if he would not show ingratitude to the school where he was taught, & to the Christian community by whom he was supported; if he would not show that ingratitude which Indians are said to be incapable of committing, one would think that he would choose to select a wife from among the daughters of his people.

But as it respects yourself, Harriett, I give you this advice, because, as I view the subject, you cannot fulfil your designs of marriage with the person in question, without an evident disregard to the interests of the School, & the cause of the missions; & a total inconsistency as it respects your Christian profession. A thing which may be right in itself, still, in given circumstances, [may] be very wrong. For instance, in itself, your Father has a perfect right to kindle a fire on his own land; but if his neighbor comes & expresses his fears that that fire so kindled, will be driven by the wind into his fields, & if there is indeed manifest reason to fear that such fire will injure his neighbour's property, then, though it be on his own ground, your Father cannot kindle such a fire without doing that which, in such circumstances, becomes absolutely wrong; & he must answer for its consequences.

On such principles we are to reason in the present case. And are you told by others, since you have concluded to marry an Indian, that there is danger? Do they point it out; & tell you what will be the consequence if you take such a step? Before you kindle the fire, which if once kindled may burn, we know not how far, nor how long, O Harriett, before you kindle the fire, remember that so far as there is danger, so far it will be wrong; & that God will hold you accountable to Him, for all the injury which His cause may this receive. You are warned that there is danger; that there is reason to fear that such a step will greatly injure the cause of Christ, both in its relation to the Mission School, & to the interests of missions from our churches to the heathen.

...

Do you hesitate? Do you fear that because you had gone so far, you cannot turn back? Yes, you can. True you have wandered; & yet you will never get right in that way. The only way is to turn back; & if you turn there will be more evidence in that you are a Christian, than you ever gave before. Do not go away like Cain, & Judas; but come back like Peter. Your friends invite, the cause of the Redeemer demands; the vows you have made to Christ require; The Providence of God has shut the door against your going; & be afraid, O my Sister, be afraid to burst it open. For if you do, all the evils which may result, thro' your life, & thro' Eternity, will stand charged against you ...

I will not mention our own feelings [illegible] brothers, & sisters. If you stay, we shall rejoice over you, & love you more than ever. But if you go, still we can bear it. We shall love each [illegible] still. When we are permitted to meet we shall rejoice; But then, in the fraternal Thanksgiving circle, we shall see that "One is not," & that one will feel that she is not. Still we can bear it.

We shall feel for our aged Parents; for their sun is near his setting; & we fear that if you go, the sun of their Christian reputation is already set. We feel for your Aged Father, (You know his worldly troubles;) & you may visit the Home of your childhood yet, ah, & so may we, & find its once happy inhabitants all gone.

But, Oh the Bar of Judgment. He that doeth evil; or becomes the voluntary cause of evil, of Him will the final Judge take account. Will you go? if you are a hypocrite, & designed for a reprobate, doubtless you will. But if you are a Christian, it must be you will listen, & regard the advice of friends, & the call of God, & his church.

Herman Vaill to Harriett Gold, 5 March 1826

Dear Sister Harriett R. Gold, whose Gold will shortly become dim, & to whom, I write now with this appellation, probably for the last time; I have long intended to write you, a sort of Adieu; or Farewell Letter; but ill health, & various calls & labours have hithero prevented. I suppose you will be going far away before long; My best wishes & my Prayers attend you.

You know, dear Sister, you know I always loved you; & that difference of opinion with regard to the propriety & expediency of your contemplated connexion, (for you are aware that I did not think just as you did,) has not abated my desire to see you happy & useful. I have the same affectionate, fraternal regard for you as ever; & hope that you will be the instrument of accomplishing much in behalf of that People whom I suppose you now consider as your Nation.

As to the Principle you know that I have maintained it as correct, & scriptural that such connexions should be formed. [I] have always, in this respect, been an advocate for intermarriage &c. The present expediency, all circumstances considered, is another thing. But as you & I talked the matter over when I saw you last, & parted amicably, I am willing it should there rest. Go dear Sister, & if you have erred, beseech God to forgive you; go, & in His cause, & in His strength, do all the good you can. And must we thus part? Am I never to see you more? Are you never more to see your dear Sister, & my dear wife, never to see our dear little Catharine Harriet [Harriett's niece and namesake]? It may be so; but—my health is at present feeble; I may be obliged to visit a milder climate again; I may go to Georgia; yes, & to your Nation, & see you there. My sister, we shall remember you; we shall remember you at the Throne of Grace; & you will there remember us. Our request is that you would always write to us—once in 3 months & we will answer you as often. My kind regards & best wishes, to Brother Boudinott; when he becomes your husband.

Discussion Questions

1. According to L'Incarnation, what kind of transformation did conversion to Christianity cause in the values and behavior of Native American girls and women? How did L'Incarnation expect these female converts to use marriage as a means of extending Christian missionary work among Native Americans?
2. According to Schaw, what are the social costs of interracial sexual unions, and to whom does she assign the blame for such activity? How does her description of white colonial women contrast with her description of female slaves? How might an African woman's description of these relationships differ from Schaw's?
3. What racial prejudices are evident in Cresswell's descriptions of the Native American women and men he encounters in the Ohio country? How might his Indian wife Nancy have explained their relationship? Do you think their relationship was strictly an economic one, or did it involve genuine emotional intimacy?
4. How does Harriett Gold's family react to her engagement to Elias Boudinot, and how does Harriett defend her decision? If the Gold family and their neighbors were so committed to converting and educating Native Americans, why do you think Harriett and Elias faced such intense opposition to their union?

Suggested Readings

The role of interracial sexuality and marriage in the fur trade is examined in Susan Sleeper-Smith, *Indian Women and French Men: Rethinking Cultural Encounter in the Western Great Lakes* (Amherst, MA: University of Massachusetts Press, 2001); Carolyn Podruchny, *Making the Voyageur World: Travelers and Traders in the North American Fur Trade* (Lincoln, NE: University of Nebraska Press, 2006); and Lucy Eldersveld Murphy, *Great Lakes Creoles: A French-Indian Community in the Northern Borderlands, Praire du Chien, 1750–1860* (Cambridge: Cambridge University Press, 2014). Juliana Barr details the connections between trade, diplomacy, and gender relations in *Peace Came in the Form of a Woman: Indians and Spaniards in the Texas Borderlands* (Chapel Hill, NC: University of North Carolina Press, 2007). Ann Marie Plane investigates the tensions between Christian and Native American practices regarding marriage and sexuality in *Colonial Intimacies: Indian Marriage in Early New England* (Ithaca, NY: Cornell University Press, 2000). For more about the controversy ignited by Harriett Gold's marriage to Elias Boudinot, see John Demos, *The Heathen School: A Story of Hope and Betrayal in the Age of the Early Republic* (New York: Random House, 2014).

For the intersection of gender, sexuality, and race in Atlantic slave societies, see Jennifer L. Morgan, *Laboring Women: Reproduction and Gender in New World Slavery* (Philadelphia, PA: University of Pennsylvania Press, 2004). For studies that focus on North America, see Wendy Warren, *New England Bound: Slavery and Colonization in Early America* (New York: Liveright, 2016); and Kathleen M. Brown, *Good Wives, Nasty Wenches, and Anxious Patriarchs: Gender, Race, and Power in Colonial Virginia* (Chapel Hill, NC: University of North Carolina Press, 1996). For the Caribbean, see *Engendering History: Caribbean Women in Historical Perspective*, eds. Verene Shepherd, Bridget Brereton, and Barbara Bailey (New York: St. Martin's Press, 1995); and Hilary Beckles, *Natural Rebels: A Social History of Enslaved Women in Barbados* (London: Zed Press, 1989). For Latin America, see Susan M. Socolow, *The Women of Colonial Latin America* (Cambridge: Cambridge University Press, 2000); and Asuncion Lavrin, *Sexuality and Marriage in Colonial Latin America* (1989; Lincoln, NE: University of Nebraska Press, 1992).

Historians have also studied the construction of gender and sexuality in early America through the lenses of religion and the law. For studies emphasizing religion, see Laurel Thatcher Ulrich, *Good Wives: Image and Reality in the Lives of Women in Northern New England,*

1650–1750 (New York: Alfred A. Knopf, 1982); and Susan Juster, *Disorderly Women: Sexual Politics and Evangelicalism in Revolutionary New England* (Ithaca, NY: Cornell University Press, 1994). For studies emphasizing the law, see Kirsten Fischer, *Suspect Relations: Sex, Race, and Resistance in Colonial North Carolina* (Ithaca, NY: Cornell University Press, 2002); Mary Beth Norton, *Founding Mothers and Fathers: Gendered Power and the Forming of American Society* (New York: Alfred A. Knopf, 1996); and Cornelia Hughes Dayton, *Women Before the Bar: Gender, Law, and Society in Connecticut, 1639–1789* (Chapel Hill, NC: University of North Carolina Press, 1995).

12 Enlightenment and Revolution

Figure 12.1 The Female Combatants (London, 1776).

This British political cartoon lampooned the outbreak of the American Revolution. Britain is depicted as the female figure Britannia, who tells her rebellious subject, "I'll force you to Obedience you Rebellious Slut." The American colonies are represented by the female Indian figure, who responds, "Liberty Liberty for ever Mother while I exist." While the artist clearly intended the image of two women engaged in fisti-cuffs to be humorous, the cartoon also reflects the Enlightenment's depiction of America as a place younger, less refined, and culturally distinct from Europe (see Selection 1). Colonial revolutionaries embraced the image of the Indian and the name "American" to set themselves apart from the Old World (see Selection 4). What positive attributes do you suppose they associated with Indians?

Introduction

The American War of Independence initiated an era of political upheaval that transformed the Atlantic World between 1775 and 1825. Wars and slave rebellions in the Americas as well as political revolutions in Europe upset the systems of trade and government that imperial powers had worked so hard to create since the time of Columbus. Revolutionary ideas followed the currents of trade and traveled back and forth across the Atlantic, spreading the contagion of rebellion and its unanticipated consequences to new regions. In this era, the Atlantic World seemed to reach its zenith and its disintegration at the same time, as the institutions that had allowed it to prosper in the first place—the slave trade, colonial empires, powerful monarchies—faced crippling attacks from the discontented and disenfranchised.

The Atlantic revolutions had many causes, each unique to particular circumstances of time and place. The American Revolution (1775–1783) and the Spanish-American revolutions (1810–1825) are best described as wars of independence led by colonial elites who resented imperial restrictions on their economic and political autonomy. By the end of the eighteenth century, there had emerged in North and South America native-born, or creole, elites descended from the first waves of European colonizers. These creole elites proudly identified themselves as "Americans," claiming a cultural and moral superiority over their African and Indian dependents, while also setting themselves apart from the European society across the Atlantic. In North and South America during the late eighteenth century, creole patriots resented the imperial officials who monopolized high offices of church and state in their colonies and attacked the arbitrary authority that European monarchies claimed over them. They fought wars of colonial independence to free themselves from the economic and political restraints imposed upon them by these monarchies, but not necessarily to extend that same freedom to the dependent peoples over whom they ruled.

In other regions, particularly the Caribbean, slave populations grew so large relative to the planter class that by the end of the eighteenth century, rebellions became more frequent and costly. The Haitian Revolution (1791–1804) toppled the colonial planter class and raised a banner for the self-emancipation of slaves throughout the Western Hemisphere. The French Revolution (1789–1799) was another species of revolution altogether, a violent convulsion from within French society that destroyed the authority of the monarchy, aristocracy, and church and initiated an age of democratic ferment that reverberated throughout Europe for fifty years.

The common connection between these various revolutionary movements was their ideological foundation in the Enlightenment, an intellectual movement that transformed European science and philosophy between 1680 and 1800. The spirit of the Enlightenment was cosmopolitan. Its adherents, often known by the French term *philosophes* (philosophers), considered themselves "citizens of the world," individuals who recognized their common humanity with others around the globe and who contemplated science, politics, and philosophy in the most universal terms possible. They believed that what was learned or uncovered in one realm of study—cosmology, botany, mathematics—could be applied to the study of another, because all of creation was rationally ordered and worked according to certain immutable natural laws. The *philosophes* most often conveyed this idea through mechanical metaphors, comparing the natural world to a machine whose blueprint could be deciphered through proper observation and experimentation. Just as a craftsman could apply his knowledge of mechanics to building a better clock, so too did the *philosophes* believe that they could apply their grasp of the laws that governed nature to making society more free, prosperous, and harmonious.

The model of a mechanical universe governed by natural laws gave rise to a belief in natural rights, universal liberties held by all people in all societies. The classic statement of natural rights philosophy comes from John Locke's *Second Treatise on Government*, written in the 1680s to justify parliamentary resistance to the Stuart monarchy in England. Locke challenged the absolutist authority of monarchs by arguing that human beings possess natural rights to life, liberty, and property. According to Locke, all governments were contractual and therefore limited in power. When a government ceased to protect the natural rights of its citizens, the people had a right to replace it.

During the Age of Revolutions, Locke's natural rights philosophy was adopted and popularized by a host of radical thinkers and revolutionaries on both sides of the Atlantic. An obvious source of the appeal of Locke's argument was its universality. While Locke wrote in a distinctly English tradition about rights and liberties, subsequent theorists applied his ideas across national and cultural boundaries. Colonial elites, political radicals, and enslaved Africans adopted natural rights rhetoric to make their own case for rebellion, and in doing so, made Lockean principles about self-government and human rights part of the common intellectual fabric of the Atlantic World. The foundational documents of the American and French Revolutions, the Declaration of Independence and the Declaration of Rights of Man and Citizen, respectively, are examples of Locke's profound influence on the Atlantic revolutions and our own modern notions of democracy.

Despite the many variations in their causes and consequences, the Atlantic revolutions shared a general commitment to replacing forms of absolutist political power with representative government. *Philosophes* challenged the divine right of kings, a political doctrine that argued that monarchs derived their power from God and therefore rebellion against them violated God's will. Political revolutionaries in Europe and the Americas extended this attack to all forms of hereditary power, including the social and economic privileges that aristocrats enjoyed by virtue of their birth. The equality of all citizens before the law became an important component of the revolutionary agenda, and the republics of ancient Greece and Rome replaced absolutist monarchies as the model for national government in the Americas. Of course, few of the Atlantic revolutions succeeded in creating stable republics, and many reverted to some form of de facto absolutist power in the form of dictators or military strongmen. Nevertheless, the Enlightenment dealt a fatal blow to the institution of hereditary kingship and made possible the emergence of modern nation states out of the colonial empires that had previously governed the Atlantic World.

The readings in this chapter examine the intersection of the Enlightenment and the Atlantic revolutions of 1775–1825. In the first selection, a French expatriate living in British North America uses Enlightenment ideas about human nature and the environment to explain how European colonists have turned into "Americans." In the second, a trans-Atlantic revolutionary uses natural rights philosophy to attack the hereditary powers of monarchs and aristocrats. In the third selection, an American abolitionist defends Haitian slaves from critics in the United States, who have condemned them for rising up against their oppressors. In the fourth selection, a Spanish American revolutionary expresses a creole nationalism grounded in Enlightenment notions about self-government. As you read these sources, try to pick out the themes and ideas that unite them. How do they make use of natural rights to attack the traditional forms of government that have ruled the Atlantic World? What types of government do they expect to replace those older models?

Selection 1: A French Expatriate Describes Colonial Society in British North America

Hector St. John de Crèvecoeur's life was buffeted and changed several times by the revolutionary struggles of the Atlantic World. He came to North America as a French military officer in 1755. After France surrendered Canada to Britain in 1763, he became a naturalized British subject, traveled throughout eastern North America, and settled in New York. His loyalism during the American Revolution forced him to return to Europe, where he published *Letters from an American Farmer* in 1782. The book's glowing descriptions of American society made him a literary celebrity, and the French Crown appointed him an ambassador to the new United States. He returned from this diplomatic service during the French Revolution, but this time avoided his political enemies by retreating to the French countryside, where he died in 1813.

Crèvecoeur's career illustrated the trans-Atlantic kinship between the American and French revolutions. Although not a revolutionary himself, he embraced Enlightenment notions about human progress, the order of nature, and the irrepressible expansion of liberty. In "What is an American?"—the most famous essay from *Letters from an American Farmer*—he described North America as a place where the environment transformed European immigrants into a society that was more equal, prosperous, and just than that they had left behind.

Credit: J. Hector St. John de Crèvecoeur, "What is an American?" in *Letters from an American Farmer* (1782; New York: E. P. Dutton, 1926), 39–44.

I wish I could be acquainted with the feelings and thoughts which must agitate the heart and present themselves to the mind of an enlightened Englishman when he first lands on this continent [North America]. He must greatly rejoice that he lived at a time to see this fair country discovered and settled; he must necessarily feel a share of national pride when he views the chain of settlements which embellish these extended shores. When he says to himself, "This is the work of my countrymen, who, when convulsed by factions, afflicted by a variety of miseries and wants, restless and impatient, took refuge here. They brought along with them their national genius, to which they principally owe what liberty they enjoy and what substance they possess." Here he sees the industry of his native country displayed in a new manner and traces in their works the embryos of all the arts, sciences, and ingenuity which flourish in Europe. Here he beholds fair cities, substantial villages, extensive fields, an immense country filled with decent houses, good roads, orchards, meadows, and bridges where an hundred years ago all was wild, woody, and uncultivated! What a train of pleasing ideas this fair spectacle must suggest; it is a prospect which must inspire a good citizen with the most heart-felt pleasure. The difficulty consists in the manner of viewing so extensive a scene. He is arrived on a new continent; a modern society offers itself to his contemplation, different from what he had hitherto seen. It is not composed, as in Europe, of great lords who possess everything and of a herd of people who have nothing. Here are no aristocratical families, no courts, no kings, no bishops, no ecclesiastical dominion, no invisible power giving to a few a very visible one, no great manufactures employing thousands, no great refinements of luxury. The rich and the poor are not so far removed from each other as they are in Europe. Some few towns excepted, we are all tillers of the earth, from Nova Scotia to West Florida. We are a people of cultivators scattered over an immense territory, communicating with each other by means of good roads and navigable rivers, united by the silken bands of mild government, all respecting the laws without dreading their power, because they are equitable. We are all animated with the spirit of an industry which is unfettered and unrestrained, because each person works for himself. If he travels through our rural districts, he views not the hostile castle and the haughty mansion, contrasted with the clay-built hut and miserable cabin, where cattle and men help to keep each other warm and dwell in meanness, smoke, and indigence. A pleasing uniformity of decent competence appears throughout our habitations. The meanest of our log-houses is a dry and comfortable habitation. Lawyer or merchant are the fairest titles our towns afford; that of a farmer is the only appellation of the rural inhabitants of our country. It must take some time ere he can reconcile himself to our dictionary, which is but short in words of dignity and names of honour. There, on a Sunday, he sees a congregation of respectable farmers and their wives, all clad in neat homespun, well mounted, or riding in their own humble waggons. There is not among them an esquire, saving the unlettered magistrate. There he sees a parson as simple as his flock, a farmer who does not riot on the labour of others. We have no princes for whom we toil, starve, and bleed; we are the most perfect society now existing in the world. Here man is free as he ought to be, nor is this pleasing equality so transitory as many others are. Many ages will not see the shores of our great lakes replenished with inland nations, nor the unknown bounds of North America entirely peopled. Who can tell how far it extends? Who can tell the millions of men whom it will feed and contain? For no European foot has as yet travelled half the extent of this mighty continent!

The next wish of this traveller will be to know whence came all these people. They are a mixture of English, Scotch, Irish, French, Dutch, Germans, and Swedes. From this promiscuous breed, that race now called Americans have arisen. The eastern provinces [New England] must indeed be excepted as being the unmixed descendants of Englishmen. I have heard many wish that they had been more intermixed also; for my part, I am no wisher and think it much better as it has happened. They exhibit a most conspicuous figure in this great and variegated picture; they too enter for a great share in the pleasing perspective displayed in these thirteen provinces. I know it is fashionable to reflect on them, but I respect them for what they have done; for the accuracy and wisdom with which they have settled their territory; for the decency of their manners; for their early love of letters; their ancient college, the first in this hemisphere; for their industry, which to me who am but a farmer is the criterion of everything. There never was a people, situated as they are, who with so ungrateful a soil have done more in so short a time. Do you think that the monarchical ingredients which are more prevalent in other governments have purged them from all foul stains? Their histories assert the contrary.

In this great American asylum, the poor of Europe have by some means met together, and in consequence of various causes; to what purpose should they ask one another what countrymen they are? Alas, two thirds of them had no country. Can a wretch who wanders about, who works and starves, whose life is a continual scene of sore affliction or pinching penury—can that man call England or any other kingdom his country? A country that had no bread for him, whose fields procured him no harvest, who met with nothing but the frowns of the rich, the severity of the laws, with jails and punishments, who owned not a single foot of the extensive surface of this planet? No! Urged by a variety of motives, here they came. Everything has tended to regenerate them: new laws, a new mode of living, a new social system; here they are become men: in Europe they were as so many useless plants, wanting vegetative mould and refreshing showers; they withered, and were mowed down by want, hunger, and war; but now, by the power of transplantation, like all other plants they have taken root and flourished! Formerly they were not numbered in any civil lists of their country, except in those of the poor; here they rank as citizens. By what invisible power hath this surprising metamorphosis been performed? By that of the laws and that of their industry. The laws, the indulgent laws, protect them as they arrive, stamping on them the symbol of adoption; they receive ample rewards for their labours; these accumulated rewards procure them lands; those lands confer on them the title of freemen, and to that title every benefit is affixed which men can possibly require. This is the great operation daily performed by our laws. Whence proceed these laws? From our government. Whence that government? It is derived from the original genius and strong desire of the people ratified and confirmed by the crown. This is the great chain which links us all, this is the picture which every province exhibits, Nova Scotia excepted. There the crown has done all; either there were no people who had genius or it was not much attended to; the consequence is that the province is very thinly inhabited indeed; the power of the crown in conjunction with the musketos [mosquitos] has prevented men from settling there. Yet some parts of it flourished once, and it contained a mild, harmless set of people. But for the fault of a few leaders, the whole was banished. The greatest political error the crown ever committed in America was to cut off men from a country which wanted nothing but men!

What attachment can a poor European emigrant have for a country where he had nothing? The knowledge of the language, the love of a few kindred as poor as himself, were the only cords that tied him; his country is now that which gives him his land, bread, protection, and consequence; *Ubi panis ibi patria* [where my bread is, there is my country] is the motto of all emigrants. What, then, is the American, this new man? He is either an European or the descendant of an European; hence that strange mixture of blood, which you will find in no other country. I could point out to you a family whose grandfather was an Englishman, whose wife was Dutch, whose son married a French woman, and whose present four sons have now four wives of different nations. *He* is an American, who, leaving behind him all his ancient prejudices and manners, receives new ones from the new mode of life he has embraced, the new government he obeys, and the new rank he holds. He becomes an American by being received in the broad lap of our great Alma Mater. Here individuals of all nations are melted into a new race of men, whose labours and posterity will one day cause great changes in the world. Americans are the western pilgrims who are carrying along with them that great mass of arts, sciences, vigour, and industry which began long since in the East; they will finish the great circle. The Americans were once scattered all over Europe; here they are incorporated into one of the finest systems of population which has ever appeared, and which will hereafter become distinct by the power of the different climates they inhabit. The American ought therefore to love this country much better than that wherein either he or his forefathers were born. Here the rewards of his industry follow with equal steps the progress of his labour; his labour is founded on the basis of nature, self-interest; can it want a stronger allurement? Wives and children, who before in vain demanded of him a morsel of bread, now, fat and frolicsome, gladly help their father to clear those fields whence exuberant crops are to arise to feed and to clothe them all, without any part being claimed, either by a despotic prince, a rich abbot, or a mighty lord. Here religion demands but little of him: a small voluntary salary to the minister and gratitude to God; can he refuse these? The American is a new man, who acts upon new principles; he must therefore entertain new ideas and form new opinions. From involuntary idleness, servile dependence, penury, and useless labour, he has passed to toils of a very different nature, rewarded by ample subsistence. This is an American.

Selection 2: A Trans-Atlantic Revolutionary's Attack on Monarchy and Aristocracy

The international revolutionary cause in the eighteenth-century Atlantic World had no voice more eloquent than Thomas Paine's. A native of England, he emigrated to Pennsylvania on the eve of the American Revolution, where he achieved fame as the author of the pro-independence pamphlet *Common Sense* in 1776. After the American Revolution, his radicalism drew him to France, where he worked as a member of the revolutionary National Assembly. Shifting political fortunes landed him in prison, where he wrote *The Age of Reason* (1794), an attack on Christianity and a defense of the Enlightenment notion of natural religion, or deism. In 1802, he returned to North America, but his reputation for atheism had soured his name, and he died in obscurity in 1809.

The most common theme in Paine's political writings was the inconsistency of hereditary privilege with natural law. Paine railed against monarchy and aristocracy as unjust systems of social and political power, designed only to perpetuate the lordship of a chosen few over the disenfranchised many. He gave fullest expression to this argument in *The Rights of Man*, his defense of the democratic principles of the French Revolution against their chief critic, the British statesman Edmund Burke. In the passage excerpted here, Paine lays out the choice he sees ahead, between a past bound by tradition and ignorance to false privilege or a future transformed by representative government and the recognition of the natural rights of all.

Credit: Thomas Paine, *The Rights of Man, Part First* (1791), in *The Political Works of Thomas Paine* (New York: Calvin Blanchard, 1860), 95–102.

Reason and ignorance, the opposites of each other, influence the great bulk of mankind. If either of these can be rendered sufficiently extensive in a country, the machinery of government goes easily on. Reason shows itself, and ignorance submits to whatever is dictated to it.

The two modes of government which prevail in the world, are, 1st, government by election and representation; 2d, government by hereditary succession. The former is generally known by the name of republic; the latter by that of monarchy and aristocracy.

Those two distinct and opposite forms, erect themselves on the two distinct and opposite bases of reason and ignorance. As the exercise of government requires talents and abilities, and as talents and abilities cannot have hereditary descent, it is evident that hereditary succession requires a belief from man, to which his reason cannot subscribe, and which can only be established upon his ignorance; and the more ignorant any country is, the better it is fitted for this species of government.

On the contrary, government in a well constituted republic, requires no belief from man beyond what his reason authorizes. He sees the *rationale* of the whole system, its origin, and its operation; and as it is best supported when best understood, the human faculties act with boldness, and acquire, under this form of government, a gigantic manliness.

As, therefore, each of those forms acts on a different basis, the one moving freely by the aid of reason, the other by ignorance; we have next to consider, what it is that gives motion to that species of government which is called mixed government, or, as it is sometimes ludicrously styled, a government of *this, that, and t'other*.

The moving power in this species of government is, of necessity, corruption. However imperfect election and representation may be in mixed governments, they still give exertion to a greater portion of reason than is convenient to the hereditary part; and therefore it becomes necessary to buy the reason up. A mixed government is an imperfect every-thing, cementing and soldering the discordant parts together, by corruption, to act as a whole. Mr. Burke appears highly disgusted, that France, since she had resolved on a revolution, did not adopt what he calls "a British constitution"; and the regret which he expresses on this occasion, implies a suspicion, that the British constitution needed something to keep its defects in countenance.

In mixed governments, there is no responsibility; the parts cover each other till responsibility is lost; and the corruption which moves the machine, contrives at the same time its own escape. When it is laid down as a maxim, that a *king can do no wrong*, it places him in a state of similar security with that of idiots and persons insane, and responsibility is out of the question, with respect to himself. It then descends upon the [prime] minister, who shelters himself under a majority in parliament, which by places, pensions, and corruption, he can always command; and that majority justifies itself by the same authority with which it protects the minister. In this rotatory motion, responsibility is thrown off from the parts, and from the whole.

When there is a part in a government which can do no wrong, it implies that it does nothing; and is only the machine of another power, by whose advice and direction it acts. What is supposed to be the king, in mixed governments, is the cabinet; and as the cabinet is always a part of the parliament, and the members justifying in one character what they act in another, a mixed government becomes a continual enigma; entailing upon a country, by the quantity of corruption necessary to solder the parts, the expense of supporting all the forms of government at once, and finally resolving itself into a government by committee; in which the advisers, the actors, the approvers, the justifiers, the persons responsible, and the persons not responsible, are the same person.

By this pantomimical contrivance, and change of scene and character, the parts help each other out in matters, which, neither of them singly, would presume to act. When money is to be obtained, the mass of variety apparently dissolves, and a profusion of parliamentary praises passes between the parts. Each admires, with astonishment, the wisdom, the liberality and disinterestedness of the other; and all of them breathe a pitying sigh at the burdens of the nation.

But in a well-conditioned republic, nothing of this soldering, praising and pitying, can take place; the representation being equal throughout the country, and complete in itself, however it may be arranged into legislative and executive, they have all one and the same natural source. The parts are not foreigners to each other, like democracy, aristocracy, and monarchy. As there are no discordant distinctions, there is nothing to corrupt by compromise, nor confound by contrivance. Public measures appeal of themselves to the understanding of the nation, and, resting on their own merits, disown any flattering application to vanity. The continual whine of lamenting the burden of taxes, however successfully it may be practised in mixed governments, is inconsistent with the sense and spirit of a republic. If taxes are necessary, they are of course advantageous; and if they require an apology, the apology itself implies an impeachment. Why then is man thus imposed upon, or why does he impose upon himself.

When men are spoken of as kings and subjects, or when government is mentioned under distinct or combined heads of monarchy, aristocracy, and democracy, what is it that *reasoning* man is to understand by the terms? If there really existed in the world two more distinct and separate *elements* of human power, we should then see the several origins to which those terms would descriptively apply; but as there is but one species of man, there can be but one element of human power, and that element is man himself. Monarchy, aristocracy, and democracy are but creatures of imagination; and a thousand such may be contrived as well as three.

***

From the revolutions of America and France, and the symptoms that have appeared in other countries, it is evident that the opinion of the world is changing with respect to systems of government, and that revolutions are not within the compass of political calculations. The progress of time and circumstances, which men assign to the accomplishment of great changes, is too mechanical to measure the force of the mind, and the rapidity of reflection, by which revolutions are generated; all the old governments have received a shock from those that already appear, and which were once more improbable, and are a greater subject of wonder, than a general revolution in Europe would be now.

When we survey the wretched condition of man, under the monarchical and hereditary systems of government, dragged from his home by one power, or driven by another, and impoverished by taxes more than by enemies, it becomes evident that those systems are bad, and that a general revolution in the principle and construction of governments is necessary.

What is government more than the management of the affairs of a nation? It is not, and from its nature cannot be, the property of any particular man or family, but of the whole community at whose expense it is supported; and though by force or contrivance it has been usurped into an inheritance, the usurpation cannot alter the right of things. Sovereignty, as a matter of right, appertains to the nation only, and not to any individual; and a nation has at all times an inherent, indefeasible right to abolish any form of government it finds inconvenient, and establish such as accords with its interest, disposition, and happiness. The romantic and barbarous distinctions of men into kings and subjects, though it may suit the condition of courtiers cannot that of citizens; and is exploded by the principle upon which governments are now founded. Every citizen is a member of the sovereignty, and as such can acknowledge no personal subjection; and his obedience can be only to the laws.

When men think of what government is, they must necessarily suppose it to possess a knowledge of all the objects and matters upon which its authority is to be exercised. In this view of government, the republican system, as established by America and France, operates to embrace the whole of a nation: and the knowledge necessary to the interest of all the parts, is to be found in the centre, which the parts by representation form; but the old governments are on a construction that excludes knowledge as well as happiness; government by monks, who know nothing of the world beyond the walls of a convent, is as consistent as government by kings.

What were formerly called revolutions, were little more than a change of persons, or an alteration of local circumstances. They rose and fell like things of course, and had nothing in their existence or their fate that could influence beyond the spot that produced them. But what we now see in the world, from the revolutions of America and France, are a renovation of the natural order of things, a system of principles as universal as truth and the existence of man, and combining moral with political happiness and national prosperity.

I. Men are born, and always continue, free and equal, in respect to their rights. Civil distinctions, therefore, can be founded only on public utility.

II. The end of all political associations is the preservation of the natural and imprescriptible rights of man, and these rights are liberty, property, security, and resistance of oppression.

III. The nation is essentially the source of all sovereignty; nor can any individual, or any body of men, be entitled to any authority which is not expressly derived from it.

In these principles there is nothing to throw a nation into confusion, by inflaming ambition. They are calculated to call forth wisdom and abilities, and to exercise them for the public good, and not for the emolument or aggrandizement of particular descriptions of men or families. Monarchical sovereignty, the enemy of mankind and the source of misery, is abolished; and sovereignty itself is restored to its natural and original place, the nation.—Were this the case throughout Europe, the cause of wars would be taken away.

It is attributed to Henry IV. of France, a man of an enlarged and benevolent heart, that he proposed, about the year 1620, a plan for abolishing war in Europe. The plan consisted in constituting an European congress, or, as the French authors style it, a pacific republic; by appointing delegates from the several nations, who were to act, as a court of arbitration, in any disputes that might arise between nation and nation.

Had such a plan been adopted at the time it was proposed, the taxes of England and France, as two of the parties, would have been at least ten millions sterling annually, to each nation, less than they were at the commencement of the French revolution.

To conceive a cause why such a plan has not been adopted, (and that instead of a congress for the purpose of preventing war, it has been called only to *terminate* a war, after a fruitless expense of several years,) it will be necessary to consider the interest of governments as a distinct interest to that of nations.

Whatever is the cause of taxes to a nation, becomes also the means of revenue to a government. Every war terminates with an addition of taxes, and consequently with an addition of revenue; and in any event of war, in the manner they are now commenced and concluded, the power and interest of governments are increased. War, therefore, from its productiveness, as it easily furnishes the pretense of necessity for taxes and appointments to places and office, becomes the principal part of the system of old governments; and to establish any mode to abolish war, however advantageous it might be to nations, would be to take from such government the most lucrative of its branches. The frivolous matters upon which war is made, show the disposition and avidity of governments to uphold the system of war, and betray the motives upon which they act.

Why are not republics plunged into war, but because the nature of their government does not admit of an interest distinct from that of the nation? Even Holland, though an ill-constructed republic, and with a commerce extending over the world, existed nearly a century without war: and the instant the form of government was changed in France, the republican principles of peace, and domestic prosperity and economy, arose with the new government; and the same consequences would follow the same causes in other nations,

As war is the system of government on the old construction, the animosity which nations reciprocally entertain, is nothing more than what the policy of their governments excite, to keep up the spirit of the system. Each government accuses the other of perfidy, intrigue and ambition, as a means of heating the imagination of their respective nations, and incensing them to hostilities. Man is not the enemy of man, but through the medium of a false system of government. Instead, therefore, of exclaiming against the ambition of kings, the exclamation should be directed against the principle of such governments; and instead of seeking to reform the individual, the wisdom of a nation should apply itself to reform the system.

Whether the forms and maxims of governments which are still in practice, were adapted to the condition of the world at the period they were established, is not in this case the question. The older they are the less correspondence can they have with the present state of things. Time, and change of circumstances and opinions have the same progressive effect in rendering modes of government obsolete, as they have upon customs and manners. Agriculture, commerce, manufactures, and the tranquil arts, by which the prosperity of nations is best promoted, require a different system of government and a different species of knowledge to direct its operations, to what might have been the former condition of the world.

As it is not difficult to perceive, from the enlightened state of mankind, that the hereditary governments are verging to their decline, and that revolutions on the broad basis of national sovereignty, and government by representation, are making their way in Europe, it would be an act of wisdom to anticipate their approach, and produce revolutions by reason and accommodation, rather than commit them to the issue of convulsions.

From what we now see, nothing of reform in the political world ought to be held improbable. It is an age of revolutions, in which every thing may be looked for. The intrigue of courts, by which the system of war is kept up, may provoke a confederation of nations to abolish it: and an European congress to patronize the progress of free government, and promote the civilization of nations with each other is an event nearer in probability, than once were the revolutions and alliances of France and America.

Selection 3: An Anti-Slavery Advocate Defends the Slave Rebels of Saint Domingue

In 1791, slaves rebelled against their masters in Saint Domingue (modern Haiti), France's most profitable colony in the Caribbean. Reports of the rebellion spread rapidly throughout the Atlantic World as white planters fled for their lives, telling stories of arson, violence, and bloodshed. The rebellion on Saint Domingue was in fact unprecedented in its scale, engulfing the entire colony, destroying its ruling class, and culminating in the creation of Haiti, the second independent nation state in the Western Hemisphere.

Anti-slavery advocates did not rush to endorse the slave rebellion on Saint Domingue. Many feared that the violence there damaged the moral authority of their cause, and others thought it presaged the exportation of the French Revolution's radical ideology across the Atlantic. In the United States, many politicians, including Thomas Jefferson, who had expressed sympathy for the French Revolution recoiled in horror at what was happening in Saint Domingue and urged the United States to aid the planters there. That hypocrisy prompted Abraham Bishop to publish an essay titled "The Rights of Black Men" in a Boston newspaper. Bishop had imbibed the democratic ideals of the American and French Revolutions, and he saw no reason why they did not also apply to the slaves of Saint Domingue. His defense of the slaves' cause is an example of how the language of liberty and equality used in the Declaration of Independence had repercussions far beyond the American Revolution.

Credit: Abraham Bishop, "The Rights of Black Men," *The Argus* (Boston), November 22, 25, and December 6, 1791.

If Freedom depends upon colour, and if the Blacks were born for slaves, those in the West-India Islands may be called Insurgents and Murder[er]s. If Freedom depends upon colour, we have only to seek for the whitest man in the world, that we may find the freest and for the blackest, that we may find the greatest slave. But the enlightened mind of Americans will not receive such ideas. We believe, that Freedom is the natural right of all rational beings, and we know that the Blacks have never voluntarily resigned that freedom. Then is not their cause as just as ours? We fought with bravery, and prayed earnestly for success upon our righteous cause, when we drew the sword, and shed the blood of the Englishmen—for what!—Not to gain Freedom; for we were never Slaves; but to rid ourselves of taxes, imposed without our consent, and from the growing evils of usurpation. Believing our cause to have been just, I believe firmly, that the cause of the Blacks is just. They are asserting those rights by the sword, which it was impossible to secure by mild measures. Stripes, imprisonment, hunger, nakedness, cruel tortures and death, were the portion of those Blacks who even talked of liberty, or who, for a moment, conducted like Freemen. Did we talk coolly about the cruel murders of our brothers and sisters at the Northward? Did we act coolly, when our officers and soldiers were loaded with irons in loathsome dungeons, and dying by hundreds in prison ships? We did not. Then shall we preach lessons of coolness and moderation to the Blacks? Alas, they are not in a situation to hear us. Gallows are erected, and tortures prepared for them at this very moment.

Review the history of their past sufferings, be but a moment in their situation, and judge whether, in a climate warm as theirs your blood would flow coolly. Let us be consistent Americans, and if we justify our own conduct in the late glorious Revolution, let us justify those, who, in a cause like ours fight with equal bravery.

We may feel in the cause of humanity, and may lament, that the blood of white men is spilling. It would be happy indeed, if the rights of man could in all countries be asserted as coolly and judiciously, as they have been in France; but, in the French West-India Islands this could not have been done. The efforts of Blacks for a peaceable assertion would have cost them their lives. Arms gave them courage in a common cause. If their Lords had kept them in savage ignorance, shall they be blamed, that they fight like savages. Had they been learnt [taught] the art of war, they might have conducted their measures more according to Baron Steuben [a German officer who trained American soldiers at Valley Forge]. Had they been treated with mildness, perhaps their measures would have been more mild.

We talked in the late war about the hand of Providence. Since then we have seen the wonders of Providence in various parts of the world, and have gloried that men, long oppressed, had dared to assert their rights. Shall we now cease to glory? Shall we now sacrifice principle to a paltry partiality for colour? Can we believe that the French people were ever as oppressed as the Blacks have been? Let those differ from me, who will, I have a firm confidence, that we shall now see the hand of Providence more visibly, than ever. *The Universal Father seems now demonstrating that of one blood, he has created all nations of men, that dwell on the face of the earth.* In the last war, we called those *savages and monsters in human shape*, who would be hired to assist in reducing us to allegiance. We agreed to ascribe all the glory to Heaven, if we might be prospered; but in all our histories since the war, have ascribed all the glory to ourselves, *politely* trusting that the goodness of our Heavenly Father needed not our praises. Zealous in the *theory* of liberty, we talked in high strains about the equal rights of man, and formed ourselves into societies for the abolition of slavery. The policy of some of the states has, to their honour, reduced this theory to practice. In other states, liberty and property clashed, and the last, as usual, gained the victory. The blacks are still enslaved within the United States. The Indians are driven into the society of savage beasts, and we glory in the equal rights of men, provided that *we white men can enjoy the whole of them*.

***

I speak the words of truth and soberness, in saying that the blacks are now fighting in a just cause. My assertion, that they are entitled to freedom, is founded on the American Declaration of Independence: Upon the language of our petitions to the English court, at the commencement of the late war: Upon the spirit of freedom, which animated and conducted to victory, the American army: Upon Paine's *Common Sense:* Upon the articles of our liberating societies, and upon the Declaration of Rights, to be seen in the different *statute-law-books* throughout the states.

Have we already forgotten the animating sound, *Liberty or Death?* That sound has gone out into the world, and is rapidly extending to the ends of the earth. From various parts of Europe we have already heard the echo, *Liberty or Death:* We have firmly asserted, *that all men are free.* Yet, as soon as the poor blacks, who we have oppressed beyond measure, who suffered, till cruelty itself cried out, *It is enough,* who bore, till patience had done its perfect work, echoed *Liberty or Death,* we have been the first to assist in riveting their chains! From us the blacks had a right to expect effectual assistance. They are pursuing the principles which had taught them, and are now sealing with their blood, *the rights of men;* yet Americans are sending assistance to their enemies. I do not suggest, that the Federal Legislature [Congress] has sent them assistance, or that any one of the States has officially afforded assistance; but vessel-loads of military stores and provisions have been sent; the public papers have been cautiously filled with reports of the whites.

Every public transaction, and most private conversations have evinced a great zeal in favor of the whites and one can hardly wish the blacks to be victorious without exposing himself to censure, calumny, and opprobrious names. That conduct and language, which in 1775, would have cost a man the loss of his liberty, will now, in 1791, be applauded. But my argument for a contrary conduct and language is made up in the following manner.

The blacks are entitled to freedom, for we did not say all *white* men are *free,* but *all men* are free. The blacks bore their conditions of slavery, till it became too terrible. The blacks took up arms to rid themselves of slavery. Arms were their only resource. They use their arms according to the best of their knowledge. They look to the liberating societies [anti-slavery societies] for that aid and support which they were taught to expect. It is cruelty then to withhold such aid and support; Worse than cruelty to assist their enemies. If, at this time, the liberating societies do not come forward, how ridiculous must appear their orations, their publications, their record; their addresses to the passions, and to the reason, in favor of the poor blacks, how profane must appear their appeals to Heaven for the sincerity of their zeal, and their resolution to exert themselves to liberate the blacks.

Selection 4: A Creole Revolutionary's Vision for the Future of Spanish America

Known as *El Libertador* in his native Venezuela, Simon Bolívar was the most famous of Latin America's creole revolutionaries. As a general and a statesman, he helped forge the independent nations of Venezuela, Colombia, Ecuador, Peru, and Bolivia, and he was an early and eloquent advocate of Latin American nationalism.

Bolívar's social background and intellectual influences resemble closely those of George Washington, Thomas Jefferson, and other revolutionary leaders in North America. His parents were members of Venezuela's planter aristocracy, and his private tutor educated him in the classic works of the Enlightenment. As a young man, he traveled in Europe and was drawn to the political radicalism of many of Latin American expatriates. Between 1810 and 1825, he led the struggle for independence in Andean South America, a conflict that Bolívar himself called a "War to the Death." After independence, he worked to forge a confederation of Andean states, but he died in 1830 after political rivals had forced him from office.

One of Bolívar's most famous works was "The Jamaica Letter," which he wrote during an interlude of Caribbean exile in 1815, in hopes of attracting British support to his cause. In this essay, Bolívar described the causes and course of the Spanish-American revolutions and his vision of a post-revolutionary South America founded on Enlightenment principles of government.

Credit: *Selected Writings of Bolívar*, compiled by Vicente Lecuna, ed. Harold A. Bierck, Jr., and trans. Lewis Bertrand, 2 vols, 2nd edn (New York: The Colonial Press, 1951), Vol. 1: 104–105, 109–112, 115–117, 121–122.

Success will crown our efforts, because the destiny of America has been irrevocably decided; the tie that bound her to Spain has been severed. Only a concept maintained that tie and kept the parts of that immense monarchy together. That which formerly bound them now divides them. The hatred that the [Iberian] Peninsula has inspired in us is greater than the ocean between us. It would be easier to have the two continents meet than to reconcile the spirits of the two countries. The habit of obedience; a community of interest, of understanding, of religion; mutual goodwill; a tender regard for the birthplace and good name of our forefathers; in short, all that gave rise to our hopes, came to us from Spain. As a result there was born a principle of affinity that seemed eternal, notwithstanding the misbehavior of our rulers which weakened that sympathy, or, rather, that bond enforced by the domination of their rule. At present the contrary attitude persists: we are threatened with the fear of death, dishonor, and every harm; there is nothing we have not suffered at the hands of that unnatural step-mother— Spain. The veil has been torn asunder. We have already seen the light, and it is not our desire to be thrust back into darkness. The chains have been broken; we have been freed, and now our enemies seek to enslave us anew. For this reason America fights desperately, and seldom has desperation failed to achieve victory.

Because successes have been partial and spasmodic, we must not lose faith. In some regions the Independents triumph, while in others the tyrants have the advantage. What is the end result? Is not the entire New World in motion, armed for defense? We have but to look around us on this hemisphere to witness a simultaneous struggle at every point.

***

It is even more difficult to foresee the future fate of the New World, to set down its political principles, or to prophesy what manner of government it will adopt. Every conjecture relative to America's future is, I feel, pure speculation. When mankind was in its infancy, steeped in uncertainty, ignorance, and error, was it possible to foresee what system it would adopt for its preservation? Who could venture to say that a certain nation would be a republic or a monarchy; this nation great, that nation small? To my way of thinking, such is our own situation. We are a young people. We inhabit a world apart, separated by broad seas. We are young in the ways of almost all the arts and sciences, although, in a certain manner, we are old in the ways of civilized society. I look upon the present state of America as similar to that of Rome after its fall. Each part of Rome adopted a political system conforming to its interest and situation or was led by the individual ambitions of certain chiefs, dynasties, or associations. But this important difference exists: those dispersed parts later reestablished their ancient nations, subject to the changes imposed by circumstances or events. But we scarcely retain a vestige of what once was; we are, moreover, neither Indian nor European, but a species midway between the legitimate proprietors of this country and the Spanish usurpers. In short, though Americans by birth we derive our rights from Europe, and we have to assert these rights against the rights of the natives, and at the same time we must defend ourselves against the invaders. This places us in a most extraordinary and involved situation. Notwithstanding that it is a type of divination to predict the result of the political course which America is pursuing, I shall venture some conjectures which, of course, are colored by my enthusiasm and dictated by rational desires rather than by reasoned calculations.

The role of the inhabitants of the American hemisphere has for centuries been purely passive. Politically they were non-existent. We are still in a position lower than slavery, and therefore it is more difficult for us to rise to the enjoyment of freedom. Permit me these transgressions in order to establish the issue. States are slaves because of either the nature or the misuse of their constitutions; a people is therefore enslaved when the government, by its nature or its vices, infringes on and usurps the rights of the citizen or subject. Applying these principles, we find that America was denied not only its freedom but even an active and effective tyranny. Let me explain. Under absolutism there are no recognized limits to the exercise of governmental powers. The will of the great sultan, khan, bey, and other despotic rulers is the supreme law, carried out more or less arbitrarily by the lesser pashas, khans, and satraps of Turkey and Persia, who have an organized system of oppression in which inferiors participate according to the authority vested in them. To them is entrusted the administration of civil, military, political, religious, and tax matters. But, after all is said and done, the rulers of Ispahan are Persians; the viziers of the Grand Turk are Turks; and the sultans of Tartary are Tartars. China does not bring its military leaders and scholars from the land of Genghis Khan, her conqueror, notwithstanding that the Chinese of today are the lineal descendants of those who were reduced to subjection by the ancestors of the present-day Tartars.

How different is our situation! We have been harassed by a conduct which has not only deprived us of our rights but has kept us in a sort of permanent infancy with regard to public affairs. If we could at least have managed our domestic affairs and our internal administration, we could have acquainted ourselves with the processes and mechanics of public affairs. We should also have enjoyed a personal consideration, thereby commanding a certain unconscious respect from the people, which is so necessary to preserve amidst revolutions. That is why I say we have even been deprived of an active tyranny, since we have not been permitted to exercise its functions.

Americans today, and perhaps to a greater extent than ever before, who live within the Spanish system occupy a position in society no better than that of serfs destined for labor, or at best they have no more status than that of mere consumers. Yet even this status is surrounded with galling restrictions, such as being forbidden to grow European crops, or to store products which are royal monopolies, or to establish factories of a type the Peninsula itself does not possess. To this add the exclusive trading privileges, even in articles of prime necessity, and the barriers between American provinces, designed to prevent all exchange of trade, traffic, and understanding. In short, do you wish to know what our future held?—simply the cultivation of the fields of indigo, grain, coffee, sugar cane, cacao, and cotton; cattle raising on the broad plains; hunting wild game in the jungles; digging in the earth to mine its gold—but even these limitations could never satisfy the greed of Spain.

So negative was our existence that I can find nothing comparable in any other civilized society, examine as I may the entire history of time and the politics of all nations. Is it not an outrage and a violation of human rights to expect a land so splendidly endowed, so vast, rich, and populous, to remain merely passive?

As I have just explained, we were cut off and, as it were, removed from the world in relation to the science of government and administration of the state. We were never viceroys or governors, save in the rarest of instances; seldom archbishops and bishops; diplomats never; as military men, only subordinates; as nobles, without royal privileges. In brief, we were neither magistrates nor financiers and seldom merchants—all in flagrant contradiction to our institutions.

Emperor Charles V made a pact with the discoverers, conquerors, and settlers of America, and this, as Guerra puts it, is our social contract. The monarchs of Spain made a solemn agreement with them, to be carried out on their own account and at their own risk, expressly prohibiting them from drawing on the royal treasury. In return, they were made the lords of the land, entitled to organize the public administration and act as the court of last appeal, together with many other exemptions and privileges that are too numerous to mention. The King committed himself never to alienate the American provinces, inasmuch as he had no jurisdiction but that of sovereign domain. Thus, for themselves and their descendants, the *conquistadores* possessed what were tantamount to feudal holdings. Yet there are explicit laws respecting employment in civil, ecclesiastical, and tax-raising establishments. These laws favor, almost exclusively, the natives of the country who are of Spanish extraction. Thus, by an outright violation of the laws and the existing agreements, those born in America have been despoiled of their constitutional rights as embodied in the code.

***

More than anyone, I desire to see America fashioned into the greatest nation in the world, greatest not so much by virtue of her area and wealth as by her freedom and glory. Although I seek perfection for the government of my country, I cannot persuade myself that the New World can, at the moment, be organized as a great republic. Since it is impossible, I dare not desire it; yet much less do I desire to have all America a monarchy because this plan is not only impracticable but also impossible. Wrongs now existing could not be righted, and our emancipation would be fruitless. The American states need the care of paternal governments to heal the sores and wounds of despotism and war. The parent country, for example, might be Mexico, the only country fitted for the position by her intrinsic strength, and without such power there can be no parent country. Let us assume it were to be the Isthmus of Panamá, the most central point of this vast continent. Would not all parts continue in their lethargy and even in their present disorder? For a single government to infuse life into the New World; to put into use all the resources for public prosperity; to improve, educate, and perfect the New World, that government would have to possess the authority of a god, much less the knowledge and virtues of mankind.

The party spirit that today keeps our states in constant agitation would assume still greater proportions were a central power established, for that power—the only force capable of checking this agitation—would be elsewhere. Furthermore, the chief figures of the capitals would not tolerate the preponderance of leaders at the metropolis, for they would regard these leaders as so many tyrants. Their resentments would attain such heights that they would compare the latter to the hated Spaniards. Any such monarchy would be a misshapen colossus that would collapse of its own weight at the slightest disturbance.

Mr. de Pradt [a French writer] has wisely divided America into fifteen or seventeen mutually independent states, governed by as many monarchs. I am in agreement on the first suggestion, as America can well tolerate seventeen nations; as to the second, though it could easily be achieved, it would serve no purpose. Consequently, I do not favor American monarchies. My reasons are these: The well-understood interest of a republic is limited to the matter of its preservation, prosperity, and glory. Republicans, because they do not desire powers which represent a directly contrary viewpoint, have no reason for expanding the boundaries of their nation to the detriment of their own resources, solely for the purpose of having their neighbors share a liberal constitution. They would not acquire rights or secure any advantage by conquering their neighbors, unless they were to make them colonies, conquered territory, or allies, after the example of Rome. But such thought and action are directly contrary to the principles of justice which characterize republican systems; and, what is more, they are in direct opposition to the interests of their citizens, because a state, too large of itself or together with its dependencies, ultimately falls into decay. Its free government becomes a tyranny. The principles that should preserve the government are disregarded, and finally it degenerates into despotism. The distinctive feature of small republics is permanence: that of large republics varies, but always with a tendency toward empire. Almost all small republics have had long lives. Among the larger republics, only Rome lasted for several centuries, for its capital was a republic. The rest of her dominions were governed by divers laws and institutions.

The policy of a king is very different. His constant desire is to increase his possessions, wealth, and authority; and with justification, for his power grows with every acquisition, both with respect to his neighbors and his own vassals, who fear him because his power is as formidable as his empire, which he maintains by war and conquest. For these reasons I think that the Americans, being anxious for peace, science, art, commerce, and agriculture, would prefer republics to kingdoms. And, further, it seems to me that these desires conform with the aims of Europe.

***

I shall tell you with what we must provide ourselves in order to expel the Spaniards and to found a free government. It is *union*, obviously; but such union will come about through sensible planning and well-directed actions rather than by divine magic. America stands together because it is abandoned by all other nations. It is isolated in the center of the world. It has no diplomatic relations, nor does it receive any military assistance; instead, America is attacked by Spain, which has more military supplies than any we can possibly acquire through furtive means.

When success is not assured, when the state is weak, and when results are distantly seen, all men hesitate; opinion is divided, passions rage, and the enemy fans these passions in order to win an easy victory because of them. As soon as we are strong and under the guidance of a liberal nation which will lend us her protection, we will achieve accord in cultivating the virtues and talents that lead to glory. Then will we march majestically toward that great prosperity for which South America is destined. Then will those sciences and arts which, born in the East, have enlightened Europe, wing their way to a free Colombia, which will cordially bid them welcome …

Discussion Questions

1. Where do you see evidence of the Enlightenment's celebration of nature, natural law, and human progress in Crèvecoeur's writing? According to him, what distinctive social factors in colonial society accounted for the transformation of Europeans into Americans?
2. Why does Paine consider hereditary power a violation of natural law? Why does he believe republican forms of government are more consistent with natural law?
3. On what grounds does Bishop compare the slave revolutionaries in Haiti to the American patriots of 1776? How does he use Enlightenment ideas to defend the Haitian revolutionaries and to call for Americans to aid them?
4. According to Bolívar, why is Spain an "unnatural stepmother" for its colonies? Bolívar lived a generation after Crèvecoeur and Paine: where do you see evidence of those two earlier writers in "The Jamaica Letter"?

Suggested Readings

For the Age of Revolutions in the Atlantic World, see Janet Polasky, *Revolutions without Borders: The Call to Liberty in the Atlantic World* (New Haven, CT: Yale University Press, 2015); and Lester D. Langley, *The Americas in the Age of Revolution, 1750–1850* (New Haven, CT: Yale University Press, 1996). Studies that examine the ricocheting impact of the American and French Revolutions include Susan Dunn, *Sister Revolutions: French Lightning, American Light* (New York: Faber and Faber, 1999); Philipp Ziesche, *Cosmopolitan Patriots: Americans in Paris in the Age of Revolution* (Charlottesville, VA: University of Virginia Press, 2010); and François Furstenberg, *When the United States Spoke French: Five Refugees Who Shaped a Nation* (New York: Penguin, 2014). For an excellent study of the global impact of natural rights philosophy, see David Armitage, *The Declaration of Independence: A Global History* (Cambridge, MA: Harvard University Press, 2007).

For the Enlightenment in British North America and Spanish America, see respectively Caroline Winterer, *American Enlightenments: Pursuing Happiness in the Age of Reason* (New Haven, CT: Yale University Press, 2016); and Stanley J. Stein and Barbara H. Stein, *Apogee of Empire: Spain and New Spain in the Age of Charles III, 1759–1789* (Baltimore, MD: Johns Hopkins University Press, 2003). For overviews of the causes and consequences of the Latin American wars of independence, see Richard Graham, *Independence in Latin America: A Comparative Approach*, 2nd edn (New York: McGraw-Hill, 1994); and John Lynch, *The Spanish American Revolutions, 1808–1826*, 2nd edn (New York: W. W. Norton, 1986). For a biography of Spanish America's most famous patriot, see John Lynch, *Simon Bolivar: A Life* (New Haven, CT: Yale University Press, 2006).

The origins and impact of the Haitian Revolution are addressed in two books by Laurent Dubois: *A Colony of Citizens: Revolution and Slave Emancipation in the French Caribbean, 1787–1804* (Chapel Hill, NC: University of North Carolina Press, 2004); and *Avengers of the New World: The Story of the Haitian Revolution* (Cambridge, MA: Harvard University Press, 2004). The reaction to the Haitian Revolution in the United States is covered in James Alexander Dun, *Dangerous Neighbors: Making the Haitian Revolution in Early America* (Philadelphia, PA: University of Pennsylvania Press, 2016). For the impact of the American Revolution in the Caribbean, see Andrew Jackson O'Shaughnessy, *An Empire Divided: The American Revolution and the British Caribbean* (Philadelphia, PA: University of Pennsylvania Press, 2000).

13 Out of the Atlantic Crucible

Figure 13.1 Europe Supported by Africa and America.

John Stedman commissioned this artwork for his narrative of his adventures in Surinam (see Chapter 6, Selection 2), depicting the three populations he encountered there—Europeans, Africans, and Indians—as three female figures with arms entwined. How does the figure of Europe differ from that of Africa and America? What is the significance of the figures' nakedness? Do you suppose Stedman meant this image to be a criticism or endorsement of the historical forces that created and sustained the Atlantic World?

Source credit: Engraving by William Blake, 1792. William Blake Archive/Wikimedia Commons.

Introduction

No singular event heralded the end of the Atlantic World System in the way that Columbus's first voyage marked its beginning. The Atlantic World had a long demise, as illustrated by the protracted battle to end slavery in the Americas. The economic and political ties that bound together Africa, Europe, and the Americas changed gradually but significantly over the course of the nineteenth century, bringing an end to the empires that had ruled and profited from the Atlantic World. Nevertheless, the Atlantic World left important legacies for the modern era, and one does not have to look far to find evidence of its continuing impact on our own world.

In 1823, the United States President James Monroe warned the nations of Europe not to interfere with the newly independent nations of Latin America. In return, Monroe promised, the United States would not meddle in the affairs of Europe. The Monroe Doctrine, as this policy became known, had no real teeth: The United States lacked the military and naval power to enforce it. More significantly, however, it gave formal expression to a reality that had been reshaping the Atlantic World since 1775. Politically, the two hemispheres were growing apart; former colonies were gaining their independence and expressing new nationalist identities that emphasized their distance and autonomy from the Old World. While some European powers retained their sugar island colonies in the Caribbean well into the twentieth century, the independent nation state had become the norm of political organization in the Americas by 1825.

While Europe's political domination of the Western Hemisphere went into eclipse, its economic power there remained strong. In nineteenth-century Latin America, British and German merchants and investors rushed to fill the gap left by the destruction of Spanish imperial rule. This reliance on European capital and industry perpetuated the economic dependence of the old colonial system in Latin America well after political independence had been achieved. In the southern United States, the plantation complex continued to thrive after independence, as planters sold their new cash crop, cotton, to textile manufacturers in Britain and the northern United States. Indeed, the explosive growth of industrial production in Britain, the northern United States, France, and Germany in the nineteenth century created a new web of international trade in which those nations with industrial capacity continued to exploit other regions of the world for their raw materials, only now on a global scale.

European imperialism, in other words, did not end with the Atlantic World. Quite to the contrary, it became even more powerful as it shifted into Africa and Asia. Powered by Industrial Age improvements in transportation (railroads, steamships, canals) and military technology (ironclad warships, machine guns), Britain, Germany, and France competed intensely for overseas empire in Africa, Asia, and the Pacific. The plantation complex traveled with them, and European investors used it to extract rubber, tea, sugar, gold, diamonds, and other raw materials from these colonies. Indigenous peoples in these regions faced the same onslaught from epidemic diseases, coerced labor, and religious missions that Native Americans had encountered in the Atlantic World.

The transoceanic migrations that shaped the Atlantic World also continued well after the decline of the Atlantic empires. Emigration from Europe to the Americas grew at an even greater pace after 1800. Latin American independence ended the restrictive immigration policy that the Spanish had imposed on their colonies, allowing British, German, and Italian emigrants to settle in South America. In North America, European immigration prior to 1850 was dominated by Irish, German, and Scandinavian peoples; after 1880, Italians, Poles, and Russian Jews made the Atlantic crossing in large numbers. The end of slavery in the New World also revived the immigration of indentured servants for the plantation economies of the Caribbean, bringing East Indians in large numbers to the British West Indies after 1833. As the nineteenth century progressed, the Pacific Ocean became another highway of migration, traveled by Chinese indentured servants to North and South America. In short, so long as the demand for labor remained high in the Americas, immigration there continued apace.

In some respects, the Atlantic World never came to an end. Rather, it morphed into something else, on a much grander scale. We live in an age of global travel and communication, of world markets and multinational corporations, of multi-ethnic communities with populations from every corner of the globe. All of these characteristics of our modern world have roots in the Atlantic World; although modern technology may make the wooden ships and muskets of the Atlantic World appear quaint by comparison, we should not let that glaring technological gap fool us. On the human scale, there is still much that bears comparison between the Atlantic World and our modern one whenever we talk about contact, exchange, and conflict between human populations around the globe.

The readings in this chapter suggest one such inquiry: What type of legacy have notions of race that were forged in the Atlantic World left for modern society? The colonization of the Americas brought together for the first time African, Native American, and European peoples, and out of this collision there emerged racial categories and social orders peculiar to the New World. As colonial empires gave way to nation states, the issue of race confronted all who contemplated the future of the Americas. In the selections in this chapter, four observers offer their differing impressions of race relations in the Atlantic World during the early nineteenth century. As you read these selections, think of the historical factors that might account for the different experiences and opinions of these writers. How did their views anticipate the continuing significance of race in the modern world's social, economic, and political systems?

Selection 1: A German Traveler Describes the Race-Based Social Order of Mexico

Alexander von Humboldt, a native of Germany, crossed the Atlantic in 1799 and spent five years in the Americas. His travels focused on the Andes and Mexico, but on his way home, he also visited Philadelphia and Washington, DC—a stop that informed his comparisons of the United States and Latin America. Humboldt's primary interests were scientific: He gathered information about flora, fauna, geology, and other aspects of the natural world. He was also a keen student of history and politics, and much of what he wrote about Latin America reflected Enlightenment-era criticism of Spain's conquest and government of its New World dominions. Upon returning to Europe, Humboldt gained celebrity for his American travels, and he spent the rest of his life working as a scientist and diplomat.

In 1811, he published his most famous work, the four-volume *Political Essay on the Kingdom of New Spain*. Most of the *Political Essay* deals with Mexico's natural resources, particularly its mineral wealth, but the picture Humboldt painted of a mature colonial society on the verge of political independence is what still attracts historians to this source today. With the voice of a detached, scientific observer, he took measure of Mexico's population and dissected its race-based social order. In the passage that follows, he comments on African and Indian slavery and the nature of the color prejudice that determined rank in this society.

Credit: Alexander von Humboldt, *Political Essay on the Kingdom of New Spain*, ed. Mary Maples Dunn (New York: Alfred A. Knopf, 1972), 84–90.

The kingdom of New Spain is, of all the European colonies under the torrid zone, that in which there are the fewest Negroes. We may almost say that there are no slaves. We may go through the whole city of Mexico without seeing a black countenance. The service of no house is carried on with slaves. From this point of view Mexico presents a singular contrast to Havana, Lima and Caracas. From information in the enumeration [census] of 1793 it appears that in all New Spain there are not six thousand Negroes and not more than nine or ten thousand slaves, of whom the greatest number belong to the ports of Acapulco and Vera Cruz or the warm regions of the coasts. The slaves are four times more numerous in Caracas which does not contain a sixth of the population of Mexico. The Negroes of Jamaica are to those of New Spain in the proportion of 250 to 1! In the West India islands, Peru and even Caracas, the progress of agriculture and industry in general depends on the augmentation of Negroes.

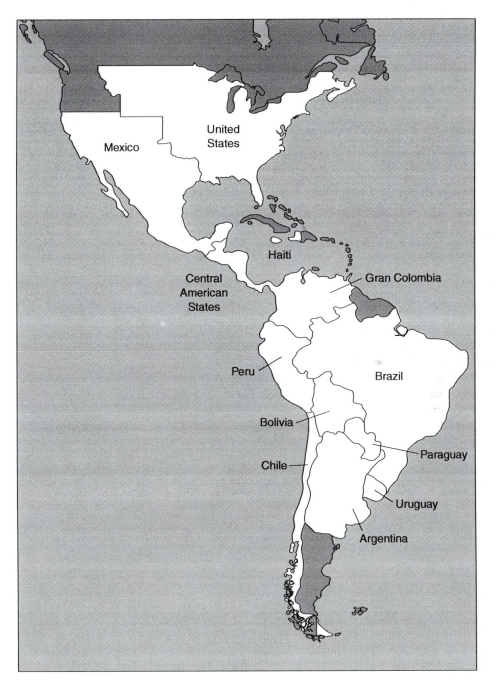

Map 13.1 Independent States in the Americas, *c.*1825.

National boundaries in Western Hemisphere.

In the island of Cuba, for example, where the annual exportation of sugar has risen in twelve years from 400,000 to 1,000,000 quintals [88 million to 220 million lbs.], between 1792 and 1803 nearly 55,000 slaves have been introduced. But in Mexico the increase of colonial prosperity is nowise occasioned by a more active slave trade, and the progress of sugar cultivation which has taken place in New Spain has not perceptibly increased the number of slaves. Of the 74,000 Negroes annually furnished by Africa to America and Asia, not above 100 land on the coast of Mexico.

By the laws there can be no Indian slaves in the Spanish colonies, and yet by a singular abuse wars give rise to a state very much like that of the African slave. In Mexico the prisoners taken in the petty warfare which is carried on almost without interruption on the frontiers of the *provincias internas* [northern provinces of Mexico] experience an unhappy fate. They are generally of the nation of the Apaches, and they are dragged to Mexico where they languish in the dungeons of a correction house. Their ferocity is increased by solitude and despair. Transported to Vera Cruz and Cuba, they soon perish, like every savage Indian removed from the high table land into the lower and hotter regions. These prisoners sometimes break from their dungeons and commit the most atrocious cruelties in the surrounding countries. It is high time that the government interested itself in these unfortunate persons whose number is small and their situation so much the easier to be ameliorated.

However, the slaves in Mexico, as in all the other Spanish possessions, are somewhat more under the protection of the laws than the Negroes of the other European colonies. These laws are always interpreted in favor of liberty. The government wishes to see the number of freedmen increased. A slave who by his industry has procured a little money may compel his master to give him his liberty on paying the moderate sum of 1,500 or 2,000 livres [French coins]. Liberty cannot be refused to a Negro on the pretext that he cost the triple of the sum, or that he possesses a particular talent for some lucrative employment. A slave who has been cruelly used acquires on that account his freedom by the law, if the judge do justice to the cause of the oppressed, but it may be easily conceived that this beneficent law must be frequently eluded. I saw, however, in Mexico in the month of July, 1803, an example of two Negroes to whom the magistrate gave their liberty because their mistress, a lady from the islands, had wounded them all over the body with scissors, pins and knives. In the course of this shocking process the lady was accused of having knocked out the teeth of the slaves with a key when they complained of a fluxion [bleeding] in the gums which prevented them from working.

To complete the table of the elements of which the Mexican population is composed, it remains for us to point out rapidly the differences of caste which spring from the mixture of the pure races with one another. These castes constitute a mass almost as considerable as the Mexican Indians. We may estimate the total of the individuals of mixed blood at nearly 2,400,000. From a refinement of vanity, the inhabitants of the colonies have enriched their language with terms for the finest shades of the colors which result from the degeneration of the primitive color. It may be useful to explain these denominations because they have been confounded by many travelers, and because this confusion frequently causes no small embarrassment to those who read Spanish works on the American possessions.

The son of a white (creole or European) and a native of copper color is called mestizo. His color is almost a pure white, and his skin is of a particular transparency. The small beard and small hands and feet, and a certain obliquity of the eyes, are more frequent indications of the mixture of Indian blood than the nature of the hair. If a mestiza marry a white man, the second generation differs hardly in anything from the European race. As very few Negroes have been introduced into New Spain, the mestizos probably compose 7/8 of the whole castes. They are generally accounted of a much more mild character than the mulattos, descended from whites and Negresses, who are distinguished for the violence of their passions and a singular volubility of tongue. The descendants of Negroes and Indian women bear the strange name of *Chino*, Chinese. On the coast of Caracas and, as appears from the laws, even in New Spain, they are called zambos. This last denomination is now principally limited to the descendants of a Negro and a female mulatto, or a Negro and a Chinese female. From these common zambos they distinguish the zambos prietos who descend from a Negro and a female zamba. From the mixture of a white man with a mulatto comes the cast of *cuarterón*. When a female cuarteron marries a European or creole, her son bears the name of *quinterón*. A new alliance with a white banishes to such a degree the remains of color that the children of a white and a quinterón are white also.

In a country governed by whites, the families reputed to have the least mixture of Negro or mulatto blood are also naturally the most honored. In Spain it is almost a title of nobility to descend neither from Jews nor Moors. In America the greater or less degree of whiteness of skin decides the rank which man occupies in society. A white who rides barefooted on horseback thinks he belongs to the nobility of the country. Color establishes even a certain equality among men who, as is universally the case where civilization is either little advanced or in a retrograde state, take a particular pleasure in dwelling on the prerogatives of race and origin. When a common man disputes with one of the titled lords of the country, he is frequently heard to say, "Do you think me not so white as yourself?" This may serve to characterize the state and source of the actual aristocracy. It becomes, consequently, a very interesting business for the public vanity to estimate accurately the fractions of European blood which belong to the different castes.

It often happens that families suspected of being of mixed blood demand from the high court of justice a declaration that they belong to the whites. These declarations are not always corroborated by the judgment of the senses. We see very swarthy mulattoes who have had the address to get themselves "whitened" (this is the vulgar expression). When the color of the skin is too repugnant to the judgment demanded, the petitioner is contented with an expression somewhat problematical—"that such or such individuals may consider themselves as whites."

The reader will no doubt desire to have a discussion of what is the influence of this mixture of races on the general well-being of society? And what is the degree of enjoyment and individual happiness which a man of cultivated mind can procure amidst such a collision of interests, prejudices and feelings?

When a European transports himself into these distant regions of the new continent, he feels oppressed at every step with the influence which the colonial government has for centuries exercised over the minds of the inhabitants. A well-informed man, who merely interests himself in the intellectual development of the species, suffers less perhaps than the man who is endowed with great sensibility. The former institutes a comparison with the mother country; from maritime communication he procures books and instruments; he sees with ecstasy the progress which the exact sciences have made in the great cities of Spanish America; and the contemplation of nature in all her grandeur and the astonishing variety of her productions, indemnifies his mind for the privations to which his position condemns him. But the man of sensibility must seek in the Spanish colonies for everything agreeable in life within himself alone. It is in this way that isolation and solitude have their attractions for him if he wishes to enjoy peaceably the advantages afforded by the excellence of the climate, the aspect of a never-fading verdure; and the political calm of the new world. While I freely give these ideas to the world, I am not censuring the moral character of the inhabitants of Mexico or Peru; nor do I say that the people of Lima are worse than those of Cadiz. I am rather inclined to believe what many other travelers have observed before me, that the Americans are endowed by nature with a gentleness of manners rather approaching to effeminacy, as the energy of several European nations easily degenerates into harshness. The want of sociability so universal in the Spanish colonies and the hatreds which divide the castes of greatest affinity, the effects of which shed a bitterness over the life of the colonists, are solely due to the political principles by which these regions have been governed since the sixteenth century. A government, aware of the true interests of humanity, will be able to diffuse information and instruction, and by extinguishing gradually the monstrous inequality of rights and fortunes, will succeed in augmenting the physical prosperity of the colonists; but it will find immense difficulties to overcome before rendering the inhabitants sociable, and teaching them to consider themselves mutually in the light of fellow citizens.

Let us not forget than in the United States society is formed in a very different manner from what it is in Mexico and the other continental regions of the Spanish colonies. Penetrating into the Alleghany mountains, the Europeans found immense forests in which a few tribes of hunters wandered up and down, attached by no tie to an uncultivated soil. At the approach of the new colonists, the natives gradually retired towards the western savannas in the neighborhood of the Mississippi and the Missouri. In this manner free men of the same race and the same origin became the first elements of a new people.

In New Spain and Peru, if we except the missions, the colonists nowhere returned to the state of nature. Fixing themselves in the midst of agricultural nations, who themselves lived under governments equally complicated and despotic, the Europeans took advantage of the preponderancy of their civilization, their cunning, and the authority they derived from the conquest. This particular situation, and the mixture of races of which the interests are diametrically opposite, became an inexhaustible source of hatred and disunion. In proportion as the descendants of the Europeans became more numerous than those sent over directly by the mother country, the white race divided into two parties, of which the ties of blood cannot heal the resentments. The colonial government from a mistaken policy wished to take advantage of these dissensions. The greater the colony, the greater the suspicion of the administration. According to the ideas which unfortunately have been adopted for ages, these distant regions are considered as tributary to Europe. Authority is there distributed not in the manner which the public interest requires, but according as the dread of seeing a too rapid increase in the prosperity of the inhabitants seems to dictate. Seeking security in civil dissensions, in the balance of power, and in a complication of all the springs of the great political machine, the mother country foments incessantly the spirit of party and hatred among the castes and constituted authorities. From this state of things arises a rancor which disturbs the enjoyments of social life.

Selection 2: A French Traveler Considers the Future of Race Relations in the United States of America

Alexis de Tocqueville was a young French nobleman who toured the United States of America from 1831 to 1832. Although the nominal purpose of his trip was to investigate reforms in the American penal system, he quickly shifted his focus to a much larger topic: how the rise of political democracy in the United States was transforming social relations. He published his observations in *Democracy in America*, the first part of which appeared in 1835 and the second in 1840. Like Humboldt before him, Tocqueville brought a spirit of a scientific observation to his work, evaluating American society as if he were encountering a new kind plant or animal species. He found in the United States a laboratory for the social transformations unleashed by the Enlightenment and Age of Revolutions, and he believed those changes would eventually sweep the Old World.

The excerpt below comes from an essay in *Democracy in America* titled "The Present and Probable Future Condition of the Three Races that Inhabit the Territory of the United States." Like the selection from Humboldt, it concerns the coming together of African, Native American, and European peoples, but describes very different results from that collision. While much of his language will strike modern readers as racist, Tocqueville nevertheless takes an unflinching look at the costs that white democracy in the United States imposed on the other racial groups living there.

Credit: Alexis de Tocqueville, *Democracy in America*, 2 vols (1835; New York: J. & H. G. Langley, 1841), Vol. 1: 362, 367–370, 386, 389–391, 404–407, 412.

The territory now occupied or claimed by the American Union spreads from the shores of the Atlantic to those of the Pacific ocean. On the east and west its limits are those of the continent itself. On the south it advances nearly to the tropic, and it extends upward to the icy regions of the north.

The human beings who are scattered over this space do not form, as in Europe, so many branches of the same stock. Three races naturally distinct, and I might almost say hostile to each other, are discoverable among them at the first glance. Almost insurmountable barriers had been raised between them by education and by law, as well as by their origin and outward characteristics; but fortune has brought them together on the same soil, where, although they are mixed, they do not amalgamate, and each race fulfils its destiny apart.

***

The Europeans introduced among the savages of North America firearms, ardent spirits, and iron: they taught them to exchange for manufactured stuffs the rough garments which had previously satisfied their untutored simplicity. Having acquired new tastes, without the arts by which they could be gratified, the Indians were obliged to have recourse to the workmanship of the whites; but in return for their productions the savage had nothing to offer except the rich furs which still abounded in his woods. Hence the chase [hunting] became necessary, not merely to provide for his subsistence, but in order to procure the only objects of barter which he could furnish to Europe. While the wants of the natives were thus increasing, their resources continued to diminish.

From the moment when a European settlement is formed in the neighbourhood of the territory occupied by the Indians, the beasts of chase takes the alarm. Thousands of savages, wandering in the forest and destitute of any fixed dwelling, did not disturb them; but as soon as the continuous sounds of European labour are heard in the neighbourhood, they begin to flee away, and retire to the west, where their instinct teaches them that they will find deserts of immeasurable extent. "The buffalo is constantly receding," say Messrs. Clarke and Cass in their Report of the year 1829; "a few years since they approached the base of the Allegany; and a few years hence they may even be rare upon the immense plains which extend to the base of the Rocky mountains." I have been assured that this effect of the approach of the whites is often felt at two hundred leagues' distance from the frontier. Their influence is thus exerted over tribes whose name is unknown to them, and who suffer the evils of usurpation long before they are acquainted with the authors of their distress.

Bold adventurers soon penetrate into the country the Indians have deserted, and when they have advanced about fifteen or twenty leagues from the extreme frontiers of the whites, they begin to build habitations for civilized beings in the midst of the wilderness. This is done without difficulty, as the territory of a hunting-nation is ill defined; it is the common property of the tribe, and belongs to no one in particular, so that individual interests are not concerned in the protection of any part of it.

A few European families, settled in different situations at a considerable distance from each other, soon drive away the wild animals which remain between their places of abode. The Indians, who had previously lived in a sort of abundance, then find it difficult to subsist, and still more difficult to procure the articles of barter which they stand in need of.

To drive away their game is to deprive them of the means of existence, as effectually as if the fields of our agriculturists were stricken with barrenness; and they are reduced, like famished wolves, to prowl through the forsaken woods in quest of prey. Their instinctive love of their country attaches them to the soil which gave them birth, even after it has ceased to yield anything but misery and death. At length they are compelled to acquiesce, and to depart: they follow the traces of the elk, the buffalo, and the beaver, and are guided by those wild animals in the choice of their future country. Properly speaking, therefore, it is not the Europeans who drive away the native inhabitants of America; it is famine which compels them to recede; a happy distinction which had escaped the casuists of former times, and for which we are indebted to modern discovery.

It is impossible to conceive the extent of the sufferings which attend these forced emigrations. They are undertaken by a people already exhausted and reduced; and the countries to which the new-comers betake themselves are inhabited by other tribes which receive them with jealous hostility. Hunger is in the rear, war awaits them, and misery besets them on all sides. In the hope of escaping from such a host of enemies, they separate, and each individual endeavours to procure the means of supporting his existence in solitude and secresy, living in the immensity of the desert like an outcast in civilized society. The social tie, which distress had long since weakened, is then dissolved; they have lost their country, and their people soon deserts them; their very families are obliterated; the names they bore in common are forgotten, their language perishes, and all the traces of their origin disappear. Their nation has ceased to exist, except in the recollection of the antiquaries of America and a few of the learned of Europe.

***

The Indians will perish in the same isolated condition in which they have lived; but the destiny of the negroes is in some measure interwoven with that of the Europeans. These two races are attached to each other without intermingling; and they are alike unable entirely to separate or to combine. The most formidable of all the ills which threaten the future existence of the United States, arises from the presence of a black population upon its territory; and in contemplating the causes of the present embarrassments or of the future dangers of the United States, the observer is invariably led to consider this as a primary fact.

***

I see that in a certain portion of the territory of the United States at the present day, the legal barrier which separated the two races is tending to fall away, but not that which exists in the manners of the country; slavery recedes, but the prejudice to which it has given birth remains stationary. Whosoever has inhabited the United States, must have perceived, that in those parts of the Union in which the negroes are no longer slaves, they have in nowise drawn nearer to the whites. On the contrary, the prejudice of the race appears to be stronger in the states which have abolished slavery, than in those where it still exists; and nowhere is it so intolerant as in those states where servitude has never been known.

It is true, that in the north of the Union, marriages may be legally contracted between negroes and whites, but public opinion would stigmatize a man who should connect himself with a negress as infamous, and it would be difficult to meet with a single instance of such a union. The electoral franchise has been conferred upon the negroes in almost all the states in which slavery has been abolished; but if they come forward to vote, their lives are in danger. If oppressed, they may bring an action at law, but they will find none but whites among their judges; and although they may legally serve as jurors, prejudice repulses them from that office. The same schools do not receive the child of the black and of the European. In the theatres, gold cannot procure a seat for the servile race beside their former masters; in the hospitals they lie apart; and although they are allowed to invoke the same Divinity as the whites, it must be at a different altar, and in their own churches with their own clergy. The gates of heaven are not closed against these unhappy beings; but their inferiority is continued to the very confines of the other world. When the negro is defunct, his bones are cast aside, and the distinction of condition prevails even in the equality of death. The negro is free, but he can share neither the rights, nor the pleasures, nor the labour, nor the afflictions, nor the tomb of him whose equal he has been declared to be; and he cannot meet him upon fair terms in life or in death.

In the south, where slavery still exists, the negroes are less carefully kept apart; they sometimes share the labour and the recreations of the whites; the whites consent to intermix with them to a certain extent, and although the legislation treats them more harshly, the habits of the people are more tolerant and compassionate. In the south the master is not afraid to raise his slave to his own standing, because he knows that he can in a moment reduce him to the dust at pleasure. In the north, the white no longer distinctly perceives the barrier which separates him from the degraded race, and he shuns the negro with the more pertinacity, because he fears lest they should some day be confounded together.

Among the Americans of the south, nature sometimes reasserts her rights, and restores a transient equality between the blacks and the whites; but in the north, pride restrains the most imperious of human passions. The American of the northern states would perhaps allow the negress to share his licentious pleasures, if the laws of his country did not declare that she may aspire to be the legitimate partner of his bed; but he recoils with horror from her who might become his wife.

Thus it is, in the United States, that the prejudice which repels the negroes seems to increase in proportion as they are emancipated, and inequality is sanctioned by the manners while it is effaced from the laws of the country. But if the relative position of the two races which inhabit the United States, is such as I have described, it may be asked why the Americans have abolished slavery in the north of the Union, why they maintain it in the south, and why they aggravate its hardships there? The answer is easily given. It is not for the good of the negroes, but for that of the whites, that measures are taken to abolish slavery in the United States.

***

As soon as it is admitted that the whites and the emancipated blacks are placed upon the same territory in the situation of two alien communities, it will readily be understood that there are but two alternatives for the future; the negroes and the whites must either wholly part or wholly mingle. I have already expressed the conviction which I entertain as to the latter event. I do not imagine that the white and the black races will ever live in any country upon an equal footing. But I believe the difficulty to be still greater in the United States than elsewhere. An isolated individual may surmount the prejudices of religion, of his country, or of his race, and if this individual is a king he may effect surprising changes in society; but a whole people cannot rise, as it were, above itself. A despot who should subject the Americans and their former slaves to the same yoke, might perhaps succeed in commingling their races; but as long as the American democracy remains at the head of affairs, no one will undertake so difficult a task; and it may be foreseen that the freer the white population of the United States becomes, the more isolated will it remain.

I have previously observed that the mixed race is the true bond of union between the Europeans and the Indians; just so the mulattoes are the true means of transition between the white and the negro; so that wherever mulattoes abound, the intermixture of the two races is not impossible. In some parts of America, the European and the negro races are so crossed by one another, that it is rare to meet with a man who is entirely black or entirely white: when they are arrived at this point, the two races may really be said to be combined; or rather to have been absorbed in a third race, which is connected with both, without being identical with either.

Of all the Europeans the English are those who have mixed least with the negroes. More mulattoes are to be seen in the south of the Union than in the north, but still they are infinitely more scarce than in any other European colony: Mulattoes are by no means numerous in the United States; they have no force peculiar to themselves, and when quarrels originating in differences of colour take place, they generally side with the whites, just as the lacqueys of the great in Europe assume the contemptuous airs of nobility to the lower orders.

The pride of origin, which is natural to the English, is singularly augmented by the personal pride which democratic liberty fosters among the Americans: the white citizen of the United States is proud of his race, and proud of himself. But if the whites and the negroes do not intermingle in the north of the Union, how should they mix in the south? Can it be supposed for an instant, that an American of the southern states, placed, as he must for ever be, between the white man with all his physical and moral superiority, and the negro, will ever think of preferring the latter? The Americans of the southern states have two powerful passions which will always keep them aloof; the first is the fear of being assimilated to the negroes, their former slaves; and the second, the dread of sinking below the whites, their neighbours.

If I were called upon to predict what will probably occur at some future time, I should say, that the abolition of slavery in the south, will, in the common course of things, increase the repugnance of the white population for the men of colour. I found this opinion upon the analogous observation which I already had occasion to make in the north. I there remarked, that the white inhabitants of the north avoid the negroes with increasing care, in proportion as the legal barriers of separation are removed by the legislature; and why should not the same result take place in the south? In the north, the whites are deterred from intermingling with the blacks by the fear of an imaginary danger; in the south, where the danger would be real, I cannot imagine that the fear would be less general.

If, on the one hand, it be admitted (and the fact is unquestionable), that the coloured population perpetually accumulates in the extreme south, and that it increases more rapidly than that of the whites; and if, on the other hand, it be allowed that it is impossible to foresee a time at which the whites and the blacks will be so intermingled as to derive the same benefits from society; must it not be inferred, that the blacks and the whites will, sooner or later, come to open strife in the southern states of the Union? But if it be asked what the issue of the struggle is likely to be, it will readily be understood, that we are here left to form a very vague surmise of the truth. The human mind may succeed in tracing a wide circle, as it were, which includes the course of future events; but within that circle a thousand various chances and circumstances may direct it in as many different ways; and in every picture of the future there is a dim spot, which the eye of the understanding cannot penetrate. It appears, however, to be extremely probable, that in the West India islands the white race is destined to be subdued, and the black population to share the same fate upon the continent.

In the West India islands the white planters are surrounded by an immense black population; on the continent, the blacks are placed between the ocean and an innumerable people, which already extends over them in a dense mass from the icy confines of Canada to the frontiers of Virginia, and from the banks of the Missouri to the shores of the Atlantic. If the white citizens of North America remain united, it cannot be supposed that the negroes will escape the destruction with which they are menaced; they must be subdued by want or by the sword. But the black population which is accumulated along the coast of the gulf of Mexico, has a chance of success, if the American Union is dissolved when the struggle between the two races begins. If the federal tie were broken, the citizens of the south would be wrong to rely upon any lasting succour from their northern countrymen. The latter are well aware that the danger can never reach them; and unless they are constrained to march to the assistance of the south by a positive obligation, it may be foreseen that the sympathy of colour will be insufficient to stimulate their exertions.

Yet, at whatever period the strife may break out, the whites of the south, even if they are abandoned to their own resources, will enter the lists with an immense superiority of knowledge and of the means of warfare; but the blacks will have numerical strength and the energy of despair upon their side; and these are powerful resources to men who have taken up arms. The fate of the white population of the southern states will, perhaps, be similar to that of the Moors in Spain. After having occupied the land for centuries, it will perhaps be forced to retire to the country whence its ancestors came, and to abandon to the negroes the possession of a territory, which Providence seems to have more peculiarly destined for them, since they can subsist and labour in it more easily than the whites.

***

If it be impossible to anticipate a period at which the Americans of the south will mingle their blood with that of the negroes, can they allow their slaves to become free without compromising their own security? And if they are obliged to keep that race in bondage, in order to save their own families, may they not be excused for availing themselves of the means best adapted to that end? The events which are taking place in the southern states of the Union, appear to be at once the most horrible and the most natural results of slavery. When I see the order of nature overthrown, and when I hear the cry of humanity in its vain struggle against the laws, my indignation does not light upon the men of our own time who are the instruments of these outrages; but I reserve my execration for those who, after a thousand years of freedom, brought back slavery into the world once more.

Whatever may be the efforts of the Americans of the south to maintain slavery, they will not always succeed. Slavery, which is now confined to a single tract of the civilized earth, which is attacked by Christianity as unjust, and by political economy as prejudicial, and which is now contrasted with democratic liberties and the information of our age, cannot survive. By the choice of the master or the will of the slave, it will cease; and in either case great calamities may be expected to ensue. If liberty be refused to the negroes of the south, they will in the end seize it for themselves by force; if it be given, they will abuse it ere long.

Selection 3: A Free Black's Incendiary Call for the Destruction of Slavery

David Walker was a shopkeeper and leader of Boston's free black community when he published *An Appeal to the Coloured Citizens of the World* in 1829. A child of a free mother and enslaved father, he had grown up in Wilmington, North Carolina and traveled in the South before settling in Boston in 1825. Like many African Americans of his era, he practiced Methodism, one of the first Protestant denominations to seek converts among free and enslaved blacks in the Americas. His Christian faith and learning influenced his attack on slavery, which relied extensively on scriptural authority and appeals to divine justice.

Walker's *Appeal* raised a militant voice for the anti-slavery cause in the Atlantic World. The book's language and imagery were incendiary, encouraging active resistance to the institution of slavery. Walker disseminated his message by distributing copies to black sailors and missionaries, who carried them into the cities and plantations of the American South and Caribbean. Slaveholders typically seized and destroyed copies of the book whenever possible and tightened anti-literacy slave laws in its wake. Most important, Walker framed his argument, as the title suggests, as a universal call to blacks, free or slave. Referring to his audience as "true-hearted sons of Africa," he gave voice to an emerging African-American consciousness in the Atlantic World that was animated and united by the anti-slavery cause.

Credit: David Walker, *An Appeal to the Coloured Citizens of the World* (1829) in *Walker's Appeal, with a Brief Sketch of His Life*, by Henry Highland Garnet (New York: J. H. Tobitt, 1848), 29–31, 40–43, 80–81.

Ignorance, my brethren, is a mist, low down into the very dark and almost impenetrable abyss of which, our fathers for many centuries have been plunged. The christians, and enlightened of Europe, and some of Asia, seeing the ignorance and consequent degradation of our fathers, instead of trying to enlighten them, by teaching them that religion and light with which God had blessed them, they have plunged them into wretchedness ten thousand times more intolerable, than if they had left them entirely to the Lord, and to add to their miseries, deep down into which they have plunged them, tell them, that they are an *inferior* and *distinct race* of beings, which they will be glad enough to recall and swallow by and by. Fortune and misfortune, two inseparable companions, lay rolled up in the wheel of events, which have from the creation of the world, and will continue to take place among men until God shall dash worlds together.

When we take a retrospective view of the arts and sciences—the wise legislators—The Pyramids, and other magnificent buildings—the turning of the channel of the river Nile, by the sons of Africa or of Ham [Noah's son, cursed by his father to serve others], among whom learning originated, and was carried thence into Greece, where it was improved upon and refined. Thence among the Romans, and all over the then enlightened parts of the world, and it has been enlightening the dark and benighted minds of men from then, down to this day. I say, when I view retrospectively, the renown of that once mighty people, the children of our great progenitor, I am indeed cheered. Yea further, when I view that mighty son of Africa, Hannibal, one of the greatest generals of antiquity, who defeated and cut off so many thousands of the white Romans or murderers, and who carried his victorious arms, to the very gate of Rome, and I give it as my candid opinion, that had Carthage been well united and had given him good support, he would have carried that cruel and barbarous city by storm. But they were disunited, as the colored people are now, in the United States of America, the reason our natural enemies are enabled to keep their feet on our throats.

Beloved brethren—here let me tell you, and believe it, that the Lord our God, as true as he sits on his throne in heaven, and as true as our Saviour died to redeem the world, will give you a Hannibal, and when the Lord shall have raised him up, and given him to you for your possession, O my suffering brethren! remember the divisions and consequent sufferings of *Carthage* and of *Hayti*. Read the history particularly of Hayti, and see how they were butchered by the whites, and do you take warning. The person whom God shall give you, give him your support and let him go his length, and behold in him the salvation of your God. God will indeed, deliver you through him from your deplorable and wretched condition under the christians of America. I charge you this day before my God to lay no obstacle in his way, but let him go.

The whites want slaves, and want us for their slaves, but some of them will curse the day they ever saw us. As true as the sun ever shone in its meridian splendor, my colour will root some of them out of the very face of the earth. They shall have enough of making slaves of, and butchering, and murdering us in the manner which they have. No doubt some may say that I write with a bad spirit, and that I being a black, wish these things to occur. Whether I write with a bad or a good spirit, I say if these things do not occur in their proper time, it is because the world in which we live does not exist, and we are deceived with regard to its existence. It is immaterial however to me, who believe, or who refuse—though I should like to see the whites repent peradventure God may have mercy on them, some however, have gone so far that their cup must be filled.

But what need have I to refer to antiquity, when Hayti, the glory of the blacks and terror of tyrants, is enough to convince the most avaricious and stupid of wretches—which is at this time, and I am sorry to say it, plagued with that scourge of nations, the Catholic religion; but I hope and pray God that she may yet rid herself of it, and adopt in its stead the Protestant faith; also, I hope that she may keep peace within her borders and be united, keeping a strict look out for tyrants, for if they get the least chance to injure her, they will avail themselves of it, as true as the Lord lives in heaven. But one thing which gives me joy is, that they are men who would be cut off to a man, before they would yield to the combined forces of the whole world—in fact, if the whole world was combined against them, it could not do any thing with them, unless the Lord delivers them up.

***

Men of colour, who are also of sense, for you particularly is my appeal designed. Our more ignorant brethren are not able to penetrate its value. I call upon you therefore to cast your eyes upon the wretchedness of your brethren and to do your utmost to enlighten them—*go to work and enlighten your brethren!*—let the Lord see you doing what you can to rescue them and yourselves from degradation. Do any of you say that you and your family are free and happy and what have you to do with wretched slaves and other people? So can I say, for I enjoy as much freedom as any of you, if I am not quite as well off as the best of you. Look into our freedom and happiness and see of what kind they are composed!! They are of the very lowest kind—they are the very *dregs!*—they are the most servile and abject kind, that ever a people was in possession of! If any of you wish to know how free you are, let one of you start and go thro' the southern and western States of this country, and unless you travel as a slave to a white man (a servant is a *slave* to the man whom he serves,) or have your free papers (which if you are not careful they will get from you) if they do not take you up and put you in jail, and if you cannot give evidence of your freedom, sell you into eternal slavery, I am not a living man; or any man of color, immaterial who he is or where he came from, if he is not the 4th from the "*Negro race*" (as we are called,) the white christians of America will serve him the same, they will sink him into wretchedness & degradation forever while he lives. And yet some of you have the hardihood to say that you are free & happy! May God have mercy on your freedom and happiness! I met a colored man in the street a short time since, with a string of boots on his shoulder; we fell into conversation, and in course of which I said to him, what a miserable set of people we are! He asked why?—Said I, we are so subjected under the whites, that we cannot obtain the comforts of life, but by cleaning their boots and shoes, old clothes, waiting on them, shaving them, etc. Said he, (with the boots on his shoulders,) "I am completely happy!!! I never want to live any better or happier than when I can get a plenty of boots and shoes to clean!!!" Oh! how can those who are actuated by avarice only, but think that our creator made us to be an inheritance to them forever, when they see that our greatest glory is centered in such mean and low objects? Understand me, brethren, I do not mean to speak against the occupations by which we acquire enough and sometimes scarcely that, to render ourselves and families comfortable through life. I am subjected to the same inconvenience, as you all. My objections are, to our *glorying* and being *happy* in such low employments; for if we are men, we ought to be thankful to the Lord for the past, and for the future. Be looking forward with thankful hearts to higher attainments than *wielding the razor* and *cleaning boots and shoes*. The man whose aspirations are not *above*, and even *below* these, is indeed, ignorant and wretched enough. I advance it therefore to you, not as a *problematical*, but as an unshaken and forever immoveable *fact*, that your full glory and happiness, as well as all other colored people under heaven, shall never be fully consummated, but with the *entire emancipation of your enslaved brethren all over the world.* You may therefore, go to work and do what you can to rescue, or join in with tyrants to oppress them and yourselves, until the Lord shall come upon you all like a thief in the night. For I believe it is the will of the Lord that our greatest happiness shall consist in working for the salvation of our whole body. When this is accomplished a burst of glory will shine upon you, which will indeed astonish you and the world. Do any of you say this will never be done? I assure you that God will accomplish it—if nothing else will answer, he will hurl tyrants and devils into *atoms* and make way for his people. But O my brethren! I say unto you again, you must go to work and *prepare the way of* the Lord.

There is a great work for you to do, as trifling as some of you may think of it. You have to prove to the Americans and the world, that we are MEN, and not *brutes* as we have been represented, and by millions treated. Remember, to let the aim of your labours among your brethren, and particularly the youths, be the dissemination of education and religion. It is lamentable, that many of our children go to school, from four until they are eight or ten, and sometimes fifteen years of age, and leave school knowing but a little more about the grammar of their language than a horse does about handling a musket—and not a few of them are really so ignorant, that they are unable to answer a person correctly, general questions in geography, and to hear them read would only be to disgust a man who has a taste for reading; which, to do well, as trifling as it may appear to some, (to the ignorant in particular) is a great part of learning. Some few of them, may make out to scribble tolerably well, over a half sheet of paper, which I believe has hitherto been a powerful obstacle in our way, to keep us from acquiring knowledge. An ignorant father, who knows no more than what nature has taught him, together with what little he acquires by the senses of hearing and seeing, finding his son able to write a neat hand, sets it down for granted that he has as good learning as any body; the young, ignorant gump, hearing his father or mother, who perhaps may be ten times more ignorant, in point of literature, than himself, extolling his learning, struts about in the full assurance, that his attainments in literature are sufficient to take him through the world, when, in fact, he has scarcely any learning at all!!!!

***

Remember Americans, that we must and shall be free, and enlightened as you are, will you wait until we shall, under God, obtain our liberty by the crushing arm of power? Will it not be dreadful for you? I speak Americans for your good. We must and shall be free I say, in spite of you. You may do your best to keep us in wretchedness and misery, to enrich you and your children but God will deliver us from under you. And Wo, Wo, will be to you if we have to obtain our freedom by fighting. Throw away your fears and prejudices then, and enlighten us and treat us like men, and we will like you more than we do now hate you, and tell us now no more about colonization [resettling free blacks in Africa] for America is as much our country, as it is yours—Treat us like men, and there is no danger but we will all live in peace and happiness together. For we are not like you, hard hearted, unmerciful, and unforgiving. What a happy country this will be, if the whites will listen. What nation under heaven, will be able to do any thing with us, unless God gives us up into his hand? But Americans, I declare to you, while you keep us and our children in bondage, and treat us like brutes, to make us support you and your families, we cannot be your friends. You do not look for it; do you? Treat us then like men, and we will be your friends. And there is not a doubt in my mind, but that the whole of the past will be sunk into oblivion, and we yet, under God, will become a united and happy people. The whites may say it is impossible, but remember that nothing is impossible with God.

The Americans may say or do as they please, but they have to raise us from the condition of brutes to that of respectable men, and to make a national acknowledgement to us for the wrongs they have inflicted on us. As unexpected, strange, and wild as these propositions may to some appear, it is no less a fact, that unless they are complied with, the Americans of the United States, though they may for a little while escape, God will yet weigh them in a balance, and if they are not superior to other men, as they have represented themselves to be, he will give them wretchedness to their very heart's content.

Selection 4: A Native American Challenges the Pilgrim Story

By the early nineteenth century, New Englanders were celebrating the Pilgrims' arrival at Plymouth Rock in 1620 in a way that anticipated the modern American holiday of Thanksgiving.

This veneration of the original colonizers of New England did not sit well with William Apess, a Pequot Indian who often advocated on behalf of the political and civil rights of the region's Indians. Apess was born in Massachusetts in 1798 and worked as a soldier and laborer before becoming an itinerant minister. His book *A Son of the Forest* (1829) is considered the first Native American autobiography published in the United States, and it gave an important voice to Indians fighting efforts by federal and state authorities to dispossess them and force their migration west of the Mississippi. In 1836, Apess gave a speech commemorating the life of King Philip (also known as Metacomet), the seventeenth-century Wampanoag Indian who had led a war against the New England colonies. He used this occasion to turn the story of the Pilgrim founding of Plymouth on its head, depicting it as a cataclysmic event for Native peoples, who were repaid with dispossession and violence for the help they had given to the newcomers.

Credit: William Apess, *Eulogy on King Philip, as Pronounced at the Odeon, in Federal Street, Boston, by the Rev. William Apess, an Indian, January 8, 1836*, 2nd edn (Boston, MA: William Apess, 1837), 10–12, 45–47.

December, 1620, the pilgrims landed at Plymouth, and without asking liberty from any one they possessed themselves of a portion of the country, and built themselves houses, and then made a treaty, and commanded them [Indians] to accede to it. This, if now done, would be called an insult, and every white man would be called to go out and act the part of a patriot, to defend their country's rights; and if every intruder were butchered, it would be sung upon every hill-top in the Union, that victory and patriotism was the order of the day. And yet the Indians (though many were dissatisfied,) without the shedding of blood or imprisoning any one, bore it. And yet for their kindness and resignation towards the whites, they were called savages and made by God on purpose for them to destroy. We might say, God understood his work better than this. But to proceed, it appears that a treaty was made by the pilgrims and the Indians, which treaty was kept during forty years; the young chiefs during this time was showing the pilgrims how to live in their country, and find support for their wives and little ones; and for all this, they were receiving the applause of being savages. The two gentleman chiefs were Squanto and Samoset, that were so good to the pilgrims.

The next we present before you are things very appalling. We turn our attention to dates 1623, January and March, when Mr. Weston['s] colony [a failed offshoot of Plymouth] came very near starving to death; some of them were obliged to hire themselves to the Indians, to become their servants, in order that they might live. Their principal work was to bring wood and water; but, not being contented with this, many of the whites sought to steal the Indian's corn; and because the Indians complained of it, and through their complaint, some one of their number being punished, as they say, to appease the savages. Now let use see who the greatest savages were; the person that stole the corn was a stout athletic man, and because of this, they wished to spare him, and take an old man who was lame and sickly, and that used to get his living by weaving; and because they thought he would not be of so much use to them, he was, though innocent of any crime, hung in his stead. O savage! where art thou, to weep over the Christian's crimes? (that is, Indians call all white people Christians, without discrimination).

Another act of humanity for Christians, as they call themselves, that one Captain Standish, gathering some fruit and provisions, goes forward with a black and hypocritical heart, and pretends to prepare a feast for the Indians; and when they sit down to eat, they seize the Indian's knives hanging about their necks, and stab them to the heart. The white people call this stabbing, feasting the savages. We suppose it might well mean themselves, their conduct being more like savages than Christians. They took one Wittumumet, the Chief's head, and put it upon a pole in their fort; and for aught we know, gave praise to their God for success in murdering a poor Indian; for we know it was their usual course to give praise to God for this kind of victory, believing it was God's will and command, for them to do so. We wonder if these same Christians did not think it the command of God, that they should lie, steal, and get drunk, commit fornication and adultery. The one is as consistent as the other. What say you, judges, is it not so, and was it not according as they did? Indians think it is.

***

How deep then, was the thought of [King] Philip, when he could look from Maine to Georgia, and from the ocean to the lakes, and the view with one look all his brethren withering before the more enlightened to come; and how true his prophesy that the white people would not only cut down their groves but would enslave them. Had the inspiration of Isaiah been there, he could not have been more correct. Our groves and our hunting grounds are gone, our dead are dug up, our council fires are put out, and a foundation was laid in the first Legislature to enslave our people, by taking from them all rights, which has been strictly adhered to ever since. Look at the disgraceful laws, disfranchising us as citizens. Look at the treaties made by Congress, all broken. Look at the deep-rooted plans laid, when a territory becomes a State, that after so many years, the laws shall be extended over the Indians that live within their boundaries. Yea, every charter that has been given was given with the view of driving the Indians out of the States, or dooming them to become chained under desperate laws, that would make them drag out a miserable life as though chained to the galley; and this is the course that has been pursued for nearly two hundred years; a fire, a canker, created by the pilgrims from across the Atlantic, to burn and destroy my unfortunate brethren, and it cannot be denied. What, then, shall we do; shall we bury the hatchet and those unjust laws and Plymouth Rock together, and become friends? And will the sons of the pilgrims aid in putting out the fire and destroying the canker that will ruin all that their fathers left behind them to destroy? If so, we hope we shall not hear it said from ministers and church members, that we are so good, no other people can live with us, as you know it is a common thing for them to say, Indians cannot live among Christian people; no, even the President of the United States [Andrew Jackson] tells the Indians they cannot live among civilized people, and we want your lands, and must have them, and will have them. As if he had said to them, ["]We want your lands for our use to speculate upon; it aids us in paying off our national debt and supporting us in Congress to drive you off.

["]You see, my red children, that our fathers carried on this scheme of getting your lands for our use, and we have now become rich and powerful; and we have a right to do with you just as we please; we claim to be your fathers. And we think we shall do you a great favor, my dear sons and daughters, to drive you out, to get you away, out of the reach of our civilized people, who are cheating you, for we have no law to reach them, we cannot protect you, although you be our children. So it is no use, you need not cry, you must go, even if the lions devour you, for we promised the land you have to somebody else, long ago, perhaps twenty or thirty years; and we did it without your consent, it is true. But this has been the way our fathers first brought us up, and it is hard to depart from it; therefore, you shall have no protection from us.["] Now, while we sum up this subject, does it not appear that the cause of all wars, from beginning to end, was, and is for the want of good usage? That the whites have always been the aggressors, and the wars, cruelties, and blood shed, is a job of their own seeking, and not the Indians? Did you ever know of Indians hurting those who was kind to them? No. We have a thousand witnesses to the contrary. Yea, every male and female declare it to be the fact. We often hear of the wars breaking out upon the frontiers, and it is because the same spirit reigns there that reigned here in New England; and wherever there are any Indians, that spirit still reigns; and at present, there is no law to stop it. What, then, is to be done? Let every friend of the Indians now seize the mantle of Liberty and throw it over those burning elements, that has spread with such fearful rapidity, and at once extinguish them forever. It is true that now and then a feeble voice has been raised in our favor. Yes, we might speak of distinguished men, but they fall so far short in the minority, that it is heard but at a small distance. We want trumpets that sound like thunder, and men to act as though they were going to war with those corrupt and degrading principles that rob one of all rights, merely because he is ignorant, and of a little different color. Let us have principles that will give every one his due; and then shall wars cease, and the weary find rest. Give the Indian his rights, and you may be assured war will cease.

Discussion Questions

1. What does Humboldt find peculiar about the racial caste system in Mexico? According to him, what historical circumstances have given rise to it? What are its long-term effects on Mexican society?
2. Summarize Tocqueville's conclusions about the fate of Indians and Africans in the United States. According to him, why have their experiences in dealing with whites followed opposite paths?
3. How did Walker make use of the Haitian Revolution, the Enlightenment, and Christianity in his call for an end to slavery? What evidence does his argument present of a distinctly African-American identity in the Atlantic World?
4. According to Apess, what made the Pilgrims savage and the Indians who greeted them at Plymouth civilized? How does his call to resist Indian removal compare to Walker's call to resist slavery?

Suggested Readings

An excellent overview of European imperialism that explores the links between the Atlantic empires and those established in Africa and Asia in the nineteenth century is D. K. Fieldhouse, *The Colonial Empires from the Eighteenth Century* (New York: Delacorte Press, 1966). Philip D. Curtin has written several books that deal with nineteenth-century imperialism in a context useful for students of the Atlantic World. See especially *The World and the West: The European Challenge and the Overseas Response in the Age of Empire* (New York: Cambridge University Press, 2000); *Disease and Empire: The Health of European Troops in the Conquest of Africa* (New York: Cambridge University Press, 1998); and *Death by Migration: Europe's Encounter with the Tropical World in the Nineteenth Century* (New York: Cambridge University Press, 1989).

A comparative perspective on the transition from colonial to national identities in the Atlantic World is provided in *Colonial Identity in the Atlantic World, 1500–1800*, eds. Nicholas P. Canny and Anthony Pagden (Princeton, NJ: Princeton University Press, 1987). Also useful in this regard for Latin America is D. A. Brading, *The First America: The Spanish Monarchy, Creole Patriots, and the Liberal State, 1492–1867* (New York: Cambridge University Press, 1991). For more on Mexico in the early nineteenth century, see *Mexico in the Age of Democratic Revolutions, 1750–1850*, ed. Jaime E. Rodríguez O. (Boulder, CO: Lynne Rienner, 1994). For more on race relations in the United States in the era of Alexis de Tocqueville and David Walker, see Thomas R. Hietala, *Manifest Design: American Exceptionalism and Empire*, revised edn (Ithaca, NY: Cornell University Press, 2002).

To learn more about William Apess, see Philip F. Gura, *The Life of William Apess, Pequot* (Chapel Hill, NC: University of North Carolina Press, 2015); and Barry O'Connell, ed., *A Son of the Forest and Other Writings by William Apess, a Pequot* (Amherst, MA: University of Massachusetts Press, 1992). David Walker's life and role in American abolitionism is examined in Peter P. Hinks, *To Awaken My Afflicted Brethren: David Walker and the Problem of Antebellum Slave Resistance* (University Park, PA: Penn State University Press, 1996). For more on Alexander von Humboldt's impressions of American nature and society, see Andrea Wulf, *The*

Invention of Nature: Alexander von Humboldt's New World (New York: Knopf, 2015); and Laura Dassow Walls, *The Passage to Cosmos: Alexander von Humboldt and the Shaping of America* (Chicago, IL: University of Chicago Press, 2009). For Tocqueville's travels in the United States, see Leo Damrosch, *Tocqueville's Discovery of America* (New York: Farrar, Straus, and Giroux, 2010).

Chronology of Important Events in Atlantic World History

c.1450	Portuguese navigators begin importing West African slaves to Europe (see Chapter 1, Selection 1).
1492–1504	Christopher Columbus completes four voyages to the Americas, initiating European colonization of the Americas (see Chapter 1, Selection 2).
1494	Treaty of Tordesillas demarcates Portuguese (eastern) and Spanish (western) claims in Atlantic World.
1500–1560	Portuguese establish first colonial settlements in Brazil (see Chapter 3, Selection 1).
1519–1521	Spanish conquest of Mexico.
1532–1533	Spanish conquest of Peru.
1542	Spanish "New Laws of the Indies" impose *repartimiento* system of tribute labor on Native Americans (see Chapter 7, Selection 1).
1585–1590	English colony at Roanoke fails (see Chapter 2, Selection 1).
1607	English establish colony at Jamestown, Virginia (see Chapter 3, Selection 2).
1608	French colonization of Canada begins in earnest with founding of Quebec (see Chapter 2, Selection 2).
1609	Henry Hudson's exploration of the Hudson River initiates the colonization of New Netherland (see Chapter 1, Selection 3).
1609–1763	Jesuits establish multiple missionary communities among Algonquian and Iroquoian peoples in New France (see Chapter 4, Selection 2 and Chapter 11, Selection 1).
1620–1680	Buccaneers dominate Caribbean piracy (see Chapter 9, Selection 1).
1640–1660	Sugar Revolution in the Caribbean expands the plantation complex and increases the Atlantic Slave Trade (see Chapter 6, Selections 1–3).
1664–1676	English conquer Dutch New Netherland and rename it New York (see Chapter 8, Selection 1).
1680	Pueblo Revolt disrupts Spanish colonization of New Mexico (see Chapter 4, Selection 1).
1697–1701, 1716–1726	British Navy fights two "wars against the pirates" in Atlantic World (see Chapter 9, Selection 2).
1707–1775	Colonial population of British North America grows rapidly because of waves of migration from Rhine River Valley, Ireland, and Scotland (see Chapter 8, Selection 3 and Chapter 10, Selections 2 and 4).
1740–1760	Protestant religious revival known as the Great Awakening sweeps through British North America (see Chapter 4, Selections 3 and 4).
1756–1763	Seven Years' War results in British conquest of Canada (see Chapter 3, Selection 3; Chapter 8, Selection 2; and Chapter 10, Selection 3).
1760–1800	Peak decades of the Atlantic Slave Trade (see Chapter 5, Selections 1–3).
1775–1783	American Revolution (see Chapter 12, Selection 1).
1775–1790	First anti-slavery societies founded; British Parliament investigates the Atlantic Slave Trade (see Chapter 5, Selection 4).
1780–1850	Rise of global whaling industry (see Chapter 9, Selection 4).
1789–1799	French Revolution (see Chapter 12, Selection 2).
1791–1804	Saint Domingue slave rebellion and Haitian Revolution (see Chapter 12, Selection 3).
1793	Philadelphia yellow fever epidemic (see Chapter 2, Selection 4).
1799–1815	Napoleonic Wars lead to increased impressment and naval warfare in the Atlantic World (see Chapter 9, Selection 3).

continued

1807	Great Britain prohibits Atlantic Slave Trade.
1808	United States prohibits Atlantic Slave Trade.
1810–1824	Spanish American Wars of Independence (see Chapter 12, Selection 4 and Chapter 13, Selection 1).
1830–1840	US government forces removal of Native Americans to territory west of the Mississippi River (see Chapter 11, Selection 4 and Chapter 13, Selections 2 and 4).
1830–1860	Abolitionist movement grows in the United States (see Chapter 13, Selection 3).
1833	British Parliament abolishes slavery in British West Indies.
1861–1865	American Civil War ends slavery in the United States.
1886–1888	Slavery abolished in Cuba and Brazil.